As He Is

*Issues in the
"Character of God"
Controversy*

BY
4TH
ANGEL
PUBLICATIONS

TEACH Services, Inc.
P U B L I S H I N G
www.TEACHServices.com

Copyright © 2012 Kevin Straub and TEACH Services, Inc.
ISBN-13: 978-1-57258-774-8 (Paperback)
ISBN-13: 978-1-57258-800-4 (Hardback)
ISBN-13: 978-1-57258-801-1 (ePub)
ISBN-13: 978-1-57258-802-8 (Kindle/Mobi)
Library of Congress Control Number: 2012936818

BY
4TH
ANGEL
PUBLICATIONS

Published by

TEACH Services, Inc.

P U B L I S H I N G

www.TEACHServices.com

Endorsements

"Nothing in the world is more important or more necessary than to get the character of God right. We can fill libraries up with religious books, all being most interesting, but if they are not telling the truth about God, it is all vain and a waste of time and space. *As He Is* should be read carefully by everybody."

Herbert Edgar Douglass, Th. D., Author of *God at Risk*

"The great controversy is about God's character, which Satan has slandered, and a deceived humanity goes right along with it. But God has only us, His faithful children, to correct this error and to show God as He is and as He has declared Himself to be. This volume clarifies that which has been confusing to us and reveals God in His true character. In this solemn hour of earth's history, moving up in understanding about who God is, is the most important thing God's people can do."

Marilyn Madison Campbell, Author, *Light Through the Darkness: A Vindication of God*

"Throughout the ages many thinkers and theologians have written works that communicate their thoughts about God. Many of these have imagined Him in ways that go beyond the written word about Him. *As He Is* presents God as One quite different from traditional notions while staying close to the inspired text. It does a superb job of bringing passages together that unveil a better picture of God than what may have been noticed before.

"Much of traditional picturing of God the Father is out of harmony with the clearly recorded character of Jesus in the Gospel account. It is fundamental to Christian faith that the Godhead be understood as being love, and love alone! As with any theological book, you may find some things in it that may not reflect some long-held ideas about God. However, I would invite all believers in God to please consider the clues in the written word that lift Him up above some ancient ideas that do not harmonize with the light we have in Jesus Christ."

D. Douglas Devnich, Minister of the Gospel in the Seventh-day Adventist Church since 1964; Pastor, Healthcare Chaplain, Teacher, Administrator

"*As He Is* definitively addresses God's unchanging character of mercy and justice in the face of sin, from its inception to its end. This penetrating study of Scripture and Spirit of Prophecy unravels and resolves a multitude of seeming contradictions that would have God's mercy be at odds with His justice. From man's fall from grace, to the great Flood, to the cross, to the final eradication of sin, we are led to appreciate God's infinitely tender love in His judgments, His vengeance, and wrath. Because we can rise no higher than our conceptions of truth, purity, and holiness, it behooves us to allow the Word to reveal the truth of God as He is, and not as we would have Him be."

James Z. Said, DC, ND, BS (ME)

"Through all of human history, and especially as we are living in the last days, Satan has been hugely successful in darkening minds with regard to the character of God. In Mark 9:37, Jesus says that anyone who welcomes Him welcomes not only Himself but also His Father. Then, in John 17:3 Jesus says that to have eternal life we need to know not only Himself but also God the Father who sent Him. *As He Is* supports Jesus' mission in seeking to dispel the lies about God and what He is really like. God is love and to know Him is to love Him. Here is victory, for it is then that we will love to obey Him."

Leighton L. Nischuk, MD

"God has not arbitrarily set a time for His second coming, but rather He is waiting for the final demonstration of the complete victory over sin in His people, through His Spirit. The body of Christ must be pure and clean, as the Head of the body is pure and clean. If we are to share His throne, then we must be like Him. This can only happen when we have a clear understanding of His character. This is what makes the subject of this book vitally important to comprehend. *As He Is* strives to answer through the inspired Word, in a logical and clear manner, many of the questions that man has asked over the years about the acts and character of God."

Edward J. Rice, Head Elder, Lacombe Community SDA Church

"Modern science has shown that 90-100% of our illnesses and diseases begin with the activity of our mind. In order to have health more abundantly we must have the mind of Christ (Phil. 2:5). *As He Is* has proven to be the grandest and most clear instruction regarding the healing knowledge of God that I have found in my 60 years. 'To know God is life eternal' (John 17:3). We can rise no higher than our concept of who God is.... So as you read this book, you can become that new creature in Christ; with new health, a new mind, and a new, closer experience in the presence of, and therefore the reflection of, the character of God."

Marilyn Dittman, Director, Whole Health Practitioner, Lifetree Wellness

Cover Picture

The enemy has obscured the truth about God in the dark shadows and thick clouds of deception and accusation. But God's own Son, Jesus Christ, came to do a glorious work of fully revealing God. This work is now carrying forward to completion. "For the earth will be filled with the knowledge of the glory of the Lord, as the waters cover the sea" (Hab. 2:14).

"The glory of the Lord is His character" (*Signs of the Times*, June 27, 1895). This glory is the light that shines out of darkness, the light of knowledge that shines into human hearts through looking to Jesus (2 Cor. 4:6; John 1:5; 8:12; 12:46; 1 John 1:4, 5). This light is not for humans only, but for all beings (1 Cor. 4:9; 1 Pet. 1:7-12).

The advancing light on God's character is present truth. It is the second and final "Advent Awakening" building up to the final "midnight cry" (*Early Writings*, p. 277; *Christ's Object Lessons*, pp. 411-415). It is the third angel's message as amplified by the expected fourth angel of Revelation 18:1. In addition to the loud cry repetition of the three angels—a message called "the truth as it is in Jesus"—the fourth angel brings more of this truth in Jesus into sharp focus by bringing "new views" to light on God's character, showing Him *as He is* (1 John 3:2-3, 7; 4:17; 1 Cor. 13:12; *Fundamentals of Christian Education*, p. 444).

As never before in history, it will be universally understood that righteousness cannot be demonstrated through any acts of violence (Isa. 53:9; Ps. 11:5; Heb. 7:26; Matt. 5:39-48). The final generation will understand this about God (2 Cor. 3:18; Isa. 60:1-3). In an age of unprecedented violence, they will proclaim it with power by their life testimony and with a strong voice (Rev. 18:1; Isa. 40:9).

This entire drama, while taking place in the lives of earth-dwellers, will soon reach a long-awaited climax that has vital ramifications at the universal level.

God is the subject of investigation. In the end all minds will come to the understanding that the sources of life and death are utterly exclusive in their relative offerings. In other words, neither can give an iota of what the other has to offer. The outcome of this investigation reveals an absolute: "Satan is the destroyer; God is the restorer" (*Ministry of Healing*, p. 113). This verdict serves to secure the eternal allegiance of the righteous and the eternal destiny of all the created inhabitants of the universe.

Kevin Straub, Compiler
straub@direct.ca
April 2012

Truth

Each progressive spirit is opposed by a thousand mediocre minds appointed to guard the past. Maurice Maeterlinck

Contempt, prior to complete investigation, enslaves men to ignorance. Dr. John Whitman Ray

In a time of universal deceit, telling the truth is a revolutionary act. George Orwell

If you want to make someone angry, tell him a lie; if you want to make him furious, tell him the truth. All truth passes through three stages. First, it is ridiculed, second, it is violently opposed, and third, it is accepted as self-evident. Arthur Schopenhauer, Philosopher, 1788-1860

As scarce as the truth is, the supply has always been in excess of the demand. J. Billings

Don't confuse your opinion with the truth. W. Erhard

The power to fit in with one's social peers can be irresistible. To a human lemming, the logic behind an opinion doesn't count as much as the power and popularity behind an opinion. Norman Livergood

Accept it or reject it; you have to know it. Mrs. McKay, my grade 11 Geology teacher, RYCI.[1]

A church endangers itself when it refuses to operate at more than one level of thinking/maturity. It's natural for someone at a lower level not to be able to under-

[1] These quotes appear in the book *How I Clobbered Every Bureaucratic Cash-Confiscatory Agency Known to Man* by Mary Elizabeth Croft

stand concepts of someone at any level above them. *That is, cognitive dissonance is experienced when you are exposed to or confronted with concepts at a higher level than where you are now. You are then faced with a choice to either be open-minded and figure out why your current understanding or doctrine is insufficient to answer the questions being asked by the "new doctrines" OR to deny, obstruct, obfuscate, twist, or attack the higher-level concepts as heresy. I don't think there is a third choice.* Dean A. Scott, MFA

Those who cannot impartially examine the evidences of a position that differs from theirs, are not fit to teach in any department of God's cause. Ellen G. White, *The Review and Herald*, February 18, 1890

He who answers a matter before he hears it, *it is folly and shame to him.* Proverbs 18:13

Preface

This is a book about the great controversy.

In today's ecumenical and interspiritual environment, there is a tendency to avoid topics of discussion that would arouse controversy. But those who seek truth, that is, the fullness of the righteousness of God as it is seen in His Son, in all their thoughts, words, and actions, will find it necessary to lay aside any fear of being out of step with prevailing ideologies that can and do breed tolerance of error. This is serious, for doctrinal error leads to behavioral error, which is unrighteousness. Relating this to the subject of this work, we find that we cannot think and act upon any higher plane than that upon which we deem God to exist. Therefore, we recognize that truly knowing God "as He is" is *everything* to us as representatives of His name as it is also in the personal development of our own characters.

The study of God's character is not merely a theme related *to* the great controversy—it is *the subject* at the very core of that conflict. If, at this late hour of earth's history, we aren't studying, discussing, reading, writing, preaching, and teaching all things *controversial*, then what is it that we are doing? Please don't misunderstand; we are not involved in generating controversy. Rather, we are answering the controverted points with regard to who God is, which deceived the entire human race, except One, into rebellion against God. This rebellion will not end until the questions, insinuations, and accusations regarding God's character and government, which Lucifer initiated in heaven and brought to this world, are finished here in earth's theater.

We are *in* this conflict; we cannot avoid it. We must understand it, for it is a war that encompasses every struggle, from the level of individuals to the level of nations. Furthermore, the final and universal verdict regarding whether or not Satan has a valid government and/ or any claim to rule rides upon the outcome of this overarching controversy. It is a war in which every human, every angel, as well as every other inhabitant of the universe, must take a stand and by which every free moral agent must choose eternal life or death.

Speaking personally, I was born and raised in a family that took the Judeo-Christian God and biblical religion seriously. We lived in reference to the Creator and the principles of the Ten Commandments. I was taught to live in the sight of the God of the Bible, as institutional Seventh-day Adventist Christianity understands Him.

I was never taught in this environment how to resolve the apparent contradiction between our understanding of the God of the Old Testament theocratic system and God as revealed in Jesus Christ. As I matured into adulthood and made the religion of three generations my own, I studied the Scriptures and the writings of Ellen G. White in an attempt to personally settle into the faith of my upbringing. As I read the inspired passages, there seemed to be, on the surface of them, a distortion of God as a Being who on the one hand grants freedom of conscience and does not rule by force, yet often appears as One who destroys those who exercise their liberty to reject Him. Or, to put it in the best light, He is seen as One who ultimately destroys those who injure His children, as one would take a shovel to the head of a rattlesnake lurking in the playground. In other words, His role as Protector of the faithful and ultimately, of eternal righteousness and peace in the universe, is seen to justify His employment of weapons of destruction, even of *mass destruction*, on those who would bring harm and ruin to future societies of righteous beings. I was beginning to get very uncomfortable with the standard paradigm of God as it was very similar to how earthly rulers operate, in that He could *break His law in order to uphold His law.*

In order to retain my belief in a loving and benevolent God and grow into a place of trust and desire to serve Him as my King, as motivated by love without fear, I had to reject that concept of a God who did not appeal to the principles of true love. The reason for this is simple. As I first heard it from a well-known Adventist preacher, it is a self-evident truth that "*love*, in order to *be love*, must be *free.*" If the Supreme Being claims to run His universe on the twin governing principles of *freedom of choice* and *noncoercion*, as rooted and grounded in *love*, then He *cannot* in *any way* be seen to exact an arbitrary, proactive, painful, destructive, or fatal punishment or judgment by His own use of creative, fiat power. It is a fundamental tenet that nothing God does can be arbitrary. His universe runs entirely on righteous principles, and "punishment," or judgment, comes only by cause and effect. The wages of sin is death, and God does not pay those wages. He simply, lovingly informs us that the result of separation from Him is a cessation of existence, for by His power alone do we live and move and have our being.

Perhaps I am running ahead of the book, but it is difficult to not burst forth with these fresh truths about God. This knowledge has eternal relevance to one's experience and never ceases to be revitalizing and full of wonder.

In the traditional paradigm, God is a King who values, above all else, subjects who freely choose to serve Him out of love, devoid of the fear of punishment, yet at the same time He warns that He will proactively rain fire and brimstone upon the heads of those who do not want Him to be their King. This sets up a condition of severe cognitive dissonance in many people's minds.

This condition has led to the development of countless self-proclaimed atheists and agnostics, of which many have come into their views honestly because Christianity has not been able or willing to offer a picture of God that is consistent with the principles of love. I like to say that the antidote for atheism is *God*. That is, to know Him "as He is" demolishes the arguments of those who hate God as they have come to understand Him, for this knowledge demolishes that concept of God which sees Him as a controlling tyrant; as the cause of bloody, fiery wars, disasters, and punishments.

Many Christian clergy and teachers have offered the unsatisfying arguments of "God's sovereignty" or His prerogatives as the Creator to create and destroy at will. Other clerics have agreed that these things are difficult and perplexing, but have counseled us to just lay them aside and look to Christ, for one day all things will be made perfectly clear. *I believe that day is now*, for it is in this time of the end that we are to understand what it is to have the name of God written in our foreheads, which is His character, which we know must be "perfectly reproduced in His people" before He comes to take us home to eternity (*Christ's Object Lessons*, p. 69). As we look to Christ, all things are made clear, indeed.

If the arguments we commonly hear from the ranks of atheism, which have largely been a reaction to standard Christian teaching that claims to be based on the Bible, cannot be answered satisfactorily from Scripture, I also would surely find God repugnant. It is quite possible that my own path would, therefore, lead to the loss of all desire to serve Him, and it would not be surprising that I would consciously turn away and live for the alternative, for if I must serve a tyrant, it may as well be this one: self.

Praise His name; I did discover the truth about God. In my searching for God, I have been delighted to find that there have been many students of the Scriptures who have studied the hard questions to a satisfying resolution. With the help of their teachings and many hours spent in personal study of Scripture and the Spirit of Prophecy, I have been relieved to find that the apparent contradictions regarding the character of God as presented to us in the "biblical language" (also known as the "language of wrath") can be harmonized by comparing scripture with scripture.

The work you hold in your hands stands upon the shoulders of light that came to the church more than three decades ago. Since then, this message has arisen in a number of places through numerous individuals and ministries who have studied carefully the issues in the character of God controversy without knowledge of or collaboration with each other. So, while this book is an abridgment, edit, and update of the presentation of an early teacher in our church who gave it to the world as "open-source" material, with the desire that the message would be widely disseminated, it is also representative of the thinking of many teachers and writers in the present day who are in agreement with regard to the advancing light on the character of God and who strictly adhere to a principled interpretation of inspiration. The studies, inspiration, and writings of each contributor is given without any names attached, so their truths can stand purely on their own merits, as self-evident and in keeping with inspired counsel. Hence, this book is published under the name of no individual, but rather that of the "4th Angel," which is to proclaim the glory of God and share the light of the knowledge of His character, shining in the face of Jesus, to the whole world:

> Those who allow prejudice to bar the mind against the reception of truth cannot receive the divine enlightenment. Yet, when a view of Scripture is presented, many do not ask, Is it True,—in harmony with God's word? but, By whom is it advocated? and unless it comes through the very channel that pleases them, they do not accept it. So thoroughly satisfied are they with their own ideas, that they

will not examine the Scripture evidence, with a desire to learn, but refuse to be interested, merely because of their prejudices.

> The Lord often works where we least expect him; he surprises us by revealing his power through instruments of his own choice, while he passes by the men to whom we have looked as those through whom light should come. God desires us to receive the truth upon its own merits,—because it is truth (*Gospel Workers*, pp. 125, 126).

This awakening to the reality of who God is can be a tremendous paradigm shift for the fundamentalist Christian who has been taught to read and believe biblical words as denoted in a human dictionary of language. For many, it is not easy to adopt these glorious truths, because faulty principles of interpretation have been ingrained from childhood. It often does not come without significant time spent in discussions, prayer, and personal study. At last, we have to *own*, for *ourselves*, what we believe about God. It has to come to an immovable settling of mind, for it is upon this very subject that the great controversy opened, and it is upon this subject that it will close. There will be two classes of people in the final generation, and each of them will be acting out the character of the God/god whom they serve. One governs on principles of pure righteousness, truth, liberty, and *agape* love, while the other governs upon principles of force, deception, hypocrisy, and arbitrary rewards and punishments.

It is necessary to state at the outset of this study that it can be expected that whenever God is at work to advance light and understanding in His great object of preparing His people for eternity—a work of God that ends the great controversy and establishes the universe on a permanently secure footing—the enemy will be at work to corrupt the message and make it of no effect. At this time, there are in circulation several aberrant theological constructs that have been attached to or associated with the so-called character of God message.

One of the more common of these is the slide into Universalism, where everyone, even Satan and his host, will be saved at last into the kingdom. We deny that there is any scriptural foundation for such a belief system. Universal salvation only serves to deter us from entering into the stern work of overcoming our defects of character through a striving to consistently submit and abide in Christ, that by His Spirit He may bring us to that place of total surrender, wherein we shall be fitted for the finishing of the work through the showing forth of God's true character in word and in life. It is through severe test and trial that the true believer enters into that special work of the final generation, in which he/she will be ripened as the harvest grain in the hot summer sun, in coming to fitness for translation into the physical kingdom. In the closing scenes of the great controversy, it will be shown that the wages of sin is death and that the mind not surrendered to Christ and not having gone with Him to second death, during its days of probationary time, will recognize its own seared condition and choose to not exist anymore. You can read details on this later, but don't skip ahead!

If anyone is looking for a message that will please the carnal mind and let us relax our war against the world, the devil, and the flesh, they will not find it here, for in the character of God message, we behold a standard of thought and conduct that reaches as high as the highest heaven where God dwells. It will at last be understood by all that there can be no life in continuing in sin, for its wages will surely be paid out in full. The character of God message seeks to bring about such a global understanding of this truth that each one can make up their mind as to where they wish to stand. Then God can at last come to claim His people, while the rest will sadly have chosen to suffer the consequences of claiming to be their own god as He departs from them.

This corrected understanding of the character of God has become a milestone in my journey toward personal sealing into Christ and His kingdom, the liberty of the good news about God. I hope and pray that for every honest seeker who embarks on this same journey the end result will be the same.

We have many lessons to learn, and many, many to unlearn. God and heaven alone are infallible. Those who think that they will never have to give up a cherished view, never have occasion to change an opinion, will be disappointed (*The Review and Herald*, July 26, 1892).

Kevin Straub, Compiler
straub@direct.ca
April 2012

Introduction

There are three facts common to us all.

1. We have a definite opinion about God's character.
2. Our attitude toward God, our treatment toward others, and our receptivity of truth are determined by these opinions.
3. All of us were born predisposed to possess a false concept of God, which in turn has been confirmed and extended by environmental educational influences. Unless delivered from this and initiated into a true knowledge of God, it will be impossible to enter into a full and perfect Christian experience, and the prospects of eternal life will be at risk.

When Christ began working miracles and proclaiming the kingdom of God, He quickly rose to great popularity as the masses hoped that He was the One to restore the lost glory that was theirs. His following continued to swell until the feeding of the five thousand, when the enthusiasm of the people had reached such a height that they were willing to make Him king by force. When He refused, the enthusiasm died away, and the crowds walked with Him no more. From that time forward every step led to the cross where those who had so ardently called for His crowning, screamed for His crucifixion.

They had a very definite concept of God's character, which was shaped by the educational processes in their environment. Jesus did not perform as their concept of God's character led them to expect and desire of Him. Thus the question of God's character became the most critical element in the mission of Jesus and the fate of the Jews.

The Pharisees "looked forward to the day when they should have dominion over the hated Romans, and possess the riches and splendor of the world's great empire. The poor peasants and fishermen hoped to hear the assurance that their wretched hovels, the scanty food, the life of toil, and fear of want were to be exchanged for mansions of plenty and days of ease" (*The Desire of Ages,* p. 299).

Because the devil had done his work well, the people believed not only that the Messiah would exalt them in this way but that He would do it by the use of the sword. They saw God as the vengeful, destroying One of the Old Testament. Their concept of the God of the Old Testament led them to believe that the God of the New Testament would behave in the same way. But because their understanding of God's character was wrong, their expectations were also wrong.

Christ had not come to fail them. He knew exactly what their true needs were, and

He had fully purposed to supply those needs. But the answer did not lie in the use of the weapons of force. It lay in the changing of their characters into the likeness of His own. But so intent were they on their long-cherished ambitions that there was no room to consider the alternative He offered.

"In their enthusiasm the people are ready at once to crown Him king.... Consulting together, they agree to take Him by force, and proclaim Him the king of Israel" (*Ibid.*, p. 378).

They could not see and were unwilling to be taught that Christ did not have this kind of character. He loved the Romans as much as He loved the Jews, neither was it His way to use force to accomplish any desired objective. Therefore, in harmony with His character, He did not permit Himself to be made king by them, nor did he use His mighty powers to advantage one class of those whom He loved above another.

The bitter complaint of the apostles against Him then was, "Why did not He who possessed such power reveal Himself *in His true character*, and make their way less painful?" (*Ibid.*, p. 380, emphasis added).

The truth was that Christ was living out His character to perfection. Thus it was that their misunderstanding of the character of God in Christ led them to expect from Him a complete deliverance from the Romans and their exaltation to the heights of material grandeur. He was a Jew like they were. He was sent as the Messiah to the chosen and favored people. He had the power. Therefore, they reasoned, it was His duty to use that power to favor them. If He refused to do it, then He was nothing short of a traitor to His own. They found Him guilty of treason and determined to be revenged.

If only they had understood the character of God so perfectly revealed in Christ, or at least been willing to be taught it, they would not have expected of Him what they did, nor would they have rejected and vengefully crucified Him. Thus the question of the character of God and Christ was the most critical element in His mission and in the fate of the Jews.

The character of God is still the most critical issue in the mission of Christ. As were the Jews, all of us have also been subjected to an erroneous education in respect to God's character. But God will not leave us in this darkness without the opportunity to escape from it. When light is presented to us, there is the terrible danger that we will repeat the history of our forefathers and reject God's message because it does not conform to our already established ideas or suit our personal ambitions and dreams.

Let there be an earnest, prayerful pleading with the Lord to open the eyes of our spiritual understanding to see God *as He really is*.

"And this is eternal life, that they may know You,
the only true God, and Jesus Christ whom You have sent" (John 17:3).

Table of Contents

Chapter One

An All-Important Theme

Study/Discussion Questions:

- **What does it mean to know God?**

- **How do we know God?**

- **We are told that those who know God will "give Him glory." How do we do that?**

- **How do we remedy a shallow Christian experience?**

Knowing God is life eternal, and life eternal is knowing God. The essential and indispensable nature of being in possession of the knowledge of God is that knowing Him *as He is* is the power of the gospel to transform the character and recreate us into the image of God. Therefore, it becomes the seeker's prime interest to know by what means this knowing can be received.

And this is eternal life, that they may know You, the only true God, and Jesus Christ whom You have sent (John 17:3).

The knowledge of God as revealed in Christ is the knowledge that all who are saved must have. It is the knowledge that works transformation of character. This knowledge, received, will re-create the soul in the image of God. It will impart to the whole being a spiritual power that is divine (*Testimonies for the Church,* vol. 8, p. 289).

The key to unlocking the power of the gospel is not hidden. It is "the knowledge of God as revealed in Christ." The full force of this truth will not be appreciated unless there is a correct understanding of what the grace and peace of God are. Let us consider each in turn.

God's grace is not merely an attitude maintained on His part toward the undeserving sinner. Rather, it is "the regenerating, enlightening power of the Holy Spirit" (*The Great Controversy,* p. 394).

Defining the grace of God as being the power of God sets it apart as the supreme force in the universe. It is the one element emanating from a creating and recreating God that lifts the lost from damnation to glorification and without which would be no hope.

Observe the media through which it will come to us: "Grace and peace be multiplied to you in the knowledge of God and of Jesus our Lord" (2 Pet. 1:2).

Likewise, the peace of God is much more than merely a mental persuasion on God's part whereby He maintains a kindly or even indulgent attitude toward those who believe in Him. Paul advises the Romans that the carnal mind is enmity against God and that being justified is to have peace with God (Rom. 8:7; 5:1).

Therefore, both enmity against God and peace with God are states of being. These two cannot coexist. The former must be removed in order to make room for the latter. Only the mighty power of God can accomplish such splendid results.

To know what God will do for us is very important. But it still will not bring us eternal life unless we understand how we can receive these blessings.

> And how can we come into harmony with God, how shall we receive His like-
> ness, unless we obtain a knowledge of Him? It is this knowledge that Christ came
> into the world to reveal to unto us (*Testimonies for the Church,* vol. 5, p. 743).

To come into harmony with God and to receive his likeness is to be justified, because "having been justified by faith, we have peace [or harmony] with God" (Rom. 5:1). To be justified is to have life eternal. But to achieve this is impossible without a true knowledge of God. He must be known *as He is.* The more fully, intimately, and accurately He is known, the richer and more glorious will be the transformation into His likeness. There is a direct relationship between the extent of our knowledge of God and the level, warmth, and power of our personal Christian experience.

For men to glorify God as God, His character must be in them and be reflected from them. Sadly, this is not what is seen by the professed people of God. They have substituted another view of God, a view according to their own vain imaginations. The first chapter of Romans tells the terrible story. They "exchanged the truth of God for the lie" and "did not like to retain God in their knowledge" (verses 25, 28); so they descended into the depths of depravity and immorality and rejected God. Subsequently, God was forced to retreat from them in order that they might have their own chosen way.

Human beings cannot enter a worse state of wickedness than described in this chapter. Remember, Paul stated by inspiration that all this was the outworking of the rejection of the knowledge of God. Rejection is the root, and unbelievable wickedness is the sure and certain fruit. To whatever degree a wrong or poor concept of God's character is held, the level of morality will match it.

> The meager views which so many have had of the exalted character and office of
> Christ have narrowed their religious experience and have greatly hindered their
> progress in the divine life (*Testimonies for the Church,* vol. 5, p. 743).

God's people ought to be "far in advance of our present position" (*Ibid.*). So, if the cause of a narrow religious experience and hindered progress in the divine life is the holding of "meager views" of the character of Christ/God, then we know the starting point for remediation of the situation.

Such a relating of cause and effect should instantly command the interested attention of all today who are aware that their experience is far from what it should be and who long for spiritual enrichment.

Only by coming into a much clearer and deeper understanding of the character of God and Christ can we advance in the truth. Such a knowledge is not acquired in a moment or by feeble intermittent efforts. Nor is the work all of a positive nature. It is a matter of both learning and unlearning.

Not only have the concepts of God's character been meager, dim, and uncertain, but in many respects, they have been quite inaccurate. In fact, calling them inaccuracies does not portray the reality of their being exactly opposite from what God really is. The devil has clouded our minds with his false representations. Never was he more successful than just before the first coming of Christ, and again during the Dark Ages. We have not yet fully escaped the effect of that midnight period. We have not yet come all the way out of Babylon.

So serious were the misrepresentations of God's character which dominated the minds of men that Jesus had to give a revelation of God exactly opposite from that which they had. "He presented to men that which was exactly contrary to the representations of the enemy in regard to the character of God" (*Fundamentals of Christian Education,* p. 177).

As we again approach the midnight darkness of the last days, the same misrepresentations of God are held by humankind throughout the world. There is much unlearning to do as well as learning, and the following chapters are designed to assist in both directions. Old concepts will be challenged, and many things will be presented about God that will be exactly opposite from what has been believed in the past. The old concepts will strive for mastery and will not go down easily, but for those who patiently and prayerfully examine the evidence, there will come such a revelation of God's character as will clear away the fog of the past, recreate the soul in the image of God, transform the believer into the likeness of God, and prepare His followers for a place in eternity.

Let this great theme of God's character become the chief and all absorbing subject of our attention, our meditation, our conversation, and our witness, for this is life eternal.

Chapter Two

Avoid Speculative Theories

Study/Discussion Questions:

- **Is the study of the character of God a realm of inquiry into which we may safely enter?**
- **In this subject are we looking into matters that God has not revealed or are we advancing in revelation into a "new development of truth"?**

In the study of the subject of God's character, there is the danger that comes with seeking a knowledge outside of what God has revealed. Therefore, any attempt to explore the unrevealed areas of divine knowledge will be strictly avoided in this study. It will be concerned only with the evidence that God has seen fit to give, and nothing else but that.

A reading of Ephesians 3:1-11 teaches us that there was a time for both angels and men when certain things were secrets still. To have attempted to search out those secrets *then* would have been dangerous, presumptuous, and speculative. But not so in Paul's day, for they had passed from the category of the secret things to the revealed.

God is infinite. We are finite. Therefore, the time will never come, even in eternity, when there will be no secret things remaining. There will always be an infinity beyond our comprehension, even though eternity "will bring richer and still more glorious revelations of God and of Christ" (*The Great Controversy,* p. 678).

> Because of the continual transfer of knowledge from the secret list to the open, that which once belonged to God alone will come to belong to us and our children forever.
>
> In every age there is a new development of truth, a message of God to the people of that generation (*Christ's Object Lessons,* p. 127).
>
> But the path of the just is like the shining sun, that shines ever brighter unto the perfect day (Prov. 4:18).
>
> In eternity we shall learn that which, had we received the enlightenment it was possible to obtain here, would have opened our understanding (*Christ's Object Lessons,* p. 134).

This statement opens the mighty possibilities of advancement in divine illumination. It is an encouragement and invitation to enter into the revelations that the Lord delights to give His people.

Yet it must be stressed that there are things that remain hidden. Our concentration of study must be in those areas where the Lord has released the light. At all costs there must be the avoidance of speculative theorizing.

> Our first parents were led into sin through indulging a desire for knowledge that God had withheld from them. In seeking to gain this knowledge, they lost all that was worth possessing.... The lesson is for us. The field into which Satan led our first parents is the same to which he is alluring men today. He is flooding the world with pleasing fables. By every device at his command he tempts men to speculate in regard to God. Thus he seeks to prevent them from obtaining that knowledge of God which is salvation (*The Ministry of Healing,* pp. 427, 428).

With such clear warnings as these before us, there can be no excuse for any indulgence in speculation about the character of God. Therefore, this study will not in any sense deviate from the strict lessons and principles contained in these warnings and instructions. It will be concerned only with that which the Lord has revealed.

While, on the one hand, there are those who would venture onto the fragile thinness of the treacherous ice of human speculation, others tend to the opposite extreme. Because God is so infinite, distant, deep, and unsearchable, they take the stand that they should not study His character at all. This is a mistake of equal gravity, completely fulfilling Satan's desire that they know not God.

> It is Satan's constant study to keep the minds of men occupied with those things which will prevent them from obtaining the knowledge of God (*Testimonies for the Church,* vol. 5, p. 740).

We are to keep a careful balance in our relation to this theme. Ever let it be remembered that there is a direct relationship between the knowledge of God and our level of righteous or unrighteous living. To know God is life eternal. To be ignorant of Him is eternal death.

Chapter Three

The Character of God in Relation to the Great Controversy

Study/Discussion Questions:

- The big question: what is the main theme of the great controversy?
- Why is it important that God's name be vindicated?
- What is the relationship between Satan's misrepresentation of the character of God and man's fall into sin?
- How was the restriction of the forbidden tree a blessing, intended to reveal the character of God?

The study of God's character is not merely a theme related to the great controversy—it is the *very subject* of the great controversy.

The awful struggle in this controversy came in at the point where, with pride-blinded eyes, Lucifer could no longer see God *as He is* and, seeing a very different character in Him, committed himself to war against God. Pride ripened into active rebellion once the misconception of the character of God settled in his mind. He understood also that in order to seed the rebellion successfully, he had to represent God as a liar and a destroyer. Satan convinced countless angels of his lies, effectively inducing them to join his ranks. This same policy was used to deceive man.

It was exactly at that point where misunderstanding of God's character first began to form that the spirit of rebellion formed. Ever since, wherever those misconceptions have taken root, rebellion has raged on. Therefore, only when those misconceptions have been completely cleared away will rebellion end and permanent, universal peace return.

This does not mean that God is seeking a personal vindication of Himself. That is the last thing He would do. He is seeking the vindication of that which will ensure the eternal life and happiness of every one of His creatures throughout the full immensity of the universe. God knows that Satan's misrepresentation and lies about God's character and government have brought only misery and death to this world. Therefore, it is to save us, not Himself, that God seeks the vindication of His own character.

This can be better appreciated when it is seen that God's law and government are an exact expression of His character. God does not have one code of behavior for Himself while He governs His people on other principles. This is so with earthly rulers, but not with God.

It is necessary, at this point, to comment further on the development of pride within the heart of Lucifer. As this leader of all the angels lived, he grew in wisdom and abilities, according to the laws that govern all of God's creatures. Marvelous was his progress, until he became the brightest of all the creatures.

The exceeding riches that he received should have elicited only perpetual gratitude and loving service, but they instead served to undo him.

> By the abundance of your trading you became filled with violence within, and you sinned (Ezek. 28:16).

The needless corruption of the covering cherub through the abundance of his talents and wealth has repeatedly destroyed humanity. The quest for greatness and material possessions has increased since the first sin was committed. Consider a fledgling movement of the Spirit upon a people. At first, they are poor in material wealth, their sense of need is proportionately great, generating a strong sense of total dependency and faith in God. God's liberal responses evoke gratitude and praise from them. This enrichment of spiritual and material wealth relieves them of the pressure of immediate necessity, but it introduces a danger against which a watchful guard must be established. That peril resides in the imperceptible but certain fading away of the positive sense of dependence on God. History verifies that most fail this test.

As the sense of dependence upon God wanes, material possessions come to be looked upon as the basis and guarantee of security. Thus it is an error to say that people lose faith. Instead, they transfer it from the God, who gave the gifts, to the gifts given by God.

So, as Lucifer descended this path, his life became increasingly self-centered and self-sufficient. Thus he, and not God, became the standard by which he judged all things. Even the Son of God came under his critical measurement. So inflated had his view of himself become that he saw himself as being actually superior to the Divine One, as it is written, "You corrupted your wisdom for the sake of your splendor" (Ezek. 28:17).

After an unknown amount of time, during which Lucifer developed his ideas and attempted to rouse sympathy amongst the angels, God convened a great assembly at which He presented the true position of His Son and the reasons for Christ occupying His exalted place in heaven. Lucifer almost yielded, but did not, and *then* the great battle began by his "leaving his place in the immediate presence of the Father," and going "forth to diffuse the spirit of discontent among the angels" (*Patriarchs and Prophets*, p. 37).

This evidence shows that a great deal happened within Lucifer *before* he went to war. The purpose of the line of thought being developed in this section is to show that it was when he lost the true knowledge of God's character and replaced it with a false concept that then, and not until then, he entered into warfare against God.

The substitution in Lucifer's mind of the false for the true concept of God's character came as the result of his incorrect evaluation of God's behavior. He attributed to God a motive that in reality was nonexistent. Let's take a closer look at how Lucifer's false concept developed.

During the time that elapsed between the first presence of pride in him and the committal to rebellion, Lucifer waited expectantly for God to elevate him to the position which, in his own mind, he judged as rightly his. He could not see nor did he want to understand that God could not promote him because Lucifer could never occupy Christ's place unless he was God as Christ was. He was not qualified and never could be.

The longer he waited, the deeper became his anxiety. He correctly concluded that something was deeply wrong, but he failed utterly to comprehend that the error lay in himself, not in God. God had not changed, but Lucifer had. He who had been the humble servant of God and his fellow creatures had become a proud self-server.

To comprehend the development of evil in Lucifer, it is only necessary to observe the same process in humanity. It is readily seen today that when a person arrives at this point, the last thing they are inclined to do is recognize that the fault lies in themselves. Everybody and everything else is to blame but never themselves.

So it was with Lucifer. The only possible conclusion left to him, in his darkened reasoning, was that the fault lay with God. Having arrived at this awful point, a radically new concept of God's character took root and thrived in his mind. Heretofore, he had *correctly* understood God to be perfectly just, fair, and impartial. He rightly knew that God assigned positions in direct relationship to each individual's fitness to fulfill the responsibility. It was in harmony with those convictions that Lucifer had expected God to exalt him. Those hopes would have been realized if Lucifer's evaluation of himself had been correct.

But, when denied the position, he erroneously concluded that God was with great partiality favoring His Son. Partiality in itself is serious enough, for it is impossible to show favor to one person except it be at the expense of another. However, charges of partiality cannot be entered against God in this case, because Christ was not in any way upon the same level of existence as Lucifer, being Himself Deity and not a created being. Lucifer had taken upon himself the work of inciting doubt regarding the supremacy of Christ. In so doing, he set about to convince everyone that God was a liar and a deceiver in that He claimed impartiality, yet He favored One above the rest.

Lucifer fully believed that he had experienced a great awakening. He felt that he had thrown off the shackles of a terrible bondage. He became hostile toward God and especially toward Christ for having, as he supposed, held the angels in deception for so long a time, and he determined to assert his rights and reform the government of God.

At this point the great controversy began, and mutiny ensued first with the angels and then with humanity, as each in turn came to share the same erroneous concepts of God's character.

Lucifer misrepresented God by:

...attributing to Him the desire for self-exaltation. With his own evil characteristics he sought to invest the loving Creator.... He led [the angels and humanity]
to doubt the word of God, and to distrust His goodness. Because God is a God
of justice and terrible majesty, Satan caused them to look upon Him as severe
and unforgiving (*The Desire of Ages*, p. 22).

By the same misrepresentation of the character of God as he had practiced in
heaven, causing Him to be regarded as severe and tyrannical, Satan induced
man to sin (*The Great Controversy*, p. 500).

Satan's objective of enlisting others in rebellion was achieved through the use of a certain very successful method. That method was to persuade angels and humans that God's
character was that of a deceiver, an oppressor and a liar. This was the method used, and to
whatever extent it was successful, rebellion followed.

In the tempting of Eve, Satan asserted that while God had assured them that they were
to have unlimited development, the real fact was that God was afraid that they would ascend to an equality with Him. Once this occurred, then He would have to share with them
all the riches He had reserved for His own pleasure. This, Satan declared, God wished to
prevent at any cost. Thus He barred them from partaking of the tree of knowledge of good
and evil, whereby such exaltation would be immediately effected. Therefore, the devil continued, God was forced to lie to them in order to protect His own position.

There was no truth in Satan's charges. God had not denied Adam and Eve access to
the tree from the motive of self-protection. Neither had He made any of His laws for this
purpose. Those principles of life were a love gift from God to protect them, not Himself.
God needs no protection from anyone, nor is it His character to restrict anyone else to His
own advantage.

The tree was a gift. It was for their benefit, designed to teach them about obedience and
respect. As they multiplied upon the earth, all that they had would have to be shared with
the increasing population. Unless the lesson of absolute respect for the property of another
was deeply ingrained into their minds, contention, strife, confusion, and open war would
develop as men sought to wrest from each other that which they desired.

In electing to believe Satan's lie, Adam and Eve transferred their allegiance from God
to Satan. They put another god in the place of the true God. To do that was also to bring
death upon themselves—practically *instant* death. They would certainly have died that
very day had not Christ interposed.

The instant man accepted the temptations of Satan ... Christ, the Son of God,
stood between the living and the dead, saying, "Let the punishment fall on
Me. I will stand in man's place. He shall have another chance" (*The SDA Bible
Commentary*, vol. 1, p. 1085).

It is the Lord that keeps all things; He sustains the heavenly bodies and systems down to the minutest atom of matter. It is the Creator of all things who maintains their proper function and place.

> God ... has in these last days spoken to us by His Son ... through whom also He made the worlds; who being the brightness of His glory and the express image of His person, and upholding all things by the word of His power, when He had by Himself purged our sins, sat down at the right hand of the Majesty on high (Heb. 1:1-3).

> "It is not by inherent power that year by year the earth yields its bounties and continues its march around the sun. The hand of the Infinite One is perpetually at work guiding this planet. It is God's power continually exercised that keeps the earth in position in its rotation. It is God who causes the sun to rise in the heavens. He opens the windows of heaven and gives rain.... It is by His power that vegetation is caused to flourish, that every leaf appears, every flower blooms, every fruit develops (*The Ministry of Healing*, p. 416).

Therefore, if any one of His creatures in any part of the vast universe—except where the presence of a Savior provides a delaying factor—puts another god in place of the real God, then the power of God as an upholder of the mighty forces of nature will have been removed from that place, and as surely, they will become uncontrolled forces of terrible destruction. In that very day, those who have made the fatal mistake will die, not because God will strike them down, but because they have placed themselves where life is impossible.

The only reason that such a cataclysm of destruction has not obliterated this earth is because of the merciful interposition of Jesus Christ. Therefore, God's instruction to Adam and Eve in the Garden of Eden not to partake of the tree was given to protect them from destruction. In no sense was it to protect Himself or His own position. Rightly understood, the "restriction" placed upon the first couple was a true revelation of the perfectly righteous character of God. It was an act of kindness and mercy. It was the work of a Savior, not that of a despot.

The study of the appearance of sin in heaven and on this earth establishes the very close connection between the misrepresentation of the character of God and the appearance of rebellion.

> It is *Satan's constant effort* to misrepresent the character of God, the nature of sin, and the real issues at stake in the great controversy. His sophistry lessens the obligation of the divine law and gives men license to sin. At the same time he causes them to cherish false conceptions of God so that they regard Him with fear and hate rather than with love. The cruelty inherent in his own character is attributed to the Creator; it is embodied in systems of religion and expressed in modes of worship. *Thus the minds of men are blinded, and Satan secures them as his agents to war against God.* By perverted conceptions of the divine attributes,

heathen nations were led to believe human sacrifices necessary to secure the favor of Deity; and horrible cruelties have been perpetrated under the various forms of idolatry (*The Great Controversy*, p. 569, emphasis added).

Therefore, the subject of the character of God is not something apart from the great controversy. It is right at the very heart of it. The weapon the devil uses to lead souls into rebellion against God is the misrepresentation of His character. The more he is able to convince men of these deceptions, the more they enter into unrighteousness and rebellion. This is the witness of the Word of God and of history. In light of these facts, what study could be more important than the one here being pursued?

Chapter Four

The Character of God and the End of the Great Controversy

Study/Discussion Questions:

- Wasn't the cross the end of the battle?
- Why are we still here?
- How is the controversy going to end?

The evidences presented in Scripture confirm the truth that the great controversy began with the misrepresentation of the character of God. Furthermore, Satan's extension and continuation of the struggle has been by the same means. Thus is revealed the cause and the effect—the cause being the establishment of an erroneous view of God, and the effect, the proliferation of iniquitous rebellion.

It is a sound principle that once the cause of a problem has been established, the remedy for it is in view. Therefore, the reversal of rebellion can be accomplished by the presentation of the truth in regard to God.

Preeminent in this work of divine restoration is Jesus Christ. When He came to earth, He came not only to save humanity from the penalty of sin by sacrificing Himself but to save people by revealing the character of God in contrast to Satan's propositions.

Christ's role as the revealer of the true character of God was as necessary to ending the great controversy and the salvation of the lost as was His supreme sacrifice on the cross. Jesus came expressly to show God to angels and people exactly as He is.

> The Son of God came to this earth to reveal the character of the Father to men, that they might learn to worship Him in spirit and in truth (*Counsels to Parents, Teachers, and Students,* p. 28).

It is also written that "for this purpose the Son of God was manifested, that He might destroy the works of the devil" (1 John 3:8).

This was no easy task. Had it simply been a contest of force versus force, it would have been over in an instant. The question is not over physical strength, but of the real nature of God's character and government.

How many times have people wished that the Lord would speak directly and audibly in a problem situation. It is firmly believed that that would settle the issue right then and there. But the witness of the ages reveals that the Word of God alone is not sufficient to settle these issues, great or small. If it was, then there never would have been a great controversy.

Once upon a time there was only the Word of God. That Word came under challenge. God explained the situation to the heavenly host in detail (see *Patriarchs and Prophets*, p. 36). Thus the word of Satan was met by the Word of God. But it did not settle the question, for it was not accepted by Satan and his followers. Therefore, time had to be given in which Satan could demonstrate the true nature of his claims while God and Christ, on the other hand, could unfold the real character of their position. It is for this purpose that the Lord has permitted the great conflict to continue through all these ages, and until that purpose has been fulfilled, the controversy will continue.

That is, the struggle will go on, Christ shall not return, sin will not be ended, and death will reign, until both angels and humanity see for themselves the real nature of God's character and government in sharp contrast to that of Satan. When that point is reached, the end will come.

While Satan's arguments drew a third of the angels to his side, two-thirds remained loyal to God. It is naturally assumed that they therefore were not all influenced by the devil's sophistries. The real truth is that *every one* of the angels was affected at least in part by the delusions of the great enemy. Uncertainties about God, His character, and the principles of His government were generated in them to the point where a definite sympathy for Satan's cause was present. Throughout the long centuries elapsing between the fall of Lucifer and the cross of Calvary, that state of affairs continued. During this period the holy angels served God with definite reservations and felt that Satan had something of a case to be argued.

> Not until the death of Christ was the character of Satan clearly revealed to the angels or to the unfallen worlds. The archapostate had so clothed himself with deception that even *holy beings* had *not* understood his principles. They had not clearly seen the nature of his rebellion....
>
> God could have destroyed Satan and his sympathizers as easily as one can cast a pebble to the earth; but He did not do this. Rebellion was not to be overcome by force. Compelling power is found only under Satan's government. The Lord's principles are not of this order. His authority rests upon goodness, mercy, and love; and the presentation of these principles is the means to be used. God's government is moral, and truth and love are to be the prevailing power.
>
> It was God's purpose to place things on an eternal basis of security, and in the councils of heaven it was decided that time must be given for Satan to develop the principles which were the foundation of his system of government. He had claimed that these were superior to God's principles. Time was given for the working of Satan's principles, *that they might be seen by the heavenly universe* (*The Desire of Ages*, pp. 758, 759, emphasis added).

At the cross the last link of sympathy between Satan and the heavenly world was broken. *The Desire of Ages* provides the following insight on the scene at the cross.

> "And I heard a loud voice saying in heaven, Now is come salvation, and strength, and the kingdom of our God, and the power of His Christ; for the accuser of our brethren is cast down, which accused them before our God day and night" Revelation 12:10.
>
> Satan saw that his disguise was torn away. His administration was laid open before the unfallen angels and before the heavenly universe. He had revealed himself as a murderer. By shedding the blood of the Son of God, he had up-rooted himself from the sympathies of the heavenly beings. Henceforth his work was restricted. Whatever attitude he might assume, he could no longer await the angels as they came from the heavenly courts, and before them accuse Christ's brethren of being clothed with the garments of blackness and the defilement of sin. The last link of sympathy between Satan and the heavenly world was broken (p. 761).

It was then that the angels saw and understood the character of God as it truly was. Christ had destroyed the works of the devil in them, and for them, the purpose of the great controversy had been achieved. Therefore, if only angels were involved in the struggle, Satan's end would have come at the cross. But what had been done for angels had to be done for humanity too, for while angels saw the real nature of the character of God and of Satan at the cross, humanity certainly did not and still has not.

We may not know it today, but even those of us who walk nearest to God still have a measure of sympathy with Satan and his ways. Not until the final time of testing will this at last be removed from us.

> The time of trouble is the crucible that is to bring out Christ-like characters. It is designed to lead the people of God to renounce Satan and his temptations. *The last conflict will reveal Satan to them in his true character,* that of a cruel tyrant, and it will do for them what nothing else could do, up-root him entirely from their affections. For to love and cherish sin, is to love and cherish its author … When they excuse sin and cling to perversity of character, they give Satan a place in their affections, and pay him homage (*The Review and Herald,* August 12, 1884, emphasis added).

Because this work has yet to be accomplished for human beings so that the purpose of the great controversy is fulfilled for them as it was for the angels, the battle was not terminated at the cross as it is written:

> Yet Satan was not then [at the time of the cross] destroyed. The angels did not even then understand all that was involved in the great controversy. The principles at stake were to be more fully revealed. And for the sake of man, Satan's existence must be continued. Man as well as angels must see the contrast be-

tween the Prince of light and the prince of darkness. He must choose whom he will serve (*The Desire of Ages*, p. 761).

The progressive development in the controversy God has with Satan is portrayed in Revelation 12. The original confrontation in heaven with the resulting removal of Satan from the celestial precincts is described in verses 7-9:

> And war broke out in heaven: Michael and his angels fought against the dragon; and the dragon and his angels fought, but they did not prevail, nor was a place found for them in heaven any longer. So the great dragon was cast out, that serpent of old, called the Devil and Satan, who deceives the whole world; he was cast to the earth, and his angels were cast out with him.

Note that it was at this time that Satan was cast *out* into the earth. The place from which he was cast *out* was heaven, but he still had the opportunity of accosting the angels as they moved to and from heaven and "before them accuse Christ's brethren of being clothed with the garments of blackness and the defilement of sin" (*The Desire of Ages*, p. 761).

But that activity was terminated when at the cross he was cast down. First, Lucifer had been cast *out*, and then he was cast *down*.

> Christ bowed His head and died, but He held fast His faith and His submission to God. "And I heard a loud voice saying in heaven, Now is come salvation, and strength, and the kingdom of our God, and the power of His Christ: for the accuser of our brethren is cast down, which accused them before our God day and night." Revelation 12:10 (*Ibid.*).

So it is written, "Therefore rejoice, O heavens, and you who dwell in them!" (Rev. 12:12). But the time for rejoicing in the unfallen universe is no time for joyous songs upon the earth, because now Satan's attention is focused only on one group: humanity. In addition, his fearful losses sustained at the cross do not discourage but only madden him into a frenzy of desperate and determined activity. Verse 12 concludes by saying, "Woe to the inhabitants of the earth and the sea! For the devil has come down to you, having great wrath, because he knows that he has a short time."

Now comes the time to discuss the achievement of the full recovery. Another great battle must be fought wherein will be accomplished for humanity that which was accomplished for the unfallen universe. This victory will be gained exactly as it was gained by Christ, for we are to overcome as He overcame (see Rev. 3:21).

How is this last battle fought and won? Counter-accusation is unproductive, becoming a contest of confusing words. The use of force often will generate sympathy for the rebel through the natural tendency to take up the cause of the underdog.

There is only one way to reveal evil and that is to expose it to righteousness. This is what Jesus did throughout His lifetime on earth. His sojourn here was able to signally defeat Satan to the point where the unfallen universe was completely and eternally delivered from the power of Satan's deceptions. But for human beings the purpose of the great controversy has not yet been fulfilled.

Christ is not returning to this earth to repeat the demonstration already given. He has other plans. This full and final display of the merciful, gracious, kind, good, and just character of God is to be given through His people. Only as He is able to do this will the purpose of the controversy be finally achieved for humanity as it was for angels. Then the Savior can and will return.

> In order to endure the trial before them, they [the people of God who will live through the final time of trouble and conflict] must understand the will of God as revealed in His word; they can honor Him only as they have a right conception of His character, government, and purposes, and act in accordance with them (*The Great Controversy*, p. 593).

The final movement of people who will provide the Lord with the means of making that ultimate manifestation of His character is prophetically described in Revelation 18:1: "After these things I saw another angel coming down from heaven, having great authority; and the earth was illuminated with his glory."

Let it be established that the message of the angel is given by a movement of people, not by a literal angel.

> Hence the movement symbolized by the angel coming down from heaven, lightening the earth with his glory and crying mightily with a strong voice announcing the sins of Babylon (*Ibid.,* p. 604).

With whose glory will the earth be lightened? To be sure, it is the glory of God, but that is not what the verse says. It says, "another angel [came] down from heaven … and the earth was lightened with *his* glory."

It is the glory of the angel that lightens the whole earth. It is true that this is also and primarily the glory of God, for it is from God that this glory is acquired. But it has been truly given to the angel that it has become his own and can be described as being his glory.

What is the glory of the angel and the glory of God? Is it merely a physical manifestation of brightness? There are numerous Scripture references to this kind of glory as an attribute of God, but there is a meaning to the word "glory" other than the outshining of radiant light and pulsing power. When Moses asked the Lord to show him His glory, the Lord hid Moses in a crack in the rocks and covered him in protection, while revealing in passing only His "back," not His face, in order that the physical glory not overpower him, causing harm. But this is not the glory God was eager to share with Moses. The Lord revealed to Moses *His character*. Here is God's response to his request.

> Then He said, "I will make all *My goodness* pass before you, and I will proclaim *the name* of the LORD before you. I will *be gracious* to whom I will be gracious, and I will *have compassion* on whom I will have compassion (Exod. 33:19).

The Lord did not show Moses the outward splendor of His being, but the wonder of His great and lovely character. From this we deduce that the glory of God is His character. When Jesus came to this earth, He left behind all the physical glory.

> He has no form or comeliness; and when we see Him, there is no beauty that we should desire Him (Isa. 53:2).

Yet despite the plainness of His outward appearance, He revealed the glory of God to those with the spiritual vision, enabling them to see it.

> And the Word became flesh and dwelt among us, and we beheld His glory, the glory as of the only begotten of the Father, full of grace and truth (John 1:14).

In *Christ's Object Lessons* the word "glory" is directly equated with character: "The light of His glory—His character—is to shine forth in His followers" (p. 414).

Back to the message of Revelation 18:1, which is summarized as follows:

- This is the *final* message to be given to the world
- The angel is the symbol of a *movement* of people
- The glory of the angel is the glory of the *character of God*

It is the angel's glory and, therefore, the character glory within the *people* of the movement that shall lighten the whole earth.

> When the character of Christ shall be perfectly reproduced in His people, then He will come to claim them as His own (*Christ's Object Lessons,* p. 69).

It is difficult to believe, as we look at ourselves with all our defects, that Christ could so reproduce Himself within a human agent that to see that person is to see the very character and nature of God. Yet, this is how it must be, for if it required a faultless manifestation of God's character to deliver the sinless beings of heaven and the unfallen worlds and thus achieve the purpose of the great controversy for them, it will require nothing less than the same faultless and complete manifestation of God's character to deliver humankind from Satan's deceptive power and accomplish the purpose of the great controversy for fallen humanity. Nothing less than this will bring the finishing of the work, and this is why "Christ is waiting with longing desire for the manifestation of Himself in His church. When the character of Christ shall be perfectly reproduced in His people, then He will come to claim them as His own" (*Ibid.*).

So it will be that "the church, being endowed with the righteousness of Christ, is His depository, in which the wealth of His mercy, His love, His grace, is to appear in full and final display" (*Testimonies to Ministers and Gospel Workers,* p. 18).

It, therefore, is of paramount concern that we appreciate the gravity of the matter. In the final work on this earth, the true understanding and manifestation of the character of God will play a vital role. Let every child of God move forward, making this topic a priority not only in study but in the living work of putting on the character of Christ and making His righteousness our own.

Chapter Five

Isaiah's Wonderful Prophecy

Study/Discussion Questions:

- **How do we fulfill the Great Commission?**
- **What is the real cause of the deep moral darkness on the earth?**
- **What is the message whose proclamation has been predicted in prophecy?**

Revelation 18 clearly foretells the time when the glory of God's character shall be revealed through His people as the final message to humanity. This message is also found in the Old Testament. One such place is Isaiah 60:1-3 (see also *Christ's Object Lessons,* p. 415).

> Arise, shine; for your light has come! And the glory of the LORD is risen upon you. For behold, the darkness shall cover the earth, and deep darkness the people; but the LORD will arise over you, and His glory will be seen upon you. The Gentiles shall come to your light, and kings to the brightness of your rising.

It is true that these verses do have an initial application to the work and ministry of Christ. Some, therefore, tend to limit the application to Him, but when it is understood that the people of the last church on earth have to reveal the character of God exactly as Jesus did, to accomplish thereby for fallen humanity what Christ accomplished for the unfallen, it will be seen that the texts do have an equal application to God's last movement on earth.

The character or righteousness of God is *not* something that is simply credited to the person; it is actually built into the person. It becomes his or her own character, so that when others look upon him or her they see the glory of God's character just as if they were looking at the Creator. There they will see the same love, justice, righteousness, peace, goodness, honesty; the same disposition to save and never to destroy.

The parable of the ten virgins parallels the teaching found in Isaiah 60. The same picture of darkness broken by clear light is presented, for the virgins are represented as sleeping until the midnight hour, which is the very darkest hour of the night. Then they arise with their lamps by which they light the way for the Bridegroom's coming. Without lighting the path, the Bridegroom could not make His way. He is dependent upon that light to make His arrival possible.

So the followers of Christ are to shed light into the darkness of the world. Through the Holy Spirit, God's word is a light as it becomes a transforming power in the life of the receiver. By implanting *in* their hearts the principles of His word, the Holy Spirit develops *in* men the *attributes of God*. The light of His glory—His *character*—is to shine forth *in* His followers. Thus they are said to glorify God, to lighten the path to the Bridegroom's home, to the city of God, to the marriage supper of the Lamb (*Christ's Object Lessons*, p. 414, emphasis added).

To be such a light requires much more than merely understanding the theory of the truth and then preaching it to others. God's Word is a light as it becomes a transforming power in the life of the receiver. This speaks of an inner working by the transforming agency of the Holy Spirit. This is the changing of the person's inward nature so that he or she becomes formed into the likeness of God.

This is not a false interpretation of these words as the next sentence in *Christ's Object Lessons*, by giving further explanation, clearly shows. "By implanting in their hearts the principles of His word, the Holy Spirit develops in men the attributes of God." Of course, these attributes are to be understood as His characteristics, His glory, His disposition, and His qualities, though not His great dynamic powers to impart life, creative power.

The purpose of the great controversy cannot be fulfilled unless this demonstration of God's character is given. Read again the quotation from *Christ's Object Lessons*, above. Could any teaching be plainer than this? Do you desire to know the way in which you can glorify God and light the way to the Bridegroom's home, to the city of God, to the marriage supper of the Lamb?

It is not by intellectual understanding of the theory of truth, nor is it by attempting to wrap Christ's covering around us through ceremonies, forms, adherence to codes, or practices of religion. It is by none of these things, though portions of all these things may have their place in our lives. *It is by having the Holy Spirit form the very character of God, His attributes, His righteousness, within the believer.* By exactly the same means through which the Savior accomplished His mission, the followers of Christ likewise must fulfill their commission in the final conflict.

It was on the earth that the love of God was revealed through Christ. It is on the earth that His children are to reflect this love through blameless lives. Thus sinners will be led to the cross to behold the Lamb of God (*The Acts of the Apostles*, p. 334).

True and necessary as these principles have been in past history, they will be even more so in the coming darkest hour of all.

The coming of the bridegroom was at midnight—the darkest hour. So the coming of Christ will take place in the darkest period of this earth's history (*Christ's Object Lessons*, p. 414).

There will be deep darkness brought by Satan's delusions, heresies, and false teachings such as there has never been in the past. But we are not left to think of the nature of the darkness of those false teachings in merely general terms. Instead, we are told specifically what they are. It is as the exact nature of those delusions are unfolded that we understand the real cause for the moral darkness in the world at the end.

> It is the darkness of misapprehension of God that is enshrouding the world. Men are losing their knowledge of His character. It has been misunderstood and misinterpreted (*Ibid.*, p. 415).

This then is the great darkness that shall blanket the world in the last days as depicted in Isaiah 60:2. It is the misunderstanding of God's character. Satan knows that rebellion against God is begun, developed, and sustained by this means. He knows also that the great conflict can never be terminated until people are set free from erroneous ideas in respect to who God really is, so he puts forth superhuman efforts to lock humanity in the gross darkness of the misapprehension of God.

As surely as we are living in this time of human history, so surely we can expect to see the Lord providing His answer to Satan's deceptions. The time has come for the proclamation of a message about the character of God and His righteousness.

It is not an idle expectation:

> At this time a message from God is to be proclaimed, a message illuminating in its influence and saving in its power. *His character is to be made known.* Into the darkness of the world is to be shed the light of His glory, the light of His goodness, mercy, and truth.
>
> This is the work outlined by the prophet Isaiah in the words, "O Jerusalem, that bringest good tidings, lift up thy voice with strength; lift it up, be not afraid; say unto the cities of Judah, Behold Your God! Behold, the Lord God will come with strong hand, and His arm shall rule for Him; behold, His reward is with Him, and His work before Him." Isaiah 40:9, 10.
>
> Those who wait for the Bridegroom's coming are to say to the people, "Behold your God." The last rays of merciful light, the last message of mercy to be given to the world, is a revelation of His character of love. *The children of God are to manifest His glory.* In their own life and character they are to reveal what the grace of God has done for them (*Ibid.*, pp. 415, 416, emphasis added).

This is not a message to be argued, debated, or contested. It is a message to be *proclaimed*, not only by the lips but by the witness of the life itself; a witness made effective by the forming of the very character of God within so that when people look upon the messenger they see the character of God revealed. Then they come to know God as God is as they see Him reflected from the transformed hearts of the believers.

The coming of this message from God is no longer a prophetic expectation but a present reality. It is a reality in your life, dear reader. As these chapters unfold the evidences for these great truths, know that they have been years in formation. With great care, every concept has been carefully checked with the correct principles of Bible interpretation until a beautiful harmony has developed.

No knowledge of the prediction that such a message would come was possessed by us when the first light of this truth opened into a fuller understanding. Otherwise we might well have gone seeking a message of our own upon the character of God, seeking to fulfill the prophecy out of our own inventions. Rather, first the light on the message came, and then we discovered that it had come in fulfillment of Bible and Spirit of Prophecy predictions.

It is hoped that by this time you will have gained some concept of the vital importance of this theme to the point of earnest study and an intense desire to understand and to possess the wonderful character of God.

Chapter Six

Approaching the Study of God

Study/Discussion Questions:

- **What reveals the true character?**
- **Why is it so difficult to see God as He is?**
- **What can we do to avoid remaining in ignorance of the nature of God's kingdom?**

Character is revealed by the way in which one acts, for the very simple reason that we do what we do because of who we are. Character is especially revealed in times of great stress, when the pressure increases under testing and difficulties.

The duress created by the sin problem made far-reaching changes in angels, humanity, and nature, but it made absolutely no change in God. He is "the same yesterday, today, and forever" (Heb. 13:8). God is unchanged and unchangeable. He declares, "I am the LORD, I do not change" (Mal. 3:6). He is "the Father of lights, with whom is no variation or shadow of turning" (James 1:17). He is "the incorruptible God" (Rom. 1:23).

These evidences confirm that God did not follow a certain line of behavior before the entrance of sin and then, when sin appeared, engage in activities utterly unknown before the uprising of evil.

Before the fall there never would have been any occasion for God to punish, so it is easy to understand that He never did such a thing. Subsequent to that sad day, however, an entirely different set of conditions demanded of God, as the responsible Ruler of all, a satisfactory and permanent solution. Because most people understand only the use of force as such a solution, they cannot see God doing anything other than bearing down with terrible punishments on the guilty. This is the common human logic that interprets all the reported actions of God in the Old Testament as being of this character. Therefore, the declaration that God did absolutely nothing after the fall that He did not do before will certainly be a startling statement that is hard to accept because it implies that God has not ever resorted to force, threats, or violence.

But it is true, nonetheless. Otherwise we are compelled to accept the thought that sin made changes in God, forcing Him, after its appearance, to do things He had never done before. This thought cannot be true if God is to remain the unchangeable, incorruptible God that Scripture says He is.

The study of what God did in the sunny days of universal innocence and harmony is the investigation of the constitution of the kingdom that He formed in such wondrous perfection. His is the only perfect rulership to ever exist.

Before continuing, you must be warned that there is a tendency to form concepts of God's government after the measure of human leadership. It is all that we know, so we tend to think of God and His kingdom as being the same. But the Word of God states, "'For My thoughts are not your thoughts, Nor are your ways My ways,' says the LORD. 'For as the heavens are higher than the earth, So are My ways higher than your ways, And My thoughts than your thoughts'" (Isa. 55:8, 9).

So it was also that Christ said:

> To what shall we liken the kingdom of God? Or with what parable shall we picture it? (Mark 4:30).

> In society He found nothing with which to compare it. Earthly kingdoms rule by the ascendancy of physical power; but from Christ's kingdom every carnal weapon, every instrument of coercion, is banished (*The Acts of the Apostles*, p. 12).

Jesus told a story, in the parable of the householder, of workers who were hired at the late hour of the day who were paid the same as those who had been hired earlier and had toiled all day.

> The householder's dealing with the workers in his vineyard represents God's dealing with the human family. It is contrary to the customs that prevail among men. In worldly business, compensation is given according to the work accomplished. The laborer expects to be paid only that which he earns. But in the parable, Christ was illustrating the principles of His kingdom—*a kingdom not of this world*. He is not controlled by any human standard (*Christ's Object Lessons*, pp. 396, 397, emphasis added).

It is impossible to learn of the heavenly kingdom from the earthly. Few, if any, consciously set out to learn of God's government in this way. The student does not even question this approach because, throughout the lifetime, no other than earthly kingdoms have been known. He comes to the study of the heavenly with definite ideas already established in his mind of what a kingdom has to be. The Scriptures are read in the light of these understandings, and the result is a view of God that is opposite from reality.

Christ's disciples took a long time to overcome this problem. When they joined the company of Christ, this misunderstanding of the true nature of the kingdom proved to be the greatest hindrance to their drawing into full intimacy with Christ in His divine mission. Despite His continual effort on their behalf, they were not delivered from this false position until after the resurrection.

We must take heed, lest we also come to the study of God's kingdom with the same preconceived ideas.

Earthly kingdoms do have a reference value only in the sense that they tell us what the kingdom of God *is not*. Let us not be among that class who "fail of a satisfactory understanding of the great problem of evil, from the fact that tradition and misinterpretation have obscured the teaching of the Bible concerning the *character* of God, the *nature* of His government, and the *principles* of His dealing with sin" (*The Great Controversy*, p. 492, emphasis added).

Chapter Seven

The Constitution of the Government of God

Study/Discussion Questions:

- After sin entered God's universe, did He do something different that He never had done before?

- Is God above His own law?

- What are the two foundational constituents of God's government?

- What is the mystery of God's will?

The full subject of this chapter would be better reflected in a longer title such as "The Constitution of the Government of God as It Was Before the Entrance of Sin." Such a study is an essential introduction to understanding God's government as it was *after* the entrance of rebellion. While such an investigation is proceeding, continually keep in mind that "tradition and misinterpretation have obscured the teaching of the Bible concerning the character of God, the nature of His government, and the principles of His dealing with sin" (*The Great Controversy*, p. 492).

Therefore, if we find the truth on this question as that truth is written in the Holy Scriptures, then we will find that which is *exactly contrary* to what is generally believed. This means we would enter into a set of wholly revised and reversed concepts of God's government and character. At the same time, there would be the continual pressure of traditionally held theories seeking to drag the mind back to the old ways again—a pressure which must be consciously resisted in order to arrive at the pure truth.

The whole structure of God's government is perfection. It cannot be improved, and there is not a single alternative to it. God's way is not the best way—*it is the only way*. While other ways have been proposed and have even existed for a time, they cannot be counted as a way of life for they shortly die by their own imperfections.

Essential in the structure of divine government is the existence of law. The necessity is there because of the provision of mighty powers without which life would be impossible but which have in them the potential for destruction. God's law is a love gift from Him to His creatures, perfectly designed to save them from destruction.

The law of God "is a transcript of His own character, and it is the standard of all character" (*Christ's Object Lessons,* p. 315). Within this truth lies something of the greatest importance. A transcription is the rewriting of something former in a new location. It does not matter whether you read the former or the latter, for the message will be the same. Inasmuch as God does what He does because of who He is, the law, being what God is, is the guide to His behavior. God will not do anything that is not in His character. Therefore, He will do nothing that is contrary to the law.

It is so natural and easy to think of the law as something that God decreed as being His wishes for our deportment but which has little or no bearing upon His own conduct. We tend to think this way because of our familiarity with human lawmakers. Professedly, in modern democracies, the same laws made to control the behaviour of the citizenry are to be obeyed by the rulers who make them. But of late the cover has been lifted to reveal that this is not so. With increasing frequency the rulers get away with breaking the laws they create. Then, when they are found out, they do not suffer the same penalties imposed upon the individual in the street who is accused of the same crimes.

The more absolute the ruler is the more open and obvious is this practice of making laws for the people that are not in any sense for the monarch. This is not so in God's government. His law is first of all His very own character. As such, it is the revelation of the way in which He will act under all circumstances. Then He simply calls upon us to behave as He does.

> For I am the LORD your God. You shall therefore consecrate yourselves, and *you shall be holy*; for *I am holy* (Lev. 11:44).

> Therefore you shall be perfect, just as your Father in heaven is perfect (Matt. 5:48).

> If you are the children of God you are partakers of His nature, and you cannot but be like Him. Every child lives by the life of his father. If you are God's children, begotten by His Spirit, you live by the life of God. In Christ dwells "all the fullness of the Godhead bodily" (Colossians 2:9); and the life of Jesus is made manifest "in our mortal flesh" (2 Corinthians 4:11). That life in you will produce the same character … as it did in Him (*Thoughts from the Mount of Blessing,* p. 78).

The areas of dispute in regard to God's behavior surface in respect to the commandments "Thou shalt not kill," "Thou shalt not steal," and "Thou shalt not bear false witness."

We know that death was not present until sin entered the world, bringing death with it. Therefore, we can know with certainty that God never once raised His powerful arm to take the life even of the minutest organism in His vast realm. Nor did He ever act deceitfully, or retrieve by force, or steal back that which He had given to any one of His creatures.

But it is contended that the fall brought about a circumstance which *required* that the Lord take decisive action to cut the sedition short and preserve the entire universe from corruption.

Most have no problem with the idea that the natural consequence of the rebellion against His word was the introduction of decay and death through separation from the source of Life. Yet many statements will surely occur in your mind, especially from the Old Testament, where it *appears* that God did come down and, by the direct and personal exercise of His mighty power, destroy, sometimes with great cruelty, thousands of people. We will later deal with many of these incidents. For now we wish to consider the nature of His character in the original kingdom and what this implies.

To recognize that God never destroyed before there was sin, and to accept the idea that He has destroyed after its emergence, is to believe that He has changed. It is to admit that with Him, of whom it is written that there is no variableness, there has been a variation. It is to believe that God respected the law in one way before iniquity arose, and then in a different and opposite way thereafter, and when sin is ended that He will return to the original pattern.

Just now you may feel disposed to discontinue the pursuance of the arguments here because they are so contrary to what you have formerly believed. We agree that they are contrary, for they are Christ's teachings, and He came to present "to men that which was *exactly contrary* to the representations of the enemy in regard to the character of God" (*Fundamentals of Christian Education,* p. 177, emphasis added).

But we implore you to bear with us until all the evidences have been considered; do not prematurely reject the conclusions.

Consideration must now be given to the way in which God keeps the law. God recognizes that if obedience to His law has to be compelled, then He would have a form of government that was short of perfection. But He will have nothing that is anything less than the ideal. He is determined on this, for He will not be content with anything less than the ultimate in happiness and prosperity for His subjects. Therefore, in God's kingdom no force is ever employed to bring about allegiance to Him or to put down rebellion. We can be certain of this, for it is plainly written that it is so.

> God could have destroyed Satan and his sympathizers … but He did not do this. Rebellion was not to be overcome by force. Compelling power is found only under Satan's government. The Lord's principles are not of this order. His authority rests upon goodness, mercy, and love; and the presentation of these principles is the means to be used (*The Desire of Ages,* p. 759).

> The exercise of force is contrary to the principles of God's government; He desires only the service of love and love cannot be commanded; it cannot be won by force or authority (*Ibid.,* p. 22).

> Earthly kingdoms rule by the ascendancy of physical power; but from Christ's kingdom every carnal weapon, every instrument of coercion, is banished (*Acts of the Apostles,* p. 12).

It needs to be fixed in our minds that because the exercise of force is contrary to the principles of God and His government, *under no circumstances* will He use force to solve any problem.

In the Old Testament, God's actions *seem to say* that He did use compelling power to achieve His righteous ends, that He did resort to force to put down rebellion, and that He did make an example of some by crushing them with terrible punishments that were often fatal.

The choice of belief between the declarations of God and the *appearances* of what God did in the human arena is before every person. The greater proportion choose to believe *what they think they see* rather than what God has said. Therefore, the almost universal belief is that God does use force, that He exterminates whole nations who have utterly rejected Him, and that He relies on compelling power to put down rebellion.

Without question, the witness of sight and circumstances is very powerful. When the Old Testament stories are read wherein it is reported that God rained fire and brimstone on the Sodomites; that He poured forth the waters of the flood until the wicked were all drowned; and so on, it is easy and natural to believe that God was personally resorting to the weapons of force.

When God's actions are correctly evaluated, it will be confirmed that His ways are so perfect and infallible that He experiences no need to turn to the use of force. There has been an aptness to conclude that there is only one possible interpretation of the Old Testament incidents. What is needed is a second and more educated investigation into those happenings. It will then be found that there are vital differences between what the Lord appears to have done and what He really did. We will take up some of these studies at the appropriate point.

We now need to consider a most important aspect of God's relationship to His subjects. It is a matter closely linked to, and consistent with, the fact that any use of force is contrary to the principles of God's government and to the purpose and nature of God's law. Only as all three of these are studied together will it be possible to understand any one of them.

This vital aspect is one of freedom, one of the most precious gifts ever given by God to His subjects. A little thought will show that as surely as God has no intention of using compelling power to enforce the observance of His law, then as certainly has He set his creatures absolutely free to serve Him or not to serve Him. The two are consistent with and inseparable from each other.

This is not to be understood as stating that the Lord gave His creatures freedom to sin with impunity. There is a doctrine abroad that paints God as being so sweetly loving that He will excuse and protect all sin and sinners rather than see anyone perish. That doctrine is not to be confused with the positions taken here. The sinner *will* die. The heavens and earth will be destroyed, and the entire universe will be rendered clean from the stain of sin. But it will not be God who wields the scourge of destruction to effect this. Rather, He will first have warned every created being of the terrible consequences attendant on choosing to take the path of disobedience. Then, when they do, He will expend every effort to save them from it, and only when they reject His saving effort, will He finally *leave* them to perish.

> The law of love being the foundation of the government of God, the happiness of all created beings depended upon their perfect accord with its great principles of righteousness. God desires from all His creatures the service of love—homage that springs from an intelligent appreciation of His character. He takes no pleasure in a forced allegiance, and to all He grants *freedom of will*, that they may render Him voluntary service (*The Great Controversy*, p. 493, emphasis added).

Observe the relationship between rendering to God a service of love based upon an intelligent conviction of God's justice and goodness and the granting to each of perfect and complete freedom to obey or not. Interestingly, the exercise of that freedom in the wrong direction immediately deprives a person of liberty, for sin is a cruel taskmaster that forces its subjects into service. It is not God who deprives of the freedom, but it is the work of sin and Satan.

Just so soon as any element of compulsion, such as the threat of punishment, is introduced, then to that extent will there be a service motivated by fear. God's subjects would then obey Him because they were afraid not to. God can never accept this form of obedience. He knows that such a kingdom cannot be blessed with flawless happiness and fullness of joy.

Thus in the kingdom of God, perfectly and fully established, there is no question of the service rendered being real or feigned. It can only be genuine. Thus God will have in eternity's coming perfection what every earthly monarch through all time has craved—the total and loving loyalty of every one of His people. No kingdom has ever been like this. Earthly kingdoms always tend to servitude in one form or another, seeking to hold the loyalty of their citizens with the threat of punishment for disobedience. No crime is considered worse than treason, disloyalty to the state.

Jesus Christ does not come to transfer the sinner from one form of bondage to another. God's object in Christ is to restore the kingdom to its original perfection, the perfection of complete freedom to serve God.

Let us for a moment examine some gems of thought from A. T. Jones' book *Ecclesiastical Empires*:

> As God made angels and men free to sin if they should choose, did He not then have to provide against this possible choice *before* they were made—did He not have to provide for the possibility of sin, before ever a single creature was made?—Assuredly He had to make such provision. And He *did* so. And this provision is an essential part of that eternal purpose which He purposed in Christ Jesus our Lord …
>
> Standing then, in thought, with Him before there was a single intelligent creature created, He desires that the universe shall be full of joyful intelligences en-

joying His love to the full. In order to do this they must be free to choose *not to serve Him*, to choose *not* to enjoy His love.... But this involves the possibility ... that some will choose not to serve Him ... Shall He then refuse to create because ... sin may enter?—This would be but eternally to remain self-centered and solitary. More than this, such a shrinking would in itself cause Him to cease to be God. For what is a god, or what is he worth, who can not do what he desires? who can not fulfill his own will? Such a god would be worthless....

He purposed to give Himself a sacrifice to redeem all who should sin; and give them even a second freedom to choose Him or themselves, to choose life or death. And those who the second time would choose death, let them have what they have chosen....

This is God, the living God, the God of love, the God and Father of our Lord Jesus Christ, who is fully able to do whatsoever He will, *and yet leave all His creatures free.* This is He who from the days of eternity "worketh all things after the counsel of His own will." *Ephesians* 1:11.

And this is "the mystery of His will, ... which He hath purposed in Himself; that in the dispensation of the fullness of times He might gather together in one all things in Christ, both which are in heaven, and which are on earth; even in Him." *Ephesians* 1:9, 10. This is "the eternal purpose which He purposed in Christ Jesus our Lord." *Ephesians* 3:11 (pp. 586-588).

Even though God thoroughly understood the possibilities of there being a period when some or even all His creatures would undertake a terrible experimentation with a supposed way of life other than His, He did not institute any safeguards involving the element of force. He would have nothing less for them than perfection; wherein lay the unlimited possibilities of infinite development.

Under restricted freedoms there can be no such thing as infinite development, for "freedom of choice is essential to intelligence" (*Ibid.*). This theme is explored in the pages of the Jones quote, above. We may confirm this by exploring in the annals of history how the freedoms brought by the Reformation resulted in great advances in intellectual development. Where freedoms are restricted there tends to be in general shorter, more toilsome lives of ignorance, poverty, and disease.

The following statements closing this chapter should be read, re-read, and pondered with the proper quality and quantity of mental taxation!

Put these two principles together again—the principle of no coercive force being used and the principle of granting absolute freedom to choose. As surely as these two things are combined in the constitution of God's kingdom, then just so surely does God place Himself where He cannot punish those who do what He said they could do, namely, choose another master if they wished.

This is a most difficult principle for people to understand because it is so foreign to their way of thinking. Civil rulers do not grant to anyone freedom of choice. Their mandate is, "Obey, or suffer at our hands." Those who make the law are the ones who punish the lawbreaker, but it is not so in God's kingdom. He has spelled out the law as the expression of His own character, but it is sin and death that enslave the transgressor.

To totally reject the use of force and at the same time grant to all freedom of will is to set up a situation wherein it would not be possible to administer punishment and death in order to correct the problem. It does not matter how it may appear that during the Old Testament period, for example, the Lord administered punishments as earthly rulers do; the fact remains that a government constituted on the lines of total rejection of the use of force as a solution, while at the same time giving freedom of choice to the subjects, *simply cannot punish those who choose to go another way*. God gave them the right to make that choice, and He cannot punish them for making the decision He Himself gave them the liberty to make.

> God does not stand toward the sinner as an executioner of the sentence against transgression; but He leaves the rejecters of His mercy to themselves, to reap that which they have sown (*The Great Controversy*, p. 36).

It was when those powerful beings stood up under Lucifer's leadership, determined to set up a rival dominion, that the first challenge to God's sincerity in His promise of freedom under His government was raised. Satan and his followers have pressed that challenge to the utmost limits, exploring, probing, and searching for some weakness whereby they might gain a foothold and topple the divine organization. God has declared that His ways are perfection, not simply for the sunny, prosperous days, but for any possible circumstances from the best to the worst. Under this searching inquisition, this endless pressure, will those principles stand or will they prove to be faulty? That is the question to be decided in the great controversy. Will it be found that God has to make modifications and concessions, that He would after all be forced to acknowledge that He has gone too far in granting such complete freedom, and that He has to withdraw it in order to rain punishments on the wrongdoers?

Satan contends that God had to resort to force to punish those who exercised the freedom He gave them not to serve Him. All too readily, humanity in general has subscribed to Satan's lies. The time is now when a revised understanding of God's actions is imperative. Such will be offered as this study progresses, but first, consideration must be given to another factor—the workings of the law of God. As already stated, the rejection of force, the granting of perfect freedom of choice to all, and the nature and purpose of God's law are three things so closely related that they must be studied in conjunction with each other for any or all of them to be adequately understood. Study has been given to the former two, so we must now consider the last.

Chapter Eight

A Perfect Law

Study/Discussion Questions:

- **Is there such a thing as free will under a system of punishment by design?**
- **Who pays the wages of sin?**
- **Is God truly jealous for His own authority?**
- **Why can only one system of law exist?**

The perfection of God's law stands in marked contrast to the imperfection of the laws framed by earthly legislators. Human beings are obliged to constantly enact new laws and to modify or repeal old ones. Behavior allowed in one country is strictly banned in another. Further, in order to ensure respect and obedience to the government and its laws, a list of punishments is formulated.

God's law, being perfect and complete, has required no modifications. It has stood as the flawless pattern for both divine and human behavior in both the sinless heavenly environment and the iniquitous situation on earth.

The life of Christ demonstrates this truth in that He kept His Father's commandments in conditions so wicked that it was described as the time "when the transgressors" had "reached their fullness" (Dan. 8:23).

Regarding the second factor in the difference between the law of God and that of humanity, consider that while people have to attach their own formulated penalties to the law, with God this is not necessary. In His system, breaking the law itself brings its own terrible fruitage in sorrow, and finally, destruction.

But let us not conclude that God deliberately or arbitrarily organized it thus. When it is understood why He formed and gave the law, it will be seen that this is the only way it could be. Essential to the successful accomplishment of the great aspirations within His creatures is the possession of tremendous power. This power was designed for blessing and benefit only, but unavoidably, it has in it the potential for destruction. Being the only way to safeguard against the destructive side of power, laws became essential. While power is handled in strict accordance with law, there is no problem. But let the law be disregarded and every kind of problem arises. Therefore, God did not formulate a law with a deliberately built-in system of punishments, but instead, He gave them a perfect protection from self-destruction.

God is only interested in voluntary obedience. It would, therefore, be impossible to give full liberty to a person to withhold obedience and then mete punishment for exercising the very freedom given to him or her. To punish under those conditions is to deny that full liberty had been given.

There are two ways in which God could have administered punishments upon those who chose to withhold obedience. The first method would be to decree what the punishment should be and then to execute it by His own direct actions. This is what the majority believe God does.

The second method would be to skillfully and deliberately build into the law punishments that would automatically fall upon the transgressor. In modern language this is called booby trapping. The farmer, for instance, has a patch of delicious melons growing, and he knows that, despite the law forbidding theft, the young lads of the village will come at night for a feast. So he installs a trip wire attached to an explosive. He has built into the law an automatic punishment that will reach out and strike the lawbreaker apart from the action of the law itself.

Whether God punishes directly by His own action or indirectly by building destruction into the law, He would still be denying that He had, in reality, given His subjects full liberty to yield or withhold obedience.

The awful punishments that fall upon the violators of God's great principles are what the law was devised to protect people from, not what it was designed to bring upon them.

What must be understood with great clarity is that the law is in no sense God's effort to protect His own position and authority. God is so completely outgoing, so utterly devoid of self-interest, self-justification, or self-protectionism in any form that He could never have formulated the law to save Himself. It is not something that He has "thought up" as His wish or pleasure whereby the people could be identified as His subjects, doing His will and obeying His commands.

We must remember that "the wages of sin is death" (Rom. 6:23). There are two masters, God and Satan, or more correctly, righteousness and sin. Neither of these masters pays the wages earned in the service of the other. Satan never pays the gifts of God. God alone pays the gift of life. It should be equally clear that the Lord never pays the wages owed by sin to its subjects. Sin and Satan alone pay those. God does not traffic in death, for He is the purveyor of life. That is His merchandise, and He dispenses no other. He does not pay wages in the currency of death.

The law was given that it might be a protection and blessing to humankind. Obedience to it ensures absolute immunity from sickness, suffering, sorrow, fear, suspicion, robbery, violence, and death. Violation of its principles guarantees the introduction of these things in their worst forms.

The first command in the Decalogue is this: "You shall have no other gods before Me" (Exod. 20:3). To the average person, this suggests a picture of God concerned about His receiving the homage, respect, service, and worship that He feels is due to Him. This perception of God is such that God is seen as demanding that we acquiesce to His position of sole and ultimate authority, and He is thought to be saying, "If I find any drifting away from Me, any rendering of homage or love to another, My anger shall become exceedingly great, and I will come in My fury to punish you without mercy." Unfortunately, a more erroneous view of God's intent could not be entertained. God had no concern for His own honor, security, and safety when He formed that commandment. He was entirely preoccupied with His subjects and their needs. He knew the danger in which they were, and to make them secure from it, He gave them this and the other commands.

God gave humanity the precious gift of life. But to give life was not sufficient. A home must be provided. Without this, what would life be but a horror of eternal drifting through cold and vast empty space with nothing to see or do. Rather, He created a home in which His children could develop and achieve the highest aspirations of their active minds. But life and a home were not enough. It was necessary that God bestow powers that would enable all of these things.

These powers may be grouped into two divisions, those within people and those outside people in the marvelous world of nature. The powers in people may be listed as the power of thought, speech, ambition, planning, reasoning, invention, love, joy, and so forth, including muscular power. The powers in the world of nature are the powers of the sun, moon, gravity, wind, water, centrifugal and inertial forces, electricity, and many more.

But giving of life, home, and all the powers was still not enough. The bestowal of the powers, while intended for the blessing and prosperity of all His creatures, inevitably possessed the potential of destruction. Therefore, God needed to add one more gift to make the work of creation complete and secure. That gift was the law.

Returning to the example of the first commandment, we can demonstrate that the law was not made by God for God, but for humanity. The sun in the heavens will serve as one example. God spoke it into existence, and His work in respect to it did not end there. The sun cannot fulfill its mission unaided. It must be directed by another power. The only power that can do this is the power which made it. The Son of God is the One who not only "made the worlds" but is constantly "upholding all things by the word of His power" (Heb. 1:2, 3).

> God is constantly employed in upholding and using as His servants the things that He has made. He works through the laws of nature, using them as His instruments. They are not self-acting. Nature in her work testifies of the intelligent presence and active agency of a Being who moves in all things according to His will (*The Ministry of Healing*, p. 416).

> You alone are the LORD; You have made heaven, The heaven of heavens, with all their host, The earth, and everything on it, The seas and all that is in them, And you preserve them all (Neh. 9:6).

It is not because of inherent energy that our hearts continue to beat and we continue to draw breath, but rather these things are evidence of the all-pervading care of Him in whom "we live and move and have our being" (Acts 17:28). Nor is it by inherent power that the heavenly bodies continue in their way, for the hand of God "brings out their host by number; He calls them all by name, By the greatness of His might, And the strength of His power; Not one is missing [not one faileth (KJV)] (Isa. 40:26).

These and many other statements teach the active presence of God as the Controller of all the powers He has installed in the universe for the good of His creatures. But this is not because God must be personally in control of all things in that He is power hungry or anxious to reserve to Himself any special position. The fact is that this is the only way it can be done. It was not possible to leave all these tremendous powers to themselves, for it is the very nature of power to be unintelligent. Power and force are just what they are, while intelligence is designed to control and guide the powers.

Therefore, the mighty sun must have a controller and guide to keep it exactly on its course and, at the same time, a source of energy to keep it forever fuelled and burning at a constant level. Should there be no controlling power, the possibilities are fearsome to contemplate.

God cannot merely appoint one of His mighty creatures to look after guiding the sun or other such tasks, for it required His own power to create it and set it up, and it requires the same power to maintain it. God gladly gives His creatures whatever He can, but this is one thing He cannot give, for there is not one of us, angel or person, who can keep those mighty powers under perfect control.

Therefore, it is essential that no other god be placed in God's position as the Controller, Guide, and Sustainer of these mighty powers. To do so would be to put in place a being who would have no hope of keeping those things under control. The heavenly powers would swiftly break out of their course in a holocaust of destruction. Some may object that God could prevent it. Certainly He has the physical power to do so, but in order for that power to be exercised to prevent that destruction, it has to be in the very place from which it has been dismissed. Once another god has been put in the place of the true God, then God can only save the situation by forcing Himself back into the place from which He has been sent away, and God will never do this. This would violate the freedom of choice that He Himself gave to His creatures and which He will never invade even to a hair's breadth.

When Adam and Eve replaced God the Father for another god, they removed from themselves the protection the first commandment was designed to give. Sudden and terrible destruction immediately threatened them. Now, it may be objected here that the whole argument is disproved by the fact that sudden destruction did not befall them as God had said it would. But God is not a liar. His word was fulfilled in that the spiritual side of their natures, the life of God in the presence of the Holy Spirit, died out of them and was replaced by another spirit, that of the devil. They would have also died physically that day had not the Lord interposed to introduce a delaying factor, designed in love, to give them a limited probationary period in which to reconsider their decision. Christ stepped in to divert the punishment to Himself.

The instant man accepted the temptations of Satan, ... the Son of God, stood between the living and the dead, saying, "Let the punishment fall on Me. I will stand in man's place. He shall have another chance" (*The SDA Bible Commentary*, vol. 1, p. 1085).

Right there in the Garden of Eden, all nature would have swung wildly out of its course with increasing ferocity had not Christ stepped in to give the world a period of probation in which to make a second choice either to serve God or to continue with the god of death and destruction. When at last the time of probation is ended and all have made their choice for eternity, this is just what will happen. Christ will step out of His place as Mediator, and all nature will collapse in a cataclysm of destruction. These "punishments" for disobedience are the unpreventable consequence of the removal of the protections the laws are designed to give.

These things must be meditated upon until the purposes and character of God are fully understood; until it is seen that God neither inflicts the punishment by His own hand, nor has He arbitrarily legislated penalties to automatically sanction or destroy those who get out of line; until it is seen that death and suffering are the direct and unpreventable result of sin. The Lord seeks to save all from such disastrous results and guide them forever in those pathways that will ensure them perfect and complete happiness.

A quick examination of the violation of the command "thou shalt not steal" will show us how it opens upon humanity the floodgates of woe. In a perfect society there would be no need for gates and locks. But suppose that one day someone enters this society and steals the property of another. As news of the event spreads through the village, the peace and happiness dies under a cloud of fear and suspicion. Steps are soon taken to bar the openings and lock the doors so that protection may be obtained against a further visit from the thief. In this, the innocent suffer with the guilty. One look at airline travel today, with all its security measures, is sufficient to illustrate this point.

Should more and more people follow the path of the lawbreaker and become thieves, then the problem will escalate into destructive proportions. As one step leads to another, what begins with theft often leads to violence and murder.

It is only because the Lord is still able to exercise some restraint over humankind that people survive at all. Should the law be totally cast aside and anarchy reign, the extermination of the race by its own hands would be the swift result. It is self-evident that the breaking of the law governing people's relationship to each other brings its own terrible results upon the world.

What kind of world would it be if all laws were done away with and every person became a thief, murderer, liar, adulterer, and so on? As this grim picture, wherein there is no stability or security, develops in your mind, ponder and see that the terrible conditions would not in any sense be the inflictions of God, but the result of removing the protection afforded by the law. Here is the revelation of the cause and effect, and no charge can be laid to God for any of it.

Not only is it against God's principles to exercise force to compel or punish people into obeying Him, but He does not need to. The removal of sin is guaranteed by the mere fact that it is, in its own nature, a way of death and destruction. There is only one life path, and that is the one God has mapped out for His people.

When the nature of the law as it really is, is truly understood, then our obedience to it will be far more willing and successful. Likewise, when the character and ways of God are genuinely comprehended and appreciated, it will be known that He did not compose the law as the symbol of His authority, imposing it upon us as the obligation of service to Him, the medium whereby He could exact our service and homage. It will be realized that the law was made for the children of God and that perfect obedience is the only protection from death and destruction. It will be recognized that when human beings cast aside both the law and Christ as their protectors, they will have exhausted all that heaven has and can do to save them.

Beyond that limit, God can go no further, for that is the totality of His resources. This leaves Him with no choice but to grant to each apostate the total separation with its attendant annihilation that he or she has chosen.

The law is a transcript of His character. His own behavior is expressed therein and is not something to which He has forced Himself to uphold as strict discipline contrary to His own nature. His promise is that He writes the same law on our hearts so that it is also a transcript of our characters. Then we can and will obey the law as He obeys it, and this will be the natural response of our regenerated inner natures.

As we have seen, we have "full liberty to yield or to withhold obedience" (*Patriarchs and Prophets*, p. 48). As surely as God gives full liberty to withhold obedience, He can never punish any one of His creatures for exercising the liberty that He Himself has given. This means then that the punishments that come as a result of turning from God's way are the fruit or result of our own course of action, not the administration of such things by the hand of God.

Chapter Nine

God's Principles Tested

Study/Discussion Questions:

- **Does the entrance of sin necessitate any change in the operation of God's government?**

- **What was God thinking in placing a forbidden tree in the garden?**

- **What were Satan's charges against God at the tree?**

God's principles of government worked perfectly under perfect conditions. So far, our study has been of that sinless period.

Now the attention must be focused on the drastically changed conditions that developed after angels and then humans exercised their God-given liberty to choose not to serve Him. With intense interest the entire universe looked on to see whether these principles could still operate without modification, addition, or any other changes. Would God find it necessary to solve the sin problem by exercising His infinite physical power to destroy the wrongdoers?

As students and others have viewed history, they have been convinced that the entrance of sin imposed on God the necessity to take actions He was never obliged to take before. They look at the flood, the burning of Sodom and Gomorrah, the plagues upon Egypt, the destruction of the rebels who worshipped the golden calf, the death of Korah, Dathan, and Abiram, the liquidation of Sennacherib's army, the stoning of the Sabbath breaker, the adulterer, Achan, and many other such instances. They read the words used to describe God's responses and conclude from this that God exercised force to put down rebellion, that He punished by His own decision and decree, that He destroyed those who rejected His last offers of mercy, and that He does not, therefore, give all individuals full liberty to yield or withhold obedience.

We recognize that it strongly *appears* that this is true, but at the same time, we know that there is more than one way of understanding what happened.

There prevails in the world today the concept that the law was made for God's personal exaltation, that it is His invention to produce and maintain His position of undisputed authority. Therefore, it is seen as a device calculated to exalt One at the expense of the rest.

What is the origin of this teaching? The answer to this question is an infallible guide as to whether it is true or not. A careful study of what took place in the Garden of Eden reveals the truth. God made the earth and equipped it with all the powerful life-support systems as a love gift to Adam and Eve. Because He was interested only in receiving from them service motivated by love, He did not place them "beyond the possibility of wrong-doing. God made them free moral agents, capable of appreciating the wisdom and benevolence of His character and the justice of His requirements, and with full liberty to yield or to withhold obedience" (*Patriarchs and Prophets*, p. 48).

There is no point in saying that one has full liberty to withhold obedience if there is no opportunity to do so. Therefore, God provided them not only with the full liberty to withhold obedience but also the means to do so by placing the tree of knowledge of good and evil in the midst of the garden. That was the one tree the Lord did not give them. It was His property, not theirs. All He asked of them was to respect it as being His. If they could always do this, and teach their children the same principles, then there would never be unhappiness in the world. There would be only perfect trust and security.

If they could learn perfect respect for another's property, there would never be any stealing, adultery, or murder. If they could respect the time belonging to another, there could never be a Sabbath breaker.

This is what the law is all about—respect for that which belongs to another. On the first table of the law is the area of respect for that which is God's, and on the second, for that which is humanity's.

When God instructed them regarding His tree, they were given the clearest warning: "But of the tree of the knowledge of good and evil you shall not eat, for in the day that you eat of it you shall surely die" (Gen. 2:17).

It is just as important to see what the text does not say, as to see what it says. It does not say that in the day when they ate of it the Lord would destroy them. It says that they would *die*. Granted, the text does not spell out the way they would die, and it could be interpreted to mean that they would die at God's hands. But Adam and Eve did not understand it that way, and Satan knew this. He knew that they understood God's words to mean that the destruction would be the result of their eating of that tree and not the act of God. Therefore, Satan set to work to destroy their confidence in that interpretation of God's word and to substitute it with one of his own.

The certainty that Adam and Eve understood God's words to mean that they would die because of their disobedience, not at the hand of a punishing God, is confirmed by Satan himself. This is deduced in the following way. Satan came, not to endorse God's truth, but to overthrow it. There were only two possible ways of understanding God's words. They either meant that God would personally kill them for disobeying Him, or they would die as a consequence of their wrong deeds. To perceive which is the error, it is only necessary to ask which of the two Satan denied and which one he supported.

Throughout that conversation with Eve, Satan worked up to and stressed the idea that there was no danger in eating of the tree. He assured her that doing so would not bring death. He insinuated that there was another reason for God's stipulations, a reason entirely motivated by self-protectionism and self-interest. Therefore, he implied, without directly saying it, that if there was any death at all it would be God's directly administered act, not the natural consequence of broken law.

He was too cunning to confront Eve with this counterinterpretation in the first moments of their contact. First, he had to inject just enough doubt into her mind to get her thoughts working in the desired direction. So he asked in an incredulous tone if it was really true that the Lord had denied to a creature so beautiful, intelligent, and worthy as herself the right to partake of the fruit of the tree. To give more power to the suggestion, "the serpent continued, in a musical voice, with subtle praise of her surpassing loveliness; and his words were not displeasing" (*Patriarchs and Prophets*, p. 54).

In her reply, Eve misquoted God's words, thus showing that doubt had begun to form. Whereas God had said, "You shall surely die," she quoted Him as saying, "You shall not eat it, nor shall you touch it, lest you die" (Gen. 3:3).

The word "lest" denies the certainty and admits only a possibility. Her use of it transmitted to the serpent the information that her conviction of the nature of God's law was weakening. Thus he was emboldened to make a direct attack on the law and the character of the One who had made it. So he said to the woman, "You will not surely die" (verse 4).

This is the attack on the law. God had said that disobedience to the law would bring death, but here Satan was saying that the law could be broken with impunity. He argued that there is nothing in keeping the law which affords a protection from death. Eve had the choice then of whether she would believe the truth as God told it or Satan's proposition.

Having made the assault on the law, Satan follows it with an attack on God's character. In order to sustain his statement that breaking the law would not bring death, he said that there was another purpose for God's saying it would. Here are his words. "You will not surely die. For God knows that in the day you eat it your eyes will be opened, and you will be like God, knowing good and evil" (verses 4, 5).

He represented God as One who was deeply concerned lest any of His creatures should ascend to a position of equality with Himself so that the glory, honor, and power which He had previously enjoyed as His own special privilege would have to be shared with others.

While God had not told them, and for very good reason, Satan insinuated that the tree held certain magical properties which would project those who partook of it into a gloriously superior station in the universe. While God had not revealed this to them, Satan continued, stating that God certainly knew about it and was desperately afraid that they would partake of the tree and thus become equal with Himself. In order to be secure from such a terrible contingency, He had placed fear in their hearts to prevent them from eating of the tree.

This was the base from which Satan would later develop the teaching that it is God who destroys. There was no need to take this teaching all the way at that time, for he could accomplish the objective of the moment without doing so.

If God was the kind of being who would stoop to inventing a lie in order to safeguard His own position, and should that lie be discovered and the people do the very thing He had commanded them not to do, then He would not quietly acquiesce to sharing His throne with them. He would naturally resort to other measures to accomplish the same purpose.

The point is that a being of the character Satan represented God to be would be unable to do anything else. Deception having failed, He would be driven to use the only other weapon available—force. He would enter into direct physical conflict with those who sought to climb into His place, and in the end, when even that failed, He would have to liquidate them.

While we are now aware of who authored these rebellious ideas, we are to understand that this does not explain how God worked these principles out in every one of the difficult complications introduced by the sin problem. But a foundation has been laid upon that such comprehensions can be built. It will now be possible to approach every situation with knowledge that the devil will continue attempting to cloud the mind with the erroneous view of what God did, exactly as he did in the Garden of Eden. There will now be the blessed tendency to reject such an interpretation and search further for the real one.

The time has come to study God's behavior as far as it can be understood during the interlude of sin.

Chapter Ten

A Summary

Study/Discussion Questions:

- **What is the relationship between the character of God and the law of God?**
- **What are the ramifications of God's granting of liberty to all His subjects?**
- **Did the constitution of God's government change in any way after the introduction of sin?**

So far, our study has been mainly given to the constitution of God's government as it was formed and operated under conditions where no sin existed. It was a perfectly idealistic situation, which worked faultlessly to the unmarred happiness of every creature in the universe.

Condensed into summary form, the character of God as revealed in that constitution is as follows:

- The laws of God's kingdom are the transcript of His character. Inasmuch as God is a Savior, His laws are also designed to be a protector and deliverer from the perils contained in the existence of power.
- The character of the law and of God are one; the righteousness of God is purely and entirely a voluntary, spontaneous obedience that is in no way forced either by Himself or by circumstances.
- This is the only kind of obedience He will accept from His creatures—a service that springs from an intelligent conviction of His goodness, impartial justice, and love.
- Because He could accept only this kind of service, God could not introduce any form of compulsion such as the threat of punishment, for this would stimulate within His children the disposition to obey because they were afraid not to. No kingdom can be truly happy when the subjects obey from fear no matter how slight that fear may be.
- Therefore, God gave every one of His created beings the full liberty and opportunity to either give or withhold obedience.

But the advent of the rebellion of the covering cherub, Lucifer, who made himself to be the devil and Satan, raised a challenge against the constitution. Before us, in the Word of God and in the annals of human history, is the record of the testing of that constitution so far as that test has gone. The final pressure is yet to be brought upon it in the earth's closing days.

God affirms that every principle of His government is eternally perfect, requires no adjustments or modifications, and is equally applicable in situations of sinfulness as well as sinlessness. He presents His law as the only standard of righteousness for the dwellers in the purity of heaven *and* for those who must dwell in the midst of a sin-cursed people.

If God is wholly correct in His assertions, then He cannot introduce any actions to deal with the sin problem different from what He did before it appeared. Therefore, as surely as He gave His creatures full liberty to withhold obedience before they fell, must He still give them the same liberty thereafter? The granting of that liberty places God where He can neither punish nor destroy those who exercise it.

Before the fall, motivated by a heart of wondrous love, God made all things to perfection and gave them freely and fully to His children. Then, to save them from the awful possibilities involved in power out of control, He expressed His love further by giving them a law to save them from suffering and death. Thus, before the fall, God fulfilled the role of a Savior. If His claims in regard to His kingdom and its rulership are correct, then after the fall He must still occupy the role of a Savior.

Before the fall, the law that, among other things, lays down the maxim, "Thou shalt not kill," was the direct expression of His character. Accordingly it was not in Him to kill. Since the fall, that law still declares, "Thou shalt not kill," and it continues to be the expression of His character. This being so, it is still not in His nature to kill, and for this reason He still cannot do it.

It is God's declaration that He changes not that He is "the same yesterday, today, and forever" (Heb. 13:8). Link this great truth with the principle that what we do is the result of what we are. Before the fall, God, in faithfully acting out His character, destroyed no one. Therefore, if after the fall, He resorted to destroying people His character would have changed in order to make this possible. But God has truthfully declared that He does not change; therefore, He has not changed.

Pitted against God's testimonies are the devil's charges. While fully admitting that before the rebellion God did not destroy anything, Satan claims that the appearance of the sin problem has imposed upon God the necessity of dealing with this by liquidating those who will not serve Him.

Therefore, it is Satan's accusation that the principles of God's government are not perfect. If the Lord had admitted that His system of government would only operate successfully with the full cooperation of every subject, requiring the introduction of death to defectors from it, then Satan would have had no case to argue. In fact, he would not have been there to argue, for as a defector he would have been eliminated immediately.

Satan is as desperately anxious to win our allegiance today as he was in the Garden of Eden. Before us, then, is the task of deciding who is correct in this great controversy. Some have been taught to almost blindly have faith in God, but this is not sufficient. Our faith must be intelligent for it to be effective. The area in which it must be truly intelligent is in this very field of the principles of the constitution of God's government. Let the gravity of the implications of this statement be fully realized by all.

> In order to endure the trial before them, they must understand the will of God as revealed in His word; they can honor Him only as they have a *right conception* of His character, government, and purposes, and act in accordance with them (*The Great Controversy*, p. 593).

The task before us now is a difficult one of searching out the operation of those principles during the period when it was under the fearful test imposed by Satan and wicked humanity. This is the area that this study now enters.

Individuals under the tutelage of Satan, by his misinterpretations of the Bible, have gained a very definite picture of God. Such a picture can only be correct if the devil is correct in his assertions that God has had to resort to acts of destruction in order to solve the sin problem.

Chapter Eleven

Contrasting Statements

Study/Discussion Questions:

- **Problems can't be solved by countering statements against statements. Are there actually any contradictions in God's Word?**

- **Do we just ignore the perplexities and hide behind blind faith?**

The vast majority of Christians are strongly convinced that necessity has demanded a punishing, destroying God since the rebellion began. In fact, the whole world lives under some form of belief in systems of reward and punishment.

There are at least two reasons for this thinking. First, the human mind has long been educated to believe that the only way to overcome rebellion is by force. A second reason is that the mind has been trained to read Scripture references according to a certain method of interpretation. When read according to that system, there are many Scriptures that will be understood as saying that God punishes, destroys, and liquidates.

Consider the following examples:

> So the LORD said, "*I will destroy* man whom I have created from the face of the earth, both man and beast, creeping thing and birds of the air, for I am sorry that I have made them (Gen. 6:7).

> And, behold, *I Myself* am bringing a floodwaters on the earth, to destroy from under heaven all flesh in which is the breath of life; everything that is on the earth shall die (Gen. 6:17).

> Then *the LORD* rained brimstone and fire on Sodom and Gomorrah, *from the LORD* out of the heavens. So He overthrew those cities, all the plain, all the inhabitants of the cities, and what grew on the ground (Gen. 19:24, 25).

> And *I will harden* Pharaoh's heart, and multiply My signs and My wonders in the land of Egypt (Exod. 7:3)

> And *He hardened Pharaoh's heart*, that he hearkened not unto them; as the LORD had said (Exod. 7:13, KJV).

> And he said to them, "Thus says the LORD God of Israel: 'Let every man put his

> sword on his side, and go in and out from entrance to entrance throughout the camp, and let every man kill his brother, every man his companion, and every man his neighbor'" (Exod. 32:27).

> It was to be impressed upon Israel that in the conquest of Canaan they were not to fight for themselves, but simply as instruments to execute the will of God; not to seek for riches or self-exaltation, but the glory of Jehovah their King (*Patriarchs and Prophets*, p. 491).

> Like the men before the Flood, the Canaanites lived only to blaspheme Heaven and defile the earth. And both love and justice demanded the prompt execution of these rebels against God and foes to man (*Ibid.*, p. 492).

> But when the king heard about it, he was furious. And he sent out his armies, destroyed those murderers, and burned up their city (Matt. 22:7).

A careful reading of the whole parable of which this last verse is a part, and the commentary on it in *Christ's Object Lessons*, pages 307-309, will show that the king is God, the armies were those of the Romans, the murderers were the Jews, and the city was Jerusalem. The text was fulfilled in the destruction of Jerusalem in AD 70.

Therefore, the text is really saying, "And when God heard thereof, *He* was wroth: and God sent forth *His* armies, the Romans, and God destroyed the Jews, and God burned up Jerusalem."

> They went up on the breadth of the earth and surrounded the camp of the saints and the beloved city. And fire came down from God out of heaven and devoured them (Rev. 20:9).

This is by no means a comprehensive list of statements of this nature. There is no special point in assembling every such quotation here. However, these are more than sufficient to provide the examples needed to show that there are many such Scriptures that, when interpreted according to the way our minds have been accustomed to interpret them, leave one with no option but to believe that God does use force to liquidate those who have rebelled against Him.

There are many people today who read these texts, interpret them according to long-accustomed methods, and are quite satisfied to believe that God behaves as an executioner to those who refuse to obey His laws. But in doing so they are ignoring several things. First, there are quite a number of statements that say the opposite from what these statements are interpreted to mean. Second, there are the great principles that are embodied in the constitution of God's government. Third, there are the terrible implications of holding such beliefs about God.

These will be considered in turn as we proceed, but first let a list be made of what some would call counterstatements. In reality they are not and cannot be counterstatements, for there are no contradictions in God's Word.

Here are some examples of such statements:

> The LORD is righteous in all His ways, Gracious [holy, KJV] in all His works (Ps. 145:17).

> Your testimonies [commandments or laws], which You have commanded, are righteous and very faithful (Ps. 119:138).

The Lord is righteous and the law is righteous. Therefore, God is what the law is. It is the "transcript of His own character" (*Christ's Object Lessons,* p. 315), and that law declares that "thou shalt not kill" (Exod. 20:13, KJV). Therefore, if it is not in the law to kill, it is not in the character of God to kill. Let's examine a number of other quotations.

> God destroys no man. Everyone who is destroyed will have destroyed himself (*Christ's Object Lessons,* p. 84).

> God destroys no one (*Testimonies for the Church,* vol. 5, p. 120).

> God does not stand toward the sinner as *an executioner* of the sentence against transgression; but *He leaves the rejecters of His mercy to themselves,* to reap that which they have sown. Every ray of light rejected, every warning despised or unheeded, every passion indulged, every transgression of the law of God, is a seed sown which yields its unfailing harvest. The Spirit of God, persistently resisted, is at last withdrawn from the sinner, and then there is left no power to control the evil passions of the soul, and no protection from the malice and enmity of Satan (*The Great Controversy,* p. 36, emphasis added).

> *Satan is the destroyer.* God cannot bless those who refuse to be faithful stewards. All He can do is to *permit* Satan to accomplish *his destroying work.* We see calamities of every kind and in every degree coming upon the earth, and why? *The Lord's restraining power is not exercised.* The world has disregarded the word of God. They live as though there were no God. Like the inhabitants of the Noachic world, they refuse to have any thought of God. Wickedness prevails to an alarming extent, and the *earth is ripe for the harvest* (*Testimonies for the Church,* vol. 6, pp. 388, 389, emphasis added).

> This earth has almost reached the place where God will permit *the destroyer* to work his will upon it (*Testimonies for the Church,* vol. 7, p. 141).

> In this age a more than common contempt is shown to God. Men have reached a point in insolence and disobedience which shows that their cup of iniquity is almost full. Many have well-nigh passed the boundary of mercy. Soon God … will say to the angels, "No longer combat Satan in his efforts to destroy. Let him work out his malignity upon the children of disobedience; for the cup of their iniquity is full. They have advanced from one degree of wickedness to another, adding

daily to their lawlessness. I will no longer interfere to prevent the destroyer from doing his work (*The Review and Herald*, September 17, 1901).

When Jesus was asked to destroy the Samaritans who had rejected Him, He replied to His disciples, "You do not know what manner of spirit you are of. For the Son of Man did not come to destroy men's lives, but to save them. And they went to another village" (Luke 9:55, 56). Consider these thoughts:

There can be no more conclusive evidence that we possess the spirit of Satan than the disposition to hurt and destroy those who do not appreciate our work, or who act contrary to our ideas (*The Desire of Ages*, p. 487).

Rebellion was not to be overcome by force. Compelling power is found only under Satan's government. The Lord's principles are not of this order. His authority rests upon goodness, mercy, and love; and the presentation of these principles is the means to be used. God's government is moral, and truth and love are to be the prevailing power (*Ibid.*, p. 759).

The exercise of force is contrary to the principles of God's government; He desires only the service of love; and love cannot be commanded; it cannot be won by force or authority (*Ibid.*, p. 22).

We know that God does nothing that is contrary to the principles of His government. Therefore, He does not use force. This principle is stated with certainty in *The Ministry of Healing*: "Sickness, suffering, and death are work of an antagonistic power. Satan is the destroyer; God is the restorer" (p. 113).

In this second compilation of statements, we have an emphatic and clear assertion that God is not an executioner, punisher, or destroyer. When these and the first set are viewed side by side, there does not appear to be any way of reconciling the two.

These apparent contradictions present the Bible student with a problem. For some, it is "solved" by simply discarding faith in the Word of God, charging it and its Author with duplicity and inconsistency. Others simply ignore the words that they are unable to understand or do not really desire to accept, while they carefully collect the opposite set, building their faith accordingly.

True students of God's Word will not make this mistake. They will ignore no statements, no matter how they may seem to contradict others. They will candidly acknowledge that so far as their understanding has developed, these statements remain for them a flat contradiction of each other, though by faith, they know that in God's Word there is no real contradiction.

Undisturbed by the clamor of voices around, they will move forward in quiet faith, patiently studying God's Word, knowing that, under God's tutelage, such revelations of the mysteries will come to them and will remove all contradictions, providing a perfect harmony where previously only confusion existed.

There will be those who will charge these careful students with twisting the Scriptures. They will accuse them of making the Word of God say what it does not. They will argue emphatically that the Bible says, "God destroyed them." Then they will ask, "What could be written more plainly than that?"

One might counter by saying, "It also says, 'God destroys no man.'" This will have no effect. Their minds have been programmed to accept only that which they have chosen to believe. No impression can be made by quoting contrary statements. They merely entrench themselves more firmly behind their list while, in growing indignation, they level the charge that the plainly written words of God are being rejected.

Two things must be established at this point. One is that this problem cannot be solved by simply countering statements with other statements. Second, it cannot be resolved by twisting or changing the statements to conform to our preferred ideas. In this study great care has been taken not to do this. Even so, we still expect that the opponents of the position taken in this book will level this accusation against us. We believe it will be found that the only interpretations given to the Scriptures will be those found in the Scriptures themselves, with no private interpretation being offered.

There has been the careful and frank quoting of the two different and seemingly contradictory compilations in order to demonstrate that there is a problem which needs solving. How can this problem be solved so as to bring the thoughtful, responsible student to an accurate knowledge of what the Word of God is teaching? That is the important question which we must now study.

Faith is a steadying factor in the problem. Faith says that there are no contradictions in God's Word. Faith says that we must take both of these statements as they read. Faith says that in due time the God of heaven Himself will provide the answers if we trust Him and continue our careful, objective study.

Then we come to the flood. The implications of the standard view of what God did in the obliteration of the human race in Noah's day are very serious indeed. The commonly accepted view of what God did suggests that He was forced to admit that righteousness was not able to withstand the crushing tide of evil, so God and Christ were obliged to step in, exercising Their own superior physical power to reverse the tide, erase the entire company of Satan's followers, and preserve alive only Their own.

It would be as if there was a conversation between the Father and the Son along these lines: "In the beginning We determined to fight this great controversy on the basis that righteousness could stand on its own merits. But now it is clear that sin has reached such proportions that it is on the verge of a world takeover. At the moment We only have eight subjects remaining, and in a short time, these, too, will die or join Satan's camp, thus making him the total victor in this struggle. So we must act now by coming to the rescue of righteousness. Let us step in with our limitless, infinite power and obliterate the entire side standing for Satan. We will preserve only our own people and thus make a complete, fresh start. Thereafter, We will maintain the use of force in appropriate places to ensure that Satan never again brings the world to this same crisis point."

This implies that God had to *revise* His method of dealing with the sin problem. It reveals Him as beginning in one way, but finding Himself later obliged to introduce measures not contemplated in the beginning. This makes God less than infinite, omniscient, omnipresent and omnipotent. It means that He is not really God because God has perfect foreknowledge, needing no revisions, compromises, or changes as time goes by.

In this way we find a serious problem on our hands. Nothing can deny the clarity of the principles underlining God's government or of His way of dealing with the sin problem. Yet, at the same time, the story of the flood seems to show a God who was later forced to introduce an element of compulsion and destruction.

Our attitude must be one of faith. We must believe implicitly that in the Word of God there are no contradictions. Those contradictions that appear as such are there only because of an inadequate understanding on our part. God will give light and understanding to those who humbly and sincerely seek it. There is a perfect reconciliation between God's stated attitude to the sin problem and the story of the flood, as well as many other accounts of what God appears to have done in history.

This chapter has been devoted to the recognition that there is a very real problem to be solved because of the existence of *apparent* contradictions in the Word of God. At the same time, we encourage each believer to realize that there are no real contradictions in God's Word, that the Bible is written for man's understanding, that these problems are therefore solvable, and that simple trusting faith in God will bring clear understandings in this connection. If we are prepared to adopt this attitude, then we are ready to proceed on to the study of the way in which the problem may be solved.

Chapter Twelve

Statements and Principles

Study/Discussion Questions:

- **We know that no scripture is to be of private interpretation. What does this really mean?**
- **How can we know when we are not applying erroneous methods of interpretation?**
- **Can we be satisfied in our beliefs when we find that it is possible to just decide that we like one over the other and build our faith upon the one we like?**

Our understanding of God's character depends on the revelation of it as given in His Word. But, if we are to arrive at a correct and, therefore, lifesaving knowledge of God's character, we must first understand what the correct principles of Bible interpretation are. This is obviously important. To begin studying the Word of God with an incorrect principle of interpretation is to end up far removed from the truth.

The fact is that few people approach the study of God's Word with any real system of interpretation clearly laid out. They search through the Word and form their own opinions of what they think the passages mean. This is a haphazard and dangerous practice.

In our approach to the subject of God's character, we dare not do this. We have before us a very real problem in the existence of two sets of statements that can and have been understood to say quite the opposite from each other. The only safe way to approach this difficulty is along the lines of correct Scriptural interpretation.

It is from the Bible itself that we obtain the guidelines for its interpretation. Not only does the Bible give us the message of truth, but it also informs us how those messages are to be comprehended. Our standing in this respect is the principle laid down in 2 Peter 1:20: "Knowing this first, that no prophecy of Scripture is of any private interpretation."

Some might tend to limit the application of this verse to those areas of Scripture foretelling future events, because this is the most generally accepted definition of the word "prophecy."

In a limited sense this is what the word "prophecy" means, but in its fuller and broader sense, "prophecy" applies to any revelations that come from the prophets. Therefore this verse plainly lays down the rule that no prophecy—no word of the entire Scriptures—is to be of any private interpretation.

We can now ask the question, "What is the difference between private interpretation and scriptural interpretation?" Private interpretation is that which emanates from the mind of human beings as their considered opinion of what the divine revelations are intended to say.

Individuals arrive at these conclusions according to the definitions of words already formed in their mind. Their mind is a dictionary to which they make reference whenever they read a word. When people encounter a word not already stored in the limited compendium of the mind, they turn to a comprehensive dictionary such as Oxford or Webster. Having obtained the meaning from there, they apply this word to the scripture being read and develop therefrom an understanding of what the scripture is supposed to say.

We may well define this method of Bible study as definitions by the dictionary. For instance, when people read in the Scriptures that God sent the flood upon the earth and that He *destroyed* humanity by raining fire and brimstone on Sodom and Gomorrah, they will without thought or question look to the definitions of the keywords "sent," "destroyed," and "rained," as those words are already defined in their minds. Such definitions paint a picture of God personally and directly using His mighty power to lash out and liquidate His enemies.

It cannot be too strongly emphasized that by using this method of interpretation, *no conclusion other than this can be drawn.* Inevitably, all who use this method must believe that God is a grim executioner and that He is doing things after the fall that He never did before.

The limited, erroneous nature of this method is exposed when it is seen that its adherents are left with inexplicable contradictions. They are left with no explanation of the other set of statements and the great principles that undergird God's character. They conveniently ignore those scriptures, concentrating their study on the ones that support their chosen view.

Those who learn and adopt the scriptural method of interpretation do not have this problem. They find that the whole of God's Word becomes one harmonious pattern of saving truth.

Why then is the method of defining by the dictionary words describing the character and behavior of God so certain to lead to erroneous views of Scripture? If we do not use the dictionary to define our terms, then to what shall we turn?

These are excellent questions.

The dictionary defines words based on human behavior. This is the key point. On this earth the dictionary is the undisputed authority for the meaning of words. But the dictionary is compiled by people who do not understand or who are not even concerned with divine behavior. If divine and human behavior were the same, then the dictionary would serve both, but they are not the same. The Lord has unmistakably warned us of this.

> "For My thoughts are not your thoughts, nor are your ways My ways," says the LORD. "For as the heavens are higher than the earth, so are My ways higher than your ways, and My thoughts than your thoughts" (Isa. 55:8, 9).

Anyone who would arrive at a correct concept of God's character must engrave this statement in their mind and continually refer to it as a guideline in their study. They should program themselves to test every assertion, every concept, and every idea in their mind by the words of this statement. Whenever, as they read the words of God, they form a picture of divine behavior as being the same as human behavior; then, in the light of this Scripture, they must know that the concept formed is erroneous.

This necessitates having two different sets of definitions for the same keywords. One set is already well known to us, being the dictionary and everyday usage of the words as they describe human behavior. What needs to be developed in human understanding is that other definition which defines the words as they are used by God to describe His own behavior. Reference is made here to such keywords as "destroy," "wrath," "justice," "judgment," "punish," and similar words.

Humanity destroys. We know that. We know how people go about it, and we have no difficulty in defining this word as it applies to human behavior.

The Bible says, "God destroys." Therefore, it is the truth that God does destroy, and no attempt will be made to deny that. But the Bible also says that God's ways are not our ways. From this we can only conclude that God's way of destroying is altogether different from humanity's way. Between them, there is no similarity.

Having determined that these alternate definitions are not written in the dictionary, the question arises as to where they can be found. The Bible is to be used as its own dictionary. Only when we have learned to use it as such can a correct comprehension of its messages be obtained.

There is no excuse for anybody not obtaining the scriptural definitions. They are there. God has provided them, and it is our duty to search them out and, having found them, apply them to the study of God's Word.

There can hardly be a more serious barrier to arriving at saving truth than that provided by preconceived opinions and ideas. There is no person alive today who is not to a larger or lesser degree afflicted with this problem. During the entire span of our lives, we have been absorbing concepts, ideas, and information. We have come to think along certain lines and these thought processes have mostly been erroneous so far as our concept of God's kingdom is concerned.

The outstanding example of this is found in the experience of Christ's apostles. They were born into a Jewish world wherein the prevailing expectation for the coming of the Messiah was the advent of an all-conquering king. As those boys grew, they heard this conversation around them. It was preached to them in church and taught to them in school. The result was the building up of strong, preconceived notions of Christ's work and ministry. When the real Savior appeared, those ideas formed a fearful barrier that for a long time made it impossible for Christ to bring to them the truth regarding His ministry and mission. Only when He was finally able to sweep away those preconceived ideas could He teach them the truth.

So it is with us today. Every one of us should humbly recognize that we do not possess accurate wisdom, knowledge, concepts, and ideas and that these erroneous thought patterns are indeed a great problem.

> The stamps of minds are different. All do not understand expressions and statements alike. Some understand the statements of the Scriptures to suit their own particular minds and cases. Prepossessions, prejudices, and passions have a strong influence to darken the understanding and confuse the mind even in reading the words of Holy Writ (*Selected Messages*, book 1, p. 20).

> The Scriptures are not to be adapted to meet the prejudice and jealousy of men. They can be understood only by those who are humbly seeking for a knowledge of the truth that they may obey it (*Christ's Object Lessons*, p. 112).

Some may feel that earnestness and sincerity compensate for accuracy. But Jesus plainly said, "And you shall know the truth, and the truth shall make you free" (John 8:32). It is the truth and not error that saves us. For this reason, God is continually seeking to send us clearer and more advanced revelations of His truth so we may correspondingly ascend into greater heights of the knowledge of Him. It is also His intent that this knowledge would translate into an ever-deepening *experience* of Him. Many people will fail to enter the kingdom of heaven because prejudice has barred the door to their receiving the truth.

Notice carefully the solemn warnings laid out in this next quotation, which begins with the question, "What shall I do to be saved?" The answer provided is an unexpected and solemn one.

> Do you ask, What shall I do to be saved? You must lay your preconceived opinions, your hereditary and cultivated ideas, at the door of investigation. If you search the Scriptures to vindicate your own opinions, you will never reach the truth. Search in order to learn what the Lord says. If conviction comes as you search, if you see that your cherished opinions are not in harmony with the truth, do not misinterpret the truth in order to suit your own belief, but accept the light given. Open mind and heart that you may behold wondrous things out of God's Word (*Christ's Object Lessons*, p. 112).

There are a number of answers that could have been given to the question "What shall I do to be saved?" Elsewhere those answers are given, but here the point is made that our salvation depends upon laying aside preconceived opinions, hereditary, and cultivated ideas.

Pains are being taken to emphasize this thought because when dealing with the topic of the character of God wrong concepts are prolific. Any emergence into this truth must be from a background of dark error and misconception. The whole world lies in ignorance as to who God really is, and those of us who have lived in this world have been unconsciously influenced by this atmosphere. There is no subject, then, in which the need to lay aside preconceived ideas and opinions is more critical than this one.

Make the Scriptures their own dictionary, their own interpreter. Do this under the blessing and guidance of the Holy Spirit, and the assurance is there that you will arrive at an accurate, comprehensive, and harmonious knowledge of saving truth.

This will take time, so it is not to be expected that every error will be immediately swept away. After all, God's truth is the expression of the mind of the Infinite. Eternity will never exhaust it. Therefore, it is too much to expect that a person using perfect methods of study would emerge in a few short years from deep darkness to a correct understanding of the great verities.

It is a common understanding in worldly churches that the fires of final purification will unceasingly burn the unrepentant wicked who will suffer unending torture and torment within those unquenchable flames. The advent message denies this concept, teaching, rather, that a short consumption of the lost will render them as though they had never been.

It is a difficult subject to present because there are certain scriptures that make it appear that the wicked will burn forever and ever.

It hardly seems necessary to quote the many statements from Scripture which tell us that the wicked will be as though they had not been, that we shall tread down their ashes, that they shall burn, leaving neither root nor branch. We know the Scriptures tell us that the dead know nothing, that their very thoughts are gone. This is one side of the question, but on the other side are statements which clearly say that the wicked will burn forever. The most noteworthy reference of this nature is in Revelation 20:10: "The devil, who deceived them, was cast into the lake of fire and brimstone where the beast and the false prophet are. And they will be tormented day and night for ever and ever."

As an exercise in the correct principles of Bible study, let this verse be taken and interpreted according to dictionary definitions of the keywords to show us the *wrong* way to interpret the Bible.

The important keywords in this particular verse are the words "forever and ever." In our minds there already exists a clear definition of this word, which is in harmony with the written definition in the published dictionary that reads as follows: "Forever means for a limitless time or endless ages, everlastingly, eternally, at all times, always, continually, incessantly." If this dictionary definition of the word "forever" is taken and Revelation 20:10 understood according to it then the only possible understanding of this verse would be that the wicked will suffer for eternity. One could only believe that there would never come a time when their agonies would end. It is hoped that no one will miss the point that a certain method of interpretation will yield its corresponding idea of what the truth is.

Serious doubt of the validity of this method is gendered when it is seen that it brings this text into sharp contradiction with other Scriptures. Here are two examples.

> For as you drank on My holy mountain, so shall all the nations drink continually; yes, they shall drink, and swallow, and they shall be as though they had never been (Obad. 1:16).

"For, behold, the day is coming, burning like an oven, and all the proud, yes, all who do wickedly will be stubble. And the day which is coming shall burn them up," says the LORD of hosts, "That will leave them neither root nor branch" (Mal. 4:1).

It is obviously impossible for the wicked to be as though they had not been and to be burned up, leaving neither root nor branch, and yet, at the same time, eternally exist. The only safety lies in discarding dictionary definitions of words wherever those words are a problem and seeking a revised understanding of the meaning of the statements. The only way to discover an alternative meaning is by making the Bible, and the Bible only, its own dictionary, and therefore, its own interpreter.

We quote now from the book *Answers to Objections* by F. D. Nichol:

We read of "Sodom and Gomorrah, and the cities about them … suffering the vengeance of eternal [*aiōnios*] fire." Jude 7. Are those cities, set ablaze long ago as a divine judgment, still burning? No; their ruins are quite submerged by the Dead Sea. The Bible itself specifically states that God turned "the cities of Sodom and Gomorrah into ashes." 2 Peter 2:6. Now the fate of these cities is declared to be a warning to all wicked men of the fate that impends for them. Therefore if the "*aiōnios* fire" of that long ago judgment turned into ashes those upon whom it preyed, and then died down of itself, we may properly conclude that the "*aiōnios* fire" of the last day will do likewise.

When we turn to the Old Testament we discover that "everlasting" and "for ever" sometimes signify a very limited time. We shall quote texts in which these two terms are translated from the Hebrew word *olam*, because *olam* is the equivalent of the Greek *aiōn*.

The Passover was to be kept "for ever [*olam*]." Ex. 12:24. But it ended with the cross. (See Heb. 9:24-26.) Aaron and his sons were to offer incense "for ever [*olam*]." (1 Chron. 23:13), and to have an "everlasting [*olam*] priesthood." Ex. 40:15. But this priesthood, with its offerings of incense, ended at the cross. (See Heb. 7:11-14.) A servant who desired to stay with his master, was to serve him "for ever [*olam*]." (See Ex. 21:1-6.) How could a servant serve a master to endless time? Will there be masters and servants in the world to come? Jonah, describing his watery experience, said, "The earth with her bars was about me for ever [*olam*]." Jonah 2:6. Yet this "for ever" was only "three days and three nights" long. Jonah 1:17. Rather a short "for ever." Because Gehazi practiced deceit, Elisha declared, "The leprosy therefore of Naaman shall cleave unto thee [Gehazi], and unto thy seed for ever [*olam*]." 2 Kings 5:27. Should we conclude, therefore, that Gehazi's family would never end, and that thus leprosy would be perpetuated for all time to come?

Thus by the acid test of actual usage we discover that in a number of cases *aiōn*, *aiōnios*, and *olam* have a very limited time value (pp. 360, 361).

It should now be clear that when the words "for ever and ever" are interpreted according to dictionary definitions, a certain understanding of that verse will emerge, while if the Bible is used to uncover its usage of the words, then a very different understanding will result.

A sound test of the true method is that it removes impossible contradictions and replaces them with harmony and cohesion. There will be no need to ignore statements that otherwise do not fit.

Once the correct method has been found, it is to be applied with unfailing consistency throughout the entire study of the Bible. One system cannot be used in one area and a different one used in another. It has been astonishing to see people having no trouble in believing that the wicked do not burn forever, and then rejecting the principle that God destroys only by trying to save. Yet exactly the same methods of interpretation used to arrive at the former were the only means of arriving at the latter.

This does not mean that every word will have a separate definition apart from the dictionary definition when used in the Scriptures. Many will have the same meaning, but there will always be keywords that do not. They are readily recognized, for whenever a word, when understood according to its common everyday usage, creates a serious problem then it is time to search out its scriptural meaning.

Chapter Thirteen

God Does Destroy—But How?

Study/Discussion Questions:

- "God said it. I believe it. That settles it." Have you heard this before, or even said it yourself? Is there a difference between human language and scriptural language? This is our study.

- Does the gospel truth only save or can it ruin and destroy?

- When God advises us that our ways are not His ways, does He leave it to us to determine in which area(s) this principle applies?

- Knowing that our thoughts and ways hold no resemblance whatsoever to God's thoughts and ways, would we be likely to find that the "God did it" form of expression we find in scriptures is to be guided by a totally different frame of reference than the human experience?

The principles of interpretation laid out in the previous chapter can now be applied to the problem of reconciling otherwise contradicting statements. In this case the concern is over the declarations that God does not destroy versus those which say He does. These principles, properly applied, are guaranteed to establish a perfect harmony where confusion previously reigned.

This application is a practical exercise. Let's begin by selecting a scripture that has frequently been offered as proof that God steps forth in almighty power and cuts down the rejecters of His mercy.

Then the LORD rained brimstone and fire on Sodom and Gomorrah, from the LORD out of the heavens. So He overthrew those cities, all the plain, all the inhabitants of the cities, and what grew on the ground (Gen. 19:24, 25).

Ponder now upon those words. Just what picture do they suggest to you? Ask the question, "What do these words tell me God did?"

The normal understanding is the view that God, after working with great love and patience to bring these rebels to repentance, finally laid aside the garments of mercy, took hold of the mighty power of fire, and personally poured it out on their unsheltered heads. The result was such total obliteration that no trace of those cities can be found today.

But the Word of God expressly advises that God's ways are entirely different from humanity's. This difference is not in one point or another but is completely so in every area. Because of this when Christ came to earth, "He presented to men that which was *exactly contrary* to the representations of the enemy in regard to the character of God" (*Fundamentals of Christian Education*, p. 177, emphasis added).

Therefore, as surely as it is established that God's ways are different from our ways, then there must be another explanation to these verses. This alternative is not found by casting around in the human mind for other possibilities. The Bible, under the illumination of the Holy Spirit, must be its own interpreter. When it is learned from there how such words are to be understood, the correct concept of God will be gained.

Within the Word of God, the same terminology is used consistently when describing God's actions in the destruction of people and cities. God does not provide a careful explanation of what He means by these words in every case, but there are two or three places where He does, and this is sufficient to inform us how every such expression is to be interpreted. Thus the truth is established in the "mouth of two or three witnesses" (Matt. 18:16).

Reference will now be made to three such witnesses to clarify from the Word itself how such statements are to be understood when used to describe God's actions. The method used in the Scriptures to make the meaning clear is to express the same truth in two different places in two different ways. In the first case, what God did will be clearly stated. Then the Lord Himself will use His own method of expressing or describing what He did. By putting these two together it will be clearly seen what God means when He says, "I destroyed them."

Remember that it is not important what we *think* the Lord meant when He uses certain expressions. Our task is to *be sure* of what the Lord meant when He used those words.

The first reference to be considered is in regard to the death of Saul, the first king of Israel.

> The battle became fierce against Saul. The archers hit him, and he was wounded by the archers. Then Saul said to his armorbearer, "Draw your sword, and thrust me through with it, lest these uncircumcised men come and abuse me." But his armorbearer would not, for he was greatly afraid. Therefore Saul took a sword and fell on it. And when his armorbearer saw that Saul was dead, he also fell on his sword and died. So Saul and his three sons died, and all his house died together (1 Chron. 10:3-6).

This is a simple, and therefore easily understood, account of Saul's death. There is a background to this event that is but the climax of that which went before. After a certain critical point in the king's life, he persistently rejected the appeals of mercy. By this means he took himself further and further outside the circle of God's protection until it was impossible for the Lord to help him. This was not because the Lord would not but only because He could not.

Thus, when he went forth to the final battle, Saul went without the Lord's protection, and he knew it. It was for this reason Saul sought guidance from the witch at Endor. Without God's presence, there was nothing to save Saul from the dreadful power of the

Philistines, resulting in his destruction. As Saul's life is considered, it will be seen that he took himself away from God, placing himself where there was no defense from Satan's power, and thus, in fact, he destroyed himself.

Having seen clearly, then, what the Lord did in respect to Saul's destruction, we are now ready to see how He described what He did.

> So Saul died for his unfaithfulness which he had committed against the LORD, because he did not keep the word of the LORD, and also because he consulted a medium for guidance. But he did not inquire of the LORD; *therefore He killed him*, and turned the kingdom over to David the son of Jesse (1 Chron. 10:13, 14).

But we know that God did not raise His hand to slay Saul. Saul killed himself just in time to save the Philistines from doing it. The Scriptures, which are the very expression of God's thought, described that in these words, "Therefore, He [the Lord God of heaven] killed him."

This is certainly not the way we would use the words, "He killed him." Describing human behavior, we would imagine the slayer coming to the victim and bringing the sword down upon the head of the guilty person. This is not how we describe the way God kills. God moves away from the person, handing them over to be the victim of other forces.

So foreign is this form of expression to what we are accustomed to that it is initially difficult to think in this new terminology. Yet, in order to truthfully understand God's thought as expressed in His word, the mind must be re-educated to think this way when reading about God's ways as distinct from our ways. There certainly will be no difficulty in seeing that the way in which God uses words and the way in which we use them are contrary to each other.

The presentation of one witness is never sufficient to establish the truth of the Bible. A second must be added.

As it was with Saul, so it was with the entire nation of Israel. Centuries of loving appeals were spurned, the prophets were persecuted and, in some cases, martyred. Eventually, the Son of God Himself came with a personal message from the Father. But they rejected Him even more emphatically.

The time came when Christ recognized that they had passed the point of no return. What did He say and do? He declared that Jerusalem was beyond hope, and then, instead of launching fiery balls of destruction upon the city, He quietly left them to their fate. Again, He did not do this because He wanted to but because there was nothing else He could do that was consistent with His character of love. Here are His sad words.

> "O Jerusalem, Jerusalem, the one who kills the prophets and stones those who are sent to her! How often I wanted to gather your children together, as a hen gathers her chicks under her wings, but you were not willing! See! Your house is *left to you desolate*; for I say to you, you shall see Me no more till you say, 'Blessed is He who comes in the name of the LORD!'" (Matt. 23:37-39).

For the same reasons, and in harmony with the same principles, God left Israel exactly as He had left Saul. Thus was removed from them the only effective defense from their many enemies.

> The Jews had forged their own fetters; they had filled for themselves the cup of vengeance. In the utter destruction that befell them as a nation, and in all the woes that followed them in their dispersion, they were but reaping the harvest which their own hands had sown. Says the prophet, "O Israel, thou hast destroyed thyself;" "for thou hast fallen by thine iniquity." Hosea 13:9; 14:1. Their sufferings are often represented as a punishment visited upon them by the direct decree of God. It is thus that the great deceiver seeks to conceal his own work. By stubborn rejection of divine love and mercy, the Jews had caused the protection of God to be withdrawn from them, and Satan was permitted to rule them according to his will. The horrible cruelties enacted in the destruction of Jerusalem are a demonstration of Satan's vindictive power over those who yield to his control....
>
> But when men pass the limits of divine forbearance, that restraint [placed upon Satan] is removed. God does not stand toward the sinner as an executioner of the sentence against transgression; but He leaves the rejecters of His mercy to themselves, to reap that which they have sown.... The Spirit of God, persistently resisted, is at last withdrawn from the sinner, and then there is left no power to control the evil passions of the soul, and no protection from the malice and enmity of Satan. The destruction of Jerusalem is a fearful and solemn warning to all [regarding] ... the certain punishment that will fall upon the guilty (*The Great Controversy*, pp. 35, 36).

Of particular value is the reference made to the common interpretation of what was done there. "Their sufferings are often represented as a punishment visited upon them by the direct decree of God." In other words, this is the way in which most people view God's actions in this incident:

"With loving appeals the Lord seeks to woo and to win until the time comes when His patience is exhausted. Then, having passed judgment upon them, He personally decides what form of punishment He will send. Will it be a fearful earthquake, a fire, a volcanic eruption, or pestilence, or shall He send their enemies among them? In the case of Jerusalem, God decided that He would send the Romans. Having made this decree, He called them to the terrible office of being the personal executioners of His vengeance on the Jews."

That is the view most people have of the judgment on the Jews in AD 70. This is the interpretation that comes of thinking that God's behavior is the same as humanity's and of defining Bible words according to dictionary meanings. While these methods are employed, it is impossible to come to any other conclusion.

Again, we read: "Their sufferings are often represented as a punishment visited upon them by the direct decree of God. It is thus that the great deceiver seeks to conceal his own work" (*The Great Controversy*, p. 35).

Then there is laid down forever the precious truth that "God does not stand toward the sinner as an executioner of the sentence against transgression; but He leaves the rejecters of His mercy to themselves, to reap that which they have sown" (*Ibid.*, p. 36). What befell the Jews was the natural *outworking* of their *own course* of action. It was not something brought upon them by God. They had sown the seed; now they had to gather the certain harvest.

We have before us a revelation of the course God pursued toward the Israelites, which is the same as that with Saul. It is now necessary to find how God Himself described what He did.

In the death of Israel's first king and the destruction of the nation in AD 70, God consistently followed the same course. In both cases He worked with infinite love and patience to win them to the ways of righteousness and safety, but they utterly rejected it, forcing Him to withdraw and leave them to the fate that lay nearest. For Saul, it was the invasion of the Philistines, for Jerusalem, the Roman onslaught.

God described what He did to Saul in words very different from the ones we would use to describe what He did. God said, "I destroyed him." We would say, "Saul destroyed himself."

Because God is consistent, it is to be expected that He would describe the same action in the fall of Jerusalem in the same language. Therefore, it must be anticipated that He would say, "I destroyed Jerusalem and killed those murderers." This is just how He did describe that terrible destruction.

In Matthew 22, there is a parable that, in its initial application, sets out the two final calls given to the Jewish people and their rejections of those calls. When the second call is complete and is rejected, the king's reaction is described in these words:

> But when the king heard about it, he was furious. And he sent out his armies, destroyed those murderers, and burned up their city (Matt. 22:7).

This verse is couched in symbolic language. God the Father was the king; the armies were the Romans under Titus; the murderers were the Jews who crucified Christ; and the city was Jerusalem. The fulfillment of this fearful prophecy came in AD 70 as verified in *Christ's Object Lessons*, page 309, where this verse is quoted, followed by these words:

> The judgment pronounced came upon the Jews in the destruction of Jerusalem and the scattering of the nation.

If we substitute the things symbolized for the symbolic words, the verse must read as follows: "But when God heard thereof, God was wroth: and God sent forth His armies, the Romans, and God destroyed the Jews, and God burned up Jerusalem."

If these words are interpreted according to normal dictionary definitions, the only possible picture of God would be identical to earthly despots. But the inspired word quoted from *The Great Controversy* confirms that an altogether different understanding is to be obtained from these verses. Therefore, the position adopted depends directly on the way in which the words are understood. The choice lies between accepting a meaning according to human or scriptural language. The former is acquired by reference to a standard dictionary, the latter by the Scriptures themselves.

The third witness will also be drawn from Israel's history. There was the occasion when the Israelites were traveling through the wilderness and once again murmured about God and Moses. Unknown to them, they were traveling through an area infested with deadly serpents and other terrors. Because of God's protecting care, they had passed through this area unharmed until that time when they drove away His protection through their own ingratitude and sinfulness. With the shield removed, there was nothing to hold back the invasion of those reptiles, and as a result many of the people died a terrible death.

Here is the description of what happened and of what God did. It needs but little comment after the two already studied, for once again it will be seen that the Lord simply left them to what they wanted. He did not decree the particular punishment; it was lurking there all the time only awaiting the opportunity to destroy them.

> As the Israelites indulged the spirit of discontent, they were disposed to find fault even with their blessings. "And the people spake against God, and against Moses, Wherefore have ye brought us up out of Egypt to die in the wilderness? for there is no bread, neither is there any water; and our soul loatheth this light bread."
>
> Moses faithfully set before the people their great sin. It was God's power alone that had preserved them in "that great and terrible wilderness, wherein were fiery serpents, and scorpions, and drought, where there was no water." Deuteronomy 8:15. Every day of their travels they had been kept by a miracle of divine mercy. In all the way of God's leading they had found water to refresh the thirsty, bread from heaven to satisfy their hunger, and peace and safety under the shadowy cloud by day and the pillar of fire by night. Angels had ministered to them as they climbed the rocky heights or threaded the rugged paths of the wilderness. Notwithstanding the hardships they had endured, there was not a feeble one in all their ranks. Their feet had not swollen in their long journeys, neither had their clothes grown old. God had subdued before them the fierce beasts of prey and the venomous reptiles of the forest and the desert. If with all these tokens of His love the people still continued to complain, the Lord would *withdraw His protection* until they should be led to appreciate His merciful care, and return to Him with repentance and humiliation.
>
> Because they had been shielded by divine power they had not realized the countless dangers by which they were continually surrounded. In their ingratitude and unbelief they had anticipated death, and now the Lord *permitted* death to come upon them. The poisonous serpents that infested the wilderness were called fiery serpents, on account of the terrible effects produced by their sting,

it causing violent inflammation and speedy death. As the *protecting hand of God was removed from Israel,* great numbers of the people were attacked by these venomous creatures (*Patriarchs and Prophets,* pp. 428, 429, emphasis added).

As in the previous illustrations, a comparison will be made between what the Lord is described as doing and His own statement of what He did. If God is consistent, and we know He is, then He will describe this in the same way as He spoke of the previous two. Again, the consistency of God stands forth without variableness or shadow of turning.

So the LORD sent fiery serpents among the people, and they bit the people; and many of the people of Israel died (Num. 21:6).

For those who want further confirmation of the truths revealed in this use of the Bible as its own dictionary, referral is made to the experience of the patriarch Job. Satan demanded the right to destroy him. God withdrew and left him to the power of the devil with one restriction—that he could not take his life. Everything that happened to Job was at the hands of Satan, not God. The picture of God's behavior was the same as previously shown except for this difference. Whereas in each of the other cases, it was the sinfulness of the rejecters of His mercy that drove God and His protection away, Job was "a perfect and an upright man" (Job 1:8). God's withdrawal from him was not the result of Job's sinfulness.

On what grounds, then, could the Lord leave Job to suffer at the devil's hands? This is a good question that finds its answer in the following principle. Every true child of God has given his life into God's hands to be sacrificed in His cause if thereby the work will be advanced. This is a privilege, and the Lord will never deny that privilege to any one of His children when the hour comes. The hour came for Job, and the Lord did not stand in the way of his offering.

Thus there are two ways in which the Lord will remove His protection from a person and leave him to the destroyer. One is by humanity's sinfulness, which drives off the Spirit of God, and the other is by the individual offering himself as a sacrifice for the cause of truth, a thing that every child of God does.

When the Lord came down to personally describe what He had done to Job, He again used the same language as previously noted.

Have you considered My servant Job, that there is none like him on the earth, a blameless and upright man, one who fears God and shuns evil? And still he holds fast to his integrity, although you incited Me against him, to destroy him without cause (Job 2:3).

Once again this is not the way we would use those words according to everyday usage. Our use of them would convey a meaning quite opposite from what God intended when He used them.

It would be impossible to arrive at the meanings of the words, according to God's usage of them, without the guidance of the Word of God. Only from there can such an interpretation be obtained. That is, it is the only dictionary which gives this definition of these words.

It may take some time to train our minds to carry these double definitions for the same words. But conscious effort must be made until it is just as natural to think of the new definition as of the old. It must become second nature to ascribe one meaning to the words when they describe divine conduct and another when they deal with the human. Here is a comparison between the two.

When human beings destroy, they move toward the victim with deliberate intention to kill.

When God destroys, He moves away from the subject with no intention of killing.

When human beings destroy, they carry the weapons of death in their hands.

When God destroys, He carries no weapons but lays down control of the destructive powers.

When human beings destroy, they guide the sword to its target.

When God destroys, there is no personal administration of punishment. Whatever comes upon sinners is the outworking of the forces of death that they themselves have set in motion.

At this point two questions are apt to arise. The first is, what is the essential difference between the direct act of destroying or that of departing to leave the person to die? In both cases it is God's action that brings about the destruction, and therefore, in each case, He is a destroyer.

This would be true if God's withdrawal was His own act, but it is not. The fact is that He is driven away.

The truth of this is stated in a paragraph from *Prophets and Kings.*

> Christ will never abandon those for whom He has died. We may leave Him and be overwhelmed with temptation, but Christ can never turn from one for whom He has paid the ransom of His own life (p. 176).

In view of the fact that Christ died for everyone, this statement is saying that it is impossible for Christ to turn away from anyone. People turn away from God. God *cannot* turn away from humanity. That is impossible.

The second question is this: If God does *not* in fact destroy, then why does He use this word to describe His actions? Does this not tend to make the Scriptures confusing?

Again, this is an excellent question. But this is the right word to use in describing God's actions, for there is a deep and important sense in which it is true that He does destroy.

As the evidences gathered here unfold, it will be seen that God comes to humanity in one role only, which is as a Savior. But the *effect* of that effort is not always a saving one. With the majority, the effect is to harden them in rebellion and to cause them to withdraw themselves from the voice of loving entreaty. Thus God destroys by trying to save. The more He exerts His saving power, the more that people reject His offer, thus leading to destruction. It is in this sense that He destroys.

This principle of truth is spelled out with great clarity in the following statement:

It is not God that blinds the eyes of men or hardens their hearts. He sends them light to correct their errors, and to lead them in safe paths; it is by the rejection of this light that the eyes are blinded and the heart hardened. Often the process is gradual, and almost imperceptible. Light comes to the soul through God's word, through His servants, or by the direct agency of His Spirit; but when one ray of light is disregarded, there is a partial benumbing of the spiritual perceptions, and the second revealing of light is less clearly discerned. So the darkness increases, until it is night in the soul. Thus it had been with these Jewish leaders. They were convinced that a divine power attended Christ, but in order to resist the truth, they attributed the work of the Holy Spirit to Satan. In doing this they deliberately chose deception; they yielded themselves to Satan, and henceforth they were controlled by his power (*The Desire of Ages*, pp. 322, 323).

It is not God that puts the blinder before the eyes of men or makes their hearts hard; it is the light which God sends to his people, to correct their errors, to lead them in safe paths, but which they refuse to accept,—it is this that blinds their minds and hardens their hearts (*The Review and Herald*, October 21, 1890).

The outstanding example of this outworking is the history of Pharaoh of Egypt. The Scriptures say, "And I will harden Pharaoh's heart, and multiply My signs and My wonders in the land of Egypt" (Exod. 7:3).

To harden is to destroy. It is not physical destruction but spiritual. This spiritual destruction is the prelude to the physical, which must inevitably follow. The Scriptures plainly say that it was God who did it and He did, but every reference that throws light on what God did shows that His action was to send spiritual light and loving appeals to Pharaoh. These were designed to soften and save, not to harden him, but that which was sent to save, destroyed him instead because he rejected it. Note carefully that it was not the light, but his rejection of it that hardened and destroyed him.

Every rejection of light hardens the heart and darkens the understanding; and thus men find it more and more difficult to distinguish between right and wrong, and they become bolder in resisting the will of God (*The SDA Bible Commentary*, vol. 1, p. 1100).

Every additional evidence of the power of God that the Egyptian monarch resisted, carried him on to a stronger and more persistent defiance of God. Thus the work went on, finite man warring against the expressed will of an infinite God. This case is a clear illustration of the sin against the Holy Ghost. "Whatsoever a man soweth, that shall he also reap." Gradually the Lord withdrew his Spirit. Removing his restraining power, he gave the king into the hands of the worst of all tyrants,—self (*The Review and Herald*, July 27, 1897).

The patience and long-suffering of God, which should soften and subdue the soul, has an altogether different influence upon the careless and sinful. It leads them to cast off restraint, and strengthens them in resistance (*The Review and Herald*, August 14, 1900).

The truth laid out in these statements is a very important one. When it is truly appreciated, there will be no careless attitude toward the revelations that are brought to us. There will be the dread of having the heart hardened and the spiritual sense benumbed.

Let ministers and people remember that gospel truth ruins if it does not save. The soul that refuses to listen to the invitations of mercy from day to day can soon listen to the most urgent appeals without an emotion stirring his soul (*Testimonies for the Church*, vol. 5, p. 134).

We must clearly understand that the only effort God puts forth is to save. That effort can and does produce two opposite effects. In the hearts and lives of those who accept God's work, it achieves its intended result. It softens, changes, cleanses, and restores. It is unto life eternal.

But in the lives of those who reject that saving ministry, there is a terrible work of destruction going forward. It is a destroying work that breaks down every spiritual response within, hardens the heart in rebellion, develops every sinful trait, and compels the Spirit of God to withdraw His presence and His protection. This leaves the individual to the choice he or she has made—a position where there is no protection whatsoever from the destructive malice of Satan and sin.

God destroys, but not as human beings destroy. Every effort on God's part is to save, but it has an altogether different result in the lives of those who reject that saving power. Therefore, we can know that, in fact, God is a Savior and a Savior only. He destroys by trying to save. The more His saving power is manifest in the world and that power is rejected, the more swiftly and terribly are the rejecters destroyed by the simple outworking of the forces involved.

This principle will come through with greater clarity and force as the individual cases of the flood, Sodom and Gomorrah, the plagues of Egypt, the crucifixion of Christ, the seven last plagues, and the final judgment are studied. These will be progressively examined. For now it is sufficient to establish the principle that the way in which the Lord destroys is by seeking to save. Thus His way of destroying is entirely different from humanity's way. Once this is clearly comprehended, it is possible to view all God's actions in a new and enlightened way. As a result, the whole of the Scriptures will emerge as one great harmonious truth.

Chapter Fourteen

The Supreme Revelation

Study/Discussion Questions:

- Is the Father the wrathful One, standing by to execute vengeance upon sinners, while the meek and gentle Jesus interposes to persuade Him to hold back His retribution?

- What does it mean that Christ and the Father "are one"?

- Is there really no difference between the Father and Son in how they relate to humankind?

- Was the Old Testament revelation not enough to know the truth about the character of God?

- Was the Old Testament revelation of God and the coming of Christ simply a shifting of emphasis from one aspect of God to another, implying that Christ's revelation of the character of God was incomplete?

There are no contradictions in the Word of God; it must not be interpreted according to private or human methods; the Bible is its own dictionary and, therefore, its own interpreter; God's ways and humanity's way are entirely different from each other; the only way in which God destroys is by trying to save; and any destruction eventuating is because of rejection by human beings and not the action of God.

This established, the groundwork has been prepared for studying the various incidents of history in which God has played a part. Reference is made here to the flood, the destruction of Sodom and Gomorrah, the plagues of Egypt, the execution of those who worshiped the golden calf, the stoning of the Sabbath breaker, the adulterer, the glutton, Achan, the slaughter of the Canaanites, the obliteration of Sennacherib's army, and many other such events, right through to the concluding one—the final liquidation in the lake of fire.

Evidence will now be presented to show that the Old Testament is not the place to begin examining the character of God. The convincing argument for this is that not even the holy angels were able to understand God's character as it was revealed in the Old Testament. Not until the advent of Christ, and ultimately the demonstration of infinite love and justice given on Calvary, were they able to see God as He really is. At the same time, Satan was revealed in his true light. For the first time, the angels were truly convinced of the righteousness of God's cause. The scriptural evidences for this have already been quoted, but it is appropriate to quote them again.

> Not until the death of Christ was the character of Satan clearly revealed to the angels or to the unfallen worlds. The archapostate had so clothed himself with deception that even holy beings had not understood his principles. They had not clearly seen the nature of his rebellion (*The Desire of Ages*, p. 758).

There is a direct relationship between the misunderstanding of Satan's character and the falsification of God's. Therefore, to whatever extent the angels were not able to see the true nature of Satan and his work during the Old Testament era, then to that extent they were unable to correctly comprehend God's principles of character and conduct. If holy angels, mighty in intellectual and spiritual power and personally involved in God's workings in the Old Testament dispensation, still had clouded views of God, then it is impossible for human minds to understand God from these evidences alone.

What was necessary for them is even more so for earthbound travelers seeking the knowledge of God, which is life eternal. This search must start with the finest and fullest existing revelation of Him—the life of Christ and the marvel of Calvary. Entering the study at this point will quickly impress on the searcher's mind the necessity of penetrating beyond the commonly held view of the Old Testament God.

For many people, the Old Testament revelation of God, compared with Christ's example in the New Testament, has provided an altogether contradictory picture. God is seen as a stern, exacting lawmaker who will not permit His will to be thwarted, while Christ is viewed as a tender, benign, loving forgiver of all sins. To God is ascribed one character and to Christ another. This destroys the precious truth that Christ and the Father are one in authority, character, spirit, aims, and works. The belief is spawned that Christ is the appeaser of the Father's fury, influencing Him to act contrary to His real character by showing mercy when it is not in His heart or nature to do so.

It is grossly inconsistent to hold such a position and only possible if the two ideas are carefully compartmentalized into separate areas of the brain so that they are never thought of at the same time. Let them be brought together, and the honest, thoughtful student will realize that one or the other has to go. Either Christ and the Father are one, or they are not.

Solving this problem is not difficult, for the Scriptures are emphatic that the Father and Son are one in every particular. Jesus testified to this repeatedly.

> I and My Father are one (John 10:30).

> If I do not the works of My Father, do not believe Me; but if I do, though you do not believe Me, believe the works, that you may know and believe that the Father is in Me, and I in Him (John 10:37, 38).

> If you had known Me, you would have known My Father also; and from now on you know Him, and have seen Him. Philip said to Him, "Lord, show us the Father, and it is sufficient for us." Jesus said to him, "Have I been with you so

long, and yet you have not known Me, Philip? He who has seen Me has seen the Father; so how can you say, 'Show us the Father'?

Do you not believe that I am in the Father, and the Father in Me? The words that I speak to you I do not speak on My own authority; but the Father who dwells in Me does the works. Believe Me that I am in the Father and the Father in Me, or else believe Me for the sake of the works themselves (John 14:7-11).

Then Jesus answered and said to them, "Most assuredly, I say to you, the Son can do nothing of Himself, but what He sees the Father do; for whatever He does, the Son also does in like manner (John 5:19).

By these words, Christ, on His Father's behalf, denied that there was any difference whatsoever between Them in character and work. Both are joined in the most intimate way, in dedicated purpose to save the perishing. Christ does not have to appease the Father, for He is doing exactly what the Father has commissioned Him to do.

Evidence was presented back in chapter 3 that the specific method employed by Satan to drive wedges between God and His creatures was the false presentation of God's character.

Sin originated in self-seeking. Lucifer, the covering cherub, desired to be first in heaven. He sought to gain control of heavenly beings, to draw them away from their Creator, and to win their homage to himself. Therefore *he* misrepresented *God*, attributing to Him the desire for self-exaltation. With his own evil characteristics he sought to invest the loving Creator. *Thus he deceived angels. Thus he deceived men.* He led them to doubt the word of God, and to distrust His goodness. Because God is a God of justice and terrible majesty, Satan caused them to look upon Him as severe and unforgiving. Thus he drew men to join him in rebellion against God, and the night of woe settled down upon the world (*The Desire of Ages*, pp. 21, 22, emphasis added).

By the same misrepresentation of the character of God as he had practiced in heaven, causing Him to be regarded as severe and tyrannical, Satan induced man to sin (*The Great Controversy*, p. 500).

Adam believed the falsehood of Satan, and *through his misrepresentation of the character of God*, Adam's life was changed and marred. He disobeyed the commandment of God, and did the very thing the Lord told him not to do. Through disobedience Adam fell; but had he endured the test, and been loyal to God, the floodgates of woe would not have been opened upon our world. *Through belief in Satan's misrepresentation of God*, man's character and destiny were changed, but if men will believe in the Word of God, they will be transformed in mind and character, and fitted for eternal life (*Selected Messages*, book 1, pp. 345, 346, emphasis added).

Satan's method of destroying the unity of the universe can only be countered by the restoration of the truth about God. That character was manifested in all God's dealings with both loyal and rebellious individuals and nations between the fall and the first advent, but human beings, influenced and blinded by Satan, were not able to see the verities offered there.

Therefore, an incontrovertible revelation of God's character had to be supplied to counteract Satan's lies and make clear the real message of the Old Testament. There was only one being who could give such a demonstration and that was Christ, "who being the brightness of His glory and the express image of His person" (Heb. 1:3) was commissioned by God to do so.

> The Saviour was deeply anxious for His disciples to understand for what purpose His divinity was united to humanity. He came to the world to display the glory [character] of God, that man might be uplifted by its restoring power (*The Desire of Ages*, p. 664).

> Christ came to the earth to reveal to men the character of His Father, and His life was filled with deeds of divine tenderness and compassion (*Patriarchs and Prophets*, p. 469).

> Jesus, the express image of the Father's person, the effulgence of His glory; the self-denying Redeemer, throughout His pilgrimage of love on earth was a living representative of the character of the law of God. In His life it is made manifest that heaven-born love, Christlike principles, underlie the laws of eternal rectitude (*God's Amazing Grace*, p. 102).

So total is the revelation of God's character as given by Christ that "All that man needs to know or can know of God has been revealed in the life and character of His Son" (*Testimonies for the Church*, vol. 8, p. 286).

There is not a single reason for doubting the veracity of these statements. Jesus confirmed the truth of it in His words to Philip, "Have I been with you so long, and yet you have not known Me, Philip? *He who has seen Me has seen the Father*; so how can you say, 'Show us the Father'?" (John 14:9).

As a description of this work, the title, "the Word of God," is most appropriate. Falling from the lips of one who is entirely honest and truthful, words are an exact expression of the thinking and character of the speaker. Upon this earth, Jesus Christ was the Word of God.

That is, He did not speak His own words but those of the Father. He did not do His own deeds but the deeds of the One who had sent Him. "He was the Word of God—God's thought made audible" (*The Desire of Ages*, p. 19).

Therefore, He declared of His mission:

> Do you not believe that I am in the Father, and the Father in Me? The words that I speak to you I do not speak on My own authority; but the Father who dwells in

Me does the works (John 14:10).

> Then Jesus said to them, "When you lift up the Son of Man, then you will know
> that I am He, and that I do nothing of Myself; but as My Father taught Me, I
> speak these things" (John 8:28).

Therefore, great care should be taken to understand this aspect of Christ's mission.
The truth that Jesus was the very expression of the thought and character of God should
hold so firm a place in the mind, that no matter what contradictory pictures of God may
be presented, the only acceptable ones are those in harmony with Christ's representations
of God. In the New Testament, Christ gave us the true picture of God. Let that truth be
forever and without question established in the mind. As surely as the Lord is consistent,
then the Old Testament presentation of Him must coincide with the New Testament. The
student must not rest until the two are harmonized.

To appreciate the full value of Christ's matchless presentation of God's character, it is
necessary to recognize how all-encompassing it was. Did Christ come to present a partial
view of God? Was it simply a shifting of emphasis? Did God, feeling that He had most
satisfactorily convinced men in the Old Testament of the sterner and uncompromising
side of His nature, leave Christ to emphasize the qualities of love, forgiveness, and mercy?

Such a view is adopted by many as a solution to what they feel would otherwise be a
contradiction between the messages of the Old and New Testaments, but it is not the message of the Scriptures themselves. Therein, it is asserted that Christ's manifestation of the
Father was complete. It leaves nothing more to be shown. This is not saying that everything
about God's character can be understood in one contact with the Savior, for it will take
eternity to see all that Christ came to tell. What must be recognized and accepted as truth
is that the revelation of God in the face of Christ is complete. Therefore it is written:

> *All* that man needs to know or can know of God has been revealed in the life and
> character of His Son (*Testimonies for the Church*, vol. 8, p. 286, emphasis added).

This statement is specific, comprehensive, and accurate. It leaves no space for the sup-
position that Christ revealed only a certain aspect of God's character or even the larger part
of it. It does not admit to the notion that Christ's ministry provided a further stage in this
revelation with final unfolding to be given in the future. All that remains is for the eager,
spiritual child of God, through earnest study and prayer, to come into possession of this
richest of all treasures. Some may counter that eternal life is the richest of treasures. This is
true and in its truth establishes this point, for the knowledge of God is eternal life.

> And this is eternal life, that they may know You, the only true God, and Jesus
> Christ whom You have sent (John 17:3).

Christ Himself declared the totality of His revelation of His Father. "Then Jesus answered and said to them, 'Most assuredly, I say to you, the Son can do nothing of Himself,
but what He sees the Father do; for whatever He does, the Son also does in like manner"

(John 5:19).

Therefore, as certainly as His life, so filled with activity, contained nothing done of Himself or from Himself, all that He did was of God and from God. It was the Father who was acting out His life and character through the medium of His beloved Son. Therefore, in Christ's every act, we see God at work and know thereby exactly what the Father does in relation to His subjects, be they sinful or righteous.

This is confirmed in Christ's words: "for whatever He does, the Son also does in like manner" (John 5:19).

The witness of Christ here is not simply in these terms, "what things He doeth," but "whatever [things] He does." The addition of this word means that *everything* the Father does is included. This is a word that carries the idea of completeness, of infinitude. Therefore, Christ is attesting that *everything* the Father does, without any exceptions, the Son does likewise.

The student must not fail to observe the insertion of the word "likewise." It adds significant meaning to the Savior's message. It is important that we believe that Christ did upon this earth *everything* the Father did. It is equally essential for us to know that He did it *likewise* as the Father did it. Not only did He do all the Father did, but He did it exactly as the Father did it.

In a further attempt to argue that the revelation of God by Christ was incomplete, it may be claimed that during the earthly interval Christ did not have a full knowledge of the works of God. Such an argument is stifled in the very next verse where Christ claimed complete knowledge of the ways and works of God.

> For the Father loves the Son, and shows Him *all things* that He Himself does; and He will show Him greater works than these, that you may marvel (John 5:20).

What a challenge this is to the old ideas about God. Every idea in which God is seen as the destroyer of those who refuse His offers of mercy, can be sustained only if we find Christ doing the same thing. What citadels of error must collapse before the onslaught of this impregnable truth! What an entirely new and glorious structure of living verities about the Father must now arise from the wreckage of those edifices of lies!

Consider the time-honored theories about God. He is viewed as One who initially seeks the salvation of His creatures. From His position of supreme authority, He calls upon human beings to repent of their sins and obey His will. He demonstrates patience while they play with His appeals, but the time comes when that patience is exhausted. Then He arises to perform His "strange act." With terrifying power, wielded in His own hands, He wipes the rebellious from the face of the earth, thus demonstrating that He is not a God to be scorned. He thus asserts His will by the naked use of destructive force, convincing men that they must obey Him or perish. This is the view of the traditionalist.

Is this what God does? Is this a true picture of His patterns of behavior? It is important to know the answer, for if it is not correct, then it is a lying representation of God designed by the devil to separate us from Him and to effect our destruction. Certainly, it is the time-honored view of God and His ways, but that does not make it the truth.

Can this pattern of behavior be found in Christ's life on this earth? It cannot be found. Search as exhaustively as possible. Investigate every word and act. Listen to His inspired utterances. See Him dealing with those who rejected His last appeals of mercy. Behold Him receiving abuse and mockery in return for love and mercy and never once can any suggestion be found of His even entertaining an idea of doing as humans have understood God to do. Not even by a thought did He enter into any work whereby He would use the mighty power available to Him to destroy the impenitent.

Humans have long seen God as having two faces. One of these is the forgiving, merciful face, which He turns toward individuals during the period of pleading for their repentance, while the other is the face of thunder as He is about to destroy them. Christ exhibited no such duality. Throughout His life only one role was ever played by Him—that of a Savior and a Savior only. Not once do we find Him lifting His hand to destroy anyone. He lived only to bless, to heal, to restore, and to save.

> How God anointed Jesus of Nazareth with the Holy Spirit and with power, who went about doing good, and healing all who were oppressed of the devil, for God was with Him (Acts 10:38).

> Christ stood at the head of humanity in the garb of humanity. So full of sympathy and love was His attitude that the poorest were not afraid to come to Him. He was kind to all, easily approached by the most lowly. He went from house to house, healing the sick, feeding the hungry, comforting the mourners, soothing the afflicted, speaking peace to the distressed…

> He came as an expression of *the perfect love of God, not to crush, not to judge and condemn*, but to *heal* every weak, defective character, to *save* men and women from Satan's power (*Welfare Ministry*, pp. 53, 54, emphasis added).

> Christ, the outshining of the Father's glory, came to the world as its light. *He came to represent God to men*, and of Him it is written that He was anointed 'with the Holy Ghost and with power,' and '*went about doing good*'" (*Christ's Object Lessons*, pp. 416, 417, emphasis added).

Some may raise the objection that Christ cursed and destroyed the barren fig tree and that He drove the moneychangers out of the temple on two occasions by using a whip to do so. Both these events will be studied in the next chapter. The presentation of scriptural evidences will show that the wasting of the fig tree was not an act of destruction on Christ's part. It will be shown that He related Himself to it exactly as He does to every sinner, by permitting His protection and life to be withdrawn from it. Likewise, it will be shown that it was not by personal, physical force that He was successful in clearing the temple of the moneychangers.

These are the only events that could be offered as an exception to the rule of Christ's ministry. When it is successfully shown that they are not an exception, then it will be recognized that Christ did only good while upon this earth. He came as a Savior only.

> For God did not send His Son into the world to condemn the world, but that the
> world through Him might be saved (John 3:17).

At this point, some will be thinking that if they accept Christ's life as the full and complete picture of who God is, then how will they ever understand God's actions in the Old Testament?

Let all be earnestly encouraged to take hold of Christ's words by faith. Jesus said that He came to do the works of His Father. He told us that to see Him is to see the Father. Therefore, *faith* in those words assures us that the picture of the Father, which Christ came to give, is the truth in regard to the Father. *Faith* then comforts us with the happy thought that there is a better and more beautiful interpretation of the Old Testament Scriptures than we have had in the past. Thus we are filled with eager anticipation as we return to the study of events prior to the first advent of the Word of God, equipped with new eyes. To our joy and peace, it will be seen that God is a Savior and a Savior only.

Chapter Fifteen

Urged to Destroy

Study/Discussion Questions:

- When the disciples called for fire on the heads of the Samaritans, who refused hospitality to Jesus and themselves, were they in harmony with the God of their Scriptures, our "Old Testament"?

- If so, why did Jesus rebuke them?

- When Jesus said He did not come to destroy people's lives, was He only referring to the specific time of His earthly mission?

- Will He at a later time come to destroy human lives?

- Was the cursing of the fig tree an act of destruction?

- Was the driving of the moneychangers from the temple an act of physical force?

God provided in Christ's life and teachings the complete and final means whereby every theory about Him can be tested. By this means, every interpretation of God's behavior can be infallibly categorized as true or false. Thus, for instance, the idea that God destroys those who defy Him is classified as erroneous.

When upon this earth, Jesus showed no disposition to reach out in acts of punishment and destruction. This fact is shown not only through the consistency of His life and ministry, but even more pointedly in the instance wherein He was urged by His disciples to raise His hand and rain fire upon those who had turned against Him.

> Now it came to pass, when the time had come for Him to be received up, that He steadfastly set His face to go to Jerusalem, and sent messengers before His face. And as they went, they entered a village of the Samaritans, to prepare for Him. But they did not receive Him, because His face was set for the journey to Jerusalem. And when His disciples, James and John saw this, they said, "Lord, do You want us to command fire to come down from heaven and consume them, just as Elijah did?" But He turned and rebuked them, and said, "You do know not what manner of spirit you are of. For the Son of Man did not come to destroy men's lives, but to save them." And they went to another village (Luke 9:51-56).

The Samaritans could have offered no greater insult to the Son of God. The offer of hospitality to a stranger is regarded in the east as being an obligation on all, and to refuse this is to indicate rejection of the worst kind. If ever, from the human point of view, a sin needed to be punished to teach a lesson of warning to all others, then this was it.

James and John were familiar with Old Testament history, and they thought they understood quite well the way in which God had dealt with similar offenses in the past. Therefore, they believed that they were asking Christ to do just what they were sure God would have done under the circumstances. Their misunderstanding of His character led them to expect Christ to endorse their suggestion.

If the disciples had been correct in their assessment of God's character; if what they thought they understood Him as doing in the Old Testament had been what He really had done, then, because Christ did only as and what the Father did, He would have called down fire from heaven there and then. This would have been a splendid opportunity for Christ to show forth the character of God as the executioner of those who rebelled against Him. Christ would have taken full advantage of such a splendid opportunity to show this aspect of God's character.

But Christ would not even consider doing such a thing. Instead, He rebuked the disciples.

> They were surprised to see that Jesus was pained by their words, and still more surprised as His rebuke fell upon their ears, "Ye know not what manner of spirit ye are of. For the Son of man is not come to destroy men's lives, but to save them." And He went to another village. (*The Desire of Ages*, p. 487).

Christ did not use this opportunity to show forth the Father as an executioner because that is not God's character. But this does not mean that He missed the chance of revealing the Father. Far from it. This was a golden opportunity to do so, and He made the most of it.

He instructed His followers that the course they proposed sprang from a spirit foreign both to Him and His Father. Such a spirit and its fruit, not being found in the divine nature, found its source in Satan's heart. It was his way, not God's, to destroy those who failed to serve him.

Having denied identification with that spirit, Christ reiterated what He had come to do. Close attention should be paid to what He said with care taken not to read into it what He did not say. Explicitly, He declared, "For the Son of Man did *not* come to destroy men's lives, but *to save them*."

He did not say, "The Son of Man came to save all who will be saved and then to destroy the remainder."

But this is what the Savior would have had to say if the accepted view of God's ways based on the Old Testament is correct. Furthermore, He would have been obliged to demonstrate the veracity of His words by destroying every Samaritan whose rejection of Him was final. But He neither spoke such words nor performed such actions.

Instead, with great plainness, He said, "The Son of Man did not come to destroy men's lives."

When Christ said that He did not come to destroy people's lives, we can be assured of the absolute reliability of those words. Therefore, we can know that He did not destroy when He came. Further, inasmuch as He did only what the Father did, then we can know that the Father does not come to destroy us. Christ came only to save. Likewise, the Father comes to us as a Savior and a Savior only.

> It is no part of Christ's mission to compel men to receive Him. It is Satan, and men actuated by his spirit, that seek to compel the conscience. Under a pretense of zeal for righteousness, men who are confederate with evil angels bring suffering upon their fellow men, in order to convert them to their ideas of religion; but Christ is ever showing mercy, ever seeking to win by the revealing of His love. He can admit no rival in the soul, nor accept of partial service; but He desires only voluntary service, the willing surrender of the heart under the constraint of love. *There can be no more conclusive evidence that we possess the spirit of Satan* than the disposition to hurt and destroy those who do not appreciate our work, or who act contrary to our ideas (*The Desire of Ages*, p. 487, emphasis added).

The Samaritans did not appreciate Christ's work, and they certainly acted contrary to His ideas. Had He shown the least disposition to hurt or destroy them, He would have given the strongest evidence that He possessed the spirit of Satan. It was because He did not possess that spirit that He did not show any such disposition.

If we project this principle back to the Father's behavior, the same conclusions must be maintained. Let the popular concept of God's character be tested.

It is true that the inhabitants of Sodom and Gomorrah did not appreciate the works of God, and they certainly acted contrary to His ideas. Consequently, popular theology declares that God destroyed them by raining fire down upon them. In the light of the statement quoted above, if this is true, then God provided all with convincing evidence that He was actuated with the spirit of the devil.

There is no other conclusion that can be drawn but this.

The stand made by Christ against His apostles in the matter of the Samaritans is a valuable revelation of His utter refusal to be involved in any kind of punitive work of destruction. He made it quite clear that such had no part with Him and, therefore, no part with His Father in heaven. The life of Christ utterly denies the idea that God destroys anyone for any reason.

There are, of course, those two instances mentioned in the previous chapter that, on the surface, would seem to provide occasions when Christ did stretch forth His hands to use force and to destroy. They are the cursing of the fig tree and the expelling of the desecrators from the temple precincts.

Let the case of the wasted fig tree be considered first.

This occurred very late in Christ's ministry. A few days before the last Passover, He had ridden triumphantly into Jerusalem. This was an act of final appeal to the Jewish leaders, their rejection of which placed them beyond any further hope of deliverance. He spent the night in Bethany and the next morning returned to the temple.

> On the way He passed a fig orchard. He was hungry, "and seeing a fig tree afar off having leaves, He came, if haply He might find anything thereon: and when He came to it, He found nothing but leaves; for the time of figs was not yet."
>
> It was not the season for ripe figs, except in certain localities; and on the highlands about Jerusalem it might truly be said, "The time of figs was not yet." But in the orchard to which Jesus came, one tree appeared to be in advance of all the others. It was already covered with leaves. It is the nature of the fig tree that before the leaves open, the growing fruit appears. Therefore this tree in full leaf gave promise of well-developed fruit. But its appearance was deceptive. Upon searching its branches, from the lowest bough to the topmost twig, Jesus found "nothing but leaves." It was a mass of pretentious foliage, nothing more.
>
> Christ uttered against it a withering curse. "No man eat fruit of thee hereafter forever," He said. The next morning, as the Saviour and His disciples were again on their way to the city, the blasted branches and drooping leaves attracted their attention. "Master," said Peter, "behold, the fig tree which Thou cursedst is withered away" (*The Desire of Ages*, pp. 581, 582).

> Jesus looked upon the pretentious, fruitless fig tree, and with mournful reluctance pronounced the words of doom. And under the curse of an offended God, the fig tree withered away. God help His people to make an application of this lesson while there is still time (*The Review and Herald*, February 25, 1902).

The strong words in these statements are "uttered against it a withering curse," and "under the curse of an offended God."

Now, pause and ponder what kind of picture these words call before your mind. Practically anyone will find that this is what they see. The unabated spirit of rejection and apostasy on the part of the children of Israel had brought God to the point where He became offended, indignant, wrathful, infuriated, and judgmental. So He cursed the fig tree whose pretentious foliage was a symbol of the Jews' hypocrisy. This act of cursing is seen as a direct sending forth of a stream of death from God to the tree. In other words, God thus *appears* as one who specifically decides what the fate of the tree will be and then administers judgment on the tree.

The Scriptures emphasize that God's ways are different from the ways of men. So we need to take a deeper look at what Christ really did there at the fig tree, for we cannot be satisfied with the popular view.

The disciples were surprised as we see in *The Desire of Ages*:

> Christ's act in cursing the fig tree had astonished the disciples. It seemed to them unlike His ways and works. Often they had heard Him declare that He came not

to condemn the world, but that the world through Him might be saved. They remembered His words, "The Son of man is not come to destroy men's lives, but to save them." Luke 9:56. His wonderful works had been done to restore, never to destroy. The disciples had known Him only as the Restorer, the Healer. This act stood alone. What was its purpose? they questioned (p. 582).

The truth of what Christ did is spelled out in the following statement. God "delights in mercy" (Mic. 7:18). "'As I live,' says the Lord GOD, 'I have no pleasure in the death of the wicked'" (Ezek. 33:11). To Him the work of destruction and denunciation of judgment is an "unusual act" ("strange work" [KJV]) (Isa. 28:21). But it is in mercy and love that He lifts the veil from the future and reveals to men the results of a course of sin.

> *The cursing of the fig tree was an acted parable.* That barren tree, flaunting its pretentious foliage in the very face of Christ, *was a symbol of the Jewish nation.* The Saviour desired to make plain to His disciples the cause and the certainty of Israel's doom. For this purpose He invested the tree with moral qualities, and made it the expositor of divine truth. The Jews stood forth distinct from all other nations, professing allegiance to God. They had been specially favored by Him, and they laid claim to righteousness above every other people. But they were corrupted by the love of the world and the greed of gain. They boasted of their knowledge, but they were ignorant of the requirements of God, and were full of hypocrisy. Like the barren tree, they spread their pretentious branches aloft, luxuriant in appearance, and beautiful to the eye, but they yielded "nothing but leaves." The Jewish religion, with its magnificent temple, its sacred altars, its mitered priests and impressive ceremonies, was indeed fair in outward appearance, but humility, love, and benevolence were lacking.…
>
> Jesus had come to the fig tree hungry, to find food. So He had come to Israel, hungering to find in them the fruits of righteousness.… But love to God and man was eclipsed by pride and self-sufficiency. They brought ruin upon themselves by refusing to minister to others. The treasures of truth which God had committed to them, they did not give to the world. *In the barren tree they might read both their sin and its punishment.* Withered beneath the Saviour's curse, standing forth sere and blasted, dried up by the roots, the fig tree *showed what the Jewish people would be when the grace of God was removed from them.* Refusing to impart blessing, they would no longer receive it. "O Israel," the Lord says, *"thou hast destroyed thyself"* Hosea 13:9 (*The Desire of Ages*, pp. 582, 583, emphasis added).

Thus Christ's act was a prophecy. He was declaring in advance just what was going to happen to the Jewish nation. In order for the prophecy to be accurate, Christ had to do to the fig tree exactly what He would later do to Jerusalem. Prophecy is valueless if it is not accurate.

It is a principle that a prophecy is never fully understood until it has been fulfilled. Jesus indicated this in these words,

> And now I have told you before it comes, that when it does come to pass, you may believe (John 14:29).

Knowing this, we find that there is an obvious advantage in that we have both the prophecy and the fulfillment of the parable of the cursed fig tree. The prophecy was made by Christ just prior to His crucifixion, and the fulfillment took place when Jerusalem fell in AD 70.

What took place in the fulfillment is very clear. As already noted from *The Great Controversy* (pp. 35, 36), God did not personally decree the nature of the punishment that should and did befall the Israelites. Instead, He sorrowfully and reluctantly submitted to their insistent demands that He leave them to their own way, thus exposing them to whatever potential destruction was nearest to them. It proved in this case to be the enraged Romans who, freed of any restriction imposed by God's presence, were able to wreak their vengeance upon the unsheltered Jews.

In order, then, for Christ to reveal in the prophecy what God would do in its fulfillment, He had to do the same in the prophecy. Therefore, Christ simply withdrew His presence from the tree, leaving it exposed to whatever plague, blight, or other destructive force was waiting to consume it.

Some may say that it must have been very convenient for a destructive power to have been overshadowing that particular tree so that it would serve Christ's purpose when He withdrew His protective power from it. But only those who do not appreciate the fact that a thousand unseen dangers are lurking over us and all of nature every moment of the day would adopt such a view. It would not matter from what point or quarter the Lord was to withdraw His protection. Destruction would come flooding in, in some form or the other. If we were more aware of this, we would maintain a spirit of gratitude and dependence toward God far in excess of that which we now display.

In this particular case the attack came at the roots of the tree, for the Scriptures expressly say, "Now in the morning, as they passed by, they saw the fig tree dried up from the roots" (Mark 11:20).

Note also that it was not until the next day that the effects of the withdrawing of the Creator's sustaining and protecting presence were apparent, whereas we would expect that if the Lord struck the tree with His own direct power, as so many suppose He did, then the tree would have instantly been blasted as if struck with lightning. But it was not so.

Thus the evidence is clear for those who will dig a little deeper that Christ did not strike the tree any more than He struck the Jews in the fall of Jerusalem when the prophecy was fulfilled. Thus is removed any possible reference to this event as an example of Christ using force or engaging in an act of destruction.

Let us now examine the driving out of the moneychangers and traffickers in the courtyard of the temple. Once again, the casual and superficial view of this incident is that Jesus drove these men out by force, but a careful study reveals another picture altogether.

Here is the Scripture record of it:

> Now the Passover of the Jews was at hand, and Jesus went up to Jerusalem. And He found in the temple those who sold oxen and sheep and doves, and the money changers doing business. When He had made a whip of cords, He drove them all out of the temple, with the sheep and the oxen, and poured out the changers' money and overturned the tables. And He said to those who sold doves, "Take these things away! Do not make My Father's house a house of merchandise!" Then His disciples remembered that it was written, "Zeal for Your house has eaten Me up" (John 2:13-17).

The natural human tendency is to interpret the words, "He drove them out," in the same way as they would be understood if used to describe human behavior. No greater mistake could be made, for the ways of God as revealed in Christ's life are so different from our ways. Christ drove them out; it is true. But He did not do so as a human would do it by dependence on physical power or force. Let there be the continual reminder that "compelling power is found *only* under Satan's government. The Lord's principles are not of this order" (*The Desire of Ages*, p. 759, emphasis added).

Therefore, compelling power or the use of physical force to achieve obedience is never found under God's government. Inasmuch, then, as Christ was fully under God's government, even being the perfect expression of that government, no physical force was ever used by Him to achieve obedience. So Christ did not drive those men out as others would have driven them out. He did not do it by physical force at all.

A little thought would show the infeasibility of His attempting to do it by physical force. He was only one man pitted against a considerable number of wily, hardened opponents. They were men whose souls were calloused with the sinful traffic of extortion. They feared no man on earth and would think nothing of resorting to physical violence to preserve their treasured gains.

So how did He do it? Christ stood before them that day in the role of the eternal and righteous Judge. Those men knew that He was reading the closely guarded secrets of their lives. They were conscious that His eyes were seeing beneath the pretentious garments of righteousness with which they had sought to cover the sickness of their sin-diseased souls.

The sinner cannot stand such examination. One compelling desire fills him—fleeing in abject terror from the presence of the Righteous One.

The truth of this is laid out in these words:

> And why did the priests flee from the temple? Why did they not stand their ground? He who commanded them to go was a carpenter's son, a poor Galilean, without earthly rank or power. Why did they not resist Him? Why did they leave the gain so ill acquired, and flee at the command of One whose outward appearance was so humble?

Christ spoke with the authority of a king, and in His appearance, and in the tones of His voice, there was that which they had no power to resist. At the word of command they realized, as they had never realized before, their true position as hypocrites and robbers. When divinity flashed through humanity, not only did they see indignation on Christ's countenance; they realized the import of His words. They felt as if before the throne of the eternal Judge, with their sentence passed on them for time and for eternity (*The Desire of Ages*, p. 162).

It was the awful power of burning condemnation that drove those men from the presence of Christ. They could not endure it. No human being ever can. God does not need to raise a single finger of physical power to drive them away. When the time comes that He must stand before them in that role, they will do nothing else but flee.

Thus we need have no misgivings of the perfection of the revelation of God in Christ. Throughout His life Christ made no concessions whatsoever to the principles of Satan's character. Flawlessly He showed that "God does not stand toward the sinner as an executioner of the sentence against transgression; but He leaves the rejecters of His mercy to themselves, to reap that which they have sown" (*The Great Controversy*, p. 36). He came to reveal God as a Savior and a Savior only, and He did it to perfection. There is not a single instance in Christ's life in which any other character but this is shown. Christ's life exposes the lie that God destroys the impenitent. He does not do this but rather leaves them to their own desires.

If every person in the world could see God in Christ with the understanding that Christ gave a full and undimmed revelation of the Father; if they could know that "*all* that man needs to know or can know of God *has been revealed in the life and character of His Son*" (*Testimonies for the Church*, vol. 8, p. 286, emphasis added), they would reject every concept that sees God as One who rises up and destroys those who are disobedient.

May the Lord open your eyes to see God as He is to be seen in the face of Jesus Christ, "the Word of God—God's thought made audible" (*The Desire of Ages*, p. 19).

Chapter Sixteen

Magnifying the Law

Study/Discussion Questions:

- What does it mean when we say that the law is holy and perfect as God is holy and perfect?
- Does God expect us to keep the law differently than He keeps it?
- What is Satan's educational system teaching about the law, through storytelling in novels and movies?
- Is it ever right that the law should be broken in order to uphold it?

There is a direct and inseparable connection between Christ's role as the Revelator of the Father's character and as the Magnifier of God's law. Scriptures have already been quoted which state that Christ came to show humanity the Eternal One as He really is. Now is presented this text in regard to the work of Christ and the law.

> The LORD is well pleased for His righteousness' sake; He will exalt the law and make it honorable (Isa. 42:21).

It would be a serious mistake to think of this as being a separate and different work from that of the unfolding of God's character.

> His law is a transcript of His own character, and it is the standard of all character (*Christ's Object Lessons*, p. 315).

Thus is made plain the truth that the character of God is directly and accurately expressed in His law. To see one is to see the other. This means that the characters of God, Christ, and the law are identical. Between them there is no difference even though it is difficult to grasp this. There is the inclination to think of God as a Being of living power with infinite possibilities of exercising His will. We tend to see the law as being a much lesser thing, merely the spoken will of the Supreme Ruler and certainly not something which is the expression of Himself.

> The law of God is as sacred as God Himself. It is a revelation of His will, a transcript of His character, the expression of divine love and wisdom (*Patriarchs and Prophets*, p. 52).

The broken law of God demanded the life of the sinner. In all the universe there was but one who could, in behalf of man, satisfy its claims. Since the divine law is as sacred as God Himself, only one equal with God could make atonement for its transgression. None but Christ could redeem fallen man from the curse of the law and bring him again into harmony with Heaven (*Ibid.*, p. 63).

> The law of God is as holy as He is holy, as perfect as He is perfect. It presents to men the righteousness of God (*Thoughts from the Mount of Blessing*, p. 54).

Therefore, to place God on a level of infinite greatness while relegating the law to a lesser plane is to hold a position of serious error. They must be thought of as being as holy, as great, as infinite, and as sacred as one another.

Likewise, the understanding that Jesus came to reveal the Father is to comprehend that Christ came to magnify the law. These were not two separate tasks to be accomplished in turn or even in concert. They were one and the same work. The revealing of God's character was the magnification of the law.

Great stress has been placed upon the truth that the last conflict will be over the law of God. This has not been overdone. Despite all the emphasis, there has not yet been conveyed the real significance of the place of the law in that final struggle. Generally, it is thought that the issue will simply be proving that the seventh day is the Sabbath, with the corresponding exposure of Sunday as being the day of the man of sin. But the issues will go vastly deeper than this. It is true that Sabbath versus Sunday will be the focal point of the issue, but the whole of the law will be contested, not just one point of it.

The deepest spiritual implications and ramifications of the law will be explored, presented, and controverted. Because the law is the very expression of the righteousness or character of God, the issue will involve the question of how God keeps that law. Does He kill, destroy, punish, annihilate, and execute? The time will come for the final settlement of the great questions of the law and the character of God to be made before the second advent.

But why should there be a controversy over the law of God? Surely the declarations of Scripture are clear enough! Surely there is need for nothing more than to prove that the Ten Commandments mean just what they say!

Surprising as it may seem, the simple commandments, "Thou shalt not steal, bear false witness, or kill," have one meaning in the Bible and another in the philosophy of humanity. This erroneous concept has its origin in Satan who has systematically inculcated these ideas into human minds for the express purpose of undermining faith in the law and of thereby fostering disobedience to it.

It was to correct this distorted understanding of God's law that Christ came to magnify the law and to make it honorable.

In the Old Testament is found the direct word of God, which says, "Thou shalt not kill, steal, or bear false witness." Of those words there are two separate and opposed magnifications. There is the one provided by Satan and generally accepted by humanity. It is a magnification as misshapen as that produced by a lens warped out of normal symmetry. No one can possibly understand the real truth of the law and character of God through this medium.

Then there is another magnification as provided by Jesus Christ. This magnification is so powerful that every detail is brought to view, leaving no remaining questions. It brings us to the position where "*all* that man *needs* to know or *can* know of God *has been revealed* in the life and character of His Son" (*Testimonies for the Church*, vol. 8, p. 286, emphasis added). The magnification has been provided. Christ is the microscope.

Let a comparative consideration be given to the magnification of the law as it exists on one hand in the minds and practices of human beings and on the other in the life of Christ, the Word of God.

Individuals actually inject another word into the Scriptures. They say that the law really means, "Thou shalt not lie, steal, or kill—unlawfully." Or they express it in these words, "Thou shalt commit no murder," a distinction in meaning being made between the words kill and murder. *Webster's Third New International Dictionary* defines "murder" in this way: "To kill (a human being) unlawfully and with premeditated malice or willfully, deliberately, and unlawfully."

In human minds there is a distinction between lawful and unlawful killing. There are three situations at least in which people regard it as being lawful to kill another human being.

At any time if the slayer can prove that he or she was forced to kill his or her attacker in order to save his or her own life, the slayer will be judged a killer within the bounds of the law and will be set free.

The second situation in which killing is judged to be lawful is when a person has been tried and found guilty of taking human life. The state then claims every right to take that person's life in return. This, they say, is lawful killing.

The third is when an alien army invades the borders. People regard it as being perfectly lawful, necessary, and expedient to slaughter as many of the enemy as necessary to prevent the invasion from being successful.

Human beings of every nation on earth throughout human history accept these as working principles. To most people's minds, not only are these guidelines right but they are the only solution to the problems involved in these situations. They firmly believe they can do it this way and still be keepers of the law. In fact, high honors are heaped upon military personnel in war who can destroy the most.

To ensure that people never weaken in these convictions, the whole educational system, built up under Satan's direction, is geared to systematically, continually, and persistently reiterate these ideas. Never in history has Satan been better equipped to do so than in this age. Now he has at his command not just the verbal storyteller, the limit of his facilities in the beginning, but the stupendous volume of cheap novels, radio, movie theaters, and now most present and insistent of all teachers, the television screen.

As people sit before these media, they think they are being harmlessly entertained, but in actual truth they are being thoroughly educated in Satan's doctrines. With every appreciative viewing of the usual television story, the watcher is more firmly entrenched in erroneous notions of God's character.

This is made apparent as soon as a candid analysis of the message of the movie is conducted. Here is the typical plot. It is found with minor variations in western, detective, police, military, espionage, and other tales. The message is always that the law must be broken in order to uphold it.

The film introduces the watcher to a segment of society. Maybe it is a ranch family or a small town in the West or a town or farmhouse in the case of a war story.

Care is taken to show this capsule of humanity as a clean, respectable, law-abiding group of people. There is love, trust, and cooperation between them. A little friction may intrude at times, but that is purely incidental and designed to show that they are not super-humans but everyday folk just like the viewers. The viewing audience has no difficulty in identifying with the people on the screen. A sense of fellowship and brotherhood is established.

Then the lawbreaker is introduced. In westerns he appears as a dark man clad in black clothes, riding a black horse, and armed with black guns. With him is a gang of men who look like their leader. They are hard-faced, tough, callous, and ruthless, with a total disregard for human life. Any who stand in their way, great or small, are simply gunned down. They achieve their ends by lying, stealing, and killing.

As they direct their attacks against the happy segment of society previously introduced, the audience is apprehensive and indignant, even more so as the victims are powerless to protect themselves from the desperadoes. Every instinct and desire of the audience clamors for the punishment of the outlaws.

Up until this point the universal problem of humanity has been presented with truthful accuracy. The people of this world, generally speaking, are, on the surface, law-abiding people. They are good neighbors; they help each other and live clean lives. They are pictured by the ranch or village as the case may be in our film illustration.

Just as those people are threatened by a desperado and his gang, so today, the world lies under the threat of Satan and his followers. Humanity is entirely unable to rescue itself from the power of the devil and his angels.

Thus Satan has presented the problem of the human family in a truly accurate form. As a problem requires a solution, one is offered in every film. In the western it is the arrival of a lone champion on a beautiful white horse. In contrast to the robber, he is dressed in white clothes, has a handsome, open face, carries white guns, and is stirred to the depths as he realizes the plight of the oppressed. Alone and unassisted, at any sacrifice even to life itself, he pledges to set them free and to relieve the earth forever from the scourge of the terrorist. For his services he seeks neither fame nor reward. He does it as a mission, his only motivation being that of dedicated service.

So far in the story there is the continued portrayal of the truth, for just as the solution to the film is found in the advent of a champion of self-sacrificing spirit and character, so

Jesus Christ came in that way to redeem humankind. Like the hero in the story, His soul was stirred with indignation as He beheld the predicament of humanity, and He resolved that He would save them, no matter what the cost. He would not do it for price nor reward but only from the motivation of love and mercy.

The great white hero with his pearl-handled guns rides forth on his white charger to deal with the liars, thieves, and murderers. But in order to outwit the liars, he lies; to catch the thieves, he steals, for if he suddenly needs a horse, saddle, or rifle, he will simply help himself to another person's; and to end the murderous reign of the killers, he kills.

When he is finished, the lawbreaking is ended. The law has been upheld. But the message of the film has been that in order to achieve this, the law had to be broken. Only by lying, stealing, and killing could lying, stealing, and killing be brought to an end. The law had to be broken in order to ensure that it was kept. This is Satan's message. He does not say that the law is wholly bad and should be entirely done away with. He admits that under certain circumstances it is good and should be obeyed. But he continues that the law is not perfect for there are situations where it must be disobeyed in order to solve the problems arising.

Both evil people and their master, the devil, want a law. They want it composed so that it protects them from other people but not other people from them. It is impossible to have such a law for every person. But it is possible for a privileged class to have it at the expense of the masses.

Such, then, is the message contained in Satan's educational program. In his classrooms there is no dissent. When the hero lies, steals, and murders, the viewers applaud. They honor him for what he has done and consider him very smart to use such weapons in his campaign.

To them the villain was unlawfully lying, stealing and killing, whereas the hero was doing it lawfully. Therefore, the villain was a criminal, but the hero was not.

Why do people take such an attitude toward this problem? There is a very real psychological reason for it. As noted above, every person consciously or subconsciously longs to be in the position where they are protected by law but do not have to keep it themselves.

Such is Satan's and, in turn, humanity's magnification of the law that states "Thou shalt not kill, lie, or steal." We know that it is of the devil because such a philosophy finds no place in the life and teachings of Jesus Christ.

Having examined the magnification of the law as set forth by the devil, the time has come to consider its enlargement as presented by Jesus Christ. Without doubt or question, we know that it will be the truth, for Christ is the very fountain of truth.

Jesus showed that there is no such thing as lawful and unlawful lying, stealing, and killing. He lived His whole life upon this earth devoted to ending all such things. Yet, in order to accomplish that, He never once lied, stole, or killed.

Under every circumstance, every possible pressure, threat, or danger, Jesus told only the truth, respected the property of all, and took the lives of none.

In doing so He demonstrated forever how we are to keep that law and how, in turn, the Father and He keep that law. He showed that when God said in a few simple words, "Thou shalt not lie, steal, or kill," He did not add provisos and exceptions. No matter what the circumstances, pressures, dangers, threats, needs, or any other seeming justification for breaking those commands might be, the words were still "Thou shalt not..." No distinction whatever exists in God's mind between lawful and unlawful killing. With God there is only unlawful killing.

God has spoken in His Word, saying, "The law of the LORD is perfect" (Ps. 19:7). It could, of course, be none other than this, seeing that it is the transcript of the character of the Eternal. He is perfection in the absolute sense. Therefore, His law is likewise perfect.

Such perfection does not mean that it is the perfect answer for certain situations but needs to be modified or even abrogated to suit other situations. On the contrary, it means that no matter what circumstance, situation, or pressure may arise the law is still the one and only code for perfect behavior.

When any person claims that it is lawful to kill when the commandments so distinctly say, "Thou shalt not kill," is in that moment saying that the law, and the God of that law, is imperfect, less than infinite, and therefore less than God. It is also to deny the whole witness of Christ's ministry. It is to declare the truth of God a lie.

The point which the devil is bent on making is that the law must be broken in order for it to be maintained. The life and teachings of Christ deny this. So does the message of God in the Old Testament.

There is the story of two people who adopted the policy of breaking the law in order to ensure that it be kept. It is the story of Jacob and his mother in their quest for the promised birthright. Before the birth of the two children, God, foreseeing with infinite accuracy the character of each, declared that Jacob should have the birthright instead of the elder son, Esau.

> And the Lord said to her: "Two nations are in your womb, Two peoples shall be separated from your body; One people shall be stronger than the other, And the older shall serve the younger" (Gen. 25:23).

Rebekah clearly and correctly understood that the last sentence in this verse was a promise to Jacob that the birthright should be his, not Esau's. Rebekah remembered the words of the angel, and she read with clearer insight than did her husband the character of their sons. She was convinced that the heritage of divine promise was intended for Jacob. She repeated to Isaac the angel's words, but his affections were centered upon his elder son, and he was unshaken in his purpose.

> Jacob had learned from his mother of the divine intimation that the birthright should fall to him, and he was filled with an unspeakable desire for the privileges which it would confer (*Patriarchs and Prophets*, p. 178).

God's selection of Jacob to inherit the birthright was not an arbitrary one. The directions given by God were done so on the foreknowledge that Esau would disqualify himself from the right to its possession. Without question, Isaac should have accepted the decree made on this basis, especially when Esau's behavior confirmed the rightness of God's decision. The law stipulated that should a young man marry among the heathen then he automatically forfeited all right to the birthright. This Esau had done polygamously, to make matters worse. "When Esau was forty years old, he took to wife Judith the daughter of Beeri the Hittite, and Basemath the daughter of Elon the Hittite. And they were a grief of mind to Isaac and Rebekah" (Gen. 26:34, 35).

Upon Esau's doing this, Isaac, in strict obedience to the law, ought to have relinquished his paternal preferences for his elder son and prepared to confer the birthright blessing on Jacob. But he allowed his affections to overrule his conscience so that he chose his own way in preference to the clear will of God.

Rebekah exerted all the influence she could to dissuade him from his fixed determination to confer the birthright blessing on Esau. She pointed out the disinterest in, and disregard, for the spiritual responsibilities involved in the birthright, which marked Esau's life. She reminded him of the prophecy made before the boys were born and of Esau's marriage to the heathen. She pointed to the contrasting spirit, attitude, and consecrated life of Jacob, but all her reasoning and pleadings were to no avail.

The only thing she did achieve was a deferment of the day when the blessing was to be bestowed. But as the infirmities of age advanced on Isaac, he realized that if he did not pronounce the blessing soon it would be too late. He determined on a secret session rather than the joyous family affair that was the usual way. He called Esau and instructed him to take his weapons and catch his favorite venison. They would have a little feast together after which the son would receive the prized blessing. It is to be noted that Esau's interest lay in the material blessing, for the spiritual had no attraction for him. Rebekah was listening in as the supposedly secret instructions were being given, and with a chill in her heart, she realized the implications of what her husband was about to do.

> Rebekah divined his purpose. She was confident that it was contrary to what God had revealed as His will. Isaac was in danger of incurring the divine displeasure and of debarring his younger son from the position to which God had called him. She had in vain tried the effect of reasoning with Isaac, and she determined to resort to stratagem (*Patriarchs and Prophets*, p. 180).

With great clarity she saw that Isaac was about to act in direct opposition to the stipulations of the law, thereby incurring Divine displeasure. She saw that by so doing Jacob would be deprived of the blessing that was rightfully his. Therefore, she reasoned, she must prevent Isaac from breaking the law, both for his own good and for the good of Jacob.

She had worked hard for years to forestall such an action by appealing to Isaac. That had proved unsuccessful, so she reasoned that she now had to use other means.

To what method did she turn?

In order to save Isaac from being a lawbreaker, she became a lawbreaker herself and induced Jacob to become one with her. They turned from God's way to their way. They acted out the same principles, or lack of them, as portrayed by the heroes of the silver screen, the novel, or any other form of fiction. It was an evil sowing that brought them a bitter reaping even though they achieved their objective to a point. Jacob did obtain the spiritual blessing, but the material wealth and power fell into Esau's hands just the same.

> Jacob and Rebekah succeeded in their purpose, but they gained only trouble and sorrow by their deception. God had declared that Jacob should receive the birthright, *and His word would have been fulfilled in His own time had they waited in faith for Him to work for them.* But like many who now profess to be children of God, they were unwilling to leave the matter in His hands. Rebekah bitterly repented the wrong counsel she had given her son; it was the means of separating him from her, and she never saw his face again. From the hour when he received the birthright, Jacob was weighed down with self-condemnation. He had sinned against his father, his brother, his own soul, and against God. In one short hour he had made work for a lifelong repentance. This scene was vivid before him in afteryears, when the wicked course of his own sons oppressed his soul (*Ibid.*, emphasis added).

Rebekah and Jacob broke the law in order to keep it from being broken. They were wholly wrong in so doing, as is proved by the sad punishment they had to bear for their mistake. Let not their mistake and its consequent troubles be of no value to those of us facing the final confrontation over what the law really means. Let it be that we shall see with great clarity that the law cannot be upheld by its being broken.

The words, "Thou shalt not bear false witness, steal, or kill," set forth the pattern of behavior no matter what the circumstances, pressures, threats, demands, necessities, advantages, or whatever else it may be. In God's kingdom and under His principles, the end can never, never, never justify the means. Therefore, in every situation, the law, and not expedience, is to be consulted and obeyed. When God has a people who will stand by these principles and be guided in this way, He will have a people whom He can trust to finish the work, and it will then be finished.

Chapter Seventeen

Go the Second Mile

Study/Discussion Questions:

- In the Old Testament, God apparently instructed the people to function under a compensatory, retributive, retaliatory legal system. It was called "eye for eye," but God came down in Jesus saying, "Not so, here is what God is like and what He wants you to be like; turn the other cheek and love your enemies." How do we deal with this dichotomy?

- Is there a "sunset clause" on God's grace and mercy and forgiveness? When is it reached?

- If we hold that God's way is not retributive, punitive, and "eye for eye," that His mercy and love endures forever, do we say that Satan and the wicked get to go on forever in their ways, never coming to full justice?

Jesus' first great sermon was a clear statement of what the law really meant, alerting the people to know that that which "was said to them of old," was not the version He had come to bring them.

But the people who gathered to hear that wonderful Sermon on the Mount recorded in Matthew 5-7, came with erroneous concepts of the law and the kingdom of God. They had been raised up to know humanity's ways so that their expectation of the Messiah's kingdom was quite different from what it would be in fact.

Before He began to explain the law as He had given it and would live it, He warned that, even though it might appear so to them, He had not come to do away with the law but to establish it. He said to them:

> Do not think that I came to destroy the Law or the Prophets. I did not come to destroy but to fulfill. For assuredly, I say to you, till heaven and earth pass away, one jot or one tittle will by no means pass from the law till all is fulfilled. Whoever therefore breaks one of the least of these commandments, and teaches men so, shall be called least in the kingdom of heaven; but whoever does and teaches them, he shall be called great in the kingdom of heaven. For I say to you, that unless your righteousness exceeds the righteousness of the scribes and Pharisees, you will by no means enter the kingdom of heaven (Matt. 5:17-20).

The Pharisees' lives were as fine an example as can be found of living the law according to human interpretation of how it should be kept. It was to deliver people from their concept of keeping the law and replace it with the true one, that Christ came to this earth.

As He progressed through His sermon, repeatedly He swept aside the law as they *understood* it to read and replaced it with the law as God *intended* that it should be read and obeyed. The hearers' evaluation of Christ's presentation and position would depend then on their having a spiritual perception of what He was saying.

Great profit would be gained by studying every statement made by Christ in this sermon, but time and space will not be taken to do this here. A selection will be made of that passage that reveals, if not better than any of the others, the principles of the law as Christ espoused them.

Jesus said, "You have heard that it was said, 'An eye for an eye and a tooth for a tooth.' But I tell you …" (Matt. 5:38, 39).

So Christ segregated the teaching of the past from His own. The old, He classified as *their* way, against which He set forth that which was *His* way. He made no attempt to compromise with the old teaching or to apologize for what He offered. It was the truth and, as such, it had to be accepted.

To many, Christ adopted a course here that laid Him open to the charge of denying the law as God in the Old Testament had taught it. It was not the writings or teachings of the heathen that Christ was disavowing here but, to all appearances, the word of God through Moses.

"And God spoke all these words, saying …" (Exod. 20:1). Then follow the Ten Commandments, after which the people are terrified and plead with Moses to speak with them instead of God. "Then the LORD said to Moses, 'Thus you shall say to the children of Israel'…" (verse 22).

Many directions follow until these verses are reached: "But if any harm follows, then you shall give life for life, eye for eye, tooth for tooth, hand for hand, foot for foot, burn for burn, wound for wound, stripe for stripe" (Exod. 21:23-25).

God spoke these words to Moses with the direction that they be told to, and obeyed by, the people. The people did obey them, confident that in so doing they were following the Lord's instructions. Then Jesus came and denied that that was His way, swept all that aside, and gave the people a new code of behavior.

The appearances certainly point to Christ as being at variance with His Father on what the law was and how it should be kept. Small wonder then that the Pharisees, who subscribed so vigorously to the old Mosaic law, should regard Christ as being the worst kind of lawbreaker.

A solution to this problem offered in our day is to teach dispensationalism. Such a belief would see one law for the people before the advent of Christ, and another and more beautiful law for the people thereafter.

Such a resolution of the problem must be rejected because the perfect law is as unchangeable as the God who gave it. If the Lord gave one law for the people in a given age and situation and subsequently changed this for later generations, then He is no better than changeable men and women who are forever modifying the laws to suit changing circumstances. Satan would then have the argument he needed to win the controversy. He would point to the changing of the law as clear proof that it was imperfect and needed to be changed.

There is yet another explanation that reveals the character of God in wonderful beauty, shows that Christ was not at variance with the Father, and establishes the truth that God has never changed His law in the slightest. It, together with its Author, is the "same yesterday, today, and forever" (Heb. 13:8).

This explanation will be fully developed when we examine the various incidents of the Old Testament period. It will be seen that God has only one way for Himself and His people. But there comes a time when the people reject His way and turn to their own, yet still desire God to be with them. In great mercy, He provides directives effecting, if obeyed, the best conditions possible under humanity's system. It will be shown when this point is reached that God acted out the role of a Savior exclusively, and that Christ's sole objective was to bring them back from their own way to God's. When this characteristic of behavior on God's part is seen, the last problems in understanding His character will disappear.

Having relegated the teaching, an eye for an eye and a tooth for a tooth, to the errors of humankind's ways, Christ then set forth His amplification of the law.

> But I tell you not to resist an evil person. But whoever slaps you on your right cheek, turn the other to him also. If anyone wants to sue you and take away your tunic, let him have your cloak also. And whoever compels you to go one mile, go with him two. Give to him who asks you, and from him who wants to borrow from you do not turn away (Matt. 5:39-42).

These are not the patterns of behavior advertised as ideal through the entertainment media. Nothing could be more contrary. To the person of the world, there is no sense in Christ's words. If the movie industry were to prepare films depicting these principles, no one would be interested in viewing them. They would be a financial failure.

The average person rejects the principles in Christ's words because they see in that way the whole world taking advantage of them to the point where they would be divested of everything they had. To them, there is a no more frightening prospect. Therefore, most people have no disposition to surrender the security provided by their defending and protecting their rights and possessions. They prefer to work at being more powerful than their enemy so that they can hit back harder than they can be hit. People find safety in this doctrine of deterrence.

Christ continued His instruction in these words:

> You have heard that it was said, "You shall love your neighbor and hate your enemy." But I say to you, love your enemies, bless those who curse you, do good to those who hate you, and pray for those who spitefully use you and persecute

you, that you may be sons of your Father in heaven; for He makes His sun rise on the evil and on the good, and sends rain on the just and on the unjust. For if you love those who love you, what reward have you? Do not even the tax collectors do the same? And if you greet your brethren only, what do you do more than others? Do not even the tax collectors do so? Therefore you shall be perfect, just as your Father in heaven is perfect" (Matt. 5:43-48).

When Jesus said, "Love your enemies," He placed no time limitation upon this stipulation. He did not say to love them as long as there was any hope of saving them, and then hate them to destruction. He simply said, "Love your enemies." Therefore they are to be loved—forever. The time must never come when the child of God ceases to love his or her enemy, blessing them and doing good to them. Christians are to know no other way.

The disciples sat nearest to Christ when He spoke these words, but they did not understand this message as is evident from the question Peter asked much later.

Then Peter came to Him and said, "Lord, how often shall my brother sin against me, and I forgive him? Up to seven times?" Jesus said to him, "I do not say to you, up to seven times, but up to seventy times seven (Matt. 18:21, 22).

Seventy times seven is four hundred and ninety times. Did Christ mean that we are to carefully count till we reach this number and then stop forgiving? No, that is not the way these words are to be understood. Rather, Christ desired to convey the idea that there is no time when we are to cease forgiving.

It is impossible to strike back at those who strike first and at the same time manifest a forgiving spirit. As surely as forgiveness is to be forever, the turning of the other cheek is likewise to be forever.

In this discourse, Christ is magnifying the law. He is explaining the way in which God desired His directives, "Thou shalt not kill, steal, and lie," to be understood. Consider the difference between humanity's philosophy and the teachings of Jesus Christ. People say that if your enemy strikes you, strike back—harder. If a person kills someone you love, kill him or her. If someone curses you, curse them in return; if an individual does you evil, return evil for it.

But Jesus said to return love for hate, blessing for cursing, and goodness for evil. If lies are told about you, do not lie in return; if they steal your goods, do not seek to steal them back again; if they seek your life, do not seek theirs. This is to say that the law is to be kept under all circumstances. There is neither time nor place where the law is to be broken in order to assure that it is kept.

Having laid out these guidelines for human behavior, Christ confirmed that this was the way in which His Father practiced the law. He told His hearers that by so doing they would "be sons of" their "Father in heaven; for He makes His sun rise on the evil and on the good, and sends rain on the just and on the unjust" (Matt. 5:45).

Jesus identified the children of God as those who obey the law in the way He declared it should be obeyed. They were such, He affirmed, because they were doing as the Father did.

A distinguishing mark of God's children is that they do turn the other cheek, do go the second mile, do love their enemies, and do bless and do good to those who return them only evil. Individuals who return evil for evil, do not turn the other cheek, do not go the second mile, and do not bless those who despitefully use them are not children of God.

This identification of the children of God is powerfully meaningful. The relationship is spiritual for it is in this, and not the physical sense, that we are God's children. It conveys the idea that there must first be the same character in the Christian as in the Father before there can be the corresponding behavior without. Those who are God's children have the same character as He has. It is a character received by the process of spiritual regeneration.

> By the transforming agency of His grace, the image of God is reproduced in the disciple; he becomes a new creature. Love takes the place of hatred, and the heart receives the divine similitude. This is what it means to live "by every word that proceedeth out of the mouth of God." This is eating the Bread that comes down from heaven (*The Desire of Ages*, p. 391).

As surely as they have the same character, they will have the same behavior. They will keep the law exactly as God, the King of Righteousness, keeps it.

> Jesus said, Be perfect as *your Father* is perfect. If you are the children of God you are partakers of His nature, and you cannot but be like Him. Every child lives by the life of his father. If you are God's children, begotten by His Spirit, you live by the life of God. In Christ dwells "all the fullness of the Godhead bodily" (Colossians 2:9); and the life of Jesus is made manifest "in our mortal flesh" (2 Corinthians 4:11). That life in you will produce the same character and manifest the same works as it did in Him. Thus you will be in harmony with every precept of His law; for "the law of the Lord is perfect, restoring the soul." Psalm 19:7, margin. Through love "the righteousness of the law" will be "fulfilled in us, who walk not after the flesh, but after the Spirit" Romans 8:4 (*Thoughts from the Mount of Blessing*, pp. 77, 78).

But it was Christ, the Truth, who testified these things of God. Therefore, they are the truth in the strictest sense. God does love His enemies.

Of all the beings who have ever existed, no one has ever hated God more fiercely, cursed Him more savagely, done evil to Him more extensively, or persecuted Him more relentlessly than Satan. Could it be possible that God loves Satan even to this very day? Could it be possible that He blesses him in return for his curses, does good to him who hates Him so much, and prays for him who so despitefully uses and persecutes Him?

Christ answers that question, testifying that the Father does all this. The form of His testimony lays out what we are to be and do in order to reproduce the behavior and character of the Father. In doing so, He makes no exception of the devil. He does not counsel us to love our enemies except for Satan. He simply says, "Love your enemies." Therefore, anyone who can be classified as an enemy is to be loved. Satan certainly comes into this classification, for he is the archenemy.

Therefore, if doing this makes us the children of God and thus the reproduction of Him, then God loves His enemies, including Satan. He blesses him as far as it is possible for the blessings to reach him, does him good where He can, and will continue to do so for as long as Satan exists. If He did not, then Christ bore a false witness of His Father.

To understand the attitude of genuine love that the Father has for His lost son, a distinction must be made between love together *with* fellowship, and love without it.

God has no fellowship with the devil. They do not see each other, nor do they work together. Their interests and objectives are completely opposite. God does not support any of the devil's activities, even though he is the recipient of God's blessings just as the most wicked person receives the outflow of God's life and love in the seedtime and harvest, the rain and the wind, and the continued protection from total and final disaster. The devil takes all these blessings and uses them to war against God, but for this God is not responsible. He gives the blessings for their good, but the perversion of them is the responsibility of those who misuse the gift.

Be assured on the strength of Christ's witness of His Father that God loves the devil and will therefore only bless and do him good. This means that God will never take Satan's life but would reach out to save him if possible. This is love on an incredible scale.

When Jesus bore this beautiful and truthful testimony of His Father, He knew all that God had done in the Old Testament. He was also familiar with the view that people took of what God had done. Human beings saw God pouring good upon the dwellers in Sodom and Gomorrah for a limited time, after which He exchanged the blessings for cursing, and the good for evil as He poured upon them the flood of fire and brimstone. They saw the same picture in the flood, the plagues of Egypt, the obliteration of the Canaanites, the death by night of Sennacherib's army, and many other instances.

If the view of those things as held by people then and now is correct, then Christ could never truthfully say what He said of His Father on the mount of blessing. Therefore, for Christ to say what He said from personal conviction, He must have held a very different view of what the Father did in the Old Testament from what people held then and since, for humanity's view of God and the picture that Christ presented of Him are two altogether conflicting concepts.

Christ lived and taught the character of God. He presented God as the perfect keeper of the law. Christ neither knew nor presented a God who had one law for Himself and another for the people.

God is in a position of power from which He can obliterate any opposition by a single word. Therefore, humanity might well tremble in dread before such a God if He were indeed altogether such as ourselves.

The law was not given by God to protect Himself from humankind. It was God's perfect love gift to human beings to protect them from themselves and from the possibility of perverting the powers given to them for life and blessing into a cataclysm of destruction. This aspect of the law was studied earlier in chapter 8.

Serving humanity in these ways, the law is a wonderful thing indeed, but the greatest wonder of all is that it actually *protects human beings from God.* In setting out the principles of that law, God has declared what He is and what He will and will not do. He has stated that He will never lie, never steal, and never kill no matter what situation may arise to call for or to justify such things. The enunciation of the law of God is God's own pledge that we are forever secure from His doing any such thing no matter how we may treat Him in return.

When God commits Himself to a pledge of that nature, there is absolute assurance that He will never vary from it in the slightest degree.

By the misrepresentation of the testimony of God's word, Satan has convinced people that, if ever God did make such a pledge, He certainly has not honored it. Because the persuasion of people to Satan's lies about God is so extensive and long-standing, it will be very difficult for the average person to accept that God has made and honored such a commitment. The mind, long trained to see the workings of God in a certain light, will swiftly object that the great rebellion demanded that God arise to cleanse the universe of the curse by actively destroying the offenders. To the human mind, this is the only available solution to the problem. People do not understand the wisdom and power of God as it will be employed to put down the great rebellion. They do not see that there is another and infinitely better way to deal with rebellion than counterforce.

Christ neither shared nor taught such a view. He presented a Father who loved His enemies and who would give them only blessing and goodness.

No ruler in human history is like unto our God. There is no king, governor, president, dictator, lord, prince, emperor, or any other kind of ruler who has pledged themselves never to lie to, steal from, or kill any one of their subjects no matter how treasonous, rebellious, slanderous, insurrectionist, arsonist, murderous, thieving, cruel, activist, reactionary, or criminal that subject may become. Earthly potentates know only one way to deal with such elements in society and that is to meet force with force. There is no turning of the other cheek, no going the second mile, no love for their enemies, and no blessing of those who do them evil.

But what no earthly ruler has ever done or ever will do, God has done. Truly, His ways are as much higher than our ways as the heavens are above the earth. When the real nature of God's righteousness is understood and appreciated, it will call forth from the hearts of those who thus see it a rapture of praise and adoration otherwise impossible. They will then begin to understand and testify with the words of the Bible writers:

> Among the gods there is none like You, O Lord; Nor are there any works like Your works. All nations whom You have made shall come and worship before You, O Lord, and shall glorify Your name. For You are great, and do wondrous things; You alone are God (Ps. 86:8-10).

Great is the Lord, and greatly to be praised in the city of our God, in His holy mountain (Ps. 48:1).

Let it be clearly recognized that while God Himself pledged that He would never destroy the violators of His principles, He did not, because He could not, guarantee that sinners would not be destroyed. On the contrary, He warned that sin is the act of separating from God, so that there remains no protection from the destructive forces thus set in motion. May you come to see God as Christ knew Him.

Chapter Eighteen

An Eye for an Eye

Study/Discussion Questions:

- Jesus started His ministry (and ended it, too), by coming in contravention to the "eye for eye" laws. Were those laws His perfect will? If not, then what would we call them?

- How does cultural context bear upon the way God works with humanity?

- Can and does God give instructions built upon imperfect, sinful foundations?

When Christ gave the Sermon on the Mount, people had assembled on the mountain expecting to hear His pronouncements of the nature of the kingdom He had come to establish. At the very outset, He warned them that He had not come to do away with the law. He said:

> For assuredly, I say to you, till heaven and earth pass away, one jot or one tittle will by no means pass from the law till all is fulfilled. Whoever therefore breaks one of the least of these commandments, and teaches men so, shall be called least in the kingdom of heaven; but whoever does and teaches them, he shall be called great in the kingdom of heaven. For I say to you, that unless your righteousness exceeds the righteousness of the scribes and Pharisees, you will by no means enter the kingdom of heaven (Matt. 5:18-20).

Having asserted that He had not come to do away with the law, He then appeared to do just that. In the Old Testament He had said to them, "An eye for an eye and a tooth for a tooth," but now He said:

> "You have heard that it was said, 'An eye for an eye and a tooth for a tooth.' *But I tell you* not to resist an evil person. But whoever slaps you on your right cheek, turn the other to him also. If anyone wants to sue you and take away your tunic, let him have your cloak also. And whoever compels you to go one mile, go with him two. Give to him who asks you, and from him who wants to borrow from you do not turn away.
>
> "You have heard that it was said, 'You shall love your neighbor and hate your enemy.' But I say to you, love your enemies, bless those who curse you, do

good to those who hate you, and pray for those who spitefully use you and persecute you, that you may be sons of your Father in heaven; for He makes His sun
rise on the evil and on the good, and sends rain on the just and on the unjust.
For if you love those who love you, what reward have you? Do not even the tax
collectors do the same? And if you greet your brethren only, what do you do
more than others? Do not even the tax collectors do so? Therefore you shall be
perfect, just as your Father in heaven is perfect" (Matt. 5:38-48).

In order to understand why Christ spoke this way with regard to the "eye for an eye"
expression, we have to understand the original intent that God had in giving the "eye for an
eye" principle in the original Mosaic law as well as the circumstances under which He gave
it and how we are to understand His "giving" of these laws. A correct understanding of this
biblical expression will also establish a foundation that is fundamental to understanding
the civil laws that are outlined in the Old Testament. It is vital that we place these laws in
a valid historical context.

Most of Christendom holds an incorrect understanding of what was intended in the
Hebrew idiom of "eye for eye" as found in three texts in the Old Testament (Exod. 21:24;
Lev. 24:20; Deut. 19:21). The "eye for eye" principle has been interpreted to indicate a *retaliatory* penal code. It is, in fact, commonly referred to as the "*lex talionis*" or "law of retaliation." An understanding of the whole tenor of the Mosaic law, however, shows a much
different picture, a picture that does not reveal a vengeful intent or retaliatory nature from
the Law-giver. We must examine each of the three uses of the "eye for eye" expression in
the Old Testament, in their full context, to better grasp how it was used and understood in
the Hebrew culture in terms of intent and meaning.

When the "eye for eye" expression, or idiom, is first introduced into the Mosaic law, it
is in relation to a situation in which a pregnant woman, as a bystander to a physical fight,
gets injured, causing her to lose the baby she is carrying. If the woman is not hurt beyond
the loss of her child, the husband is entitled to compensation only for the loss of the child.
If "mischief follows" and the woman dies, then the statement is made that there should be
"life for life, eye for eye, tooth for tooth, hand for hand, foot for foot, burn for burn, wound
for wound, stripe for stripe" (Exod. 21:23-25). In the commentary of a Hebrew Bible, *The
Living Torah*, it is footnoted that "these expressions, however, are meant idiomatically and
not literally." Therefore, the Hebrew Bible translation reads:

> However, if there is a fatal injury [to the woman], then *he must pay full compen-
> sation* for her life. *Full compensation must be paid* for the loss of an eye, a tooth,
> a hand or a foot. *Full compensation must [also] be paid* for a burn, a wound, or
> a bruise.

We can see this same understanding of the "eye for eye" principle played out in other
laws of the Bible. For example, in Exodus 21:18, 19 there is a case of bodily injury which
could be compared to that in Exodus 21:24.

> If men contend with each other, and one strikes the other with a stone or with *his* fist, and he does not die but is confined to *his* bed, if he rises again and walks about outside with his staff, then he who struck *him* shall be acquitted. He shall only pay *for* the loss of his time, and shall provide *for him* to be thoroughly healed" (Exod. 21:18, 19).

In this case, no injury is to be inflicted on the person who caused the original injury. Instead, provision is made for a fair payment of the medical costs and loss of livelihood of the injured party to be taken care of as compensation. It is reasonable, therefore, to apply this same principle of fair and equal compensation as being awarded to the case of bodily injury to the pregnant woman. Contextually, the culture of the time was governed by a system that put economic value on people. In fact, people were bought and sold as slaves and fixed prices were put on individuals of both genders and various ages. This context must be kept in mind when reviewing the civil laws of the Israelite people.

In Leviticus 24:19, 20 the "eye for eye" idiom is used again. Here, it is in relation to bodily injury, once again, wherein if a man is maimed, then there is to be "eye for eye" compensation. This example requires a close inspection of the context and original language used in order to gain a clear picture as to how the expression is to be understood. One could interpret these verses to mean that the person who caused the injury should be disfigured, also, as a retaliatory measure, but the *contextual evidence* doesn't indicate this because directly surrounding these verses the principle of equal payment is again reiterated, specifically with regard to the loss of animals.

"Whoever kills an animal shall make it good, animal for animal" (Lev. 24:18). "And whoever kills an animal shall restore it" (Lev. 24:21).

In addition to this contextual evidence, the Hebrew language in Leviticus also supports the understanding that fair compensation is the primary intent here, also, in this "eye for eye" expression. Leviticus 24:19, 20 states, "If a man causes a disfigurement of his neighbor, as he has done, so shall it be done to him—fracture for fracture, eye for eye, tooth for tooth; as he has caused disfigurement of a man, so shall it be done to him."

In these verses the verb "done" is used three times, twice in verse 19 and once in verse 20. However, the word used in each of these verses is different. The concise use of each Hebrew word provides the clearly desired meaning of the original text. In verse 19 the Hebrew word used is "*asah*," which has a primary meaning of "do" or "make." When used in conjunction with other words, it can also mean "execute (put in execution), govern, bring forth, deal (with), grant, have the charge of," among others. Read in this context, verse 19 could be understood to mean "as he hath done, so shall it be 'executed/governed/dealt with.'"

To know for certain that this is what is meant, we only need to compare it with the following verse. In verse 20 the Hebrew word for "done" is a totally different word, "*nathan*," which means "to give." The Strong's Concordance says this word is "used with great latitude of application." It can be used to mean "put" or "make," but it is commonly expressed as "add, apply, appoint, ascribe, assign, bring forth, charge, commit, consider, grant, lay unto charge, recompense, render, requite, restore, set (forth)." The common connotation that all of these words have is one implying a judgment, not an executed action. The Hebrew mind would have understood it that way, and a scholarly examination of biblical language will render the same understanding.

One issue that can confuse our thinking about the "eye for eye" expression is an incorrect understanding of the difference between what this expression was intended to mean within the Hebrew language and mind-set as unrelated to the use of capital punishment as one of the sentences used in the civil Mosaic laws. In Leviticus 24:21, in the second half of the verse, capital punishment is mandated. It states, "And whoever kills an animal shall restore it; but whoever kills a man shall be put to death" (Lev. 24:21).

Since this verse is in proximity to the "eye for an eye" expression, given in verse 20, it can create a misunderstanding about the meaning of the expression. In reality, we must simply differentiate between the expression and the unrelated punitive sentence of death, which comes afterwards. There are many crimes in the civil law for which the death sentence was given. Some of these crimes included kidnapping for slavery, murder, cursing or hitting parents, adultery, incest, bestiality, Sabbath breaking, human sacrifice, witchcraft, false prophets, defiling the priesthood/sanctuary, and blasphemy. The fact that all of the crimes which result in the death sentence are not given with any reference at all to the "eye for an eye" expression is, actually, further confirmation that the original intent of the use of this expression was not one of retaliation, vengeance, or physical violence.

In Deuteronomy 19:16-21 we have the last incidence where the "eye for eye" principle is mentioned. In this case it is in regard to a false witness. It does not concern any kind of injury or loss of life at all. The law states that if a man bears false witness and it is discovered he is to receive that penalty, or fine, that he wished to have brought upon the person against whom he acted as a false witness. This is described as a directive, not to show pity but rather to give equal punitive judgment on the false witness, and it is described using the language "life *shall be* for life, eye for eye, tooth for tooth, hand for hand, foot for foot" (verse 21).

From this examination of the three instances where the "eye for eye" figure is used, it can be seen that the original intent was to administer justice according to the principle that fair and equal compensation was to be granted to those who received any kind of a loss.

This, of course, was the directive given *within the framework of humanity's decision* to be ruled by human laws and systems. *Do not miss this point, as it is the crux of understanding.* This is God working in the mode of "permissive will," which is the term we apply in reference to allowances made "for the hardness of people's hearts." Confusion arises when we read permissive will as the actual (perfect) will of God. Such confusion will bring us to distorted views of God's character. So, when God is forced to work with people that insist on functioning using their own methods and ways, He is still merciful and continues to guide them toward the best actions that can be used within their chosen systems. As they respond to His leading and fully surrender their wills to Him, He will lead them out of their own erroneous ways and choices and will redirect them toward His ways, truths, laws and principles.

When Jesus came He contrasted humanity's principles with the principles of the kingdom of God. He took the minds of the people to a higher standard of righteousness than they had chosen to live under in the Old Testament time. His expansion on God's ideal principles of righteousness challenged the people to live under a system where His *perfect*, rather than *permissive*, will could be understood and lived out. In actual fact, the ultimate goal of salvation must see redeemed human beings entirely cleansed of all that pertains to the ways of the carnal heart; self-rule in any particular must be rooted out at last, for anything less than God's perfection of character and conduct leads to death, for anything not of God is sin.

The Education of Israel

Christ wanted to direct the people to God's perfect will on the Sermon on the Mount. The fact that the Sermon on the Mount teachings differ from the teachings of the Mosaic law can only be rightly understood when we examine the situational context and purpose of the giving of the Mosaic law.

Prior to the exodus there were laws and ordinances that were kept by the people of God. The Scriptures affirm that Abraham kept the laws, statutes, and judgments of God (Gen. 26:5). They were known and passed down from generation to generation (*The Spirit of Prophecy*, book 1, p. 264). Some of these included the sacrifice of the lamb, keeping the Sabbath, tithing, and later, the rite of circumcision. Because the Israelite people had been in slavery and had not been permitted to walk in the ways of the Lord for many generations, many of the laws were no longer held in regard or practiced. God had to remind the people of their heritage and teach them about the plan of salvation, which had been almost completely lost to them as they became steeped in the customs, religious practices, laws, and ancestral/historical influences of the land of their captivity over hundreds of years.

In order to re-educate the people of Israel, the Lord started instituting various symbolic methods of leading them to more than a cursory knowledge of Him.

> Victims of lifelong slavery, they were ignorant, untrained, degraded. They had little knowledge of God and little faith in Him. They were confused by false teaching and corrupted by their long contact with heathenism. God desired to lift them to a higher moral level, and to this end He sought to give them a knowledge of Himself (*Education*, p. 34).

God teaches people in a manner that is both progressive and responsive. His teaching must be progressive because we can only handle so much at a time. Our cultivated tendencies and cultural influences can have a significant bearing on whether we are prepared to accept God's ways and truths. Though He has much to teach us, He only gives us what we can bear, as a corporate body and as individuals (John 16:12). He wants to reveal His complete will to us but He must first prepare our minds to be receptive to His teaching. Our readiness is, then, reflected not only in the desire that He has created within us to know the truth but to walk in it.

True education is not the forcing of instruction on an unready and unrecep-
tive mind. The mental powers must be awakened, the interest aroused. For this,
God's method of teaching provided. He who created the mind and ordained its
laws, provided for its development in accordance with them. In the home and
the sanctuary, through the things of nature and of art, in labor and in festivity,
in sacred building and *memorial stone*, by methods and rites and symbols unnumbered, God gave to Israel lessons illustrating His principles and preserving
the memory of His wonderful works. Then, as inquiry was made, the instruction
given impressed mind and heart (*Education*, p. 41, emphasis added).

God's methods seek to engage the mind of those He is trying to teach, speaking to them
in ways they can understand and to which they can relate both intellectually and emotion-
ally, while introducing deep spiritual truths and implications. This frame of reference will
vary greatly according to time, culture, geographical location, or any other influencing
factors that may surround the people He is seeking to reach. The ancient Israelites, recently
delivered from slavery, were no exception to this rule. So, from the Exodus onward, we can
see old laws reintroduced and new systems and types added to draw the people to Christ
in a way they could understand and accept.

First, God introduced the Passover and Feast of Unleavened Bread as they exited
Egypt to teach them that they had a Deliverer and Redeemer, the Lamb that was slain
(Exod. 12:43). Also, the people were called to sanctify all the firstborn of humans and beast
unto the Lord (Exod. 13:2, 15), which was in commemoration of how the Lord protected
and saved all the firstborn from the destroyer when the last Egyptian plague killed all the
firstborn of those who were dedicated unto the Egyptian gods at birth. Those who did not
mark their doors with the symbolic blood of the Lamb, thereby accepting God's authority and protection, were given over to the destroyer, who was the entity behind the god to
whom they were dedicated and whose priest they would grow up to be in their own future
households.

Next, God reintroduced His desire for them to keep the Sabbath. The people were
already aware of the Sabbath, but God had to illustrate the importance of it in a way that
would impact the people experientially, so they would come to understand its significance
and meaning. This was necessary because, as slaves, they had not been able to practice
their religion, which included keeping the Sabbath, for centuries. He did this by providing
manna for the people, providing a test of faith and dependence as well as an object lesson
that would recommit them to the Sabbath blessing and truth:

The Creator's rest-day was hallowed by Adam in holy Eden, and by men of God
throughout the patriarchal ages. During Israel's long bondage in Egypt, under
taskmasters that knew not God, they could not keep the Sabbath; therefore the
Lord brought them out where they could remember his holy day (*Signs of the
Times*, February 28, 1884).

> Then the LORD said to Moses, "Behold, I will rain bread from heaven for you. And the people shall go out and gather a certain quota every day, *that I may test them, whether they will walk in My law or not*" (Exod. 16:4).

The next law to be proclaimed was the moral law given from Mount Sinai. Had the people been willing to simply obey His voice and let Him lead them in righteousness on a daily basis they would not have needed these written laws, but they were afraid of God speaking directly to them. So the Lord had to provide the moral law in written form, utilizing Moses as a mediator, as per their demand. In the Ten Commandments, God wished to reveal to the Israelites His goodness and give them a right understanding of His character and righteousness. Through the tabernacle services, He wanted to teach the plan of salvation, wherein Christ would not only pardon, forgive, and redeem but would also dwell in them and save them from being slaves to sin.

> So to Israel, whom He desired to make His dwelling place, *He revealed His glorious ideal of character*. The pattern was shown them in the mount when the law was given from Sinai and when God passed by before Moses and proclaimed, "The Lord, The Lord God, merciful and gracious, long-suffering, and abundant in goodness and truth." Exodus 34:6. But this ideal they were, in themselves, powerless to attain. The revelation at Sinai could only impress them with their need and helplessness. Another lesson the tabernacle, through its service of sacrifice, was to teach—the lesson of pardon of sin, and power through the Saviour for obedience unto life (*Education*, pp. 35, 36, emphasis added).

The descendants of Abraham had almost completely lost their knowledge of God and His ways. They no longer had an understanding of the principles and promises of God revealed in the Abrahamic covenant; they had no true conception of the holiness of God or of their own sinfulness. They did not realize their need of a Savior or of their own inability to obey God's laws in their own strength. They were conditioned to believe that the practices of the land they lived in were perfectly acceptable, even righteous, and justified in their own eyes. They had no experiential knowledge of Him that would create trust and loyalty in them. God had to teach them His ways and who He was all over again.

> In their bondage the people had to a great extent lost the knowledge of God and of the principles of the Abrahamic covenant. In delivering them from Egypt, God sought to reveal to them His power and His mercy, that they might be led to love and trust Him. He brought them down to the Red Sea—where, pursued by the Egyptians, escape seemed impossible—that they might realize their utter helplessness, their need of divine aid; and then He wrought deliverance for them. Thus they were filled with love and gratitude to God and with confidence in His power to help them. He had bound them to Himself as their deliverer from temporal bondage.
>
> But there was a still greater truth to be impressed upon their minds. Living

in the midst of idolatry and corruption, they had no true conception of the holiness of God, of the exceeding sinfulness of their own hearts, their utter inability, in themselves, to render obedience to God's law, and their need of a Saviour. All this they must be taught (*Patriarchs and Prophets*, p. 371).

Even the civil laws of the heathen lands they lived in were completely ingrained into the Israelites' way of thinking and sense of justice. They had been slaves for hundreds of years and were conditioned to obey or be punished. They were ruled by fear, serving out of compulsion. They were used to being ruled by human laws with human penalties, with the predominate code of law being the *Code of Hammurabi*, instituted by a Babylonian king of centuries past. Therefore, the Israelites chose their own system of civil law early in their freedom when Moses' father-in-law, Jethro, advised him to put into effect a legal code with additional judges to help judge the issues of the people.

And you shall teach them the statutes and the laws, and show them the way in which they must walk and the work they must do. Moreover you shall select from all the people able men, such as fear God, men of truth, hating covetousness; and place *such* over them *to be* rulers of thousands, rulers of hundreds, rulers of fifties, and rulers of tens (Exod. 18:20, 21).

Because of the people's action of taking on their own civil law system, God had to react by introducing to them a system of civil law designed to begin leading them back to the principles of His kingdom. These laws incorporated higher levels of morality than any other laws to which they had already been exposed. They were designed to progressively lead them back to God's ideal of righteousness and point them to Christ. He gave these to Moses at the same time as He gave the Ten Commandments. The Ten Commandments outlined principles of righteousness and the judgments expanded these principles into practical applications. These laws had to allow for their freedom of choice and had to be given in relation to what the people were able to bear, taking into consideration their current level of morality and all their cultural biases and influences. His great task in this was to direct the people to a higher morality and to advance them in righteousness and knowledge of Him without interfering with their freedom of choice.

Unfortunately, their current level of righteousness, as reflected in the neighboring nations and cultures, was so debased that the Lord could only advance them in controlled doses of the light of truth. The Mosaic law was unique and was far more righteous and superior to any preexisting codes of law. Furthermore, the Lord wove into these laws deep spiritual symbolisms and lessons that would direct them to a new way of thinking and living. However, there was much in it that reflected the laws they already understood and which had already to a certain extent been incorporated within their culture, by their choice.

The civil and ceremonial laws were included in the Book of the Law kept in the side of the ark of the covenant.

After speaking all these laws, God called Moses, Aaron, and seventy elders to meet with Him on the mountain. He asked Moses to stay up on the mount to receive the tables of stone and listen to God recite the judgments again.

> Moses wrote these judgments and statutes from the mouth of God while he was with him in the mount. *If the people of God had obeyed the principles of the ten commandments, there would have been no need of the specific directions given to Moses*, which he wrote in a book, relative to their duty to God and to one another. The definite directions which the Lord gave to Moses in regard to the duty of his people to one another, and to the stranger, *are the principles of the ten commandments simplified and given in a definite manner*, that they need not err (*Spirit of Prophecy*, book 1, p. 265, emphasis added).

God also foresaw the need of the tabernacle service for the people, and so He started to instruct Moses about the pattern of the earthly sanctuary while he was on the mount. God instituted the tabernacle service in response to their choice to have a tangible representation of their God and ritualistic services. God knew in advance that the children of Israel would regress to idolatrous practices of their own if they did not have a system of religion that involved form, rite, and visible representations. He also knew they would corrupt any system of worship they were given with the heathen customs they had observed and in which they had participated in Egypt. So God gave them a form of ritualistic service, but He also provided guidelines in order to mitigate the corruption He could foresee they would introduce into this system. God provides instruction based on the necessity He sees will arise.

> *Accustomed as they had been in Egypt to material representations of the Deity,* and these of the most degrading nature, it was difficult for them to conceive of the existence or the character of the Unseen One. *In pity for their weakness*, God gave them a symbol of His presence. "Let them make Me a sanctuary," He said; "that I may dwell among them." Exodus 25:8 (*Education*, p. 35).

> If man had kept the law of God, as given to Adam after his fall, preserved by Noah, and observed by Abraham, there would have been no *necessity* for the ordinance of circumcision. And if the descendants of Abraham had kept the covenant, of which circumcision was a sign, they would never have been seduced into idolatry, nor would it have been *necessary* for them to suffer a life of bondage in Egypt; they would have kept God's law in mind, and there would have been no *necessity* for it to be proclaimed from Sinai or engraved upon the tables of stone. And had the people practiced the principles of the Ten Commandments, there would have been no *need* of the additional directions given to Moses.
>
> The sacrificial system, committed to Adam, was also *perverted* by his descendants. Superstition, idolatry, cruelty, and licentiousness corrupted the simple and significant service that God had appointed. Through long intercourse with idolaters the people of Israel had mingled many heathen customs with their worship; *therefore the Lord gave them at Sinai definite instruction concerning the*

sacrificial service. After the completion of the tabernacle He communicated with Moses from the cloud of glory above the mercy seat, and gave him *full directions concerning the system of offerings and the forms of worship* to be maintained in the sanctuary (*Patriarchs and Prophets*, p. 364, emphasis added).

Unfortunately, the Israelites fulfilled their own desire for a visible God to worship even before Moses returned from the mountain by making the golden calf. God knew that transforming these people out of their paradigm of thought and experience would not be accomplished overnight. It would involve advancing them slowly. *It had to allow freedom, even to choose error or unrighteousness.* It could not be done by force or compulsion. So we see a progression of laws and structures being added in order to reach them in a way they could relate to. They were babes in their concept of God and His righteousness. This they had to learn, one step at a time.

Each time the Israelite people made a choice that was contrary to God's ideal will for them, God had to react in righteousness. He did not forsake them. He strove to bring them back to His way by giving them an alternative that would advance them in righteousness while still allowing them to walk in the ways of their choice. Here are some examples of the instances we have thus far discussed:

The Israelites demand food and complain, desiring to return to the flesh pots of Egypt.	God gives them manna and the Sabbath to teach them how to rest in and trust Him.
The Israelites refuse to hear from God, directly.	God gives them Moses as a mediator and a written law.
The Israelites promise to "obey" all that God says, choosing a system of works (Exod. 19:8).	God gives them the Ten Commandments, promises of what He will fulfill in them by faith.
The Israelites choose a civil system, as instituted by Moses under advisement of Jethro.	God gives them civil laws to govern them, more righteous than any others in the land (Deut. 4:8).
The Israelites demand a tangible form of worship with celebrations and rituals, as demonstrated at the golden calf incident.	God gives them the sanctuary, feast days, and ceremonial laws, which all point to Christ as their Deliverer and Redeemer.

God, in His mercy, always meets people where they are and respects their choices. The eternal principles of His kingdom only allow for freedom of choice and service of love. So, when human beings go astray and choose their own way, God strives to pull them back to His ways and to advance them in righteousness as quickly as they are able to bear.

Hammurabi's Code of Law

While working with the Israelites within the framework of their own choices, God still desires to lead His people into further blessings and righteousness. The Mosaic law is an amazing example of how God achieves His purposes, working all things together for good without infringing on people's freedom to choose their own systems. We have established that Moses set up a system of laws prior to those given at Mt. Sinai. Without input from God, we could safely assume that the laws they would have chosen would have been laws that reflected the extant code of law by which their contemporaneous surrounding nations were governed.

One of the predominant legal systems that was used at that time is Hammurabi's Code of Law. It is one of the oldest sets of laws discovered by archaeologists. It predates the Mosaic law by hundreds of years, and yet there are great similarities between the two systems of civil law. The Hammurabi's Code of law is inscribed on a seven-foot-tall diorite stele (ancient upright stone pillar bearing markings) that is currently on display in the Louvre Museum in Paris. Having the history and exploits of nations inscribed upon buildings, walls, or monuments was a common practice in ancient times, and we derive a great amount of historic knowledge from these kinds of archeological finds. It was also the custom of these ancient civilizations to engrave the laws of the land on stone and publically display them before the surrounding nations so that none need be unaware of what was expected of them by the governing lands. Interestingly enough, Israel also participated in this ancient custom. We see evidence of this as outlined in Deuteronomy in God's instruction to His people:

> And it shall be, on the day when you cross over the Jordan to the land which the LORD your God is giving you, that you shall set up for yourselves large stones, and whitewash them with lime. You shall write on them all the words of this law, when you have crossed over, that you may enter the land which the LORD your God is giving you, 'a land flowing with milk and honey,' just as the LORD God of your fathers promised you. Therefore it shall be, when you have crossed over the Jordan, *that* on Mount Ebal you shall set up these stones, which I command you today, and you shall whitewash them with lime. And there you shall build an altar to the LORD your God, an altar of stones; you shall not use an iron *tool* on them. You shall build with whole stones the altar of the LORD your God, and offer burnt offerings on it to the LORD your God. You shall offer peace offerings, and shall eat there, and rejoice before the LORD your God. And you shall write very plainly on the stones all the words of this law (Deut. 27:2-8).

When Joshua led the tribes of Israel over the Jordan, we see that he did as the Lord commanded, writing the laws upon large stones and setting them up near Mount Ebal, which was near Shechem (Josh. 8:32). This area surrounding Shechem was later referred to as "the plain of the pillar" (Judg. 9:6, KJV). The Lord intended for all the surrounding nations to benefit from the instructions that were given to the Israelites, too. This radically advanced law was to be Israel's wisdom in the sight of the nations that surrounded them:

> "Surely I have taught you statutes and judgments, just as the LORD my god commanded me, that you should act according to *them* in the land which you

go to possess. Therefore be careful to observe *them*; for this *is* your wisdom and your understanding in the sight of the peoples who will hear all these statutes, and say, 'Surely this great nation *is* a wise and understanding people.' "For what great nation *is there* that has God *so* near to it, as the LORD our God *is* to us, for whatever *reason* we may call upon Him? And what great nation *is there* that has *such* statutes and righteous judgments as are in all this law which I set before you this day?" (Deut. 4:5-8).

God knew that His statutes and judgments were far more righteous than those of the prevailing civil law systems of the day. As per the inscription on his stele, Hammurabi was a Babylonian king who lived about the time of Abraham and was a self-proclaimed "deity" to be worshipped and revered in his kingdom (similar to Nebuchadnezzar and the Egyptian pharaohs). On his stele, Hammurabi also declares both himself and his laws as altogether righteous. His law was the prevailing standard of conduct influencing the nations of that time, especially since most of them were under the control of the Babylonian empire. Hammurabi's name is not mentioned in biblical record, but some biblical scholars have equated him with King Amraphel who was the king of Shinar mentioned in Genesis 14:1. The land of Shinar is equated with Babylon in that Nimrod was the first Babylonian king who established his kingdom in the land of Shinar.

And it came to pass in the days of Amraphel king of Shinar (Gen. 14:1).

And the beginning of his [Nimrod's] kingdom was Babel, Erech, Accad, and Calneh, in the land of Shinar (Gen. 10:10).

As mentioned, there are many apparent similarities between the Hammurabic and Mosaic laws, in addition to their manner of public presentation on pillars. There are many internal biblical evidences that indicate that the people of Israel were familiar with this law and would have been ruled within its framework. Abraham came out of the land of Ur, which was ruled by Babylon, so he would have been directly governed by Hammurabi's Code of Law or a modified version of it. In Abraham's immediate family, we can see evidence of the influence of the Code of Hammurabi in an example where Judah, Jacob's son, applied its principles to a family situation. This is recorded in Genesis:

And it came to pass, about three months after, that Judah was told, saying, "Tamar your daughter-in-law has played the harlot; furthermore she *is* with child by harlotry." So Judah said, "Bring her out and let her be burned!" (Gen. 38:24).

Judah's judgment upon Tamar seemed to indicate that death would be a normal penalty to inflict upon women accused of adultery. The *SDA Bible Commentary* provides us with some insight into this occurrence:

Let her be burnt. Judah gave this order by virtue of his authority as head of the family. This probably seemed to him a fortunate opportunity, furthermore, to extricate himself from his obligation to provide her with a husband. Tamar was regarded as the bride of Shelah, and as such was to be punished for a breach of chastity. The Mosaic law provided for stoning under such circumstances (Deut. 22:20–24). Only in the case of a priest's daughter, or of certain forms of incest, was burning enjoined (Lev. 21:9; 20:14). Judah's sentence, therefore, was more harsh than later Israelite law required. Whether he acted according to the custom of his time, or on other grounds, cannot be determined. The Code of Hammurabi lists two crimes for which the punishment is burning. Section 110 of the code states that a "devoted one" (see on Gen. 38:21) who opens a wineshop or enters a wineshop for a drink shall be burned alive, and section 25 provides that a thief shall be cast into the burning house from which he had attempted to steal property (*The SDA Bible Commentary*, vol. 1, p. 430).

The Code of Hammurabi specifically placed the death penalty by drowning upon the crime of adultery, as per Hammurabi code #2 (H2). However, as mentioned in *The SDA Bible Commentary*, burning was another form of capital punishment used in Babylon (see also the case of the three worthy Hebrews). Death by drowning could only occur in close proximity to water, of course. Judah's encampment was in the desert, so other forms of capital punishment would have had to be enjoined. In any case, we can see that he was at least familiar with a course of law that called for death for adultery and the Code of Hammurabi was the most likely law to have influenced him.

In order to grasp at least a minimal understanding of the extent that Hammurabi's Code of Law influenced the minds, behaviors, and laws of the Israelite people, it would be helpful to chart some examples of the resemblances of the two codes of law. The first resemblance we can see is found in the similar structures of the two laws:

Exodus 21:18-27	Hammurabi's Code of Law
Verses 18, 19: bodily injuries received during a fight	H206-208: bodily injuries received during a fight
Verses 22, 23: injuries of a pregnant woman during a fight, causing miscarriage	H209-212: injuries of a pregnant woman during a fight, causing miscarriage
Verses 24, 25: the "eye for an eye" principle	H196, 197, 200 injuries to the eye, bone. and tooth (to the upper class); *lex talionis*
Verses 20, 21, 26, 27: injuries to slaves	H199: injuries to slaves

The above section of law shows how the Mosaic laws are written in similar sequence and with similar penalties, in some cases, to the Code of Hammurabi. This is not an isolated case of sections of law being similar, though. Other examples show similarity in form and content, in groupings of laws, as indicated in the table below:

Exodus 22:10-14	Hammurabi's Code of Law
Verse 10: If a man deliver unto his neighbour an ass, or an ox, or a sheep, or any beast, to keep; and it die, or be hurt, or driven away, no man seeing *it*:	H263: If he lose an ox or sheep intrusted to him, he shall compensate the owner, ox for ox, sheep for sheep.
Verse 11: Then shall an oath of the LORD be between them both, that he hath not put his hand unto his neighbour's goods; and the owner of it shall accept *thereof*, and he shall not make *it* good.	H266: If a stroke of God (accident) happen in a stable, or a lion kill it (any beast), the shepherd shall declare his innocence before God, and the owner of the stable shall suffer the loss.
Verse 13: If it be torn in pieces, *then* let him bring it *for* witness, *and* he shall not make good that which was torn. Verse 14: And if a man borrow *ought* of his neighbour, and it be hurt, or die, the owner thereof *being* not with it, he shall surely make *it* good.	H267: If a shepherd overlook anything (negligence), and an accident take place in the stable, the shepherd shall make good in cattle or sheep the damage for which he is at fault, and give to the owner.

There are also many more examples of laws that are listed singularly with the same uncanny similarity. Without taking an exhaustive approach to comparing these laws, we can point out a few of the most striking cases where the two codes of law show resemblance:

Mosaic Law	Hammurabi's Code of Law
Exodus 22:18; Leviticus 20:27: Death penalty for sorcery	H1: Death penalty for sorcery
Exodus 22:1-4: Fines for theft of animals	H8: Fines for theft of animals (death if not paid)
Exodus 21:16: Death for kidnapping and selling people	H14: Death for kidnapping the son of a freeman
Deuteronomy 22:21, 24; Leviticus 20:10: Death penalty for adultery	H129: Death penalty for adultery
Deuteronomy 22:25: Death to one who violates a betrothed virgin	H130: Death to one who violates a betrothed virgin
Genesis 29-30: The Mosaic law has no parallel, but the story of Isaac with Rebekah and Hagar bear huge similarities; Exodus 21:8 disallows concubines from being sold.	H144-147: A childless wife can give a maid to bear a child in her place; she's never to be equal; she can be treated as a servant or sold.

There are many more examples of similarities between the two codes of law in areas of civil law such as issues surrounding land rental, inheritance, items held in trust or hired out, slaves as payment for debt, cultivation of new land, stewardship of the land, negligence of work or toward hired property, etc. All these similarities in structure and content show a heavy dependence on the Code of Hammurabi.

The Lex Talionis in Hammurabi's Code of Law

The strength of the literary dependence of the Mosaic law upon Hammurabi's Code of Law could be considered as indicative that the *literal* interpretation of the *lex talionis* principle could also be predominately influenced by or derived from the Code of Hammurabi's use of the *lex talionis* expression. Let us examine the most compelling examples of "eye for eye" laws written in Hammurabi's Code of Law.

Hammurabi's Code of Law: *lex talionis origins*
H116: If the one seized die of blows or of bad treatment in the house of his distrainer … be he son of a freeborn man, then the son of the merchant shall be put to death.
H196: If a man destroy the eye of another man, they shall destroy his eye.
H197: If any one break a man's bone, one shall break his bone.
H200: If a man knock out the teeth of a man who is his equal in rank, one shall knock out his teeth.
H209: If a man strike a free-born woman and produce a miscarriage, he shall pay 10 shekels of silver for the loss (of that in her womb). H210: If that woman die, one shall put his daughter to death.
H229: If a builder build a house for any one and do not build it solid; and the house, which he has built, fall down and kill the owner; one shall put that builder to death. H230: If it kill a son of the owner of the house, one shall put to death the son of the builder.
H263: If he lose an ox or sheep intrusted to him, he shall compensate the owner, ox for ox, sheep for sheep.

We can clearly see that the Code of Hammurabi was utilized in ancient Babylon hundreds of years before the Mosaic law came into existence, and it used the "eye for an eye" expression. Anyone who would have been governed within that time and in those regions would have been familiar with this expression. This weight of evidence confirms that although used in a specific manner in the Mosaic law the "eye for eye" principle did not originate in the Mosaic law. As a matter of fact, many of the ancient laws, even those predating and contemporary with the Code of Hammurabi, reflected the "eye for eye" principle. Most of them, however, took a literal approach to the application of these laws. This is precisely the mind-set out of which God wished to bring His people. In the Exodus 21 usage of the *lex talionis* (which is the first mention of this expression), we find the following statements in *The SDA Bible Commentary*:

> Life for life. This seemingly excessive penalty for an injury that was largely accidental and with no intention of taking life, was probably the reflection of an old law like that of the "avenger of blood".… It must be remembered that there were certain provisions in these laws that Moses tolerated, such as the "bill of divorce-

ment," because of the "hardness" of their "hearts" (Deut. 24:1–4; Matt. 19:3–8). It is also to be kept in mind that some of these Mosaic enactments were not absolutely best from the divine viewpoint, but were imperfect (Ex. 20:25; Ps. 81:12). They were relatively the best that God's people, at that time and in their state of moral and spiritual development, would receive and obey....

Eye for eye. This law was also quite general among ancient nations. Solon introduced this law, in part, into the code of Athens, and in Rome it was included in the Twelve Tables. Numerous laws of a similar nature were included in the ancient Code of Hammurabi, a king of Babylon who lived about the time of Abraham....

If the literal interpretation of this law were insisted upon in our Lord's day (see Matt. 5:38–42), it must have been by the Sadducees, for they refused to read into the law a spiritual interpretation. No good would have been served by requiring, literally, "eye for eye." It would have meant great loss to the individual doing the injury, without bringing the least gain to the one injured. Persistent requirement of compensation is quite different from a passionate desire for revenge (vol. 1, p. 615).

When we compare other biblical texts, we can see that "eye for eye," applied in a literal way, has no place in God's thinking or methodology. Jesus further clarified that it has no place in God's thinking even when applied in a figurative way, for the "turn the other cheek" principle is one that foregoes any notion of compensation. God is consistent, and His principles are everlasting. Even when working with us within our own paradigms, He strives with people to bring them toward principles of mercy and righteousness. He teaches principles of reaping and sowing and of loving our neighbors as ourselves:

> You shall not take vengeance, nor bear any grudge against the children of your people, but you shall love your neighbor as yourself: I *am* the LORD (Lev. 19:18).

If we are to bring intellectual honesty to bear on these issues, we are faced with questions requiring careful contemplation. Traditional belief held to scrutiny can reveal inherent contradictions. For example, was providing cities of refuge for the manslayer in agreement with principles of a literal application of *lex talionis* (see Num. 35; Deut. 19:5, 6; Josh. 20:3-5)? When David thought to avenge himself against Nabal's refusal to send provisions for his soldiers in exchange for their protection, did God not send Abigail to divert him from this course of action (1 Sam. 25:32-34)? Does God work against Himself and the laws He has put in place? Or are we just failing to understand the cultural and moral context, purpose, and intent of the laws that were instituted in the Old Testament? If we do not diligently strive against reading through the filters of our assumptions, which results in the building of belief systems based on appearances, we will completely fail to understand how God patiently works with flawed people, within their flawed paradigms, to work out His purposes in His time and wisdom.

The principles of God's kingdom are infinite, timeless, and absolute, and the Lord has made it clear in His Word that we are not to take vengeance into our own hands. God's purposes are always accomplished in righteousness and self-sacrifice.

> Beloved, do not avenge yourselves, but *rather* give place to wrath; for it is written, "Vengeance is Mine, I will repay," says the Lord (Rom. 12:19).

> … that no one should take advantage of and defraud his brother in this matter, because the Lord *is* the avenger of all such, as we also forewarned you and testified (1 Thess. 4:6).

> For though we walk in the flesh, we do not war according to the flesh. For the weapons of our warfare *are* not carnal but mighty in God for pulling down strongholds (2 Cor. 10:3, 4).

> Now therefore, it is already an utter failure for you that you go to law against one another. Why do you not rather accept wrong? Why do you not rather *let yourselves* be cheated? (1 Cor. 6:7).

When God says not to avenge ourselves, it goes beyond giving up notions of retaliatory satisfaction. It includes not demanding compensatory action or replacement of any material goods that were lost. When He says He will repay, our thinking has been that He would strike down the perpetrator Himself, in *lex talionis* fashion, but by now we should be able to see that God Himself repays His enemies the same way that He asks us to repay: by rendering good for evil. Another consideration and level of meaning we can confidently assign to God's method of repayment is with regard to "our compensation." He will repay us, as well. Our reward is given in Christ, all of heaven poured out for us and the inheritance, with Him, of all things. Another gem of truth to apply here is to think of the potential result of repaying our enemy with good. God's intent is to win that person to Himself, and what if He should succeed? What more wonderful repayment could we receive than to gain a friend for eternity who would rather lay down his own life than to see us harmed? The one who had wanted to take from us for his or her own pleasure now wants to serve and please us through the ceaseless ages to come!

Advancing in Righteousness

Although we have established that there are strong resemblances between the Mosaic law and the Code of Hammurabi, we must also acknowledge some fundamental differences in various areas. Also, many laws from the Code of Hammurabi have no parallel laws in the Mosaic law. These differences and omissions speak volumes when understood. As God chose to work with the Israelite people, He incorporated as many changes as they would allow and could bear. Again, these changes were always in the effort to lead people further into His righteous ways. This is a principle that must ever be borne in mind as we learn to understand God operating in the mode of permissive will, which carefully pulls errant humans in His direction, through processes that take generations, even eras, to accomplish.

The first fundamental difference is that the Mosaic law was designed in a system where homage was due to God and not any man or monarch. It was also acknowledged as the most righteous law that any of the surrounding nations would have been exposed to:

> "Surely I have taught you statutes and judgments, just as the LORD my God commanded me, that you should act according *to them* in the land which you go to possess. Therefore be careful to observe *them;* for this *is* your wisdom and your understanding in the sight of the peoples who will hear all these statutes, and say, 'Surely this great nation *is* a wise and understanding people.' For what great nation *is there* that has God *so* near to it, as the LORD our God *is* to us, for whatever *reason* we may call upon Him? And what great nation *is there* that has *such* statutes and righteous judgments as are in all this law which I set before you this day?" (Deut. 4:5-8).

The issue of personal responsibility for individual sin stressed in the Mosaic law stands out in distinct contrast to many of the *lex talionis* laws contained in the Code of Hammurabi. For example, many Hammurabic laws called for the death of a person other than the one who was directly responsible for the crime committed. In some cases, a guilty person's child was to be killed in exchange for something they did which caused death to another person's child. For example:

Laws of Hammurabi (LH)

209: If an *awilu* [referring to the societal classification system] strikes a woman of the *awilu* class and thereby causes her to miscarry her fetus, he shall weigh and deliver 10 shekels of silver for her fetus. 210: If that woman should die, they shall kill his daughter.

229: If a builder build a house for any one and do not build it solid; and the house, which he has built, fall down and kill the owner; one shall put that builder to death. 230: If it kill a son of the owner of the house, one shall put to death the son of the builder.

In contrast, the Mosaic law did not allow for the taking of an innocent life for someone else's crime, specifying in particular that a child was not to be put to death in place of their father. It had to be stipulated precisely because the concept of direct personal responsibility, although to us today being self-evident as correct and normative in today's laws, was an extremely radical advance in righteousness in the minds of the people living in those ancient cultures and, therefore, requiring the clarification we read in Deuteronomy:

> "Fathers shall not be put to death for *their* children, nor shall children be put to death for *their* fathers; a person shall be put to death for his own sin" (Deut. 24:16).

There are many additional examples of how the Mosaic laws pointed people to a higher knowledge of the principles of heaven while allowing them their choice to be ruled under a flawed human system of law. For example, the Code of Hammurabi is pervaded with laws that involve mutilations. Here are a few examples:

- cutting off the hands of a physician who makes a surgical error that causes a man to lose his eye
- cutting out the tongue of an adopted son for denying his foster parents
- cutting off an ear if a slave strikes a freeman
- cutting off the hands of a child who strikes his parent
- cutting off the breast of a wet nurse who tries to substitute another baby in the place of a baby who dies while in her care and upbringing for other parents and the switch is discovered

These are just a few examples among many others. All these types of laws strive to create punishments that relate to the crime but they are extreme and cruel sentences. In contrast, the Mosaic law only has one law involving mutilation (Deut. 25:11, 12).

The Hammurabic three-tiered system of law, which assigns value to the lives of people relative to class, is also noticeably missing. Value is placed on all life, equally. The Lord even specifically calls for the same system of law to be given for the Israelite and the stranger (Exod. 12:49; Num. 15:16), and the Israelites are instructed not to make slaves of their brethren, but they are to redeem them if they somehow find themselves in this unfortunate position.

The Mosaic law still allowed for slaves in some circumstances, so we can deduce from this that to have completely abolished all systems of slavery at that time would have been a concept too difficult for the people to accept. It was a system in which they had been too deeply entrenched for a long period of time, and the surrounding nations were all still practicing it as a way of life. Slavery continued to be a generally accepted practice thousands of years later during the time of Christ and the apostolic ages (1 Cor 7:21-24; Gal. 3:28; Eph. 6:5, 6; Col. 3:13; Philemon).

Slavery was not even abolished in our own civilization until the nineteenth century. In any case, all Mosaic laws pertaining to slaves show a much higher level of fairness, respect, and mercy than those of the Code of Hammurabi. For example, in war, if a woman was captured as a slave and desired by an Israelite, he was to allow her a grieving period, and then he could marry her, treating her as a wife, thereafter. Also, after an Israelite's slave's years of service were ended, the slave was not released empty-handed but was given animals and possessions to take with him or her. If a slave lost an eye or tooth, by accident or mistreatment, he or she was to be set free. In fact, after six years of service all slaves were to be set free; the seventh year was considered to be their "year of release." According to Hammurabi, fugitive slaves were to be detained and returned to their masters. Failure to do this resulted in death, as did any effort to assist a fugitive slave (H16-20). In contrast, Israelites were commanded to house and feed fugitive slaves, allowing them to reside there free from oppression (Deut. 23:15, 16).

A comparison of laws regarding military service will also reveal advanced principles of righteousness. There were very distinct laws concerning conscripted soldiers. In the Hammurabic law, failure to fulfill military duties in the slightest had deadly consequences. In contrast, God desired only those who were unafraid and who were wholeheartedly committed to be in His army (Judg. 7:3; 1 Sam. 14:6):

> "Then the officers shall speak to the people, saying: 'What man *is there* who has built a new house and has not dedicated it? Let him go and return to his house, lest he die in the battle and another man dedicate it. Also what man *is there* who has planted a vineyard and has not eaten of it? Let him go and return to his house, lest he die in the battle and another man eat of it. And what man *is there* who is betrothed to a woman and has not married her? Let him go and return to his house, lest he die in the battle and another man marry her. The officers shall speak further to the people, and say, 'What man *is there who is* fearful and fainthearted? Let him go and return to his house, lest the heart of his brethren faint like his heart'" (Deut. 20:5-8).

Other distinct advances in righteousness included going the extra mile to find the owner of an animal or article that was found, rather than simply holding it until someone could prove it was theirs; fines being allotted for various crimes of theft rather than the death penalty; not charging usury (interest) for charitable loans to brethren; and instituting the "law of jealousies," outlined in Numbers 5:12-28, in place of throwing a wife suspected of adultery into the river to be proclaimed innocent or guilty through an "ordeal by water."

The many ways in which the Mosaic law portrayed higher moral ideals reveal God's desire for His people to come to a knowledge of His character and of His ways that they might be called out of darkness into His marvelous light. He wanted their transition and transformation to come out of their own personal choice, as He placed the desire in their hearts to go beyond that which they had known all of their lives as slaves in Egypt.

The SDA Bible Commentary sums it up very well:

> These civil ordinances were based upon and dealt with social customs of the day. In some points the ordinances simply reaffirm legal practices already in effect. Some of them are similar to laws of the Code of Hammurabi.... It may seem out of keeping with our concept of the character of God that He should at least tacitly approve of such things as servitude, concubinage, and seemingly harsh forms of punishment. However, it should be remembered that in bringing the Hebrew people forth from the land of Egypt God took them as they were, with the purpose of gradually making them over into what He wanted them to be—fit representatives of Himself.
>
> Though the new birth imparts to a man new ideals and divine power for attaining them, it does not bring instantaneous understanding of the fullness of

God's ideal for man. The understanding of, and the attaining to, that ideal are the work of a lifetime (see John 1:12; Gal. 3:13, 14; 2 Peter 3:18). God does not work a miracle to accomplish this in a moment of time, particularly when the habits in question are matters of general custom and practice. Were He to do so there could be no character development. For this reason God takes people as He finds them, and through the increasingly clearer revelation of His will leads them ever onward to loftier ideals. Thus, with some of the civil laws given at Sinai, God for the time being permitted certain customs to continue but erected a safeguard against their abuse. Final abandonment of the customs themselves came later. This principle of an increasingly clearer and more complete revelation of God's will was enunciated by Christ (Matt. 19:7-9; John 15:22; 16:13; Acts 17:30; 1 Tim. 1:13) (vol. 1, p. 610).

Christ Upholds the Truth

Christ was born to bear witness to the truth (John 18:38), and every word He spoke brought new light to the minds of people. The Sermon on the Mount was designed to proclaim hidden truths that radiated out the everlasting righteous principles of His kingdom. During this discourse, Christ challenges several misunderstandings of the people. Some of these misunderstandings were derived from ideologies found in the Old Testament. As with the misunderstanding of the "eye for eye" principle laid out in the Mosaic law, Christ challenged their ideas on divorce and marriage, love for enemies, and issues of oath taking, for example.

In addressing the issue of divorce, Christ was really reestablishing His intent for marriage as a symbol of the union between Himself and His church, which He had instituted at the creation of the earth, proclaiming that the two would become one. When the Pharisees asked if it was lawful to put away one's wife, Christ replied saying, "Therefore what God has joined together, let not man separate" (Matt. 19:6). He also went on to explain that although, because of the hardening of people's hearts, Moses had allowed for a certificate of divorcement, it was not God's will or directive and that in allowing for divorce one was bringing the sin of adultery upon their spouse (Matt. 5:32, 19:9; Mark 10:4). The Code of Hammurabi gave detailed instructions regarding divorce, and Moses would have, no doubt, been exposed to and influenced by these as much as by many of the other laws of Hammurabi. Jesus, however, made it clear that it was not so at the beginning of time and was still not ordained of God.

Other customs and traditions had also made their way into the practices of the Israelites that were not instituted by God and upon which Christ brought light to bear. Consider the tradition of Levirate marriage, which is outlined in Deuteronomy 25:5-10. This custom is referred to in the stories of Tamar in Genesis 38 and Ruth and Boaz in Ruth 4:5, 6. Christ's treatment of this law avoided controversy or explanations by simply stating that in the resurrection people would neither marry nor be given in marriage. He pointed to a more elevated concept that people would be as the angels, not subject to laws of the flesh or death (Matt. 22:30; Mark 12:25; Luke 20:34, 35).

It is interesting to note that both of these issues pertaining to marriage are not found in Exodus in the laws that were recited to Moses on Mount Sinai but were later noted in some of the other books containing laws. Christ made it clear that Moses had allowed for divorce. Is it not also possible that he allowed for some other laws and traditions?

> "Many of these Mosaic laws were undoubtedly old ones that had been in force for some time, all were now to be enforced with divine approval. Some provisions may have come from judicial decisions rendered by Moses in the wilderness" (*The SDA Bible Commentary*, vol. 1, p. 615).

We need to consider this with prayerful deliberation when we look at the Old Testament laws and endeavor to ascertain how they did or did not reflect the ultimate will and character of a loving, all wise God.

Even when unrighteous men tried to trap Jesus by presenting situations from which they felt He could not escape condemnation, He used these situations to reveal the heart, wisdom, and eternal purpose of His Father. Knowing full well that the Mosaic laws demanded death for adultery, they brought a woman, caught in the act, before Him to test Him before the people, seeking to entrap Him (John 8:7). In His infinite wisdom, He was able to find a response where mercy and justice kissed. He did not demand a literal *lex talionis* punishment. Instead, He brought forgiveness and redemption and a higher knowledge of righteousness to the world. Just as the enacted parable of the book of Hosea reveals God's heart toward humankind, the revelation of His grace in the treatment of the adulterous woman also revealed His heart and true method of dealing with sin and the sinner.

Christ was ever seeking to teach people, reaching them in their limited understanding and weak state. He is ever lifting people up to a standard of holiness that can only be found in His infinite touch of grace. In teaching people to pray, He said, "Your kingdom come, Your will be done, on earth as it is in heaven" (Matt. 6:10). He came as a Mediator so that He could grasp the hands of mortal human beings and connect them with the outstretched, loving hand of the heavenly Father. On our own our minds cannot even imagine all that God has prepared for us:

> "For My thoughts *are* not your thoughts, Nor *are* your ways My ways," says the LORD. "For *as* the heavens are higher than the earth, So are My ways higher than your ways, and My thoughts than your thoughts" (Isa. 55:8, 9).

We can aspire to understand and know God only because He *wants* us to know Him and sent His Son to reveal Him, that we might have eternal life (John 17:3). However, we shall only find Him if we seek Him with all our hearts. One day we will come to understand that God does not need nor want a system of human law that deals with crimes and metes out punishments. The principles of His law are to be written in the heart and will produce only the fruit of complete peace and righteousness. To this kind of heart, written laws will be a foreign concept as it was to the angels:

The will of God is expressed in the precepts of His holy law, and the principles of this law are the principles of heaven. The angels of heaven attain unto no higher knowledge than to know the will of God, and to do His will is the highest service that can engage their powers.

But in heaven, service is not rendered in the spirit of legality. When Satan rebelled against the law of Jehovah, the thought that there was a law came to the angels almost as an awakening to something unthought of. In their ministry the angels are not as servants, but as sons. There is perfect unity between them and their Creator. Obedience is to them no drudgery. Love for God makes their service a joy. So in every soul wherein Christ, the hope of glory, dwells, His words are re-echoed, "I delight to do Thy will, O My God: yea, Thy law is within My heart." Psalm 40:8 (*Thoughts from the Mount of Blessings*, p. 109).

Chapter Nineteen

The Mystery of Iniquity Satan's Masterpiece of Deception

Study/Discussion Questions:

- The Roman Church has given us a view of God as one who initially seeks to win by affection, but if the subject remains noncompliant, the time comes to change face and work by coercive measures, eventually killing. Is this the correct representation of God?

- If God does not change face toward those who reject Him, then what is the reward of the wicked? From where does it come?

- Does the Bible reveal clearly the identity of the perpetrator of all the deaths in the world as Satan or a combination of God and Satan?

- What are the implications of the French Revolution in the context of the papal misrepresentation of God's character, and what does that history teach us about the gravity of this subject?

- The papal and Protestant leaders will continue to misrepresent the character of God. This time, can we expect any different results than were seen in the French Revolution?

Reference has been made to the works of fiction as presented by the storyteller in the novel and on the movie screen as the specific media through which Satan has been educating an unwitting world in his misrepresentations of God's character and law.

But there is yet another medium through which Satan works with great effectiveness to achieve the same ends. This is the mystery of iniquity, otherwise known as Babylon; Babylon the Great; the mother of harlots; the man of sin; the son of perdition; and the antichrist. It has appeared in various forms during the ages. Its earliest champion subsequent to the flood was Nimrod and his followers, after which came the builders of the tower of Babel, the worshipers of Baal, the Assyrians, Babylonians, Greeks, Romans, and the papacy. It will come to a full manifestation in apostate Protestantism and finally in Babylon in the very last days.

Here is Satan's masterpiece of deception, the instrument through which more than any other he promulgates his lies about God.

> It is Satan's *constant* effort to *misrepresent* the character of God, the nature of sin, and the real issues at stake in the great controversy. His sophistry lessens the obligation of the divine law and gives men license to sin. At the same time he causes them to cherish *false conceptions* of God so that they regard Him with fear and hate rather than with love. The cruelty inherent in his own character is attributed to the Creator; it is embodied in systems of religion and expressed in modes of worship. Thus the minds of men are blinded, and Satan secures them as his agents to war against God. By perverted conceptions of the divine attributes, heathen nations were led to believe human sacrifices necessary to secure the favor of Deity; and horrible cruelties have been perpetrated under the various forms of idolatry.
>
> The Roman Catholic Church, uniting the forms of paganism and Christianity, and, like paganism, *misrepresenting the character of God*, has resorted to practices no less cruel and revolting (*The Great Controversy*, p. 569, emphasis added).

> Rome had misrepresented the character of God and perverted His requirements (*The Great Controversy*, p. 281).

> The teachings of popes and priests had led men to look upon the character of God, and even of Christ, as stern, gloomy, and forbidding. The Savior was represented as so far devoid of sympathy with man in his fallen state that the mediation of priests and saints must be invoked (*The Great Controversy*, p. 73).

Everyone must make a choice regarding how they view God's character. There are only two options: follow Babylon's depiction of God and His law or choose Christ as the revelation of God and His ways. It is impossible for both to represent the same thing, for one is Christ and the other is the antichrist.

It is a mistake to suppose that Babylon used only the weapons of force. So terrible and extensive was her use of the weapons of compulsion to persecute into submission those reluctant to obey her that this is all that is apt to be seen of her character and activities.

> Force is the *last* resort of every *false* religion. At first it tries attraction, as the king of Babylon tried the power of music and outward show. If these attractions, invented by men inspired by Satan, failed to make men worship the image, the hungry flames of the furnace were ready to consume them. So it will be now. The papacy has exercised her power to compel men to obey her, and she will continue to do so. We need the same spirit that was manifested by God's servants in the conflict with paganism (*Signs of the Times*, May 6, 1897, emphasis added).

The study of history shows that initially the antichrist comes without a sword. Her first ambassadors were priests and missionaries who, with humility and self-sacrifice, sought to win the populace to their theology by teaching and eloquent arguments.

If this was successful, they were elated. But if the people would not submit to their religion, then the sword was unsheathed. At first the persecutions were relatively mild, but as time went by and the desired objective was not achieved, they became increasingly severe until the death penalty was rigorously enforced.

In the sixth century Pope Gregory determined to convert Great Britain to Catholicism. Accordingly, he sent forty-one missionaries in the summer of 597. They were led by Augustine who settled on Canterbury as the center of his activities in Britain. The *true* Christian religion had preceded him. It was established among the original Britons but had not yet converted the Anglo-Saxon invaders from northern Europe and Scandinavia. To convert these Britons was the immediate objective. For this purpose Augustine convened a general assembly in 601. But "to no purpose did the archbishop lavish his arguments, prayers, censures, and miracles even; the Britons were firm" (J. H. Merle d'Aubigne, *History of the Reformation of the Sixteenth Century*, vol. 5, p. 36).

This council having failed, Augustine tried again with the same tactics of a peaceful, persuasive approach, but again he failed. Perceiving that he would gain nothing by these means, he rose to his feet and said,

> "If you will not receive brethren who bring you peace, you shall receive enemies who will bring you war. If you will not unite with us in showing the Saxons the way of life, you shall receive from them the stroke of death." Having thus spoken, the haughty archbishop withdrew, and occupied his last days in preparing the accomplishment of his ill-omened prophecy. Argument had failed: now for the sword! (*Ibid.*, p. 37).

What took place there in the early history of Britain has been repeated in every place where the papal shoe has rested. To millions, it is a familiar pattern.

Rome appears upon the scene acting peacefully and lovingly. She blesses those who will receive her blessings, seeking to win them to her creed. She manifests considerable long-suffering and patience in her work, and her emissaries make great personal sacrifices for the cause. But eventually she judges that any further endeavor along these peaceful lines will be fruitless. She then turns to the use of persecution, which increases in severity until those who will not obey under any pressure are put to death.

In all this she gives an impression of God that, tragically, is the one accepted without question by the majority. To be convinced of this, it is only necessary to compare the view of God as held by most with the papal representations of Him.

Most see God looking down upon the unconverted as Pope Gregory looked upon the Britons. In His great love for the lost and the dying, they see God sending His personal ambassador, the Holy Spirit who works through self-sacrificing human agents, to woo and win the erring. They believe that during this period the Lord withholds His judgments and administers blessings as an incentive to the people to follow Him. But time goes by and the blessings received are turned into a curse as in the case of the Sodomites, the Egyptians, and the Israelites. What now happens, in reality, is that the people move away from God into that area where they make it impossible for Him to protect them from the threatening destructions poised above them. But people see in these calamities the hand of God trying to enforce an allegiance where persuasion has failed. When even this fails, they see God destroying the wicked from the face of the earth.

Therefore, as surely as we know that Babylon's representation of the Deity is a misrepresentation, it must be wholly rejected. A moment's reflection will show that the representation of God given on the movie screen and that given by the papacy are identical. In both cases the law is broken in order to bring about the keeping of the law. The papacy kills those who will not obey. By killing, she *disobeys* God's commands in order to do away with those whom she judges are disobeying God's commands.

Therefore, she is of the world, and not of God in any sense. Every principle of her character and behavior is a denial of the revelations of the Deity mirrored in the life of Christ and espoused in His teachings. She fulfills most adequately Satan's objectives in misrepresenting the character of God.

The existence of Babylon and her teachings versus the presence of Christ and His provides for everyone the choice of which representation of God they will believe. It is impossible to consistently believe both. Babylon offers a picture of God as One who loves His enemies, blesses them, does them good, and forgives them—for a time. Then His face changes, and He arises to do to them the very things He has commanded them not to do. He first treats them cruelly; then he finally kills them.

But Christ came to show us a Father who loves His enemies, blesses them, does them good, and forgives them—forever. He never rises to do that which He has instructed His children not to do. He is the God of righteousness.

The choice then is Christ or the antichrist, God or the devil, the heavenly Jerusalem or Rome. There can be no difficulty in knowing which of these is the one to choose. Yet some will hesitate in uncertainty, even confusion.

Let such people who are struggling open the history books and examine the outworking of Rome's doctrines. Through the pages of God's Word, the Holy Spirit has shown that He has neither overlooked her real character nor been deceived by her pretentious outward appearance.

> The woman was arrayed in purple and scarlet, and adorned with gold and precious stones and pearls, having in her hand a golden cup full of abominations and the filthiness of her fornication. And on her forehead a name was written: MYSTERY, BABYLON THE GREAT, THE MOTHER OF HARLOTS AND OF THE ABOMINATIONS OF THE EARTH. I saw the woman, drunk with the blood of the saints and with the blood of the martyrs of Jesus. And when I saw her, I marveled with great amazement (Rev. 17:4-6).

And in her was found the blood of prophets and saints, and of *all who were slain on the earth* (Rev. 18:24).

The last verse in this extract is worthy of special attention for the charge is laid by God that the blood of *all* men who have died is the work of the man of sin. Satan has sought to lay this blood to God's charge. Human beings have been prepared to believe Satan at least to some extent, for while it is clear at least to most that sin and the devil have taken the lives of millions, it is also believed that God has done His share of killing too. But this verse does not subscribe to such teaching. Here it is stated that *all* the blood of *all* the dead is attributable to the man of sin. This text is a strong Bible witness to the truth that God does not destroy, for if the man of sin has killed *all* who have been killed, then the Lord has killed *none*.

Study must be devoted to the history of Rome's doctrines and the fruit of those teachings about God's character. If they have been productive of a warm, trusting love for God and one's neighbors; if they have brought peace and prosperity to the earth; if they have lifted oppression and set men free; if they have opened the doors to the advance of knowledge and skills, then we can know that they are a truthful presentation of the character of God. It must be so for God is righteousness and:

Righteousness exalts a nation, but sin is a reproach to any people (Prov. 14:34).

He who follows righteousness and mercy finds life, righteousness, and honor (Prov. 21:21).

The work of righteousness will be peace, and the effect of righteousness, quietness and assurance forever (Isa. 32:17).

If this is the record of Rome's work, then her representation of the righteousness or character of God is truthful, accurate, and to be followed. But if the results are the opposite, then it is deceitful, inaccurate, and to be shunned.

The records of history are clear. Wherever Rome has trodden, she has left behind her ignorance, immorality, strife, wars, bloodshed, murders, and hatred and total rejection of God's very existence. The fruitage of her work has been the exact opposite from that outlined in the verses above. It has not led to love and loyalty to God but to fear and hatred of Him and finally to infidel rejection of His very existence.

Rome had misrepresented the character of God and perverted His requirements, and now men rejected both the Bible and its Author. She had required a blind faith in her dogmas, under the pretended sanction of the Scriptures. In the reaction, Voltaire and his associates cast aside God's word altogether and spread everywhere the poison of infidelity. Rome had ground down the people under her iron heel; and now the masses, degraded and brutalized, in their recoil from her tyranny, cast off all restraint. Enraged at the glittering cheat to which they had so long paid homage, they rejected truth and falsehood together; and mistaking license for liberty, the slaves of vice exulted in their imagined freedom (*The Great Controversy*, pp. 281, 282).

This paragraph was written as a comment on the French Revolution with direct reference to the cause of it. It was a reaction, a striking back by the oppressed against those who had for so long held them in mental, physical, and spiritual bondage. No better revelation can be found of the effect of Rome's character and practice than this violent reaction. Everything that developed and transpired in that awful time was the direct fruitage of Catholic policies.

> It was popery that had begun the work which atheism was completing. The policy of Rome had wrought out those conditions, social, political, and religious, that were hurrying France on to ruin. Writers, in referring to the horrors of the Revolution, say that these excesses are to be charged upon the throne and the church... In strict justice they are to be charged upon the church. Popery had poisoned the minds of kings against the Reformation, as an enemy to the crown, an element of discord that would be fatal to the peace and harmony of the nation. It was the genius of Rome that by this means inspired the direst cruelty and the most galling oppression which proceeded from the throne (*The Great Controversy*, pp. 276, 277).

The revolution would never have been so cruel, bloodthirsty, and horrible, and people would never have gone so far in their total rejection and hatred of God, if they had seen the papacy as being a representative of no more than itself. But she presented herself to the world as God's direct agent and representative, and to millions she was the only picture of God that they knew. Therefore, they rejected not only the Roman Catholic Church but also the God of that church. Because they believed that the God of heaven was the God represented by that church, they rejected Him in the most tragic and hateful way.

Nothing could have pleased Satan more. With the masses he has been all too successful, yet the very devices he employs to misrepresent God, provide the spiritually enlightened with the proof that God is not as the world and the churches view Him. By tracing the results of papal teaching from its beginning to final culmination, we are equipped to discern the connection between the Babylonian philosophies about God and the sure outworking of bloodshed, tortures, mistrust, hatred, violence, atheism, immorality, and multiplied other horrors. Nobody desires these troubles to come upon themselves. Therefore, when it is understood that they result from those erroneous views of God, then they will likewise reject them, and there will be a turning toward those revelations of God that will breed love, joy, peace, gentleness, long-suffering, mercy, patience, and such.

The papal understanding is that God is a being above law. While God calls upon His people not to kill, lie, or steal, He is not bound by these things in His relation to them. The papists believe that the law is to protect God and the pope from the masses, but not the masses from them. Because the pope believes that he is God upon this earth, he acts out these principles in his dealing with people.

But people will not love and serve such a God. As surely as this concept of God's character is projected, so surely will people reject such a God. The great reaction of the French Revolution proves that. The message which burst from the hearts and throats of the populace then was that if this was God they wanted none of Him at all—forever.

It may be countered that there are millions today who believe that God mercifully entreats the people to repentance at first but uses destructive force to kill them if they will not repent, and yet, while believing this, love and serve Him. It is true that for a time this is so. Think of the centuries during which the people of the Middle Ages continued to serve God as the Romanists represented Him to be, but it could not and did not go on forever. There came a time when the reaction set in and the rejection of that kind of God was total.

Once again, the earth is moving toward another such absolute rejection of God. When that time comes, all the horrors of the French Revolution will be re-enacted, but not within the limited confines of national scale. It will be global.

In the coming and final conflict, every person on earth will be obliged to take his stand on one side or the other of the great controversy. Have you carefully, prayerfully, and honestly considered the implications of your present understanding of God's character?

If you believe that God does not concern Himself with personal lawkeeping; does as He pleases in the sense that people do as they please; and designed the law to protect Himself from the people but not the people from Him, then you are on the side of the greatest agency of all time through which Satan has misrepresented the character of God.

If you believe that God at first seeks to win by loving entreaty and merciful dealings but in the end uses force to wipe out those who do not serve Him, then your position is no different from that of the Roman Catholic Church or, in fact, from that of the mainstream Protestant theology of today.

It is commonly held by the majority of Christians, through misunderstanding of Bible language, that God seeks to win our allegiance and love through the picture of Himself as given in the life, ministry, and cross of Christ, but ultimately He will see to it that those who finally reject His invitation to life will burn in a never-ending torment of unthinkable intensity and magnitude. At best, according to the minority view, He will use His miracle-working power to burn up the impenitent in raining molten sulfur while miraculously exercising His power to sustain their lives. In this, He consigns them, by the exercise of inescapable divine force, to endure this tortuous rain of fire and swim in the molten elements until they, according to the scale of their wickedness in life, fulfill their preappointed duration of time as sentenced and finally die the second death. If any of these views reflect your position, you will be the devil's delight, for his purposes in you are being achieved.

On the other hand, if these things have never occurred to you before in quite this way, then the decision must be made sooner or later to either cling to these views or reject them in exchange for something better. If the right choice is made, then one more step will be taken out of Babylonian darkness.

"To know God is to love Him" (*The Desire of Ages*, p. 22). Such a statement can only mean that to know God as God is, is to love Him. Therefore, to know God as God is not is to hate and reject Him as is so clearly proved by the French Revolution.

To fill us with supreme joy and happiness, God unmasks Satan's lies about His righteousness and gives to all a true knowledge of His character. As this is understood and then experienced, believers will love God and their fellow human beings as they never thought possible.

May such glorious prospects be incentive enough to lead each and all to reject Satan's teachings through the papacy and the world and to accept both intellectually and in personal practice the truth of God's righteousness.

Chapter Twenty

The Mystery-unfolding Cross

Study/Discussion Questions:

- **The wrath of God fell upon Jesus at the cross. Did the Father kill the Son?**
- **What is it about the sufferings of Christ in the atoning sacrifice that reveals God's character, particularly in the subject of the final disposition of sin and impenitent sinners?**
- **What does it mean when we say that Jesus "took the sinner's place" on the cross?**

"The mystery of the cross explains all other mysteries. In the light that streams from Calvary the attributes of God which had filled us with fear and awe appear beautiful and attractive. Mercy, tenderness, and parental love are seen to blend with holiness, justice, and power. While we behold the majesty of His throne, high and lifted up, we see His character in its gracious manifestations, and comprehend, as never before, the significance of that endearing title, 'Our Father'" (*The Great Controversy*, p. 652).

It is impossible to understand the character of God as it really is until every mystery about it is taken to the light shining from Golgotha. Not even the angels could comprehend God's character and be delivered from Satan's devilish charges against the Omnipotent One until Jesus cried, "It is finished" (*The Desire of Ages,* p. 764).

Therefore, if the angels could not understand all of God's workings in the Old Testament period until they saw them in the light of the cross, then we have no possibility of grasping those mysteries in any other way.

> In order to be rightly understood and appreciated, every truth in the Word of God, from Genesis to Revelation, must be studied in the light which streams from the cross of Calvary, and in connection with the wondrous, central truth of the Saviour's atonement. Those who study the Redeemer's wonderful sacrifice grow in grace and knowledge (*The SDA Bible Commentary*, vol. 5, p. 1137).

This is quite a statement. It establishes that there is not a single Bible truth that can be rightly understood except in the light which streams from Calvary. This means, consequently, that it is impossible to know God as He is, impossible to rightly understand His character and the nature of His law, unless all this is studied with continual reference to the cross of Calvary.

In light of these things, it comes as no surprise to find that those who insist that God destroys reject the cross as having any helpful or significant bearing on the question of God's character. In all their arguments, they make no appeal to it and expressly reject any witness from it which counters their fixed ideas of God's behavior.

Such an attitude is tragic, for there is no mightier revelation of His character than the cross of Calvary. Before it all other arguments sink into insignificance and all errors are exposed for what they are.

> It was on the earth that the love of God was revealed through Christ. It is on the earth that His children are to reflect this love through blameless lives. Thus sinners will be led to the cross to behold the Lamb of God (*The Acts of the Apostles*, p. 334).

> The cross of Calvary challenges, and will finally vanquish every earthly and hellish power. In the cross all influence centers, and from it all influence goes forth. It is the great center of attraction; for on it Christ gave up His life for the human race. This sacrifice was offered for the purpose of restoring man to his original perfection. Yea, more, it was offered to give him an entire transformation of character, making him more than a conqueror.

> Those who in the strength of Christ overcome the great enemy of God and man, will occupy a position in the heavenly courts above angels who have never fallen.

> Christ declares, "I, if I be lifted up from the earth, will draw all men unto Me." ...Christ on the cross was the medium whereby mercy and truth met together, and righteousness and peace kissed each other. This is the means that is to move the world (*The SDA Bible Commentary*, vol. 5, p. 1113).

It was an awareness of and appreciation for these great truths that caused Paul to testify: "But God forbid that I should glory except in the cross of our Lord Jesus Christ, by whom the world has been crucified to me, and I to the world" (Gal. 6:14).

Therefore, he said, "For I determined not to know anything among you except Jesus Christ and Him crucified" (1 Cor. 2:2).

These words provide the fullest encouragement to proceed into the study of God's character with the assurance that when that theme is brought into the light flooding from the cross every mystery will be solved.

The particular problem before us concerns the way in which God deals with the unrepentant sinner. The emergence of sin imposed upon God the greatest test of character ever. It is true that the greater the test the greater the manifestation of the character present. Therefore, the contemplation of the way in which God deals with the sinner reveals more of the wonder of God's character than any other study could.

The cross is God's personal demonstration of the way in which He will deal with the finally impenitent. Christ took the sinner's place, and God dealt with Him exactly as He has dealt with every sinner throughout the annals of time. This is the point that must be clearly seen and accepted. God did not relate Himself to Christ any differently from what He does to the sinner. It is exactly the same. It must be, for if God should do otherwise, then Satan would be very quick to justly charge God with partiality.

Christ wholly took the sinner's place. This was so real, so complete, that it was as if He were the sinner. It was thus that God saw Him in Gethsemane and on the cross, and it was as a lost and condemned sinner that God treated Him. It was no make-believe substitution. Had it not been absolutely real all would have been lost, for if Christ's standing in the place of sinners came short in the least degree, then to that degree the ransom was not fully paid.

Christ in no way received any "preferred Son" treatment from His Father, resulting in His being punished in a different way from that of the lost and unrepentant sinner. Look to the cross of Calvary for a clear view of the way God acted there, and you will know exactly how God acts when a sinner has eternally refused the offer of repentance.

Back in the Garden of Eden, despite the warnings given them from God, Adam and Eve chose to go the way of transgression. That way incurs a punishment. God has given people life, a home, and mighty powers to enable them to live to full happiness and achievement in that home. But power with its capacity to maintain life on the best of levels also has the potential for doing away with it altogether.

To protect humanity from the latter eventuality, God gave them the law as a love gift from heaven. Obedience to it would perpetuate their eternal and perfect happiness, but disobedience would unleash all those powers in a destructive role. That destruction would in no way be the working of God's personal retaliation against the sinner. It would be the inevitable outworking of the sinner's own course of action.

When the first pair sinned, they took another god in place of the real God, making it impossible for Him to continue as the Sustainer of all the powers of nature without His forcing His presence where it was not desired. Therefore, at the very moment in which they turned out of the pathway of righteousness, there were poised and ready to strike mighty powers, which, though provided for their blessing, had been perverted to destroy. They would have died that very day as God had said, but for one contingency.

> The instant man accepted the temptations of Satan, and did the very things God had said he should not do, Christ, the Son of God, stood between the living and the dead, saying, "Let the punishment fall on Me. I will stand in man's place. He shall have another chance" (*The SDA Bible Commentary*, vol. 1, p. 1085).

The substitution of Christ in humanity's place was complete. Christ bears the same punishment and stands in the same place to receive it. To determine the nature of the sentence to fall upon humanity, study need only be given to the way Christ died. There are two ways in which it could have happened.

One is under the power of an offended God rising to vindicate His authority. The death would then be the result of God's direct act. If this is the way the sinner was to die then Christ must die in an identical fashion. God cannot administer one sentence on the sinner and a different one on Christ, for if He did, He would deny the truth that Christ took humanity's punishment and stood in their place.

The other possibility is for God to leave sinners to the fate they have chosen, once they have rejected every possible effort on God's part to save them. His death would then be the outworking of the broken law. If this is the way people are to die, then that is the way Christ died.

In short, the question is, does God kill the sinner or is it sin that destroys him or her? Whichever it was destroyed Christ when the punishment fell upon Him.

The reading of individual statements would certainly give the impression that it was God who personally administered the punishment on the sinner according to His judgment of what it should be. Here is a sample of such a statement.

> There are limits even to the forbearance of God. The boundary of His long-suffering may be reached, and then he will surely punish. And when he does take up the case of the presumptuous sinner, he will not cease till he has made a full end.
>
> Very few realize the sinfulness of sin; they flatter themselves that God is too good to punish the offender. But the cases of Miriam, Aaron, David, and many others show that it is not a safe thing to sin against God in deed, in word, or even in thought. God is a being of infinite love and compassion, but he also declares himself to be a "consuming fire, even a jealous God" (*The Review and Herald*, August 14, 1900).

Because we have been so long accustomed to interpret words such as these in the same way as we would if they were describing human behavior, we see in them the description of God as the One who, with patience exhausted, arises to personally punish those who have offended Him. But the witness of the cross does not support this interpretation.

> The death of Christ was to be the convincing, everlasting argument that the law of God is as unchangeable as His throne. The agonies of the Garden of Gethsemane, the insult, the mockery, and abuse heaped upon God's dear Son, the horrors and ignominy of the crucifixion, furnish sufficient and thrilling demonstration that God's justice, when it punishes, does the work thoroughly. The fact that His own Son, the Surety for man, was not spared, is an argument that will stand to all eternity before saint and sinner, before the universe of God, to testify that He will not excuse the transgressor of His law. Every offense against God's law, however minute, is set down in the reckoning, and when the sword of justice is taken in hand, *it will do the work for impenitent transgressors that was done to the divine Sufferer.* Justice will strike; for God's hatred of sin is intense and overwhelming (*The SDA Bible Commentary*, vol. 3, p. 1166, emphasis added).

Reference is made in this quotation to the working of God's justice. A caution again needs to be sounded that God's ways are not our ways, and therefore, God's justice and humanity's justice are not the same. More will be studied on this later.

Again, note that the *same* work, when the "sword of justice is taken in hand" by God, will be done in destroying the impenitent as was done to Christ when He died. Therefore, His death is a revelation of the work of God in the death of the wicked. By this means we can understand the Bible meaning of how God punishes the sinner.

Before we do look at the cross to see just what the Father did there, let a further statement be studied to strengthen the point made in the one just quoted, namely that the death of Christ was exactly as the death of the sinner will be.

> It is a fearful thing for the unrepentant sinner to fall into the hands of the living God. This is proved by the history of the destruction of the old world by a flood, by the record of the fire which fell from heaven and destroyed the inhabitants of Sodom (*The SDA Bible Commentary*, vol. 5, p. 1103).

This is the first part of what is to be quoted here from this statement. From what has been read thus far, the impression will be formed that God is the destroyer. When we hear a human being speak of his or her enemy in these words, "If that person should ever fall into my hands," we know that that person purposes to use all his or her powers to personally crush and destroy the other individual. So we are apt to think of God in the same terms because of our familiarity with the earthly meaning of such an expression. But as the statement continues, it gives us again the guideline of the experience of God and Christ at the cross to enable us to understand the real meaning of those words.

> But never was this [the fearful thing of falling into the hands of the living God] proved to so great an extent as in the agony of Christ, the Son of the infinite God, when He bore *the wrath of God* for a sinful world (*Ibid.*, emphasis added).

People who look first and only at what they *think they see* taking place at the flood and at Sodom and Gomorrah will arrive at an incorrect view of what it means to fall into the hands of the living God. But if they look first at the death of Christ and understand from the revelation there what it means to fall into the hands of the living God, then they will have the right view of the character and justice of God.

The revelation of this truth is strengthened as we read further in the paragraph.

> It was in consequence of sin, the transgression of God's law, that the Garden of Gethsemane has become pre-eminently the place of suffering to a sinful world. No sorrow, no agony, can measure with that which was endured by the Son of God.
>
> > Man has not been made a sin-bearer, and he will never know the horror of the curse of sin which the Saviour bore. No sorrow can bear any comparison with the sorrow of Him upon whom the wrath of God fell with overwhelming force. Human nature can endure but a limited amount of test and trial. The finite

can only endure the finite measure, and human nature succumbs; but the nature of Christ had a greater capacity for suffering; for the human existed in the divine nature, and created a capacity for suffering to endure that which resulted from the sins of a lost world. The agony which Christ endured, broadens, deepens, and gives a more extended conception of the character of sin, and *the character of the retribution* which God will bring upon those who continue in sin. The wages of sin is death, but the gift of God is eternal life through Jesus Christ to the repenting, believing sinner (*Ibid.,* emphasis added).

So Christ said, "Let the punishment fall on Me. I will stand in man's place." And this is what happened:

- The punishment fell on Christ
- The sword of justice did to Christ exactly what it would have done to sinful people and will do when the finally impenitent suffer their ultimate destruction
- Jesus received the full outpouring of the wrath of God
- Jesus fell into the hands of the living God; and thus died as people will die *if they remain in sin.*

This being so, there remains only the need to study how Jesus died on the cross to understand how God will relate Himself to the sinner; to understand what the wrath of God is; and to know what the punishment of sin consists of.

On the cross of Calvary, Christ died the death of the sinner. It was a death that met the full demands of God's law. It was God's punishment on sinners, but it was not at the hand of God that Christ died. *The Father did not slay His Son.*

It was sin that slew the Son of God. The Father simply *withdrew* from the Son and *left* Him to perish because there was nothing else He could do. Christ stood in the very position of the sinner who wants nothing of God and demands His withdrawal. With the withdrawal of the sustaining, life-protecting, life-giving power of God, there was nothing to save Christ from the awful, destructive power of sin. Its fearful weight crushed the life forces into extinction.

> But it was not the spear thrust, it was not the pain of the cross, that caused the death of Jesus. That cry, uttered "with a loud voice" (Matthew 27:50; Luke 23:46), at the moment of death, the stream of blood and water that flowed from His side, declared that *He died of a broken heart. His heart was broken by mental anguish. He was slain by the sin of the world* (*The Desire of Ages*, p. 772, emphasis added).

There can be no mistaking the way in which Christ died. Accordingly, there is no difficulty in knowing how people will die at the destructive hands of sin. At the cross, when the full penalty which Christ undertook to bear in humanity's place was exacted, Christ did not find the Father waiting for Him there as an executioner to extinguish every ray of hope and element of life. It was sin which, in that role, awaited Him.

So human beings will never find God waiting as their executioner. Satan makes it *appear* that He does, but it is not so. The cross of Calvary proves that. Sin is the destroyer that awaits the condemned sinner.

> God does not stand toward the sinner as an executioner of the sentence against transgression; but He leaves the rejecters of His mercy to themselves, to reap that which they have sown (*The Great Controversy*, p. 36).

This is that to which people are left. This is how humanity perishes.

> Those who reject the mercy so freely proffered, will yet be made to know the worth of that which they have despised. They will feel the agony which Christ endured upon the cross to purchase redemption for all who would receive it. And they will then realize what they have lost,—eternal life and the immortal inheritance (*The Review and Herald*, September 4, 1883).

Nothing can deny the truths presented by Christ on the cross. He took the punishment due to fall on humanity in the way in which it will eventually fall on sinners at the final reckoning. In this is given to us the most accurate picture of the nature of God's wrath and the punishment of human beings that could ever be given.

The finally impenitent will suffer an agony of soul, a mental stress that is incomparable to anything that any human except Christ has yet endured, for no person has yet been made to feel the full burden of sin upon their being. They will experience the full realization of the magnitude of sin and its results, which is the final and ultimate separation from the Life-giver and Sustainer, a sinking into the everlasting darkness of nonexistence, the second death.

> We read of *chains of darkness* for the transgressor of God's law. We read of *the worm that dieth not*, and of *the fire that is not quenched*. Thus is represented *the experience* of every one who has permitted himself to be grafted into the stock of Satan, who has cherished sinful attributes. When it is too late, he will see that sin is the transgression of God's law. He will *realize* that because of transgression, his soul is cut off from God, and that God's wrath abides on him. *This* is a fire unquenchable, and *by it* every unrepentant sinner will be destroyed. Satan strives constantly to lead men into sin, and he who is willing to be led, who refuses to forsake his sins, and despises forgiveness and grace, will suffer the result of his course (*The Signs of the Times*, April 14, 1898, emphasis added).

This is how it was with Christ upon the cross and how it will be with every sinner who perishes in the resurrection of the unjust. The protecting presence of God will be withdrawn, leaving the sinner exposed to all the destructive power of an evil conscience within and the unleashed forces of nature without.

God does not come to the sinner equipped with the weapons of destruction to execute His own decrees against the impenitent. This is not His way. That is the way of Satan and his followers.

157

God's way was to give human beings the law in the first instance as a protection and a savior from death. Then when people cast away that savior, He gave Himself to save them. When, in turn, they reject this means of salvation, then there is nothing further the Lord can do. He has no option but to leave them to perish.

Chapter Twenty-One

The Way of the Cross

Study/Discussion Questions:

- Why is the cross foolishness to the world?

- The religionist of modern times would point to the icons that decorate the church and deny that the cross is foolishness, but if he truly understood the cross of Christ, would he still?

- At the cross, both Satan and Christ fully manifested and demonstrated the principles of two opposing governments. The symbol of the cross is derived from the ancient mystery religion out of Babel and from that side, Satan's side, it speaks of another principle of operation. What is that principle?

The witness of the cross is not limited to proving that God does not destroy the rejectors of His mercy. To see nothing more in Calvary's testimony than this is to be handicapped with an imbalanced view of its wonderful light.

The revelations of God's character and purposes as given at the cross are infinite in their scope. They are inexhaustible and utterly limitless. Eternity will never exhaust the beauty, the power, and the wonder of God's character, and as we learn new delights of wisdom in the unfolding of that character, the more wonderful will be the joy and satisfaction that will permeate every soul.

> Our little world is the lesson book of the universe. God's wonderful purpose of grace, the mystery of redeeming love, is the theme into which "angels desire to look," and it will be their study throughout endless ages. Both the redeemed and the unfallen beings will find in the cross of Christ their science and their song (*The Desire of Ages*, pp. 19, 20).

> You may study that love for ages; yet you can never fully comprehend the length and the breadth, the depth and the height, of the love of God in giving His Son to die for the world. Eternity itself can never fully reveal it. Yet as we study the Bible and meditate upon the life of Christ and the plan of redemption, these great themes will open to our understanding more and more. And it will be ours to realize the blessing which Paul desired for the Ephesian church when he prayed "that the God of our Lord Jesus Christ, the Father of glory, may give

unto you *the Spirit of wisdom and revelation in the knowledge of Him*; the eyes of your understanding being enlightened, that ye may know what is the hope of His calling, and what *the riches of the glory* of His inheritance in the saints, and what is *the exceeding greatness of His power* to usward who believe" (*Testimonies for the Church,* vol. 5, p. 740).

The focal point of all that glory is the cross of Christ. The beholding of the glory of that revelation will change us into the same image from glory to glory as it is written: "But we all, with unveiled face, beholding as in a mirror the glory of the Lord, are being transformed into the same image from glory to glory, just as by the Spirit of the Lord" (2 Cor. 3:18).

This is the way to become like Christ. It is not by the threat of punishment or the offers of eternal riches that one is motivated to develop a fitness for heaven. It is by devoting the life to the intensive study of God's wonderful character in response to the drawing power of infinite love that one is changed into the very likeness of God.

> It is not the fear of punishment, or the hope of everlasting reward, that leads the disciples of Christ to follow Him. They behold the Saviour's matchless love, revealed throughout His pilgrimage on earth, from the manger of Bethlehem to Calvary's cross, and the sight of Him attracts, it softens and subdues the soul. Love awakens in the heart of the beholders. They hear His voice, and they follow Him (*The Desire of Ages*, p. 480).

If the full implications of this truth could be grasped as it should be there would be such an intensive study of the sacrifice of Christ as this world has never seen. Paul appreciated this so that he "determined not to know anything among you except Jesus Christ and Him crucified" (1 Cor. 2:2).

We are not sent to debate or to deliver dissertations on this and that Bible subject. We are to preach the gospel of Jesus Christ with its great central point, the cross. Paul affirmed the truth of this for himself and us in the words in 1 Corinthians 1:17, "For Christ did not send me to baptize, but to preach the gospel, not with wisdom of words, lest the cross of Christ should be made of no effect."

> When the Lord arrested Paul's mad course of destruction and set him forth as a missionary to the Gentiles, He gave him this specific commission to *preach the gospel of the cross*, but in doing so God only reiterated the gospel commission. Before He left this earth, Christ gathered His beloved followers around Him and solemnly outlined their mission to them. "Go into all the world," He instructed them, "and preach the gospel to every creature" (Mark 16:15).

For the faithful fulfillment of his commission, Paul had to know just what the preaching of the gospel really was. The master counterfeiter was as wide awake then as he is today. In this concluding era of human history, he has his spurious version of the preaching of the cross being vigorously advocated throughout the religious organizations under his control. So did he likewise in Paul's time. Enlightened by the ministry of the Spirit, the inspired apostle was well able to detect the deception while comprehending the wisdom and power resident in the true gospel of the genuine cross. Thus he was competent to present the saving cross as distinct from the false version.

Therefore, when he observed that "the message of the cross is foolishness to those who are perishing, but to us who are being saved it is the power of God" (1 Cor. 1:18), he expected it to be understood that the cross about which he was speaking was not the cross as known and held by the world but as presented in the life and death of Christ. The principles embodied in one are the direct and hostile opposite from those incorporated in the other. Never shall the two come into any kind of harmony or cooperation. Where one is upheld, the other is despised and rejected. On God's side it is the symbol of the very spirit of self-denying, self-sacrificing, self-abnegating love. It is the ultimate declaration that God will never use the limitless powers at His command to compel any to follow and serve Him. On Satan's side the cross is the revelation of the spirit of selfishness at its fully matured worst. It is the declaration that those who will not submit to the one in power will be subjected to the cruelest torture and death.

So despised was the true cross by the unbelieving world that to them it was foolishness and to the Jews a stumbling block. Neither of them saw in it any beauty, power, or attractiveness.

> For Jews request a sign, and Greeks seek after wisdom; but we preach Christ crucified, to the Jews a stumbling block and to the Greeks foolishness, but to those who are called, both Jews and Greeks, Christ the power of God and the wisdom of God. Because the foolishness of God is wiser than men, and the weakness of God is stronger than men (1 Cor. 1:22-25).

It is not to be supposed that times have changed since Paul's day. There are many who would argue that they have. The popular churches would ridicule any suggestion that to them the cross was either foolishness or a stumbling block. To support their contention, they would point to the dominant place it holds in their literature, preaching, and worship and its prolific use in the adornment of their religious houses and persons.

They would then inquire if this was not sufficient evidence to prove that, far from being foolishness to them, the cross was the very heart and life of their religion. This argument does seem to be conclusive, and it is the claim of modern evangelical Protestantism that they preach nothing but Christ and Him crucified.

But there has been no change. The true cross of Christ is just as much foolishness today as it ever was in Paul's day. The careful and thoughtful student of God's Word will come to see that the modern religionist is not worshiping the cross of Christ as he or she thinks and professes to be, but another cross altogether.

This means that there are two crosses—the cross of Christ and the Babylonian cross, usually referred to as the Christian cross. Again, the former is the revelation of God's character while the latter symbolizes the spirit that actuates the devil and his breed.

The enemy did not institute his cross when he took Christ to the hill of sacrifice. Neither the Jew nor the Greek beheld it then for the first time. That evil cross dated back to the setting up of the counterfeit kingdom shortly after the flood. There was a "mighty hunter before the Lord" whose name was Nimrod and whose brief mention in Scripture appears in Genesis 10:8-11.

The description of him as being "before the Lord" is to be understood in the sense that he placed himself before God or in the place of God for whom he had neither respect nor regard.

His life ended in a violent and untimely death, which his wife, Semiramis, and others upheld as a voluntary sacrifice on his part. It was taught that if the Babylonians would revere this noble offering they would be preserved forever. As a fitting reward, Nimrod was given deification as the sun god, and the first day of the week was set aside as his day.

Once the dead hero had been deified, then the secret mysteries of the Babylonian religion were set up. In due course, the licentious Semiramis bore an illegitimate son. Semiramis and the upholders of the secret mysteries taught that this child was the reincarnation of the dead hero. Thus Nimrod was represented as being both the father and the son while the child was also declared to be both her husband and her son. The name Tammuz was given to the child, the significance being that this had been Nimrod's name too. But, whereas a son is simply named after his father without in fact being the father himself, in this case the name was given because it was believed that the father had actually reappeared. It was not purported to be a birth in the normal sense. It was regarded as an incarnation.

It is immediately apparent that in all this the mystery of God is remarkably counterfeited. Christ was to come and die a sacrificial death, the acceptance and recognition of which would restore eternal life. He was, in His incarnation, both the Father and the Son, while the Son of Mary was, in a certain sense, also her Husband. Let it be emphasized that we say this is true in **a** *certain very special sense* as you should well understand. This unique role of being both the Father and the Son was the subject of a difficult and, for them, unanswerable question put to the Pharisees by Christ.

> While the Pharisees were gathered together, Jesus asked them, saying, "What do you think about the Christ? Whose Son is He?"
>
> They said to Him, "The Son of David."
>
> He said to them, "How then does David in the Spirit call Him 'Lord,' saying: 'The Lord said to my Lord, "Sit at My right hand, till I make Your enemies Your footstool"'? If David then calls Him 'Lord,' how is He his Son?"
>
> And no one was able to answer Him a word, nor from that day on did anyone dare question Him anymore (Matt. 22:41-46).

The incontrovertible witness of the Scriptures was that the Messiah was the Lord or spiritual father of King David, yet at the same time, the Word testified that He would be

David's son. It is the mystery of God that the same being can be both the father and the son, and it is the mystery of iniquity to pretend that it is so in a created being apart from the only One who could be such.

Tammuz then, as the supposedly reincarnated one, was exalted to the place of highest honor in the ancient mysteries and appeared under different names in various religious orders. The whole system was designed by Satan to assist him to more effectively war against God. While its structure held the appearance of being a reproduction of the divine mysteries, its every spirit and principle of operation was so far separated from, so hostile to, and so dedicated to war against the divine principles that there could be no real similarity between them. The deceptive appearance was skillfully crafted to ensnare to destruction the bodies, minds, and souls of men.

It is characteristic of every system of human devising to erect a visible symbol as a means of identification. Thus nations have their flags, armies their uniforms, organizations their badges, special groups their insignias, and so on. God, too, has His identifying signs, but they are not material things made of cloth, bronze, silver, or gold. They are spiritual in nature and cannot be discerned except with the enlightened eye.

Thus the secret mysteries needed a symbol to give them a distinguishing identification. Such a sign must center in the being who, it was believed, had come back from the dead—Tammuz. Accordingly, the first letter of his name, which in its ancient form was in the shape of a cross—"T"—became the insignia of that vast apostate and rebellious religious system. It was as fully important and sacred in that ancient system as it is in the papal orders today. Alexander Hislop has made this point very strongly in the following extract.

> In the Papal system as is well known, the sign of the cross and the image of the cross are all in all. No prayer can be said, no worship engaged in, no step almost can be taken, without the frequent use of the sign of the cross. The cross is looked upon as the grand charm, as the great refuge in every season of danger, in every hour of temptation as the infallible preservative from all the powers of darkness. The cross is adored with all the homage due only to the Most High; and for any one to call it, in the hearing of a genuine Romanist, by the Scriptural term, "the accursed tree," is a mortal offence. To say that such superstitious feeling for the sign of the cross, such worship as Rome pays to a wooden or a metal cross, ever grew out of the saying of Paul, "God forbid that I should glory, save in the cross of our Lord Jesus Christ"—that is, in the doctrine of Christ crucified—is a mere absurdity, a shallow subterfuge and pretense. The magic virtues attributed to the so-called sign of the cross, the worship bestowed on it, never came from such a source. The same sign of the cross that Rome now worships was used in the Babylonian Mysteries, was applied by Paganism to the same magic purposes, was honoured with the same honours. That which is now called the Christian cross was originally no Christian emblem at all, but was the mystic Tau of the Chaldeans and Egyptians—the true original form of the letter T—the initial of the name of Tammuz …

> The mystic Tau, as the symbol of the great divinity, was called "the sign of life"; it was used as an amulet over the heart; it was marked on the official garments of the priests, as on the official garments of the priests of Rome; it was borne by kings in their hand, as a token of their dignity or divinely-conferred authority. The Vestal virgins of Pagan Rome wore it suspended from their necklaces, as the nuns do now. The Egyptians did the same, and many of the barbarous nations with whom they had intercourse, as the Egyptian monuments bear witness …
>
> It was already in use as early as the fifteenth century before the Christian era. There is hardly a Pagan tribe where the cross has not been found (Alexander Hislop, *The Two Babylons*, pp. 197-199).

Paul's statement that the cross was foolishness to the Greek cannot be rightly understood except it be known that the cross was as much an integral and important part of Greek and Roman religion then as it is of papal and Protestant religion today. Consequently, if Paul's words had been reported to a Greek or Roman of that time, they would have ridiculed the idea as being utterly false, exactly as a modern religionist would, if it was suggested to them that the cross was foolishness. They would point to the dominant role of the cross in their religious rites and ceremonies, to its multiplied appearances in every church function and on every person and building, offering these things as evidence that the cross is anything but foolishness and that it is an object receiving the deepest reverence and continual adoration in their worship.

They (the Greeks and Romans) would have contended that Paul's assertion, not the cross, was the foolish thing.

Thus there existed the testimony of God's Word through the inspired apostle versus the counterclaim by the Greek and Roman. The former taught that the cross was foolishness to the Greek while the latter disclaimed such a charge. It must be conceded that the Greek would be entirely sincere in what he said, believing that he, and not Paul, spoke the truth.

The real fact is that both the Spirit of God and the Greek were giving an honest assessment of their thinking because they were speaking about two different crosses. The cross as Paul knew and taught it was utterly foolish to the Greek while the cross as the Greek knew it was anything but that. Nothing has changed since that day. The cross of Christ with all it stands for is still foolishness to the world, including the modern religionist, while the cross known and understood by the world is the epitome of human wisdom and ways.

In short, while the cross as Paul knew, lived, and taught it was the revelation of God's character, the other cross was the manifestation of the character of the man of sin, the son of perdition, as the Babylonians knew, lived, and taught it. Therefore, while the cross as a symbol did not appear till the days of Tammuz, that which it represents dates back to Lucifer's defection when the counter-philosophy was established.

The way of the living God is self-sacrificing, self-renouncing love. It is God's infinite wisdom that there should be a circle of love reaching out from Him to the uttermost limits of the universe and returning to Him to flow out again in a transcendent glory of joy and praise. No one is to receive merely for his own gratification and advantage. Each is to be a channel so that everything received is passed on to those around for them to administer the same blessing to still others and they to others yet beyond.

While that beautiful stream flowed in unbroken rhythm, no note of sadness or jarring discord broke the sweet harmonies of the universal kingdom. Lucifer, the covering cherub, was as happy as the rest as he faithfully fulfilled his appointed mission of service.

But the time came when his fidelity to this principle began to waver and then break down. He was the brightest and, therefore, most privileged of all the angels. He held the highest position available to a creature. He had developed the most brilliant talents, and his arrival at this pinnacle of power and glory was the result of the gifts showered upon him by his Creator combined with his own diligent effort. At first, he felt only gratitude to God for His wonderful love, his heart daily responding to the life flowing from God to him. But the passing of time eventually brought him imperceptibly to the point where he came to be increasingly aware of himself and his brilliance and less aware of the God who had given it all to him.

With marvelous perception, the Scriptures discern the cause of Lucifer's fall from his lofty elevation: "By the abundance of your trading you became filled with violence within, and you sinned" (Ezek. 28:16).

The nature of the merchandise that dethroned the beautiful one is not known to us. Earthly merchandise is salable goods from the commonest to the most valuable form. They are eagerly sought by the world, for possession of them assures freedom from want and security, comfort, and power.

Whatever form they took in heaven is not important. Merchandise meant for Lucifer the increase of personal possessions, power, and wealth. It had the same effect upon him as it has had upon earth-dwellers through all time, apart from those rare exceptions who have taken hold of the spirit of self-sacrificing love that they escape that snare.

That effect caused Lucifer to gradually transfer his faith from the Giver of all good things to the gifts provided by the Giver. He began to realize that if he retained that which came into his possession then he would accumulate so much more of these delightful things. Thus the already wealthy angel would become just that much wealthier.

All this is not so easily seen in Lucifer's life as it is in the lives of men and women. The procedure has been repeated countless times since Satan came to Eve at the forbidden tree. It is most noticeable in the history of movements that have been raised up by God to effectively demonstrate His character and thus bring about the termination of sin and its attendant horrors.

Such movements are born out of times of great spiritual apostasy. The exodus movement from Egypt lifted the people out of the deep darkness of the long Egyptian night. So it was with the return to the Promised Land after the Babylonian captivity. Later, the apostolic church emerged from the darkness of the long Jewish rejection of divine principles as did the reformation churches from the papal midnight.

The windows of heaven are opened and light, power, and material aid are directed to the movement of God. With consecrated devotion and faith, His followers throw all they have into the battle, looking to God and God alone for their guidance and support. The sense of need during this period is very great, resulting in a total absence of self-sufficiency.

As time goes by, great victories are achieved, numbers are added to the ranks, and the initial struggles are followed by a relatively quieter period. God continues to deliver His wonderful blessings to them for the purpose of their using them to reach out still further with the message of power.

But, like the Israelites of Joshua's day who did not push the battle to the utmost ends of the land but allowed pockets of rebellion to remain, so the believers do not follow the directive to go beyond Jerusalem and Samaria to the uttermost parts of the earth. Privation, self-denial, and sacrifice are not attractive to human beings who prefer rest from battle, ease, pleasure, comfort, and, above all, security. The temptation to turn aside, at least in part, from the heat of the battle is so attractive as to win little by little. More and more of God's gifts are appropriated for personal security and comfort.

As a firm base of material security is formed, the intense sense of need that previously drew them to God as the Supplier of all good things diminishes while the emphasis is placed more and more on worldly acquisitions. Eventually the whole mission of the church is lost as the accumulation of personal wealth becomes the one great objective. Such have lost faith in God. But it is important to understand that they have not lost faith. Instead they have *transferred* it from the Great Giver of all things to the gifts given by the Giver.

Increasing pride and personal satisfaction is taken in their enlarging prosperity. They view with gratification their industrious labor, their honest, faithful payment of accounts, and their scrupulous attention to their various obligations as proof that they have gained their wealth blamelessly. They feel entitled to all that they have. They consider themselves blessed of heaven, possessors of no more than their just rights. This conviction develops in them the spirit of contention for those rights, so that, if anyone should threaten to relieve them of the least part of their gains, they will resist and even counterattack to the limit of their powers.

The human tragedy is that the real nature of what they have done is hidden from them. That which they regard as being a perfectly legitimate course is in fact one of fraud and embezzlement, for they have misappropriated the goods entrusted to them to a purpose other than that designated by the Giver.

This earth is not heaven. It is a wilderness of suffering and despair created by the entry of sin. A crisis situation exists that the Father and the heavenly ministers are devoted to ending as soon as possible. But it is impossible to accomplish this without the entire cooperation of the human family. God does not leave those who accept their responsibility to do this work alone. He has made available every necessary facility. But none of this is given to humanity to make this earth into a paradise for themselves while the vast majority suffer want, disease, afflictions, and degradation. All these gifts are given for carrying forward the vast program of salvation. Some of it is needed to house, feed, and clothe the ones who are participant in the work, just as a soldier in the field must be personally sustained. Beyond what is strictly needed for this purpose, the facilities provided by the grace of God and the diligent industry of the believer are to be returned to the Lord with interest. But instead of being strictly faithful stewards, they have misappropriated into other uses that which the Lord gave for specifically designated purposes.

This is only the early stages of human defection. The Scriptures tell us that in Lucifer's case the multitude of his merchandise filled the midst of him with violence (Ezek. 28:16). Therefore, the decay is not complete until it develops into violence. This it will always do.

As individuals become obsessed with the drive to accumulate more and more material merchandise, they show less and less consideration and regard for their fellow human beings. Should others stand in the way, they will oppress them. But if they can be used to assist them in building their empire, they will not hesitate to exploit them.

While they retain a superior advantage, they will successfully rise in power and wealth by this means. Yet continually, there will be a growing resentment on the part of those being used that will eventually break out into open violence. Throughout earth's history it is possible to find examples of this as long oppressed races rise against their overlords. Rivers of blood are shed, great changes are made in the political structure of the world, and the scepter of power passes from one group to another.

The ruling elite's development of a power structure through the heavy oppression of the masses had been achieved by the Jewish hierarchy at the time of Christ's first advent. God had appointed the Jewish nation to carry the truth of His righteousness to the farthermost parts of the habitable globe. To them had been given every possible advantage and blessing as equipment for the speedy and complete execution of their calling. But they had turned from living by the law of self-renouncing service to others to gathering power and glory to themselves. They had fully transferred their faith from God to earthly possessions, and by the time Christ came, their lives manifested all the results of such a course.

Every principle of operation among them was that of Babylon which declares that you either serve the powers that be as they want you to serve them or you perish. This is the very heart and substance of Babylonian philosophy by which she seeks to justify her mass slaughter of those who dare refuse to subscribe to her philosophy. That is her religion, and her cross, dating back to Nimrod and Tammuz, is the symbol of it.

Into that darkness and sorrow Jesus came to shed forth the light of the opposite principles of self-serving and self-sacrificing love. The Pharisees and Sadducees found themselves confronted with a threat, the like of which they had never known before. The peril of losing their authority, power, wealth, and all else that they had so painstakingly and untiringly worked to achieve suddenly became terribly imminent to them.

Jesus brought an entirely different method of working. He did not seek their power and wealth as a primary or any other objective. He came to *implant* in the hearts of all people a new principle that in reality is the oldest principle of all, for it had operated throughout the limitless eternity of the past. (The Pharisees' principles had not existed till sin appeared.) That principle is the cross of Christ as distinct from the cross of Tammuz. It is the guideline for living in which "the love which 'seeketh not her own' has its source in the heart of God" (*The Desire of Ages*, p. 20).

Every word spoken by Christ taught these principles. Every act of His life was a living, practical demonstration of them. His teaching and example reached out to encircle even those who had devoted their entire lives to self-aggrandizement. For the most part, those proud and sensual minds, recognizing the call to an entire change in their attitudes and procedures, involving the surrender of that which they cherished as their rights, resisted with increasing vehemence the Savior's loving ministry.

The more earnestly Christ worked to save them the more decidedly they entrenched themselves in their way and devised every means possible to prevent Him from reaching the minds of the people. They hoped that mild measures would intimidate and turn Him from His mission, but as this did not affect the desired objective, they went on under the command and leadership of Satan, their master, until they had Him nailed to the cross.

One of the greatest possible tests that can be imposed on human nature is to call upon it to serve others at its own expense. When that expense calls for the supreme sacrifice, exacted under conditions of extreme torture and fearful mental suffering, then the test has achieved maximum intensity. "Greater love has no one than this, than to lay down one's life for his friends" (John 15:13).

This was the service that Christ came to give, thereby demonstrating the very heart of the nature of God's character. As that marvelous revelation of God is portrayed before the wondering gaze, it is to be known that thereby God through Christ has declared that He will serve even the creatures He has made, no matter what the cost to Himself. God declared before sin ever entered that this was what He would do as the outworking of His nature. When rebellion arose, then that declaration was tested to the uttermost. God in Christ demonstrated that God is true, that He is motivated by the principle of service to others no matter what the cost to Himself. If Calvary does not prove this, then it proves nothing.

Inasmuch as Satan understood that his principles could become the established way only by the dethronement of God's way, he worked relentlessly to make Christ's service as costly as possible, hoping the time would come when His humanity would protest to the point where He would proceed no further in paying the price for others.

But no matter how Satan levied upon Him cost and added cost, the Savior continued with undeviating consistency toward the moment of total sacrifice. Not only on Calvary but at every step toward that pivotal point in eternity Jesus lived out the principle of serving with no regard of the cost to Himself. Therefore, the crucifixion was nothing new to Him. It was but the ultimate confirmation of what He had been and lived eternally and would continue to live forevermore.

The revelation of God's character as the One who serves others irrespective of the cost to Himself was only one side of the picture. On the other side, Satan's continual exaction of the highest possible cost to the Son of God was revealing in him that character whereby he would gain his ends no matter how high the cost to be paid by others.

Likewise, Calvary was nothing new for Satan. It was the ultimate manifestation of his character of total selfishness. As we behold his behavior there, we are given a glimpse of the nature of his principles and their ultimate outworking. It is seen that there is no length to which he will not go, no suffering he will not cause, no price he will not exact even to taking the life of the very Being who gave him life and everything he ever had—the One who had given him only kindness, love, justice, mercy, and every other goodly thing.

Thus on Calvary's hill the cross on which the Savior hung was, in reality, two crosses. There was the Roman or Greek cross that antedated back to the initiation of satanic rebellion. It was the statement, in its most cogent expression, of Satan's principles of operation.

There Satan demonstrated to every creature in the universe what he would do to them if they did not pay the price whereby he could have the best for himself. Every person, system, and organization that has followed his leadership operates under the same principles to whatever extent they have the power to enforce their wills.

There is nothing foolish to the Greeks in this cross. They understand and accept its message. That is the only way of life they know, for to them it is the secret both of survival and access into the comforts and powers that the sinful human nature craves.

The greatest contradistinction to this cross and its message is the cross of which Paul spoke so reverently and enthusiastically. From Christ's cross we have a view to the beautiful and touching submission of Christ to the demanding cost of our salvation and the call to take up our individual cross and follow where He has led the way.

> "If anyone desires to come after Me, let him deny himself, and take up his cross, and follow Me" (Matt. 16:24).

These directives are not fulfilled by wearing a cross on a cord about the neck or by fixing it on doors, walls, or any other part of our homes. This is an invitation to abandon forever the Babylonian, Greek, Roman, and heathen principle of making the service of self foremost no matter what the cost may be to others. It is a challenge to so utterly deny self that service to the needs of others will be life's first and greatest mission no matter how costly such a work may become.

To the unsanctified mind, the mind of the Greek, this is indeed foolishness. He can see no sense in it. But he can see much sense in the sacrifice of another on his behalf. Therefore, if the cross were no more than Christ giving His all for others, then it would not be foolishness to the Greek or anyone else. But when it calls on him to follow in the same pathway, to live as Jesus lived, to serve others no matter how great the cost to himself, then that to the Greek is foolishness indeed.

There are indeed heights and depths in the cross of Christ as distinct from the cross of Tammuz, the Babylonians, the Romans, the Greeks, and the heathen, which eternity itself can never exhaust. When it is truly seen, it constitutes the finest revelation of God's character available. The Lord of glory and His righteousness will appear at their wondrous best while Satan and his unrighteousness stand forth at their very worst.

The cross proves that God does not destroy as humans do, for should He do so in order to preserve His kingdom, then He would be serving Himself and His loyal subjects at terrible cost to others. That is not the way of the cross of Christ, and it is not the way of God's character. But, while it proves this point, the cross is vastly more of a message to God's people than that, vitally important as that truth is.

Calvary challenges every individual in the universe to find and follow the way that received its most magnificent, explicit, and comprehensive exhibition on Golgotha's hill. Look again, deeper and still deeper into its splendors. When the lessons to be learned at the foot of the cross are truly comprehended and daily and more deeply refreshed, there will walk this earth a transformed people through whom at last the finishing of the sin problem can be accomplished.

Chapter Twenty-Two

God Is Not a Criminal

Study/Discussion Questions:

- **When we read the account of the contest between God and Pharaoh in the deliverance of His people, what is our understanding of God's methods?**

- **Does God's mode of dealing with the Egyptians differ from mafia strong-arm tactics? How?**

There can be no mistaking the kind of heavenly Father introduced to us by the Savior in every act and word of His ministry. It is the picture of a God filled with love and compassion, whose mercy endures forever, who does not condemn or destroy but seeks only and ever to save.

But this is not how we have viewed Him in the Old Testament. There we have seen Him as a stern God who has maintained His authority by superiority of power and knowledge. We have seen Him as One who spelled out His law *as the symbol of His authority* and called upon people to obey it so He could feel the satisfaction of being in power. Thus, even though unwittingly, we have seen Him as a self-centered God. We have failed entirely to see the provision of the law as a love gift to save us from destruction. Therefore, we have failed to see God as One in whom there is no self-centeredness.

Having seen the nature of the law in this light, it has been natural to conclude that when the plagues fell upon Egypt, the fire upon the Sodomites, the flood upon the world in Noah's time, and every other such incident, God was demonstrating that He was not to be ignored, trifled with, or disobeyed. We looked upon God as personally upholding His position and authority. We have regarded the utter destruction of lives and property as a just act on God's part to terrify the remainder into obedience and thus into personal favor with God. Most people hold this concept of God.

But it is not the view of God that Jesus held. Nor is it the picture of God that Christ presented. It was an altogether different God of whom Jesus came to speak.

What then? Are we to hold two differing views of God, one as presented in the Old Testament and the other as proclaimed by Christ? If we cannot hold any other view of God than that presented by Christ, how are we to understand God's actions in the Old Testament? The majority will object that the pictures in the Old Testament are so clear that it would be impossible to view God in any other way than the traditional light.

This is exactly where people make a mistake. There is more than one way of looking at God's actions in the Old Testament. Viewed through the colored lens of human preconceptions, *it seems* that there is only one way to view it—the obvious way. But this is not so. Furthermore, when the implications of the standard view of God as held in the past are considered, then God is characterized in the worst possible light. The time has come, therefore, to reconsider God's ways in the Old Testament. This time His actions will be studied in the light which streams from the cross of Calvary and flowed from the life and lips of Christ.

A beginning might be made almost anywhere in the Old Testament wherein are recorded numerous incidents where God appeared as an actor in the human arena. The starting point chosen will be the well-known story of Pharaoh, king of Egypt.

The mighty Pharaoh, the greatest king in the world in his day, stood in determined defiance of God's purpose to release His people from Egyptian bondage. But when a certain point of time was reached, the Lord called Moses and sent him with a message to the king. Moses commanded the Pharaoh to set the people free with the warning that should he refuse plague after plague would descend upon the hapless Egyptians. The king refused, and the plagues came until the king's power was broken and he was obliged to release the captives.

In studying this event, the average person sees God as the Almighty One whose power is limitless. Backed by that power and the right to do so by virtue of His position as Creator and Ruler of the universe, He rightly and justly orders Pharaoh to release the Israelites. But Pharaoh is defiant and is prepared to resist God's power. This, it is generally accepted, leaves God with no option but to obtain *by force* what the king will not surrender willingly. People generally do not question either God's justice or right in dealing with the monarch as they see Him doing.

The dreadful outpouring of destruction on Egypt and the king's steady resistance of this pressure until the very end is seen by most as being a contest of power between God and the king. They see it as physical power versus physical power.

In viewing this as a contest between two great powers, people see the plagues as direct instruments wielded *in the hand of God* against the Egyptians. These things were sent upon the Egyptians, it is believed, because God decided that this was the way they should be humbled. Then, having *decided* it, the Lord specifically gathered these forces and *directed* them against His enemies.

Nor is this all. Because the Lord desired to really show the nations of the world that He was not One to be trifled with, He raised up a Pharaoh who was unusually tough, defiant, powerful, and resilient. Such a king, because he would fight doggedly to the very end, provided God with the opportunity to manifest how great He was, whereas a weaker king would have given in before the Lord had the chance to demonstrate the full range of His judgmental powers.

There is no denying that when interpreted in the usually accepted way that is what the Scriptures can be understood to say. For instance, consider such verses as the following:

So the Lord said to Moses: "See, I have made you as God to Pharaoh, and Aaron your brother shall be your prophet. You shall speak all that I command you. And Aaron your brother shall tell Pharaoh to send the children of Israel out of his land. And I will harden Pharaoh's heart, and multiply My signs and My wonders in the land of Egypt. But Pharaoh will not heed you, so that I may lay My hand on Egypt and bring My armies and My people, the children of Israel, out of the land of Egypt by great judgments. And the Egyptians shall know that I am the Lord, when I stretch out My hand on Egypt and bring out the children of Israel from among them" (Exod. 7:1-5).

For the Scripture says to Pharaoh, "For this very purpose I have raised you up, that I may show My power in you, and that My name may be declared in all the earth" (Rom. 9:17; see also Exod. 9:16).

The Lord would give the Egyptians an opportunity to see how vain was the wisdom of their mighty men, how feeble the power of their gods, when opposed to the commands of Jehovah. He would punish the people of Egypt for their idolatry and silence their boasting of the blessings received from their senseless deities. God would glorify His own name, that other nations might hear of His power and tremble at His mighty acts, and that His people might be led to turn from their idolatry and render Him pure worship (*Patriarchs and Prophets*, p. 263).

Still the heart of Pharaoh grew harder. And now the Lord sent a message to him, declaring, "I will at this time send all My plagues upon thy heart, and upon thy servants, and upon thy people; that thou mayest know that there is none like Me in all the earth.... And in very deed for this cause have I raised thee up, for to show in thee My power." Not that God had given him an existence for this purpose, but His providence had overruled events to place him upon the throne at the very time appointed for Israel's deliverance. Though this haughty tyrant had by his crimes forfeited the mercy of God, yet his life had been preserved that through his stubbornness the Lord might manifest His wonders in the land of Egypt. The disposing of events is of God's providence. He could have placed upon the throne a more merciful king, who would not have dared to withstand the mighty manifestations of divine power. But in that case the Lord's purposes would not have been accomplished. His people were permitted to experience the grinding cruelty of the Egyptians, that they might not be deceived concerning the debasing influence of idolatry. In His dealing with Pharaoh, the Lord manifested His hatred of idolatry and His determination to punish cruelty and oppression (*Ibid.*, pp. 267, 268).

These are the references and statements to which people point as support for their view that God wielded the powers of force in His own almighty hands to compel Pharaoh to release the Israelites. To human minds trained for so long to think of God as doing things our way, the Scriptures provide weighty support to such arguments and views. The deeper and correct message of these writings totally escapes those whose interpretations of God's Word are guided by this concept. It is hoped that what follows will correct such sad misconceptions of our wonderful Father.

That which should alert every mind to the erroneous nature of such conclusions is the extremely bad light into which God is placed by them. Such teachings, no matter how well meaning the teacher may be or how deeply sincere their love for God is, declare that the ways of God and of criminal organizations are identical.

Note the following comparison.

The agents of a large criminal organization come to a certain businessperson from whom they wish to obtain regular payments. The services they offer are "protection."

The businessperson courageously refuses to make these "contributions" whereupon the syndicate resorts to a tried and proven method of obtaining their objective. They possess powers of force in the form of destructive weapons. These they now wield, though they do not, at first, go all the way. They begin by smashing the business's plate glass store windows and emptying the displays into the gutter.

This first blow is relatively mild, but as the owner continues to refuse, they hit harder and harder, even to the point of threatening the lives of the owner's family, until he or she is literally pounded into submission.

Here is how the Almighty is understood to have solved the Egyptian problem. God desired the release of His people. He came to Pharaoh and demanded this, but the courageous king refused to obey. In God's hands were mighty weapons of destruction, and with these, He struck the Egyptian monarch a deadly blow. He did not unleash all He could have so as to give opportunity for compliance with His demands.

When this was not forthcoming, God struck Egypt again and again, even to the slaying of the firstborn of every noncompliant family, until king and people were pounded into submission. Thus the nation did under compulsion what it would not do any other way.

Anyone who candidly thinks about the standard view of the Egyptian plagues will recognize that this is a correct analysis of how God is seen as behaving.

Immediately it is evident that this places God in the same class as the crime syndicate. It means that the methods used by the world's leading criminals to secure their ends are those used by God.

Once this realization comes, the question of how we shall relate to it arises. There should be a great awakening to the need of obtaining a reversed and corrected view of God's activities in Egypt.

But this is seldom so. Marvelous are the powers of the human mind to rationalize.

There are those who will readily admit the uncanny similarity between God's action against Egypt and the strong-arm tactics used by organized crime. But there is offered a rationale for this. "Yes, it looks very much like God uses the same methods as the extortionist. What makes the difference is God's *intention*. He does it with a good intention for the benefit of others, while the criminal does it for greedy self-gain."

In this we are asked to accept that the end justifies the means. The means used by the criminal are *unjustified* because the end is *selfish*. The same means used by God are *justified* because the end is *unselfish*.

Once this line of reasoning has become established, any crime can be justified. During the Dark Ages millions of people were martyred on the basis of this rationale. Therefore, I offer that the end can *never* justify the means. Let every child of God forever reject such a philosophy. There is no place for it in the ways, character, and government of God's church. God has never worked like this and never will.

All His ways are ways of righteousness and peace. Any belief that God and criminals use the same methods must be forever denied by the testimony of God Himself when He said, "'For My thoughts are not your thoughts, nor are your ways My ways,' says the Lord" (Isa. 55:8).

We, therefore, reject the long-held traditional view of God's behavior in Egypt because it makes God's ways conform to the ways of wicked men.

There is no issue in regard to God's *intentions* versus the *intentions* of criminals. They are different. This we accept as a fact. What this book is devoted to proving is that the *methods* of God and of men are different. It aims to develop the unshakable conviction that God's words in Isaiah 55:8, 9, mean exactly what they say. It will demonstrate that the methods used by God when dealing with those who oppose Him are totally different from humanity's ways. No resemblance between them can be found.

God is not a God of force. This is a weapon He *never* uses.

> God could have destroyed Satan and his sympathizers as easily as one can cast a pebble to the earth; but He did not do this. Rebellion was not to be overcome by force. *Compelling* power is found *only* under Satan's government. The Lord's principles are not of this order. His authority rests upon goodness, mercy, and love; and the presentation of these principles is the means to be used. God's government is moral, and truth and love are to be the prevailing power (*The Desire of Ages*, p. 759).

> The exercise of force is contrary to the principles of God's government; He desires only the service of love; and love cannot be commanded; it cannot be won by force or authority (*Ibid.*, p. 22).

> Earthly kingdoms rule by the ascendancy of physical power; but from Christ's kingdom every carnal weapon, every instrument of coercion, is banished (*The Acts of the Apostles*, p. 12).

> In the work of redemption there is no compulsion. No external force is employed. Under the influence of the Spirit of God, man is left free to choose whom he will serve. In the change that takes place when the soul surrenders to Christ, there is the highest sense of freedom (*The Desire of Ages*, p. 466).

> God does not employ compulsory measures; love is the agent which He uses to expel sin from the heart (*Thoughts from the Mount of Blessing*, p. 77).

The message of these statements is clear. The use of compelling power is found only under Satan's government. Herein lies at least one great distinction between the way of God and the ways of Satan and human beings. The only course they know by which to build their kingdoms and achieve their ends is by employing force. If God builds His kingdom by using compelling power, as so many believe, then His and humanity's ways are the same. But they are not. People rule by compulsion. God does not employ this means at all.

Therefore, the standard view of what God did in Egypt is a false one, needing to be replaced by another. The correct understanding of the role played by God must harmonize with the following principles:

- God must be seen as doing only that which Christ lived and taught.
- He must not be seen relating to this problem as sinful human beings would relate to it, e.g., by using force to solve it.
- Everything must be done in righteousness. As the law is the definition and limitation of righteousness, and as God's character is the transcript of the law, then all that God did must be within those principles. As the law says, "Thou shalt not kill," then God did not destroy or kill in the land of Egypt.
- Any teaching or view that sees God as operating other than within these limits is erroneous and must be rejected as such. It is not the teaching of Christ and is, therefore, of the devil.

The evidences argued here call for a restudy of the Egyptian incident. The long-closed case must be reopened and a new verdict obtained—one that will indeed reveal God as He is—the Lord our righteousness.

Chapter Twenty-Three

Rods and Serpents

Study/Discussion Questions:

- If, in "sending" the plagues upon Egypt, God did not either: 1) exercise His creative word to produce them by fiat, ex nihilo activity, or 2) by the application of His power, execute a direct manipulation of existing elements of nature, then how is it that He brought them upon the heads of the Egyptians?

- Of what was Moses' rod a symbol?

- Why, if God can exercise His will by force, did He leave the Israelites in such misery for all those generations of grinding servitude?

- What about Christ in the temple with the cord of whips in His hand? Was this not a demonstration of a God of force?

This chapter is devoted to the study of what really happened in Egypt. Of necessity, it will be a radical departure from the traditionally accepted concept. But it will be in harmony with the life and teachings of Christ, the principles of God's character, and God's eternal upholding of His sacred law.

By sending Moses and Aaron to enact the parable of the rods and the serpents, God detailed before Pharaoh exactly what was about to transpire. The Lord would have spelled it out in words, but the monarch's mind was so darkened by sin that it was necessary to tell it in the clearest and most dramatic way—in pictorial form.

Millions of other darkened minds since have failed to read correctly the message God sent to the king that day. It has been almost universally read as the ultimatum of an all-powerful executioner who had come to personally administer His judgments.

But "God *does not stand* toward the sinner as an executioner of the sentence against transgression; but *He leaves the rejectors* of His mercy to themselves, to reap that which they have sown" (*The Great Controversy*, p. 36, emphasis added).

Correctly read, this was the message delivered to the haughty monarch. God had ever looked with saving love upon the land of Egypt. It was not alone for the salvation of Israel that Joseph had been kidnapped to the southern kingdom. It was that Egypt might also hear the tender voice of mercy.

While God was working for their salvation, Satan masterminded a plot for their total destruction. He knew he could touch neither them nor the Israelites while they remained obedient to God. So he worked with unflagging diligence to turn the eyes of Egypt to their marvelous, God-given prosperity, diverting their attention from the God who had blessed them to the blessing received from God. As usual, he was successful. Egypt became proud, self-confident, self-serving, and oppressive. This led to their becoming taskmasters over the Israelites through whom all their blessings had come.

Thus Satan engineered a situation wherein the Israelites were not able to serve God fully except at the direct cost of their lives. The daily sacrificial system ceased, the Sabbath was hardly kept, if at all, and the people became degraded in sin.

This was just as Satan wanted it, for he knew that once he had led Egypt into the full practice of self-service and utter rejection of God they would move outside the circle of God's mercy and would be in his destructive power.

As generation after generation of Egyptians descended more deeply into the mire of abandoned iniquity, Satan saw the day drawing nearer when there would be none of God's protection left. He exulted in the increasing depravity of the Israelites, for this meant they had less and less of God's protection also.

Plotting every move with calculated care, he proposed to involve the land of Egypt in a destructive cataclysm of such proportions as to exterminate every Israelite, thus certifying that the Redeemer would never be born. If this necessitated obliterating every Egyptian as well, Satan would not hesitate.

It must be emphasized that, as the day of Egypt's doom approached, God did not wish to withdraw His protective presence from them. *They* were taking *themselves* outside it. *They* were making it impossible for God to remain.

Meanwhile, Satan was marshaling destructive forces that encircled the whole nation. The stage was set so that when the Egyptians finally dismissed God from His position as Protector the plagues would begin.

It would be well if every person on the earth were to know that all nature, from the instant Adam and Eve rejected the law as their savior, is deranged and poised to collapse into all-obliterating devastation.

The reason it has not done so is because "Christ, the Son of God, stood between the living and the dead, saying, 'Let the punishment fall on Me. I will stand in man's place. He shall have another chance'" (*The SDA Bible Commentary*, vol. 1, p. 1085).

When humanity rejected the law as their savior, God gave Himself to be the Savior. Ever since the fall in Eden Christ by His personal power has been holding under control that fearsome wrath all around us.

Should sinful, defiant, desperate human beings, during any period of history, make a total rejection of that Savior, then they dismiss Christ from His post, His restraining power is removed, and the flood of death pours upon the unprotected.

But the Egyptians neither understood nor believed this. They had advanced from one depth of wickedness to an even greater level and had come to the point of making the final dismissal of Christ from their world.

It was now that Moses and Aaron appeared with the rods. This was God's last love message to the haughty king. It was a futile attempt to explain to him the principles laid out above. The message was given in the simplest possible form—pictorially, in an acted parable.

The symbols God used were Moses, Aaron, the rods, and the serpents.

Moses was the representative and symbol of God. He portrayed before the monarch God's role in the coming time of terrible trouble. This is certified in God's own words.

> So the Lord said to Moses: "See, I have made you as God to Pharaoh, and Aaron your brother shall be your prophet" (Exod. 7:1).

Moses had not become God. By no means could this be true. He was still Moses, but he portrayed God's role to Pharaoh. He demonstrated God's behavior and appealed to the rebel to recognize and accept the petition of love being presented to him.

The rod in the hand of Aaron, who held it on Moses' behalf, was the symbol of the powers God had given to humanity for their blessing, which, because of sin, were poised to destroy, but which, because of Christ's interposition, still remained in God's hands and under His control.

> "In place of a shepherd's crook a rod of power had been given him [Moses] ..." (*Patriarchs and Prophets*, p. 396).

It is important to distinguish between the powers that God gives to human beings and the powers of God Himself. The distinction is well illustrated by this parable wherein Moses stands as a symbol of the Almighty. Allowing the rod to symbolize the powers given by God to human beings, it is not difficult to distinguish between that and the powers in Moses. The rod of power could be separated from him and pass out of his control and direction, but not so the powers within him. While he lived, they were inseparable from him.

So with God. The mighty powers given to humankind can and have passed out of His control, but the powers within Himself can never be separated from Him. This distinction must be clearly seen for the Egyptian incident to be correctly evaluated.

Finally, there was the serpent into which the rod turned. No one will have any difficulty in recognizing the serpent as a symbol of the destroyer.

Now that the symbolism has been established, we return to the story.

> So Moses and Aaron went in to Pharaoh, and they did so, just as the Lord had commanded. And Aaron cast down his rod before Pharaoh and before his servants, and it became a serpent. But Pharaoh also called the wise men and the sorcerers; so the magicians of Egypt, they also did in like manner with their enchantments. For every man threw down his rod, and they became serpents. But Aaron's rod swallowed up their rods. And Pharaoh's heart grew hard, and he did not heed them, as the Lord had said (Exod. 7:10-13).

As the brothers stood before the king, the rod was held firmly in Aaron's hand and was under his personal control. While that rod remained thus, it never became a serpent. Only when it passed out of his hands and control did it change and instantly so. As long as this situation remained, it continued to be a serpent, but the moment it returned to his hand it again became a rod. (Note that when Aaron handled the rod, he did so only on Moses' behalf and at his direction, therefore, we will refer to Moses' rod rather than to Aaron's in these pages.)

With what simple and beautiful clarity, the Lord sought to communicate to Pharaoh the vital truth that *at no time whatsoever*, while the powers of nature were still in God's hands and under His control, could they be agents of destruction. Only when out of His hands and control could they be such.

This truth is not limited to those days or to that particular situation. The Lord does not change. Ever since Adam and Eve fell until today and beyond to the final annihilation at the end of the thousand years, the truth revealed in the rods and the serpents is the same. Never while the powers of humanity and nature are in God's hands and control can they be destroyers. *That is impossible.*

This is beautifully illustrated in the experience of Elijah at Horeb. He had fled from Jezebel in fear and discouragement to take refuge in a cave.

> And there he went into a cave, and spent the night in that place; and behold, the word of the Lord came to him, and He said to him, "What are you doing here, Elijah?"
>
> So he said, "I have been very zealous for the Lord God of hosts; for the children of Israel have forsaken Your covenant, torn down Your altars, and killed Your prophets with the sword. I alone am left; and they seek to take my life."
>
> Then He said, "Go out, and stand on the mountain before the Lord." And behold, the Lord passed by, and a great and strong wind tore into the mountains and broke the rocks in pieces before the Lord, but the Lord was not in the wind; and after the wind an earthquake, but the Lord was not in the earthquake; and after the earthquake a fire, but the Lord was not in the fire; and after the fire a still small voice.
>
> So it was, when Elijah heard it, that he wrapped his face in his mantle and went out and stood in the entrance of the cave. And suddenly a voice came to him, and said, "What are you doing here, Elijah?" (1 Kings 19:9-13).

Do not miss the point. Had God been in the elements, that is, had those forces been in His hands and under His control, no storm would have been possible. There would have been only peace and blessing. This truth needs to become forever settled in the minds of every child of God.

This is the message with which God sought to convict and convert the heart of the king of Egypt. This picture showed that, despite the many decades during which Egypt had sunk into deeper iniquity, the mighty powers of nature were still under God's control and direction.

But the time had come when, unless immediate steps were taken in repentance and obedience, the powers of nature would pass out of God's hands and from His direct and complete control. Instantly, they would then become fearful scourges of destruction, even as the rod released from Aaron's hand turned into a serpent. What those powers did to Egypt while out of God's hands and control *were not God's work or responsibility*. He had exhausted every possible means to save them from coming to this point.

The king's response revealed the extent to which self-sufficiency had become his. He simply called in his magicians who threw down their rods. Satan, through witchcraft, made it appear that they were also turned into serpents.

> The magicians did not really cause their rods to become serpents; but by magic, aided by the great deceiver, they were able to produce this appearance. It was beyond the power of Satan to change the rods to living serpents. The prince of evil, though possessing all the wisdom and might of an angel fallen, has not power to create, or to give life; this is the prerogative of God alone. But all that was in Satan's power to do, he did; he produced a counterfeit. To human sight the rods were changed to serpents. Such they were believed to be by Pharaoh and his court. There was nothing in their appearance to distinguish them from the serpent produced by Moses. Though the Lord caused the real serpent to swallow up the spurious ones, yet even this was regarded by Pharaoh, not as a work of God's power, but as the result of a kind of magic superior to that of his servants (*Patriarchs and Prophets*, p. 264).

Thus the monarch displayed a terrible and dangerous ignorance of the extent and magnitude of the powers that had, to this point, been held under control by a merciful and loving God. Knowing nothing of the might of those powers, he was likewise ignorant of the strength of the God who held them in check. Therefore, he had no fear, no realization of the awful danger he was in, no sense of his need of God, and no trust in Him.

This is a revelation of self-sufficiency at its very worst. It had been developing in the king and his kingdom for a very long time until it had reached this state of maturity. Having rejected any sense of need of God, the king and his subjects were in effect, and in fact, rejecting all connection with and dependence upon Him.

Filled with an altogether false and grossly exaggerated view of his own powers, and a terribly deficient concept of the magnitude of the powers around him, the king was confident that he could easily handle anything God might release. The sight of his numerous serpents advancing against one reinforced that conviction.

It was not possible for the king to have a more misleading or dangerous self-assurance. His puny power could never withstand the onrush of the mighty forces of nature out of God's hands, direction, and control. Such ignorant and foolish thinking in the face of this loving appeal from God could only serve to separate him entirely from God and to place himself outside the circle of God's protection.

Even though the king rejected God's call, God did not abandon him to his errors but continued to seek to save him. To accomplish this, the Lord demonstrated the futility of the king's forces to contain the powers symbolized by the one serpent. Though to all appearances hopelessly outnumbered, the one serpent busily swallowed the rest. This was a message to the king, if he could only see it, that no matter how great an effort he might put forth to hold in check and redirect the forces released against him, he would be unable to do it. He and his people would be consumed while the mighty powers remained as undiminished as if they had not been touched at all.

This was the message brought to him through the rods and the serpents. It was a message of love designed to soften and save.

The king resisted the loving appeals of the Holy Spirit, who was there to bring home God's message with convicting power. By so doing, he took the final step, whereby he placed himself and his nation outside the limits of God's protection. Having cast aside God's law as his savior, he now cast aside Christ, the Savior, too.

There was no more God could do. The control of those assembled forces of destruction passed out of His hands and the plagues began. Yet, even so, God's love for Egypt and His reluctance to see the people suffer was so great that He only released His grip as far as He was compelled to. He could have taken Himself completely away and left the land to be swamped with all the plagues at once, but instead He went back only one step at a time, each move being forced upon Him by Pharaoh's increasing stubbornness.

While Israel was the primary target of Satan's wrath, the plagues did not consume them for the simple reason that, even though they were far from fully righteous, there were at least a goodly number among them who loved and served God the best they could under those circumstances. They had not cast aside either the law or Christ. Consequently, Christ, who will always protect even sinful, ungrateful people as long as possible, was able to shield the house of Israel from the successive pestilences.

Those plagues that devastated the Egyptians were the forces out of the hands and control of God. Furthermore, they were taken from His grasp, not because He had chosen to release them but because the Egyptians themselves had displaced Him from His position as their Protector.

Thus the plagues were not what God did to the Egyptians. They were altogether what they did to themselves.

So it will ever be. God never changes. He does not do one thing to the sin-cursed Egyptians and something different to rejecters of His mercy in another age. Therefore, whenever we are witness to the desolating march of plague, fire, earthquake, tempest, or pestilence across the land and are tempted to think God is at work, let us remember the message of the rods and the serpents. Then we will know the real truth of what is happening.

Why Not Before

To believe that God forcibly subdued the Egyptians in order to effect the release of His people is to level, by implication, a terrible indictment against the Lord. It is to charge Him with deliberately and callously leaving the Jews to suffer for centuries when they could have been released long before they were.

He who is in possession of omnipotent power and uses it as the means of executing his will can do what he wishes when he chooses. If this is God's way, as so many suppose, then every day that the Israelites continued in servitude, every searing lash received across the back as they made bricks in the hot sun, could be attributed directly to God's will for them simply because He chose to not yet release them. God could not be a God of love and at the same time behave in this fashion.

The truth is that God has committed Himself never to solve problems by the use of force. Therefore, the timing for the Israelites' release was determined, not by God's own personal choice, but by the effects of the Egyptians' deepening apostasy. This brought about a separation from God that released destructive powers upon them until they had destroyed their capacity to hold their slaves. Then and only then could the Israelites go free. When these principles are understood, no problem will be seen in their being left in servitude for so long.

God will not deviate from His ways, for He knows that the use of force is self-defeating. Had it been His principle to rule by force then He would have stamped rebellion out of existence as soon as it manifested itself initially. There would have been no long period of sin in this world.

But sin must be allowed to run its course until it ultimately destroys itself and all who cling to it. Then the Lord will be free to make the new heavens and the new earth with no danger of their defilement.

Christ and the Scourge

The same message that God sought to convey to the stubborn Egyptian ruler, Christ endeavored to impress upon the minds of the traders in the temple when He cleansed it for the first time.

The declaration given by Christ when He held the scourge is the exact counterpart in the New Testament of what Moses did in the Old Testament when he held the rod in his hands. The symbolism is identical.

As has already been established, the rod Moses held symbolized God's powers in nature still under His control and direction. As Moses gripped the rod, so Christ held the scourge, which likewise symbolized God's powers in nature. Just as Moses' rod could not, and did not, turn into a serpent while it remained in his hands, so the scourge could not and did not strike a single person while it was in Christ's control.

The story can be as easily misinterpreted as was the Egyptian episode. Most would argue that, while it is true that Christ did not actually strike the offenders in the temple, He most certainly threatened to and would have done so if they had resisted Him. To adopt this view is to regard the character of Christ as being identical with that of human beings, while missing the message that the Savior desired to convey.

He had come upon them while they were practicing serious iniquity. This could only serve to separate them from the protection of God so that they would be left exposed to the terribly destructive forces surrounding them. Christ desired to save them from this, so

183

He portrayed before them the situation which was developing. He wished them to understand that the usually mild and beneficent forces of nature were being transformed into a punishing scourge. That they had not yet been smitten by this whip was due alone to the fact that Christ still held it under His control and would continue to do so until the period of their probation ended.

For them, that was still several years away. During the ensuing interval of time, God's presence was progressively withdrawn from the land. Christ announced His eternal departure from the temple in the sad words, "See! Your house is left to you desolate" (Matt. 23:38). This was just before His final sufferings and death. In AD 34, probation closed on the nation as a whole in accordance with the prophecy of Daniel 9, but the retribution still tarried. Christ still held the scourge in His hands until in AD 70 He laid it down and wrath was released in the form of the unrestrained passion in the hearts of the Roman soldiery as they unleashed that rage upon the unprotected heads of the Jews.

Some may argue that Christ overturned the tables and scattered their money thereby establishing the fact, as they see it, that *He* would destroy their possessions. But, again, He was only giving them an object lesson of the real truth that all the earthly treasure in which they were putting their trust would be no support to them in the hour of trouble. Instead, it would be swept away, even as the coins were scattered in hopeless confusion across the floor.

Rightly considered, in the temple Jesus Christ did exactly what He and His Father had done in the land of Egypt. He came to both with the offer of forgiveness, protection, and life. He showed each of them the terrible consequences of their continuing in their present course, in the hope that the realization of their need would prompt them to reach out for God's solution to it.

In both of these situations, God and Christ lived out the maxim of their lives, in contrast to that of the devil who is the destroyer. Christ expressed the truth of this in these words: "The thief does not come except to steal, and to kill, and to destroy. I have come that they may have life, and that they may have it more abundantly" (John 10:10).

Christ's sorrow remains in the fact of this realization: "But you are not willing to come to Me that you may have life" (John 5:40).

Chapter Twenty-Four

The Upraised Rod

Study/Discussion Questions:

- The rod figures in the record of the enactment of many of the plagues that came upon Egypt, as it was apparently used to smite or release the elements for the purpose of destruction. How is this consistent with the lesson of the rod turning to a serpent, where we previously learned that it symbolized the release of God's protective control over the powers?

- We are invited to take up the challenge to come to the Scriptures and see the language in a consistent fashion. If, as in one example, we read that "God slew Saul" and realize by the same scriptures that he died by suicide, we have a key to interpret this "God-did-it" language. Is it therefore valid for us to go to another instance of destruction and read the same language, yet interpret it differently only because we aren't given the exact mechanism of destruction?

By using the parable of the rod and the serpent, God communicated to Egypt's proud ruler exactly how He would be acting in the coming devastations of the land. Thus He assured Pharaoh that the impending plagues would be neither by His decree nor by His administration. Their advent would be occasioned by His withdrawal from the scene, not His intrusion into it.

Before each plague began, God instructed Moses, as His direct agent and representative, to perform an act with the rod. Before the river turned to blood, Moses was directed to strike the water; before the frogs covered the land, Moses was to hold the upraised rod over the waters of Egypt, and so on, through each succeeding calamity. These actions are usually interpreted in the wrong way.

In the initial demonstration, the rod was separated from Moses' hand and control, indicating that the powers would descend on the hapless heads of the Egyptians because God no longer had command of them. But before each plague came, Moses held the rod firmly in his hands and control while he touched or indicated with it the place where the trouble would come. This made it appear that God decided just where each should strike, what its nature would be, and then personally directed the blow. Here, for instance, is the inspired description of the coming of the first plague.

So the Lord said to Moses: "Pharaoh's heart is hard; he refuses to let the people go. Go to Pharaoh in the morning, when he goes out to the water, and you shall stand by the river's bank to meet him; and the rod which was turned to a serpent you shall take in your hand. And you shall say to him, 'The Lord God of the Hebrews has sent me to you, saying, "Let My people go, that they may serve Me in the wilderness"; but indeed, until now you would not hear! Thus says the Lord: "By this you shall know that I am the Lord. Behold, I will strike the waters which are in the river with the rod that is in my hand, and they shall be turned to blood. And the fish that are in the river shall die, the river shall stink, and the Egyptians will loathe to drink the water of the river."'"

Then the Lord spoke to Moses, "Say to Aaron, 'Take your rod and stretch out your hand over the waters of Egypt, over their streams, over their rivers, over their ponds, and over all their pools of water, that they may become blood. And there shall be blood throughout all the land of Egypt, both in buckets of wood and pitchers of stone.'" And Moses and Aaron did so, just as the Lord commanded. So he lifted up the rod and struck the waters that were in the river, in the sight of Pharaoh and in the sight of his servants. And all the waters that were in the river were turned to blood. The fish that were in the river died, the river stank, and the Egyptians could not drink the water of the river. So there was blood throughout all the land of Egypt.

Then the magicians of Egypt did so with their enchantments; and Pharaoh's heart grew hard, and he did not heed them, as the Lord had said. And Pharaoh turned and went into his house. Neither was his heart moved by this. So all the Egyptians dug all around the river for water to drink, because they could not drink the water of the river. And seven days passed after the Lord had struck the river (Exod. 7:14-25).

There is a sharp contrast between the way the rod is used at this time and how it was handled in the king's court when it turned into a serpent. Whereas on the former occasion it was separated from Aaron's hand and control, here it remained firmly in his grasp, and while under his control and direction, it descended upon the water. The moment the water was smitten, it turned into blood.

Without question, God was again communicating a message to Egypt's leader; otherwise the whole drama would never have been deliberately enacted in his presence. God determined that he should be eyewitness to it. The matter is on record in the Scripture as a message to us as well. God expects that we shall rightly understand what He was doing there and why.

On the surface of it, this use of the rod seems to be contrary to the enacted parable of the rod and the serpent. Does God announce on one day what He will do and then on the next do the very opposite? That is, does He on the first day declare that only when the powers of nature pass out of His control do they become destroyers, and then on the second proceed to take those powers and use them as instruments of devastation?

Is that consistency? Is that the kind of God we serve? Most certainly not!

Therefore, when God had Moses smite the water with the rod firmly held in his hands, He was neither saying nor doing anything different that day from what He had announced the previous day.

First, let reference again be made to the earlier discussion on the Bible being its own interpreter in which it was clearly shown how such expressions as "the Lord *sent* fiery serpents," "And He [God] sent out His armies, *destroyed* those murderers, and *burned* up their city," and "He [God] *killed* him [Saul]" are to be understood.

By careful comparison of scripture with scripture, letting the Bible be its own dictionary and interpreter, it was learned that the Lord expects us to understand such pronouncements as meaning that He had been obliged to withdraw His protection and leave the sinner to his or her fate. Admittedly, this is the opposite meaning from what it would be if human beings were using those words to describe their activities. But when the Lord indicates that this is how they are to be understood, then truth can be known only if His directions are followed unerringly.

The expression "the Lord had struck the river" is another such statement and must be understood in the same way, for the Bible is consistent in its use of language. Only confusion would result if certain word combinations were to be understood to convey one idea in one place and something different in another.

We have previously given careful consideration as to how the words of *Matthew 22:7* were to be understood. This verse reads: "But when the king [God] heard about it, he [God] was furious. And he [God] sent out his armies [the Romans], destroyed those murderers [the Jews], and burned up their city [Jerusalem]."

The matching of this verse with an inspired explanation of its meaning plainly reveals how God expects it to be understood. That explanation is found in *The Great Controversy,* pages 35, 36.

> By stubborn rejection of divine love and mercy, the Jews had caused the protection of God to be withdrawn from them, and Satan was permitted to rule them according to his will. The horrible cruelties enacted in the destruction of Jerusalem are a demonstration of Satan's vindictive power over those who yield to his control.

God's own explanation of what He meant by Matthew 22:7 is opposite from what humans would expect of those words. It is made clear that the Lord was not present there but that He had been obliged to depart, leaving them in the unmerciful hands of Satan and the Romans.

Therefore, the identical phraseology found in Exodus 7:25, "the Lord had struck the river," is to be understood exactly as the Lord has shown how Matthew 22:7 is to be comprehended. These words inform us that the Lord had released His grip upon the forces around Egypt, and for this reason the Nile turned to blood.

Herein is demonstrated the importance of being established in correct principles of Bible interpretation. It is vital that the tendency to interpret these things according to our human senses be resisted and the mind be disciplined to read them according to God's directions. In this is complete safety.

Recently I had this lesson firmly impressed on my mind. I was engaged in a flight lesson. To simulate instrument conditions, a hood was placed over my head, shutting out the view of all but the instrument panel. I was instructed to hold a course due north. Soon I had the aircraft established on this heading. The compass indicated that we were flying straight forward, while other instruments showed correctly that we were climbing to an assigned altitude of three thousand feet.

But in a very compelling way, my senses told me that I was turning to the left while the compass assured me I was flying straight ahead. Every instinct called on me to deny the instrument and fly by my feelings. It required a decided act of will to resist this deadly influence and fly by the instruments. It is a lesson that has to be thoroughly learned by every pilot. Many have gone to their deaths because they did not overcome their feelings in favor of the readings on the gauges.

Likewise, it is essential that every Bible student learn to ignore their feelings and instincts and discipline their mind to accept only the methods of interpretation that the Lord has revealed as being the correct ones. It takes training to achieve this, but it can be mastered.

While God was showing the haughty ruler what He was about to do when He directed the rod and serpent demonstration, the next day, when the water was struck, He was saying something further.

It was important for the ruler's own good that he should understand the connection between the withdrawal of the presence and protection of God and the onslaught of the plague which immediately followed. Therefore, God sent Moses to use the rod to designate the exact time and place from whence God would step back. It was an impressive demonstration. There stood Aaron with the pointer in his hand. The river flowed on as usual with no indication of brooding trouble. Aaron brought the rod down to strike the surface of the waters, by so doing declaring to the king that the time had come and this was the place from whence the presence of God would be withdrawn. Horror blanched the defiant face of the royal observer as he saw the waters turn to the ghastly color of blood. Thus he was deprived of any opportunity to rationalize and claim that all this was but a happenstance that had no connection with Moses' predictions and would have happened anyway. It was love that directed the action, and it was love that the king spurned.

The succeeding plagues all came as did the first one, with God continuing to play His stipulated role. Once the first one is correctly understood, no problem should be encountered until the last one is reached. Then the question must arise as to why the last one was so selective. If God's protection had been removed from every house but those upon whose doors the blood was sprinkled, why did only the firstborn die? How did the rest escape?

God said:

> For I will pass through the land of Egypt on that night, and will strike all the
> firstborn in the land of Egypt, both man and beast; and against all the gods of

Egypt I will execute judgment: I am the Lord (Exod. 12:12).

There is no problem now with the language of this verse for we have learned how God intends us to understand these words. The problem of selectivity remains.

First, let it be established that it was not God, the Savior, but Satan, the destroyer, who took those lives.

At least three times in *Patriarchs and Prophets* the one who slew the firstborn is named. Here are the sentences.

> All who failed to heed the Lord's directions would lose their firstborn by the hand of the *destroyer.*... The sign of blood—the sign of a Savior's protection—was on their doors, and the *destroyer* entered not.... All the firstborn in the land, "from the firstborn of Pharaoh that sat on his throne unto the firstborn of the captive that was in the dungeon; and all the firstborn of cattle," had been smitten by the *destroyer* (pp. 278-280, emphasis added).

Who is the destroyer? The answer is clearly found in *Testimonies for the Church*, volume 6. It states:

> *Satan is the destroyer*. God cannot bless those who refuse to be faithful stewards. All He can do is to permit Satan to accomplish his destroying work. We see calamities of every kind and in every degree coming upon the earth, and why? *The Lord's restraining power* is not exercised. The world has disregarded the word of God. They live as though there were no God. Like the inhabitants of the Noachic world, they refuse to have any thought of God. Wickedness prevails to an alarming extent, and the earth is ripe for the harvest (pp. 388, 389, emphasis added).

Therefore it was the destroyer, Satan, who slew the firstborn. But why did he select only one in every family?

The killer found a barrier of protection around all but the firstborn, which could have been provided only by God. He would also have protected the firstborn, but for some reason, they were situated where this had become impossible. What was it then that had exposed the eldest child to the malice of the destroyer while the rest could not be touched by him?

No direct revelations in the Scriptures tell the answer, but there is information to strongly indicate what could have caused this to be so. From his earliest moment, the first child in the family was dedicated to Satan's service. Following this dedication, he was continually trained to fill the office and role of the priesthood in his own family at least. Others of them went on to fill national positions. Thus they were joined to Satan and separated from God more than any other persons in the land. As such they were definitely the ones who would be found without God's protection even when He was still able to extend it to the rest of the family, though marginally so.

Finally, those who escaped the silent death that deprived them of their firstborn plunged with blind and senseless stupidity after the Israelites as they crossed the Red Sea. Where the Israelites were, the power of God operated to withhold the tremendous forces of nature, but the rebellion and defiance of the Egyptians was so total that there was no possibility of their permitting the Holy Spirit to remain where they were. Thus they forced the powers of the waters out of the hand and control of God with only one possible result. Unmeasured tons of water rolled over them, destroying every last man.

The whole experience is a revelation, paid for at terrible cost by those idolaters, not of what God sent upon the Egyptians but of what they brought upon themselves despite God's best efforts to preserve them from it. No blame can be laid to God who emerged from the scene as impeccably perfect as ever:

> A perfect law keeper;
> Who did not break the law in order to preserve it;
> A loving and complete Savior;
> Who was not the destroyer;
> Nor the one who executed the impenitent.
> He was exactly what Christ later revealed Him to be.

Chapter Twenty-Five

The Showing of God's Power

Study/Discussion Questions:

- Why was God so anxious to give a demonstration of His power to the people of that day?

- How was the revelation of that power given?

- In what way did God place the hardened monarch upon the throne just at that time?

- Why did God wait so long before delivering His people?

- Is it God's will that despots come to rule over others?

- Does He specifically manipulate events to get men such as Pharaoh, Nero, Hitler, and Stalin into power?

Before leaving the story of the plagues in Egypt, another aspect of the case should be considered. God saw and accepted the opportunity to salvage from the disaster a saving blessing, expressed but rarely understood, in the following words:

> But indeed for this purpose I have raised you up, that I may show My power in you, and that My name may be declared in all the earth (Exod. 9:16).

> Still the heart of Pharaoh grew harder. And now the Lord sent a message to him, declaring, "I will at this time send all My plagues upon thy heart, and upon thy servants, and upon thy people; that thou mayest know that there is none like Me in all the earth.... And in very deed for this cause have I raised thee up, for to show in thee My power." Not that God had given him an existence for this purpose, but His providence had overruled events to place him upon the throne at the very time appointed for Israel's deliverance. Though this haughty tyrant had by his crimes forfeited the mercy of God, yet his life had been preserved that through his stubbornness the Lord might manifest His wonders in the land of Egypt. The disposing of events is of God's providence. He could have placed upon the throne a more merciful king, who would not have dared to withstand the mighty manifestations of divine power. But in that case the Lord's purposes would not have been accomplished. His people were permitted to experience

the grinding cruelty of the Egyptians, that they might not be deceived concerning the debasing influence of idolatry. In His dealing with Pharaoh, the Lord manifested His hatred of idolatry and His determination to punish cruelty and oppression (*Patriarchs and Prophets*, pp. 267, 268).

He [Moses] was informed that the monarch would not yield until God should visit judgments upon Egypt and bring out Israel by the signal manifestation of His power. Before the infliction of each plague, Moses was to describe its nature and effects, that the king might save himself from it if he chose. Every punishment rejected would be followed by one more severe, until his proud heart would be humbled, and he would acknowledge the Maker of heaven and earth as the true and living God. The Lord would give the Egyptians an opportunity to see how vain was the wisdom of their mighty men, how feeble the power of their gods, when opposed to the commands of Jehovah. He would punish the people of Egypt for their idolatry and silence their boasting of the blessings received from their senseless deities. God would glorify His own name, that other nations might hear of His power and tremble at His mighty acts, and that His people might be led to turn from their idolatry and render Him pure worship (*Ibid.*, p. 263).

These statements inform us that God realized a purpose in His dealing with that rebellion. It was that Egypt, Israel, and the nations beyond, were given the opportunity of seeing something of the magnitude of God's power, the corresponding futility of human resources to either control or contain what it had required God's power to withhold, and therefore, the utter necessity of human recognition of, and dependence upon, the arm of the Almighty. Implicit in all was the message that the protection of the All-powerful One was available only to the obedient.

But essential to the success of the divine plan was the presence upon the Egyptian throne of an extremely stubborn king. It was by God's providence that just such a king was there at the very time when the hour for Israel's deliverance had come. Alternatively, God could have placed upon the seat of power a more pliable ruler.

Once again, unless these words are read in the light that streams from the life and teachings of Christ in a spiritual depth exceeding the rather humanistic superficial study of the past, they will be misunderstood.

If God is obsessed, as earthly rulers generally are, with the demand that all men give unqualified acknowledgment of His position and authority as the absolute ruler of the universe, then His motivation in exhibiting His infinite power would be to instill respect, thus insuring that He be given the homage He feels is His due.

Thus His message to all nations would have been, "Take warning, people of the earth. I am making an example of the Egyptians so you will know how I treat those who do not give Me the respect I deem Mine. Dismiss any thought of resistance, for My power is such that none can contend with Me. This Pharaoh of Egypt was the greatest on earth. He was more hardened and stubborn than all of you. He dared to resist My will. See him now shattered and dead. Now serve Me, or I shall deal with you likewise. Know that I will take no insubordination nor even the ignoring of My claims upon you."

The vast majority are convinced that this is the message the Lord communicates through His activities in Egypt. But careful reflection upon the implications of this assessment of God's behavior in Egypt quickly reveals that it cannot be true. For God to conduct His affairs as outlined above would show Him to be self-centered, self-exalting, self-loving, and therefore totally unrighteous.

God is love to the infinite degree. It is impossible for Him to be love and at the same time manifest any selfish characteristics. Both views cannot be held. The two positions are entirely incompatible and, in fact, hostile to each other.

To maintain the concept that God did act from self-interest is to make Him like every Caesar, dictator, emperor, king, despot, potentate, and, in short, every unconverted individual. The further such depart from righteousness, the more acutely they exhibit this supreme concern for self, and its attendant preoccupation with demanding homage and respect from others. On the other hand, the nearer human beings approach God and become like Him in character, the more this disposition diminishes.

As we behold Christ we cannot find a character more devoid of selfishness. He gave no place for even the faintest suspicion that He had come to establish recognition of His position and authority for His own sake. Christ, as the revelation of the Father's character, swept away forever any basis for the notion that God unveiled His power in Egypt to bring the world to heel.

Therefore, He is not burdened with any concern over His position or of the giving of recognition and obedience to Him for His own sake. Thought of Himself and His position never troubles Him.

But He is actually aware of the fearful peril in which every human being on the earth stands. He knows that in the Garden of Eden humanity cast away the protection of the law and instituted, in God's place, one who could not control the powers surrounding this earth.

He knows that only because of the interposition of His Son are these perils held in control during the period of probation. He knows Christ cannot maintain His station as Protector of the people of the earth while their mounting attitude and spirit of self-sufficiency demand He vacate that role. Therefore, as a loving Father, He views with deepest distress the developing self-centeredness and foolish, self-destructive boldness that is edging His wayward children nearer and nearer to the abyss. As such a situation develops, He will do anything within the limitation of law to save them.

Humanity is unaware of how they benefit from God's power; that they are living under a divinely supplied umbrella of protection. In their folly, they leave God out of their reckoning. They do not recognize His power or how it is at work, and so they remain in ignorance of it and what it is doing for them.

Therefore, for those who had not the eye of faith and could not see God's wondrous

193

power, the revelation could only come by the power being withdrawn. Then, as storm, tempest, fire, earthquake, or pestilence ravaged them, they could see by the might of what came, the measure of the power that had previously held it all back.

This is not the way God desires His might to become known to humanity, for it exacts tremendous cost to life and land. Therefore, He labors with all the resources of heaven to prevent such a crisis from developing. But He cannot compel people to obey. They must serve Him from love—intelligently, or not at all.

> Since the service of love can alone be acceptable to God, the allegiance of His creatures must rest upon a conviction of His justice and benevolence (*The Great Controversy*, p. 498).

> He takes no pleasure in a forced allegiance, and to all He grants freedom of will, that they may render Him voluntary service (*The Great Controversy*, p. 493).

But despite the utmost entreaties of infinite love, humans such as the Egyptians will press on in defiance of love and entreaty to that point where God's power will be revealed by its withdrawal.

When God is forced to remove His hand from the helm, He still continues to work from the same love. While the loss to life and property will be enormous, He will work to salvage much from the wreckage.

First, He will endeavor to arouse individuals from the very midst of the unrepentant to an awareness of their need of that power which alone can withhold the fearful forces of nature and humanity. Likewise, He will seek to impress the same saving truths upon the thinking of the onlookers near and far to encourage them not to act with rash irresponsibility.

God will never engineer these conditions in order to convey these lessons, but when they develop in spite of His best efforts to prevent them, then He will use them to fulfill a valuable service to the needy.

This work is not done in vain. When the Israelites left Egypt, many of the people went with them. During the time of the plagues, when Moses announced the coming of the hail, a number of the farmers revealed their newly formed convictions by hurrying their livestock into shelter.

In Exodus 9:18, 19 it says, "Behold, tomorrow about this time I will cause very heavy hail to rain down, such as has not been in Egypt since its founding until now. Therefore send now and gather your livestock and all that you have in the field, for the hail shall come down on every man and every beast which is found in the field and is not brought home; and they shall die."

Here we have a wonderful example of God's saving character in action. If He had been desirous of destroying the Egyptians and their possessions by the hail, then why did He warn them of its coming and tell them to seek shelter? Not only did He try to save them from the hail but He also designated the approximate time that it would come so that no one would have to guess and be uncertain. This incident clearly shows that God did not send the hail to destroy them. It came in spite of His best efforts to prevent it, and when that failed, He did as much as He could after that to warn them that it was coming in order to save as many as were willing to be saved.

> He who feared the word of the Lord among the servants of Pharaoh made his servants and his livestock flee to the houses (Exod. 9:20).

These were not the only people helped. It was a lesson to the Israelites as well as the far away Canaanites, who would have had cause to take a pause in their headlong rush into total iniquity and its attendant destruction. Thus God achieved a saving purpose through events that He had untiringly worked to prevent.

Naturally, the more intense, prolonged, and total the destruction; the more emphatic the lesson; the more God's message was underscored. Such it could not be without the presence on the throne of a Pharaoh who was especially stubborn and rebellious. As we read in the opening statements of this chapter, the Scriptures declare that God's providence saw to it that this haughty tyrant would be upon the throne in order that God's purposes might be accomplished (see *Patriarchs and Prophets*, pp. 267, 268).

The same truth is repeated in Daniel 4:17:

> This decision is by the decree of the watchers, and the sentence by the word of the holy ones, in order that the living may know that the Most High rules in the kingdom of men, gives it to whomever He will, and sets over it the lowest of men.

These Scriptures likewise call for a careful, thoughtful, and above all, prayerful consideration, for they can be seriously misunderstood.

If, for instance, it is to be drawn from these words that God personally determines who shall occupy positions of leadership over the nations and elects those men or women irrespective of the wills of the people and their nations, then serious questions about God's character must assert themselves.

It would mean that in the great democracies when people cast their votes they are merely puppets in God's hand to execute His will. Worse still, some rulers only come to power through rigged elections, lobbying, threats, and many other unrighteous methods. Some rise to power along a path slippery with the blood of their opponents.

Does God work through such measures as these?

Furthermore, if God purposefully arranged for men like Nero or Hitler to assume absolute authority, then the reigns of terror and the awful atrocities must be charged to God. He becomes responsible for the torture of innocent victims, mass executions, and even for heaping difficulties in the way of His own church.

This is not to argue that the words of this Scripture are false. It is to argue that what, to minds trained in the human processes of thinking, would appear to be the correct interpretation is false. Once again a deeper, more spiritual and correct understanding must be gained.

Why then did God set upon the throne a very tough and hardened king when He might have put a milder person there?

The answer lies in *the way* in which God sets up a ruler as distinct from *the ways* of human beings. When people set out to make a ruler, they first determine who shall be that man or woman. Then they bring to bear every pressure of force, bribery, or persuasion at their command to effect their wishes. The greater the power at their disposal, provided it is skillfully used, the more successful they are.

God is possessed of infinite power and wisdom. Therefore, if He was to operate in the human sphere as people do with their lesser power, then only those of God's specific choice would ever occupy any positions. We would expect of God the very best choices from what is available—the selection of wise, strong, merciful, and just rulers. But the annals of history reveal very few such people ever rising to the seat of power. Instead, most rulers have been despotic, unjust, and cruel. If men like Nero, Hitler, and Pharaoh were specifically chosen by God and exalted to the position of ruler, then some serious questions must be asked in respect to God's character.

The only occasions in history when God has made direct choices of individuals are when the church has been working in harmony with Him or when there is an individual He can use who has been totally submitted to His ways and will. Examples of these people are Noah, Abraham, Moses, Joshua, Samuel, the various prophets, John the Baptist, Paul, and many others. It is noteworthy that every one of these individuals had a character like unto that of God and was very different from the kings of the earth.

The setting up of kings is all according to law, either used or misused. It is the result of the working out of all the powers God has invested in humankind, irrespective of whether those powers are rightly or wrongly, justly or unjustly used. As those powers are of God, then in this sense it is God who sets up and takes down kings.

Examine the rising of all great empires of history. As they are coming up, they are a very hardworking, self-sacrificing people. Before them is a mighty objective of conquest and acquisition to be achieved. Closely united and intensely loyal to each other and their leaders, they are strong.

God's laws provide that abstemiousness, self-sacrifice, hard work, unity, and the mighty stimulus generated by the prospect of great achievements will elevate and establish those who obey them. Therefore, those kings who obeyed these principles were certainly "set up."

As God is the One who provided these blessings by which kings are set up, then in this sense can it be said that He sets up kings and puts them down. The military campaign by which they ascend to the throne of power may be totally unjust and cruel, yet it is the outworking of these God-ordained principles that brings success, even though it is the illegitimate use of God's blessings.

Not only do God's laws set up kings but they also bring them down. The conquest achieved, the riches of the world flow into the hands of the conquerors. A life of ease, luxury, and licentiousness takes the place of industry, hardship, and self-denial.

By God's laws, the fruit of these is weakness, division, and internal strife. The weakness is not only physical and moral but it is also mental. Their wisdom is turned to corruption. Thus comes the period of decline during which a neighboring nation is on its way up. At a certain point the balance tips in favor of the rising power and the once proud lord of the earth is ground into the dust.

Thus, by the natural course of God's law, the nations rise and fall. As those laws are of God, and as He forever upholds and maintains them, it is He who in this way sets up kings and puts them down. It is not a personal election on God's part. It is the outworking of His will as expressed in that law.

These principles established, it is simple to understand how God placed upon the Egyptian throne a leader of exceptional stubbornness.

It must be remembered that the fullness of wickedness is developed in a man when the Spirit of God, through one of God's chosen messengers, has appealed mightily to him, and he has chosen to reject that loving ministry. To resist this appeal requires a decided spiritual effort, and this effort exercises and, therefore, strengthens the will to resist. Thus there is a hardening of the spiritual muscles—the heart, the conscience.

Therefore, in order for Pharaoh to be as hardened as he was, he must have been subjected to the strong wooing of the Spirit and persistently resisted it. There is evidence for this.

Moses spent forty years in the land of Egypt before fleeing to Midian. He was placed there by God to bring a powerful and saving witness to the court. He was successor to the throne, yet faithfully refusing to enter the priesthood, he stood as a pillar of light for God's truth.

> By the laws of Egypt all who occupied the throne of the Pharaohs must become members of the priestly caste; and Moses, as the heir apparent, was to be initiated into the mysteries of the national religion. This duty was committed to the priests. But while he was an ardent and untiring student, he could not be induced to participate in the worship of the gods. He was threatened with the loss of the crown, and warned that he would be disowned by the princess should he persist in his adherence to the Hebrew faith. But he was unshaken in his determination to render homage to none save the one God, the Maker of heaven and earth. He reasoned with priests and worshipers, showing the folly of their superstitious veneration of senseless objects. None could refute his arguments or change his purpose, yet for the time his firmness was tolerated on account of his high position and the favor with which he was regarded by both the king and the people (*Patriarchs and Prophets*, p. 245).

The strength of Moses was his connection with the Source of all power, the Lord God of hosts. He rises grandly above every earthly inducement, and trusts himself wholly to God. He considered that he was the Lord's. While he was connected with the official interests of the king of Egypt, he was constantly studying the laws of God's government, and thus his faith grew. That faith was of value to him. It was deeply rooted in the soil of his earliest teachings, and the culture of his life was to prepare him for the great work of delivering Israel from bondage. He meditated on these things; he was constantly listening to his commission from God. After slaying the Egyptian, he saw that he had not understood God's plan, and he fled from Egypt and became a shepherd. He was no longer planning to do a great work, but he became very humble; the mists that were beclouding his mind were expelled, and he disciplined his mind to seek after God as his refuge (*The SDA Bible Commentary*, vol. 1, pp. 1098, 1099).

When he fell from grace and fled to Midian, he vacated his prospects to another who was to be the Pharaoh when he returned with the rod of power in his hands. That other man, as the second in line to the throne, had inevitably been in close daily contact with Moses and, therefore, the beautiful circle of spiritual influence that surrounded the servant of God. Through this heavenly radiance, the Lord's designs were to soften and convert the hearts of the entire Egyptian court, including the young man who would later be the Pharaoh in Moses' place.

But that which had been sent to save was resisted and rejected. The spiritual power in Moses must have been very great, for the resistance to it developed in that other prince a *hardening* of his heart to an *exceptional* degree. No doubt the burning demon of jealousy intensified the worsening condition in the man.

The placing of Moses in the court was a masterstroke of love on God's part. Moses was God's direct and personal messenger by which God offered to Egypt complete and saving conversion. Had this taken place, Moses would have been the leader of Egypt at the death of the existing ruler. Actually, so great was the wisdom and power from God in Moses that he would have been the *effective* ruler long before the older man's death.

Placing Moses in Pharaoh's court was not an arbitrary act on God's part. It was not something that had to happen because He decreed it. God merely took advantage of the circumstances. He knew Pharaoh's daughter came down to wash, that she was lonely for a baby, and that this particular babe would touch her heart. So all He had to do was to instruct Amram and Jochebed to hide the child in the reeds and nature took care of the rest.

If placing a spirit-filled messenger in the royal court for forty years gave occasion for the development of a king so hard and stubborn, failure to place Moses there would have produced a king of far less determined defiance.

Thus God did place on Egypt's throne an exceedingly wicked king by putting Moses in the court. He could have had a much softer king by *not* putting Moses there. Herein is the principle demonstrated that the same sun that melts the wax will also harden the clay.

The light that shines upon our path, the truth that commends itself to our consciences, will condemn and destroy the soul, or sanctify and transform it (*Testimonies to the Church*, vol. 1, p. 307).

Let ministers and people remember that gospel truth ruins if it does not save. The soul that refuses to listen to the invitations of mercy from day to day can soon listen to the most urgent appeals without an emotion stirring his soul (*Testimonies to the Church*, vol. 5, 134).

Also, the principle of God giving two calls to a people but never a third as set out in Matthew 22:14 is clearly revealed in the history of that great nation.

In Joseph's day, the word of God was obeyed. Then followed the usual apostasy. This placed them in need of a call from God, which He sent to them as soon as He found His opportunity, in Moses. By life and word, during the years of his presence in the Egyptian court, Moses conveyed to those in authority the love and justice of God. But the call was rejected.

There could remain only the second call, which was again given through Moses when he returned with the rod that became a serpent. The call began when the rod was cast down and continued to be sounded as plague after plague fell. But that second call was not heeded.

Not until the second call had come and been refused, did God separate His people. The period of servitude spanned several centuries. Why did God wait so long to free His people?

He had no other choice. The constitution of His government, which is His character of love, would not allow it. First, He could not do it by force for "compelling power is found only under Satan's government" (*The Desire of Ages*, p. 759).

> "Whereunto," asked Christ, "shall we liken the kingdom of God? or with what comparison shall we compare it?" Mark 4:30. He could not employ the kingdoms of the world as a similitude. In society He found nothing with which to compare it. Earthly kingdoms rule by the ascendancy of physical power; but from Christ's kingdom every carnal weapon, every instrument of coercion, is banished (*The Acts of the Apostles*, p. 12).

Second, He will not *voluntarily* withdraw His presence to unleash the deranged forces of nature to break the hold of the oppressor.

Egypt itself would break its own power to hold the people of Israel, thus leaving God with perfect freedom to take His people out. Note how God waited till Pharaoh said, "Rise, go out from among my people, both you and the children of Israel. And go, serve the Lord as you have said" (Exod. 12:31).

The long servitude of the Israelites and God's refusal to move them out until Pharaoh released them is clear proof that God does not use force, and therefore, the commonly understood views of what God did in Egypt are erroneous.

God is bound by the principles of righteousness to act only within the limitations of the law. Therefore, He had to wait until the inevitable outworking of Egypt's wickedness brought its own harvest of self-destruction and the consequent release of Israel. This does not mean that God did nothing at all. He was ever there working to save.

It is recommended that you now reread the texts quoted at the beginning of this chapter. If the principles outlined in these pages have been grasped, they will be read in a new light altogether. A picture of God will be seen that is consistent with the life and teachings of Christ, thus establishing a perfect harmony between the Old and New Testament revelations of God.

Chapter Twenty-Six

The Flood

Study/Discussion Questions:

- **What caused the flood?**
- **Describe the pre-flood weather conditions. Was there a hydrologic cycle similar to that of today?**
- **What was the weather distribution pattern?**
- **Were there hot and cold areas of the world?**
- **In the restoration of all things, there are going to be tremendous changes to the sun and moon. What are they?**

In the Egyptian episode, the rods and serpents supply us with God's statement of how He would conduct His affairs. But a clear scientific explanation is not provided of how the water turned to blood, how each plague followed, and how the firstborn of the land died. It would be of considerable help if it were, but such information is not essential to faith.

In the report on the flood, however, it is different. God has given us sufficient evidence in various parts of the Bible to establish the scientific way in which the flood came. The study of this great cataclysm will be taken up from this angle.

When it is seen what caused the flood and how it came, powerful confirmation will be given to the truth that God does not execute the sinner nor destroy the earth. Far from actually sending the flood, God held it back as long as He could. It finally came because He could no longer prevent it without forcing His presence where it was no longer desired. There is no difference between God's behavior during the flood and the decimation of Egypt.

Conditions before the flood were radically different from what they have been since. The key to that difference lies in the state of the sun and moon, the former having been seven times as hot as it now is and the latter having been equal to our present sun. This meant that eight times today's heat and light was being beamed upon the earth before the flood.

The scriptural evidence is found in Isaiah 30:26:

> Moreover the light of the moon shall be as the light of the sun, and the light of the sun shall be sevenfold, as the light of seven days, in the day that the Lord bindeth up the breach of his people, and healeth the stroke of their wound (KJV).

This is both a prophecy of the future and a description of the past. God is telling what He will do when He will bind up "the breach of His people" and will heal "the stroke of their wound." This is restoration, the bringing back of that which was already there. If this involves increasing the sun to seven times its present intensity and the moon to equal the present sun, then this is how it was before "the *breach* of His people" and the infliction of "the *stroke* of their wound."

It will be when the Creator makes a new heavens and earth that this restoration will be achieved.

Therefore, for the moon to increase in brightness to equal that of the sun in its present state, it will have to become a self-luminous body. It will cease to be a reflector and will be "upgraded" to a little sun.

With these two orbs of fire jointly serving the new heavens and new earth, a vastly changed condition of things will prevail from what they do now. This would appear so drastic as to cause many to think that the Scripture predicting this has to be understood only figuratively. The words are to be understood literally. Of that time it is proclaimed,

> All nature, in its surpassing loveliness, will offer to God a tribute of praise and adoration. The world will be bathed in the light of heaven. The light of the moon will be as the light of the sun, and the light of the sun will be sevenfold greater than it is now. The years will move on in gladness. (*The Ministry of Healing*, p. 506; see also *The Review and Herald*, November 26, 1903).

It is logical to query whether this statement can be literally accepted on the obvious expectation that *eight times* more heat would be unendurable. What hope would anyone have if the temperature rose to 960°F (about 587°C)?

While this overheating would be unendurable if the present atmospheric conditions existed, the placement of a layer of water above the earth would solve the problem. This protective covering would absorb all but the heat necessary to produce a perfect climate on the entire surface of the earth below.

The conditions existing on this planet before God began to form it into a habitable home were reproduced during Noah's time. When the ark rode the stormy seas, the flooding was so complete that no dry land appeared. The record in Genesis 1 shows that it was the same in the beginning.

> In the beginning God created the heavens and the earth. And the earth was without form, and void; and darkness was upon the face *of the deep.* And the Spirit of God was hovering over the *face of the waters* (Gen. 1:1, 2).

Not one square inch of rock, sand, or soil penetrated the unbroken expanse of water. It was not until the third day that the dry land appeared.

> Then God said, "Let the waters under the heavens be gathered together into one place, *and let the dry land appear*"; and it was so.... So the evening and the

morning were the third day (Gen. 1:9, 13).

These verses establish that the entire earth was submerged prior to the third day. What is of great interest now are the events of the second day. Thereon God took a tremendous quantity of water and elevated it above the surface of the earth where it remained in a state of suspension. Some concept of the volume of water thus raised is given by the story of its return to earth to produce Noah's flood.

And the rain was on the earth forty days and forty nights (Gen. 7:12).

This was no localized storm. It rained over every square inch of the earth's surface for forty days and nights in an unbroken downpour the like of which has never been repeated.

We do not know how deep the flood was in the early creation days. We are told that even after the Lord had elevated an enormous amount of water, that which remained had to be gathered in one place in order, even then, for the dry land to appear. This would be achieved by reshaping the earth's surface. Some parts must be heightened, others lowered. The water would then naturally gravitate to the lower areas, thus forming seas.

This meant that a great deal of the land was higher than when the entire surface was flooded. Yet when, in Noah's day, the waters that had been placed high above the earth on the second day of creation returned to the earth, it was so vast in quantity that it flooded the world again. From these evidences it is established that an enormous volume of water was lifted into suspension on that second day.

Then God said, "Let there be a firmament in the midst of the waters, and let it divide the waters from the waters." Thus God made the firmament, and divided the waters which were under the firmament from the waters which were above the firmament; and it was so. And God called the firmament Heaven. So the evening and the morning were the second day (Gen. 1:6-8).

The marginal reading for "firmament" is expanse. The word "heaven" has several applications. There is the heaven where God dwells, the starry heavens, and finally, the atmospheric area around this earth where birds fly and clouds float. It is this last to which reference is made here.

Thus, in God's creative organization, He left some water upon the earth, but the remainder He stationed high above and completely around the world. In between there was an atmospheric heaven. How high that mantle was we do not know.

God made reference to it in His conversation with Job when He said, "Where were you when I laid the foundations of the earth?… When I made the clouds its garment, and thick darkness its swaddling band" (Job 38:4, 9).

Thus a deep, protective, insulating mantle of water vapor cocooned the earth, just as clouds partially and periodically do today. The height and thickness of this was precisely calculated by the Creator to produce the perfect climate upon earth.

Having positioned the water vapor, the Lord then commissioned the sun and moon to hold it there, as well as to give light to the earth.

> Then God said, "Let there be lights in the firmament of the heavens to divide the day from the night; and let them be for signs and seasons, and for days and years; and let them be for lights in the firmament of the heavens to give light on the earth"; and it was so. Then God made two great lights: the greater light to rule the day, and the lesser light to rule the night. He made the stars also. God set them in the firmament of the heavens to give light on the earth, and to rule over the day and over the night, and to divide the light from the darkness. And God saw that it was good. So the evening and the morning were the fourth day (Gen. 1:14-19).

The sun and moon were not established in their appointed orbits to give only light to the earth. Scripture clearly testifies that they were to "give light upon the earth," *and* "to rule over the day and over the night," *and* "to divide the light from the darkness."

The purpose of giving light to the earth is easily understood, but more study needs to be given to the meaning of the phrase "to rule over the day and over the night." To rule is to govern, to exercise a controlling influence of some nature or the other. In the light of Scripture's evidences revealing the physical conditions existing at the time of creation, something of the nature of this rulership becomes apparent.

The sun and moon shared a responsibility beyond that of lighting the earth. An enormous amount of water had been elevated above the globe where it rode in suspension to form a complete mantle. To hold it there required a considerable supply of heat, without which there would be a cooling that would result in condensation and precipitation.

The arrangement was a masterpiece of balanced technology. The amount of heat produced from the sun was calculated to keep just the correct volume of water vapor at the optimum altitude. The percentage of heat energy absorbed in this process left sufficient sunlight to filter through, providing the needed heat to warm the earth and the dwellers thereon.

But effective as the water mantle was in absorbing the greater part of the sun's energy, and thus protecting the world below from its searing blast, God's purpose for it did not end there. It served to conserve, distribute, and equalize the warmth reaching the surface.

Today, the cloud cover is never completely around the globe, but it was in the original design. This resulted in there never being a loss of the accumulated warmth near the earth's surface. There was a limit to the rise of the convection currents that obliged them to flow upward and then outward, generating breezes and gentle winds that evenly distributed the warmth from pole to pole. Thus there was a relatively uniform climate all over the planet, devoid of sweltering tropical regions and frozen polar zones. No more perfect conditions could be imagined.

In effect, the earth was located within a giant greenhouse with the temperature inside being maintained at the best possible comfort level for people, animals, and plants. With no adjacent areas of great temperature differences, there was nothing to generate storms, low- and high-pressure systems, or any form of violent weather. Instead, there was a climatic pattern of perfect stability and reliability.

The witness of fossils is of great value in the search for information about the antediluvian world. They verify incontrovertibly that there was a uniform climate over the entire planet prior to the cataclysm that produced those fossils. In the frozen north are fossil remains originating from plant and animal forms that are now found only in the temperate regions further south. As these plants and animals are only able to grow in temperate zones, it can be concluded that those which are now frozen wastes were then beautiful, verdant, temperate climes.

Perhaps the most amazing finds of all are those of the mighty mastodons, which were the elephants of that antediluvian period. These have been discovered frozen in the icy wastes of Siberia in perfect condition. The evidence shows that they were overwhelmed by a most sudden catastrophe, for in the mouths of some were **yellow buttercups** that had not been chewed but were perfectly preserved. Such vegetation does not grow in frigid regions, and its presence in the mouths of these great beasts testifies to two things. First, the climate in that part of the world which is now frozen waste was such as to support the vegetation and provide the animals with a climate in which they could live, and second, it proves that they were overwhelmed suddenly and disastrously.

The location of modern coal and oil fields also provides us with evidence of the geographical distribution of ancient forests. These are not confined only to those areas where the climate today is such as would produce mighty forests, but are also to be found in the frigid regions of the earth.

In the past few years, tremendous stores of crude oil have been discovered in the frozen wastes of northern Alaska, from where, despite the forbidding nature of the terrain and the present climate, people are determined to bring the oil out to the world. Likewise, there is a vast coalfield in Antarctica.

All these things tell their own story of what was there in the past, leaving no doubt that the overall climate of the earth was such as to produce vast forests that were not restricted to the temperate and tropical zones as we now know them.

Evidence has already been advanced to show that the moon was then a heat generator equivalent in power to our present sun. God carefully designed it to fulfill a specific and important role, which in the Scriptures is declared as being to rule the night while the sun ruled the day.

There certainly have been far-reaching changes since Adam's time, for not only has the moon been extinguished but it no longer occupies the night sky alone. At times it rides the daylight hours with the sun. Its original appointment was the night while the sun commanded the day. Each was faithful to its appointed sphere so that they never appeared at the same time.

The scientific necessity of this is readily discerned. During the day the enormous heat energy from the sun kept the canopy of water vapor in place, but as the earth turned away, there would be a cooling of this mantle to the point where flooding rains would mar each night. A lesser light was required to give just enough heat to prevent the excessive cooling of the water vapor, and yet not too much heat so as to allow some condensation to irrigate the vegetation. The moon, riding the night sky opposite the sun, provided exactly what was needed. Each night there was just sufficient cooling to produce a ground fog that bathed all the plant life with a gentle dew, thus meeting the moisture requirements for the day.

> For the Lord God had not caused it to rain on the earth, and there was no man to till the ground; but a mist went up from the earth and watered the whole face of the ground (Gen. 2:5, 6).

No more perfect system could have been devised. There were no pounding, windswept rains deluging one area at the expense of another, leaching the soil of its life-giving nutrients and eroding the land into the sea. There were no severe contrasts of climate, ranging from the blistering heat of today's tropics to the frigid cold of the polar regions. Everywhere there was a pleasant, balmy climate and atmosphere, which was delightful, invigorating, and congenial. Neither were there vast oceans as we have them today. All that water was suspended far above. The earth was almost entirely elevated land with only pleasant rivers and lakes well distributed by the perfect design of a marvelous Creator.

Any comparison between things as they then were and are now immediately shows that great changes have taken place. The sun has been reduced to one seventh of its brightness, and the moon has gone out. The great water canopy is no longer suspended as a protective veil and insulating blanket above and around the earth. The moon and the sun no longer sustain the same relationship to each other.

The climate has changed. Deserts dominate vast areas; huge, restless oceans occupy the greater part of the globe; great mountain ranges divide nations, control the weather, and create useless wastelands on their lee side; and the northern and southern caps are frozen solid. The earth is now watered by leaching rain in place of the gentle mist in Adam's garden.

When and how did all these changes take place? Were they gradual, occupying centuries or millenniums of time, or were they climactic, happening in a few days or weeks?

God has not left this as a matter of guesswork. The Scriptures plainly tell when and how it took place.

Certainly the changes did not take place to any significant degree prior to the flood. When Noah announced the coming of a deluge by a global rainstorm to last for forty days and nights, the antediluvians scoffed at the idea. It had never rained in all of human history.

> In the days of Noah a double curse was resting upon the earth in consequence of Adam's transgression and of the murder committed by Cain. Yet this had not greatly changed the face of nature. There were evident tokens of decay, but the earth was still rich and beautiful in the gifts of God's providence. The hills were crowned with majestic trees supporting the fruit-laden branches of the vine. The vast, gardenlike plains were clothed with verdure, and sweet with the fragrance

of a thousand flowers. The fruits of the earth were in great variety, and almost without limit. The trees far surpassed in size, beauty, and perfect proportion any now to be found; their wood was of fine grain and hard substance, closely resembling stone, and hardly less enduring. Gold, silver, and precious stones existed in abundance (*Patriarchs and Prophets*, p. 90).

Furthermore, the great scientific minds of that day could prove mathematically that no rain was possible because of the continued generation of heat by the sun during the day and the moon by night. They also boldly declared, as scientists do today, that the sun would continue its radiation of heat energy for millions of years yet. Like the Pharaoh who was not yet born, the people of that age had lost sight of the essential knowledge that nature is not self-acting but requires the continued presence, control, and sustenance of God.

The world before the Flood reasoned that for centuries the laws of nature had been fixed. The recurring seasons had come in their order. Heretofore rain had never fallen; the earth had been watered by a mist or dew. The rivers had never yet passed their boundaries, but had borne their waters safely to the sea. Fixed decrees had kept the waters from overflowing their banks. But these reasoners did not recognize the hand of Him who had stayed the waters, saying, "Hitherto shalt thou come, but no further." Job 38:11.

As time passed on, with no apparent change in nature, men whose hearts had at times trembled with fear, began to be reassured. They reasoned, as many reason now, that nature is above the God of nature, and that her laws are so firmly established that God Himself could not change them. Reasoning that if the message of Noah were correct, nature would be turned out of her course, they made that message, in the minds of the world, a delusion—a grand deception. They manifested their contempt for the warning of God by doing just as they had done before the warning was given. They continued their festivities and their gluttonous feasts; they ate and drank, planted and builded, laying their plans in reference to advantages they hoped to gain in the future; and they went to greater lengths in wickedness, and in defiant disregard of God's requirements, to testify that they had no fear of the Infinite One. They asserted that if there were any truth in what Noah had said, the men of renown—the wise, the prudent, the great men—would understand the matter (*Patriarchs and Prophets*, pp. 96, 97).

For the first time ever, rain fell, beginning its torrential and incessant downpour seven days after the closing of the door. Thus the change came suddenly. Up to a certain day, it had never rained. With the advent of that day, it rained, not gently and then increasingly, but in an absolute deluge.

The water literally dropped out of the sky. At the same time, mighty underground supplies burst forth out of all control.

But this change could not have occurred unless changes had first taken place in the sun and moon. There is only one way in which rain can come. Suspended water vapor must cool down to condensation point. Today this takes place when rain clouds drifting in from warmer areas either encounter a cold air front or are forced to rise to cross a mountain chain. In each case the saturated air is cooled. The water vapor turns to heavier-than-air water droplets, and rain is the result.

But there were no great mountain barriers in Noah's day, nor was it possible for traveling saturated air to encounter a cold front, for there were no polar regions to generate them.

There was only one way for the water vapor above the earth to be chilled and that was for the moon and sun to begin to wane in heat production. This they did. The moon went out altogether, and the sun faded to one seventh of its former brightness.

The first appearance of rain in Noah's day is positive proof that it was then that the extinguishing of the moon and the dimming of the sun took place. Confirmation of this is provided by both Isaiah and Peter. The evidence from Isaiah has already been quoted. Here it is again.

> Moreover the light of the moon shall be as the light of the sun, and the light of the sun shall be sevenfold, as the light of seven days, in the day that the Lord bindeth up the *breach of His people*, and healeth the *stroke of their wound* (Isaiah 30:26, KJV).

A healing is the restoring to an original condition. If, in this healing work, the sun and moon are to be brought back to what they were, then it had to be at the making of the breach and the wounding that the sun and moon suffered their reductions.

There is only one point of time when a great stroke was delivered against humankind that produced a terrible breach on human population and that was at the flood. It was not when Adam and Eve sinned, for the punishment did not fall on them at that time due to the instant interposition of Christ. So great was the stroke and the resulting breach in the human family that total extermination almost resulted.

What caused the sun and moon to lose their powers is a question yet to be determined, but the answer will come as we proceed. First, some consideration must be given to New Testament evidences that great changes took place at the flood.

Chapter Twenty-Seven

Great Changes

Study/Discussion Questions:

- There is a promise in Isaiah 60:20 that in the new earth the sun will no longer go down nor the moon withdraw. What is the physical restoration reality of nature in this, which is a reflection of the spiritual restoration reality of the character of God in humanity?

- According to Peter, the power of God's word "reserves" our present world until judgment, at which time fire will break forth. That same word reserved the old world until water broke forth. What is he talking about? How does God's word "reserve"?

- What happens when there is no more reservation?

- Why is the radiocarbon dating method inaccurate when testing pre-flood material, and how does it actually confirm the Scriptures? Hint: It has direct relation to antediluvian meteorological or atmospheric conditions.

In the Old Testament it is Isaiah who provides the information that there was a great change at the time of the flood. In the New Testament it is Peter. In fact, the latter writer is even more specific in that he names the flood as the great point of change.

> Knowing this first: that scoffers will come in the last days, walking according to their own lusts, and saying, "Where is the promise of His coming? For since the fathers fell asleep, all things continue as they were from the beginning of the creation." For this they willfully forget: that by the word of God the heavens were of old, and the earth standing out of water and in the water, by which the world that then existed perished, being flooded with water. But the heavens and the earth which are now preserved ["kept in store," KJV] by the same word, are reserved for fire until the day of judgment and perdition of ungodly men (2 Pet. 3:3-7).

In these words, Peter divides history into two periods—antediluvian and post-diluvian. In doing so he uses the expression "the world that then was" to indicate the world as it was before the flood and which was destroyed by the flood. When referring to the world after that catastrophe, he speaks of "the heavens and the earth which are now."

He does not speak only of the earth that is now as being different from what it was before. He also includes the heavens in the change. The heavens, which changed at the time of the flood, were those governed by the sun and the moon of this solar system.

Before the flood the sun was seven times brighter and the moon was as bright as the sun. The sun ruled the day and the moon the night. There was a wonderful mantle of protective vapor around the earth, and the climate from pole to pole was of pleasant, even temperatures. It never rained, but a gentle mist rose each morning to water the earth. Storms, tidal waves, earthquakes, blizzards, hurricanes, and hailstorms were completely unknown. That was the heavens and the earth that were before the flood.

But how different are the heavens and the earth that are now. The sun is dimmed to one seventh. The moon has gone out. The mantle of protection is not there. Wide diversity of climate covers the earth. Fierce storms, terrible earthquakes, destructive blizzards, pulverizing hailstorms, and a thousand other scourges blast the earth.

These are the great changes of which the scientists of today are ignorant, and willfully so. It is not that they do not believe in the flood, for many of them do, but the deluge is seen as if it were no more than the same disasters that occur today, but on a greater scale. They fail to acknowledge the real changes that took place back then.

We see from a more thorough and careful study of the Scriptures that the changes were much more far-reaching than that. It is needful that their full extent be understood, together with the causes, namely, the dimming of the sun and the extinguishing of the moon.

When Noah emerged from the ark, God made a special promise and prophecy to him that there would never be a flood upon the earth again. That promise is repeated again in Isaiah.

> Your sun shall no longer go down, nor shall your moon withdraw itself; for the Lord will be your everlasting light, and the days of your mourning shall be ended (Isaiah 60:20).

In what sense are these words to be understood? Usually we refer to the sun as "going down" when it appears to sink below the western horizon, but this is an erroneous expression, for the sun does not go down in relation to the earth. It only appears to. The disappearance of this heavenly body over the horizon is caused by the rotation of the earth on its own axis so that, as the earth turns, we are the ones who "go down," not the sun.

Because of its scientific inaccuracy, this understanding of the expression "go down," as used in the scripture under consideration, must be highly suspect. That it is not the correct interpretation is made evident by certain facts revealed in the Word of God.

The first creation was perfect, and the second will be a reproduction of it. There can be no differences between the second and the first because perfection cannot be improved, any modification being an admission that the first was imperfect and thus required improvement. In the first creation there was day and night occasioned by what we term the "going down" of the sun. If the promise of Isaiah 60:20 provided that the sun would never set in the western sky, then there would be no day and night as in the original, perfect creation. In fact, only one side of the earth would ever see the sun while the other would see only the moon, so it is easily seen that this is not the meaning of Isaiah 60:20.

Some may point to the reference in Revelation 22:5, "There shall be no night there: They need no lamp nor light of the sun, for the Lord God gives them light. And they shall reign for ever and ever," and claim this teaches that there will not even be a sun in the new earth, for it will not be needed.

However, most will recognize that this Scripture is not describing conditions in the new earth generally but as they will be in the New Jerusalem (see Revelation 21:23). Even then it does not say there will be no sun but only that there will be *no need* of it for there will be the greater light streaming from the presence of God. So far as the rest of the earth is concerned, it will have, as promised in Isaiah 30:26, a blazing sun and a brilliant moon. The earth will still rotate on its axis, and each evening the sun will *appear* to "go down" behind the western horizon as it does today.

Furthermore, why should the Lord make a special promise that the sun would never go down again behind the western horizon each evening when such an event was no trouble or problem? It is a perfectly normal and desirable occurrence, introducing the blessings of night. Therefore, if this is all the Lord was offering in that scripture, it could hardly be regarded as a precious promise.

The promise is made in respect to new earth dwellers who will again be enjoying perfect climatic conditions under the protective and insulating canopy supported by the sun and the moon as they will then be. They will know what happened when the sun went down in intensity and the moon withdrew itself in the days of Noah. The Hebrew words for "go down" in Isaiah 60:20 are transliterated as *"bo shaw-KHAW,"* (references 935 and 7812 in the Hebrew and Chaldee Dictionary as found in *Abingdon's Strong's Exhaustive Concordance of the Bible*, pp. 19 and 114). The proper sense of these two words in this context would be "depart," "be fallen," and "depress," "to fall down flat." This is what happened to the sun and is the sense in which the redeemed will understand the Hebrew text. To them, the promise that this will not happen again is a very valuable and precious one, for by this means they are assured that never again will their beautiful home be flooded to destruction.

It is the utter failure by modern scientists to understand the full extent of these changes that has led them into erroneous conclusions in all matters of carbon dating beyond existing historical records. While the earth is, in fact, close to six thousand years of age, they date it in the hundreds of millions of years.

Great excitement was experienced during the 1940s when the radiocarbon method of dating was developed. Careful testing of the procedure with materials of known age proved its accuracy. Thereupon, the dating of materials of otherwise undetermined age was undertaken and, to the delight of the scientists, the readout agreed with established postulations of the age of the earth and life upon it. Whereas the biblical record allows for only about six thousand years, they confirmed figures running into millions.

At the time, faithful Bible students were perplexed to some extent by this, for the evolutionists felt that they had a sure upper hand in the everlasting debate on the age of the earth. There seemed a real possibility that the Bible, after all, could be proved to be in error. Those of us, however, who understood, even back there, the full extent of the changes that took place at the flood recognized immediately the defect in their calibrations. The relaying of this information to the perplexed among God's children quickly set their minds at rest.

There is a continual bombardment of this earth by cosmic rays from outer space. These rays, interacting with the nitrogen in the atmosphere, cause all living organisms to absorb radiocarbon 14. This continues until the death of the living thing, be it plant, animal, or human. Thereafter, the radiocarbon 14 breaks down at an accurately known rate. To determine how long since death took place, the residual radiocarbon in the specimen is measured. If half the original activity remains, then it is known that the age of the subject is very close to 5,568 years.

As mentioned above, when the procedure was tested using samples with ages already established through other means, it always checked out accurately. It was natural to assume then that it would be equally reliable in testing materials for which there was no definite way of determining age. Coal was an excellent example of this kind of matter.

When samples were tested, there was found to be a complete absence of any radiocarbon 14. It was natural to conclude that it had been there in the usual strength in the original living trees, but these had been dead for so long that complete disintegration of the radioactive material had taken place. Knowing that this could happen only over an exceedingly long period of time, they dated the coal as being many hundreds of thousands of years old.

In doing so they did the very thing God, through Peter, foretold they would do. They denied that there had ever been a great change in the heavens and the earth and worked on the assumption that "all things continue as they were from the beginning of creation" (2 Pet. 3:4).

Had they understood that the earth was mantled by that protective water vapor, they would have known that before the flood cosmic rays could never have penetrated into our atmosphere as they do today. Plants and animals did not absorb any radiocarbon 14 before the flood because the band of moisture filtered the rays out before they ever reached the nitrogen in the earth's atmosphere. Therefore, scientists found no radiocarbon in the coal—not because it had all disintegrated but *because it was never there originally.* Thus the radiocarbon clock, far from denying the truth of the Bible, actually serves to confirm it.

Some may question the effectiveness of the moisture mantle in screening out the cosmic radiation, but the fact is that even the limited presence of moisture and atmosphere around our earth today is a protection from this problem. When supersonic jets traverse the oceans at altitudes that practically take them out of this earth's atmosphere, it is necessary to keep a continual watch on solar flares. Should these break out while they are in flight, they must immediately return to a lower altitude to place atmosphere between themselves and open space so as to obtain protection from this radiation.

The Word of God offers us wonderful insight regarding the conditions as they were before the flood, the scientific forces which maintained those conditions, and the changes in those forces that produced the flood. This information is of tremendous value in searching out the specific role the Lord played in that fearful stroke of their wound, which made such an enormous breach upon the people.

The revelation of the scientific causes of the flood is a strong confirmation of the truth that God does not execute the sinner but that the catastrophes which destroy humankind are the outworking of natural forces no longer under God's control and supervision. While the Lord has not supplied the same detailed information about the scientific basis of the Egyptian plagues, faith is strengthened by the evidences of the flood, knowing that they had a scientific basis too.

Chapter Twenty-Eight

Concepts Reviewed

Study/Discussion Questions:

- How is it that the effect of humanity's rejection of God was seen in the reduction of the sun and moon?

- Review: Is the great controversy about who has greater power over the physical universe, or is it about who has greater governing principles?

- Why was there no way, in righteousness, that God could have prevented the flood?

- What caused the disaster to the sun and moon to end before reaching the point where any continuance of life on earth would have become impossible?

The biblical evidences gathered so far confirm the scientific nature of the flood. The perfect arrangement of balanced heat supply and protective mantle, producing a mild and equalized climate over the earth, was critically dependent on the uniform production of heat from the sun and the moon. When that failed, the flood was inevitable.

The question now remaining is why the sun came to be dimmed and the moon extinguished. If this was God's deliberate act performed at a moment dictated by Him, then God certainly was an executioner of the sentence against transgression. He did not leave the rejecters of His mercy to themselves to reap that which they had sown. He was a destroyer. Undeniably, He departed from His stated principles and resorted to measures foreign to Him and His kingdom prior to the entrance of sin.

This is, of course, the view generally adopted together with its implications which, unfortunately, are rarely considered. If people contemplated the full import of what they believe, they would heartily reject many errors.

From the outset of the study of the great controversy, as it arose in heaven, it becomes increasingly and sharply clear that the struggle was not a contest instituted to prove who was physically stronger, for there could be no doubt of God's infinite superiority in this field. Neither Lucifer nor any other creature challenged this. Furthermore, had that been the issue then God could have resolved it with one overwhelming demonstration of His almighty power. It would not have been necessary to wait for almost two thousand years and then bring the flood to prove that He was physically stronger than Satan and his hosts.

The contest was over the respective merits of two opposing and irreconcilable systems of government, the one long established by God versus that newly espoused by Satan. God declared that His system was perfect and needed no modifications or improvements. He also guaranteed, for those who faithfully respected it, the permanence of eternal life, prosperity, and advancement. Satan counterclaimed that the divine order was not all it pretended to be, a point having been reached where it had ended its effective reign. Far from being a system designed for the universal good of all, he charged that it was a master plot formulated for the special exaltation of the Father and the Son. Because of this, he insinuated, an oppressive era was about to be introduced that would increase in severity as eternity dragged on. While he admitted that up until that time conditions could not have been better, he declared that the future would certainly reveal the defects in the divine system. He agitated that it was imperative that every member of the angelic hosts stand up for themselves before they were so circumscribed by bondage that they would be powerless to assert their rights.

Satan's attack was upon the principles of God's character and thus of His government. The question was whether the established ways of God's government could emerge impeccably from subjection to the most searching test Satan could give it, or whether defects would become evident.

God was confident that it could emerge immaculate, and therefore, He had no hesitation in submitting it to the ultimate test. Let the devil attack! Let him use all the weapons of force and deception! God knew that His system would come through vindicated and perfect.

So God entered into the great controversy for which this earth and its people became the testing ground. It is of critical importance to understand what was under test, what was at stake, and the limitations placed upon God by His own acceptance of this challenge. God did not permit the testing of His system of government to preserve His personal honor and word, for God is not self-centered. He did it for the salvation of the creatures in His universe.

A clear distinction must be seen between the principles of God's government and the personal power resident in God by which He could enforce the observance of His ways if He chose to use those methods. When this distinction is seen, it then follows that if God's principles are under test then they must stand or fall on their own merits. If the Lord should find it necessary to introduce another factor, such as the use of omnipotent power, to settle the controversy, then this would depart from His original committal to leave the principles of righteousness to stand or fall on their own merits. It would also be an admission that they were defective and could not stand by virtue of their own intrinsic qualities. It would give Satan the whole argument, for this action would prove the adversary correct in his charges.

The question may be asked where it is recorded that Satan brought forth the challenge that God would resort to force, even lethal force, if His subjects should choose to reject Him and His governance. It is a most important question.

Although we may extrapolate the answer by all of the testimony of Scripture and especially of the life of Christ, who said that He did not come to destroy but to save and that He came to show us the Father, there is given to us the key proof of this challenge right in the words of that old serpent who spoke from the tree of knowledge of good and evil.

There, he issued the statement that laid bare the fundamental charges against God and His government. He said that in the day that they ate of the forbidden tree they would not die as God had said, but rather that their eyes would be opened and they would see the true nature of their existence—that they were actually gods, implying that they could function perfectly on their own without Him.

Therefore, God was charged with being a thief, for in restricting their innate natural tendency to progress to godhood, he was stealing their destiny. God was also charged with being a liar, because He said they would die if they went against His command. In this, Satan also charged God with being a murderer. He did not say so directly, but it was there by implication in his "ye shall not surely die" retort. Obviously, Satan did not want them to suspect that *he* had anything to do with death. He was presenting himself as a great benefactor to humans. Rather, it was his suggestion that if they did die it would come by another means than the natural result of transgression. He was not willing that they should understand the nature of sin, that it would disconnect them from God, the Source of life, and result in death. He did not want them to fear and shun sin, for his philosophy was and is that we can have an innate righteousness and can do our own will, even contrary to God's will, and live in it.

There is a common belief that people are basically good and that humanity is now evolving to a higher level of consciousness through the realization of "who we really are." This is the New Age spiritualism that is taking hold of many minds today. The prevalence of this philosophy is evidence that the "god within you" doctrine is alive and well. There are still two trees from which we may choose to eat.

So, if Satan disavows any notion that *he* is the destroyer or that *sin* is the destroyer, there is only one other place to look for the cause of any such death as God would have warned them about. Satan did not have to overtly develop the idea at this time, as he would later put his lying interpretation on the consequences of sin as he well knew that the progression of ages to come would reveal them. For now, he left it to the simple implication that God, being jealous for His authority and sole proprietorship of the universe, was wielding the threat of destructive power by His own hand in order to maintain His position unchallenged. So, in all of this it is seen that Satan was attributing to God all that was within his own character. Jesus made this clear when He said,

> The thief does not come except to *steal*, and to *kill*, and to *destroy*: I have come that they might have life, and that they may have it more abundantly (John 10:10).

> He was a *murderer* from the beginning, and does not stand in the truth, because there is no truth in him. When he speaks a lie, he speaks it from his own resources, for he is a *liar* and the father of it (John 8:44).

So, as we settle into the proper understanding of the nature of the contest between God and Satan and come to view what happened in the flood, we find that the traditionally-held view is in sharp conflict with the principles of God's position in the great controversy.

On one side we see clearly that the Father and Son have allowed the conflict to play itself out upon the stage of this earth. They declared that the victory for the cause of righteousness must and would come by the application of its own power and rightness—not because of the interposition of omnipotent power on God's part being used to destroy the nonconforming.

But, on the other hand, it is clear that as time passed and people began to multiply upon the face of the earth things went from bad to worse for God's cause. Continually, in increasing numbers, the inhabitants of the earth joined Satan, while God's accounting finally showed only eight to His credit. Yet even among them, the loyalty was far from absolute, as demonstrated by Ham's behavior after the flood.

There are no records in Holy Writ showing just how many inhabitants the earth then supported, but we can safely assume that the eight that boarded the ark would have been a very small fraction of a percent. Every appearance then suggested that Satan was about to emerge as the outright winner in the great controversy, that his ways were so superior to the ways of God that everyone on the earth was for them except for the eight. In time these few would either die or possibly defect anyway.

It was desperately important to God that the situation not be allowed to continue to the point where there was no one left on His side because it was essential to the ultimate success of His plan that the Redeemer be born through the righteous line. Should the righteous line be cut off, then God's plan would have failed.

It could have failed, not simply because the intention of God to save the human family would be frustrated, but because God would be deprived of the means of removing the cause of the rebellion. That cause, as has been demonstrably proved earlier in this book, was the misrepresentation of the character of God, first in the mind of Lucifer and later through him to the other creatures.

The only satisfactory and successful way to solve a problem is to remove the cause of it. Once the problem of sin, which is rebellion against the principles of God's government, entered the universe all the resources of heaven were devoted to its solution. It is a mistake to limit the solution to the cleansing of sin from those who will be saved while the rest are simply left to their annihilation. The problem will not be solved until the cause has been removed from the mind of every creature who has ever come into existence, including all those who will, in the end, be eternally lost.

Inasmuch as the cause of all the trouble is the misrepresentation of God's character, so long as that misconception remains in the minds of angels and human beings, the rebellion must continue. Therefore, to end it, that misconception must be corrected. This cannot be done merely by declarations on God's part or by the use of force. There is only one way to accomplish it. The character of God must be manifested by One who was equal with God. Only Christ could do the work.

But it was impossible for Him to do it successfully in the perfect environment of heaven. It could be done there to a certain extent but not wholly. There is a very valid reason for this. In heaven, Satan had not developed the fullness of his attack against the character of God. It remained for him to do that on this earth. This imposed on Christ the necessity of coming right to the place where Satan was perpetrating the fullness of his lies against God and there, side by side with the character of Satan, provide the contrasting revelation of God's character. Only as humans and angels were able to see both of them side by side could the revelation of God and Satan be so fully given that the cause of the struggle could be erased from angelic and human minds.

For Jesus Christ to come into this position, He must be born into the human family. He could and would not force any woman to be His mother. The one through whom He would enter the earthly arena must be absolutely willing to perform this office. We can be assured that no one who was on Satan's side would undertake such a commission. Satan knew this. Therefore, he realized that one way to secure the victory in the contest was to either win every human being over to his side or to win all he could and then use them to exterminate the rest.

Satan was terribly afraid that if Christ appeared on the earth He would be successful in exposing the lies he had leveled against God, with the result that he would be rejected with loathing by all the creatures whose support he so desperately sought. He knew that everything depended on his successfully preventing such a demonstration from being given. Therefore, he worked with fanatical and unsleeping zeal to win as many of the human family as possible to his side and to destroy the remainder. Success in so doing would deprive God of the means whereby Christ could enter the earthly arena of battle.

Never did Satan's goals come so close to absolute success than just prior to the flood. God saw His forces of loyal followers dwindle down to a mere and doubtful eight while the devil numbered all the rest of civilization as his. It was all too obvious that but a short time would elapse before death and apostasy would swing the balance totally in Satan's favor.

With the future of the entire kingdom of God throughout the infinite reaches of His domains at stake, such a development placed enormous pressure upon God to step in and take direct and decisive action to save the situation from total and eternal disaster. If the traditional view of what God did at the flood is correct, then God succumbed to that pressure. Popular theology asserts that the Lord had to step in with the flood to thoroughly curb the advancement of Satan's cause.

If this is what God did, then He made a complete farce of the original statement of willingness to submit the case to fair contest and of His expression of confidence that the principles of righteousness could survive such a test.

Once it is clearly understood that God's character and government would stand on its own merits without the interposition of arbitrary power, it will likewise be seen that should God at the last moment have resorted to the use of destructive power to wipe out the efforts of His competitor then no one would believe in Him and He would literally give the case away to Satan.

Satan would ask how he could ever fairly demonstrate his claims when the Lord lets him go until he is on the very brink of success and then, because He is the possessor of omnipotent power, uses that to wipe out all Satan has achieved. Satan could rightfully complain that he never would have any real chance of proving anything. God would have no defense against this argument, and it would actually serve to increase the spirit of rebellion in the universe. No fair-minded person could honestly stand on God's side based upon any verifiable demonstration of equal contest once these issues were clearly understood.

It is unacceptable to the thinking person that God, who knows all things from the beginning, would commit Himself to a position that would later get completely out of hand, forcing Him to introduce methods He had originally declared would never be used. If God did this, He would reveal that He was governing by imperfect standards, subject to revision and change, thereby calling into question any and every other claim that could be made with regard to His character and government.

When God committed all the resources of heaven to ending the great controversy, He knew already the coming numerical imbalance at the flood. It did not catch Him by surprise, and He had made full provision to meet the emergency. Therefore, when He promised the ultimate triumph of truth and predicted Christ's coming to the earth as an essential part of the plan, He was well aware how narrowly the scheme would come short of failure in Noah's day. Knowing all this in advance did not perturb Him in the slightest. He made no provisions for it outside of His eternal principles of truth. He still committed Himself to a fair and open contest.

God did not send the flood to obliterate Satan's forces. On the contrary, He did His very best to keep the flood from coming for as long as He possibly could. When it finally came, it was not because He sent it but because He could no longer prevent it.

Two principles must be kept ever in our mind if we would find our way to forever discard the notion that God overruled with use of physical might in the contest with Satan. The first is that God will never force His presence where it is not desired, and the second is that every power in nature is directly and continually dependent on God's creative power to keep it on station to fulfill its appointed task.

Therefore, in the era leading up to the deluge, the sun and the moon, which were critical factors in the coming of the flood, were dependent on the presence of God's power to keep them burning at exactly the correct heat level and stationed at the proper distance from the earth. Let the Lord's hand be removed from the control and direction of those two orbs of fire, and the flood had to follow.

Under Satan's determined and relentless influence, humanity increasingly desired total separation from God. They wanted nothing of His ways or principles. God, knowing the dreadful consequences of such a course, sent message after message pleading with them to correct their drift, but they steadily insisted on His departure. Because He will never force His presence where it is not desired, He had no choice but to depart. In doing so, He gave them over to their "vain imaginations" wherein their "foolish hearts were darkened" (Rom. 1:21). Refusing to glorify God, they instead worshipped the things of nature. Displacing their faith in the Creator as the Life-giver and Sustainer with faith in the things of creation, they had reached their maximum in idolatry and were in essence telling God to leave.

Job 22:15-17 spells it out clearly, reminding us to see how the wicked of that time were cut down, in that they said, "Depart from us," by asking the question, "What can the Almighty do to them?" So the Lord had to abandon them to the effects of nature itself abandoned. Left in this state of affairs long enough, the earth and its environs would have returned to the same state as it was prior to creation week: "without form, and void."

The moon, being nearer to the earth, was the first to feel the effect of God's departure. It went out entirely. The sun, much further away from earth and much larger than the moon, took longer to diminish completely. Before it could do so, the wicked had perished, and suddenly the situation was reversed. Whereas the majority had been against God, now the changed situation placed the majority on His side. They were only eight in number but still the majority.

These, of course, desired the Lord to fill His office and do His work of sustaining the powers of heaven and earth. Thus the returning Spirit of God was able to arrest any further decay in the sun and maintain it at the diminished level. It has remained that way ever since.

With the moon out and the sun at diminished output, there was neither the heat energy to return the water to its proper place nor the energy to maintain it there. Nor was it possible for the surviving remnant to live on an ocean without a shoreline. The water had to be relocated to expose sufficient land to produce food for people and beast. This was accomplished by the violent up thrusts of landmasses that formed the great mountain chains and peaks found in the Himalayas, Andes, Alps, Rockies, and so on. Additionally, enormous quantities of water were held in cold storage at the poles.

Artists' representations of conditions experienced by the disembarking voyagers give the impression that the water gently subsided and Noah and his family emerged to a scarred but peaceful earth. This has to be far from true. We have no concept of the titanic convulsions that all but tore this earth apart. There were no great mountain chains between the creation and the cataclysm. The earth was beautifully formed with pleasant undulating land, low hills, verdant valleys, and slowly moving rivers. Think, then, of the energy necessary to open up the almost bottomless ocean depths and thrust those huge mountain chains into the air as high as 29,000 feet.

During the cataclysm, the mantle of the earth broke apart. This allowed the molten interior of the earth to find pathways to the surface in explosions and fiery issues. Volcanoes circled the globe. It also created the conditions of geological instability that lead to earthquakes and ocean disturbances which have destroyed many thousands of lives since that time.

It was not God's direct act by which the moon was extinguished and the sun dimmed. This happened not because God caused it but because He could not stop it. Those who believe that there are two sides to the character of God—the loving side and "His strange act"—see the flood coming as a result of God's changing from the former to the latter. The real truth is that the flood proved inevitable, not because God changed His tactics but because He remained undeviatingly the same. With Him, the use of force has ever been excluded. Therefore, to have prevented the flood once His final appeals had been rejected would have required Him to change to forcing His presence where it was emphatically not desired. This He could not do, thus leaving nothing to prevent the onset of disaster.

Again, there is absolutely no difference between God's conduct at the flood and His conduct during the plagues on Egypt. In both cases the rod of power had to be relinquished before it became a serpent of destruction.

Chapter Twenty-Nine

Sodom and Gomorrah

Study/Discussion Questions:

- **Was the rainbow an arbitrary sign? Why a rainbow?**
- **The time of the flood introduced vast changes that brought a curse to the earth in many ways. Describe these.**
- **How is it that the earth is now held in reserve for destruction by fire, as pointed out by Peter?**
- **Why would the sovereign and omnipotent God choose fire to punish the wicked? Do nations that allow Christian freedoms exercise the death penalty by torturous means?**
- **Did God specially create the molten fire that rained on Sodom and Gomorrah?**
- **Can we find any modern histories of fiery destruction that would give us a parallel to what happened in the cities of the plains?**

Noah and his family emerged from the ark to tread a shattered earth. The destruction was beyond description. They needed no convincing that the flood had come, but they did need a very real assurance that it would not happen again. This the Lord gave them.

> "Thus I establish My covenant with you: Never again shall all flesh be cut off by the waters of the flood; never again shall there be a flood to destroy the earth." And God said: "This is the sign of the covenant which I make between Me and you, and every living creature that is with you, for perpetual generations: I set My rainbow in the cloud, and it shall be for the sign of the covenant between Me and the earth. It shall be, when I bring a cloud over the earth, that the rainbow shall be seen in the cloud (Gen. 9:11-14).

These words assure us that there will never again be a repetition of the deluge that twice before has covered the earth, first in the opening days of creation, and second during Noah's time.

It is interesting to note that the token of God's assurance that there would never again be a flood is in itself an indicator that points us to the fact that there had been a monumental change in the environment. Specifically, the conditions required to produce the rainbow never existed before the water mantle broke. The water vapor held in the atmosphere would have been a barrier to the direct sunlight required in order to refract and produce the colors of the visible light spectrum. Now that the more heavily condensed band of water above the earth had passed away, direct visible sunlight could readily pass through the thin dispersion of water droplets in the earth's atmosphere and create the rainbow phenomenon. So, here we have yet another example of biblical language in that God says that He "set the rainbow in the cloud." The rainbow is a natural phenomenon, but God takes the responsibility for it since He is the Creator of all nature.

The Noachic flood was none of God's doing; it came in spite of His efforts. Therefore, His statement that there would never again be a flood of water was not an undertaking to restrain Himself but a *prediction* of what the future held. Specifically, the prophecy is limited to a flood of water. It does not ensure against the deluge of fire by which the earth will finally be consumed (2 Pet. 3:5-7).

For there to be another flood of water, the conditions necessary to produce it must exist as they did before Noah's time. The only way total flooding could reoccur would be for the polar caps to melt, the mountain chains to be leveled into the ocean depths, and, in general, the landmasses reduced to about the same elevation. All the water that covered the earth in the first days of creation and which returned to submerge it again is still here. Therefore, it would cover the earth if it was evenly distributed over the surface again.

Should the Lord withdraw His sustaining presence from the earth, convulsions of this magnitude are not impossible and, in fact, will happen again, but the result is not seen in a flood of water. Rather, a flood of fire will engulf the planet.

These floods, first of water and lastly of fire, are not disconnected. The former is the parent of the latter. This relationship should be clearly understood.

It is not usual to think of water producing fire, for water is the most commonly used means of extinguishing a conflagration. However, the waters of the flood were the means whereby enormous amounts of fuel were buried under the earth and will be provided to fire that last great holocaust.

Moreover, the flood, though itself long since over, lives on in the form of offspring. Some roam the earth as storms, hurricanes, tornadoes, cyclones, and tempests, others are confined to specific locations such as volcanoes, geysers, and any other geothermal activities, while still others break forth in expected and unexpected spots as earthquakes and tidal waves. All are devoted to missions of destruction.

The flood marks the time division between original tranquility and the aberrations of nature. Of every one of these deviations from God's original scheme of things, the flood is also the parent. These disturbances may be divided into two categories: those found in the earth, and the others in the atmosphere.

The first of these include volcanic eruptions, thermal activities, earthquakes, and tidal waves. In the latter are storms, tempests, hurricanes, blizzards, tornadoes, typhoons, floods, and droughts.

At the time of the flood, "the fountains of the great deep were broken up" (Gen. 7:11), and water came up from below, in addition to the great downpour from above.

> Jets of water burst from the earth with indescribable force, throwing massive rocks hundreds of feet into the air (*Patriarchs and Prophets*, p. 99).

Problems arising within the earth were spawned when the earth's crust suffered this breakage. The inner molten materials are now brought near the surface in many locations and in many cases erupt onto the surface of the earth. Water and other substances, such as coal, sulfur, and other minerals, may interact with the hot material in the depths, resulting in other disruptive occurrences. The tensions and pressures built up at fault lines result in sudden shifts of the rocks beneath the surface, resulting in earthquakes. When earthquakes or volcanoes occur under the sea, tidal waves and tsunamis are launched.

Thus, the flood is truly the parent of all these troubles within the earth itself.

Weather as it is today is the product of conditions brought about by the deluge. The redistribution of land and water masses, the location of mountains and flat lands, and the inequalities of climate, all formed by the flood, are the determining factors in producing atmospheric problems from their mildest to their wildest forms.

What tremendous changes the flood set up, producing results that reach down to the end of time. The destruction initiated at the flood but halted before it consumed all things will then break forth to completion. Those fires that contribute to the decimation of the earth at the second coming and finally at the end of the millennium will also be the offspring of the flood, as remaining deposits of coal and oil in the earth will contribute to the fuels of these final conflagrations. Undoubtedly, there will be other sources of fire coming in at that time, as well. The inner molten materials will be released at unprecedented rates and volume, as there are no restraining protections in place to keep the mantle of the earth from breaking apart in continuance of the chaos initiated at the flood. As the liquefied elements release under great pressures, they will spew high into the atmosphere, as did the waters from under the earth during the time of the flood, to rain back down upon the earth in torrents of molten fire, as "from God out of heaven" (Rev. 20:9).

We have no way of knowing for certain what other mechanisms may contribute to the fires, but it is not outside the realm of possibility that there may be burning materials coming in from outside of earth's atmosphere in the form of meteoric showers or other material.

Additionally, it seems probable that humanity's activities will play their role. We know that under the sixth plague the forces of the world will turn upon the New World Order/Babylonian system and "burn her with fire" (Rev. 17:16; see also Rev. 18:8, 9). Satan delights in war and bloodshed, and by this point in earth's history, there will be a tremendous buildup of horrific weapons of mass destruction. Undoubtedly, as the earth has been completely given over to the control of Satan, these will be unleashed, and the conflagration will be unlike anything the world has ever witnessed.

Drought and flood, tempest and earthquake, tidal wave and hurricane, volcano and fire are the cataclysm's unruly children that will plague earth dwellers till the end and especially at the end as we can read in Revelation 16 pertaining to Armageddon and the closing scenes at the second coming of Christ (see also Rev. 6:14-17).

Not every area is afflicted with all these scourges. In fact, some parts are apparently free from them. This explains why some centers of sin pass unscathed year after year while others seemingly less iniquitous are struck down with shocking suddenness. Those cities located right where one of these children of the flood resides need to be far more careful than those in positions more favored. For years the giant of destruction will remain unseen or manifest itself only in mild forms, because the restraining power of God holds it in check while He seeks to woo men and women from their danger and while there remains in the city a faithful remnant for whose sake He will continue His restraint. But during this time the unwitting inhabitants continue to resist His appeals until finally He has no choice but to leave them to their desires.

The unfettered monster then bursts with unannounced fury upon the unprotected heads and homes of the abandoned sinners, whose destruction may be as total in the area where they are as it was over the whole earth when the flood came.

Sodom and Gomorrah were a case in point. The Scriptures report the devastation of those cities and their peoples in the same way that all the other destructions which fell upon abandoned sinners are described.

> Then the Lord rained brimstone and fire on Sodom and Gomorrah, from the Lord out of the heavens. So He overthrew those cities, all the plain, all the inhabitants of the cities, and what grew on the ground (Gen. 19:24, 25).

To millions of Bible readers, these words have pictured God as personally pouring great sheets of liquid fire from His own hands upon the hapless victims below. But those who have come to learn and accept the principles of God's character, as explored in this study, and who have learned to use the Bible as its own dictionary, know that such an interpretation is wholly incorrect.

Rather, the true biblical interpretation of these words is that the Lord had no option but to withdraw and leave the wicked to the fate they had chosen. This He did only when every means and appeal had been totally exhausted and there was nothing more He could do. Then, whatever potential destruction was lurking in the area was unleashed. The result was terminal.

There is always great value in assessing the implications of a certain belief, so study will now be given to see in what image God is cast by the belief that He personally poured fire down upon the dwellers on the plains. Only a certain kind of God would do this.

Death by fire is one of the cruelest and most feared ways to die. On February 1, 1974, a fire started in Sao Paulo, Brazil. Read the following excerpt from the *1975 Britannica Book of the Year*:

> A fire, started by an electrical short-circuit in an air-conditioner, engulfed the

upper fourteen stories of a newly constructed twenty-five story bank building, trapping hundreds of workers as the flames fed on combustible interior-finish materials; due to inadequate escape facilities, at least two hundred and twenty-seven persons lost their lives (p. 238).

Those in the higher floors above the fire found themselves cut off. As the fire advanced upwards, many chose to die by leaping from the upper levels rather than face the hungry flames.

In the jungles and forests it is the thing most feared by the animal kingdom. Beasts and reptiles lose all fear of each other as they flee pell-mell from the roaring flames. There is good reason, for death by fire is a *horrible* death.

Think of yourself as facing the death penalty, the only consolation being that the choice of how you will die is given to you. The choices are firing squad, gassing, the electric chair, beheading, hanging, or being burned alive. None of these is a pleasant prospect, but when you sit and think of your body being roasted while you are still alive, you know that that is the very last choice you would make. It is not difficult to realize that this is the kind of death which a judge or king would impose upon a person whose death he wished to make as painful as possible.

It is not a pleasant scene to dwell upon. Yet it must be visualized as realistically as possible so that it can be comprehended that no God of mercy, justice, and love would ever behave in such a way to personally and deliberately inflict a death of this nature upon anyone.

The ability to do certain things reveals the disposition within the doer. It is not possible for any being in the universe, including God, to do everything. The truth of this statement is confined to the spiritual and ethical side of the person. Admittedly, God has the physical power by which He can do anything. But while He has the might, there are some things His character will never permit Him to do. If God poured the fire and brimstone on Sodom and Gomorrah, it could only be because it was in Him to do so. It had to be a part of His character. Therefore, God has within Him a spirit of cruelty by which He is motivated to select the cruelest possible death for those who have refused to obey Him. Without that, He could never have treated the Sodomites as He is accused of having done.

But that is not God's character. He is not cruel, sadistic, and revengeful. He would never select the worst conceivable punishment and then administer it to those who did not appreciate His ways and acted contrary to His ideas.

Terrible are the implications of believing that God determined that the cities of the plain should be consumed by fire and then proceeded to do so. It is to equate Him with the papacy, whose constant practice was to burn to death those who refused to submit to her assumed authority. Something of the seriousness of this is manifested when it is recognized that the papacy is Satan's masterpiece of misrepresentation of God's character. If we wish to understand what God is not, then behold the principles and practices of the papacy. The way God is supposed to have behaved at Sodom and Gomorrah is exactly as the papacy would have behaved if she had been in God's position. Therefore, how God is thought to have behaved is certainly not the way He conducted His affairs there.

The papacy went forth to convert the people to her religious beliefs and service. When her first efforts were unsuccessful, she began to exert pressure upon them until, when it was clear that the subjects of her ministrations had no mind to ever obey her, she cruelly destroyed them with fire. In doing this, she represented herself not only as administering the will of God but of doing so as she and Satan would have it believed God does it.

In all of this the papacy was carrying out Satan's plans. The very fact that this is the way of the papacy is certain denial of its being God's way, for if anyone wishes to know what God is not, let him behold what the papacy is and what she does. Contrariwise, if anyone wishes to know what God is, let him look at the life of Jesus Christ. Never will the two witnesses agree.

The ultimate witness to the character of God is found in those who have drawn so near to Him as to possess His character. Such a people cannot be brought to take up any weapon of destruction against anyone, not even their very worst enemies. They would much rather die themselves than take the life of another. That is the example of the life of Christ. He would rather die Himself than require that the life of another be taken. This is the ultimate outliving of the injunction to turn the other cheek and go the second mile. A God who counseled this kind of behavior as the reflection of His own could never pour fire on Sodom and Gomorrah. He did there just what He did on every other occasion. He did not "stand toward the sinner as an executioner of the sentence against transgression" but He left "the rejecters of His mercy to themselves, to reap that which they have sown" (*The Great Controversy*, p. 36).

If the Lord of heaven did not act the part of an executioner and personally pour fire on those cities, then how were they destroyed? Are we left with no scientific information to reveal the nature of that disaster?

There is a considerable amount of information available if careful search is made for it, though hampering the search is the relative uncertainty as to where these cities actually stood.

There are those scholars who have looked for the cities on the northern side of the Dead Sea, but

> Other scholars seek these cities underneath the waters of the southern end of the Dead Sea. Arguments for this view are more numerous and weighty: (1) The "vale of Siddim" in which these cities were located is identified with the "salt sea" in Genesis 14:3. The northern two-thirds of the present Dead Sea reaches a depth of one thousand, three hundred and twenty-eight feet, and must have existed as early as Abraham's time, but the depth of the southern part nowhere exceeds sixteen feet. Submerged trees show that part of this area was dry in relatively modern times, and accurate measurements have shown that the level of the sea has been steadily rising during the last century....
>
> (2) Asphalt is found at the southern end of the Dead Sea, while the Vale of Siddim is said to have been "full of slimepits," RSV "bitumen pits" (Genesis 14:10). Bitumen, or asphalt, still erupts from the bottom of the southern part of the Dead Sea and floats to the shore.

(3) Statements made by classical authors, Diodorus Siculus (ii. 48. 7-9), Strabo (Georgr. xvi. 2. 42-44), Tacitus (Hist. v. 6. 7), and Josephus (*War* iv. 8. 4), describe an area south of the Dead Sea (presumably now covered by its rising water) as scorched by a fiery catastrophe that destroyed several cities whose burned remains were still visible in their day. Foul gases are said to emerge from fissures of the ground. Compare Deut 29:23.

(4) Geologists have found oil and natural gases in the ground at the southern end of the Dead Sea, which is at the same time an area frequently disturbed by earthquakes, hence furnished all the conditions for the catastrophe described in the Bible, if God used natural means in the destruction of the cities (see above). Furthermore, Jebel Usdum, the 'Mount of Sodom,' at the southwestern shore of the Dead Sea, consists of 50 per cent rock salt. Some have conjectured that in an upheaval during the destruction of Sodom some of this salt may have been dislodged and may have buried Lot's wife, piling over her to form a "pillar of salt" (Genesis 19:26)....

(5) A number of streams enter the southern part of the Dead Sea from the east, in a region that is still very fertile, and it is reasonable to believe that the whole valley now forming the southernmost part of the Dead Sea was once that exceptionally fertile plain, one fitting the Bible description which compares the land with the Garden of Eden and the Nile valley (ch. 13:10)....

In 1924 W. F. Albright discovered *Bâb edh-Dhrâ*, a site on the *El Lisan* peninsula in the southern part of the Dead Sea ... and thought it to be a religious and rallying center of the cities of the plain, now covered by the waters of the Dead Sea. (*Seventh-day Adventist Bible Dictionary*, vol. 8, p. 1051).

This statement gives excellent reasons for concluding that the site of those ancient cities was at the southern end of the Dead Sea. But it also tells some further interesting facts about the area.

"Bitumen, or asphalt, still erupts from the bottom of the southern part of the Dead Sea and floats to the shore... Geologists have found oil and natural gases in the ground at the southern end of the Dead Sea, which is at the same time an area frequently disturbed by earthquakes."

In ancient times the Elamites, Chaldeans, Akkadians, and Sumerians mined shallow deposits of asphalt, or bitumen, for their own use. Mesopotamian bitumen was exported to Egypt where it was employed for various purposes, including the preservation of mummies. The Dead Sea was known as Lake Asphaltites (from which the term asphalt was derived) because of the lumps of semisolid petroleum that were washed up on its shores from underwater seeps (*Encyclopaedia Britannica*, "heavy oil and tar sand").

Even today the southern region of the Dead Sea is rich in asphalt.... Inflammable gases still escape from rock crevices in the area. Asphalt rising to the surface of the southern part of the Dead Sea gave to it the name Lake Asphaltitis in classical times. Massive lumps of asphalt floating on the surface are often of sufficient size to support several persons. Asphalt, sulphur, and other combustible materials have been reclaimed and exported from this region for years (*The SDA Bible Commentary*, vol. 1, p. 335).

Asphalt, oil, natural and highly inflammable gases, and earthquakes are not common to every part of the world, but they are a combination often found together. Where they are found indicates a spot where enormous amounts of vegetable material in the form of plants and trees together with animal and human carcasses were buried at the flood. Where such materials are found there is the formation of coal, oil, gas, and petroleum that may or may not ignite. If it does, thermal activity will result, usually accompanied by earthquakes and tremors.

Before the flood there were immense forests. The trees were many times larger than any trees which we now see. They were of great durability. They would know nothing of decay for hundreds of years. At the time of the flood these forests were torn up or broken down and buried in the earth. In some places large quantities of these immense trees were thrown together and covered with stones and earth by the commotions of the flood. They have since petrified and become coal, which accounts for the large coal beds which are now found. This coal has produced oil. God causes large quantities of coal and oil to ignite and burn. Rocks are intensely heated, limestone is burned, and iron ore melted. Water and fire under the surface of the earth meet. The action of water upon the limestone adds fury to the intense heat, and causes earthquakes, volcanoes and fiery issues. The action of fire and water upon the ledges of rocks and ore, causes loud explosions which sound like muffled thunder. These wonderful exhibitions will be more numerous and terrible just before the coming of Christ and the end of the world, as signs of its speedy destruction.

Coal and oil are generally to be found where there are no burning mountains or fiery issues. When fire and water under the surface of the earth meet, the fiery issues cannot give sufficient vent to the heated elements beneath. The earth is convulsed—the ground trembles, heaves, and rises into swells or waves, and there are heavy sounds like thunder underground. The air is heated and suffocating. The earth quickly opens, and I saw villages, cities and burning mountains carried down together into the earth (*Spiritual Gifts*, book 3, pp. 79, 80).

Noting the expressions pertaining to underground thunder in the above text, we need only do a little searching to find out that these events are now happening. We can find many instances in the news reports from recent years of these muffled explosions being heard in various locations. In an article titled "Mystery of 'The Earthquake Boom'—a real earthquake," we read:

> On June 11, 2003 the first volcanism article, *Volcanoes In California, Idaho, and Pacific Northwest Building Towards Catastrophic Eruptions*, reveals a startling discovery to science—the 'earthquake boom'.... Currently a mystery to seismologists, a powerful explosion sound which eludes detection by the best of seismographs, is a real earth event and should be correctly classified as an 'earthquake'. The rare earthquake boom is part of a 'family' of five types of events the earth can generate of which only two are known by science. It is important for residents near volcanoes to be aware of the 'earthquake boom', although an unnerving experience, doesn't indicate an actual explosion occurred or that an eruption is imminent....
>
> [An] Earthquake Boom is a very loud, deep sounding explosion, which emanates from the earth. If directly above emanation, directional determination may be difficult as sound is not from a distinct direction as it is from a wide area of earth's surface. It is a higher frequency audio form of the traditional shaking earthquake even though current seismographs cannot 'see' or 'record' them. Scalar devices are able to clearly 'see' these events along with the rest of the earthquake 'family' of earth-generated events such as the 'silent' or 'slow' earthquake. Another relative to the 'family' is the earth 'lurch' and a 'fast version of slow' earthquake—these yet to be discovered by mainstream science.
>
> These loud explosions have been witnessed by many over the years. They also accompany traditional earthquakes as these are part of the mix of seismic activity (earthquake & earthquake boom) (Larry Park, TERRA RESEARCH LLC, http://www.terraresearch.net/articles/earthquakeboom_article1.htm [accessed February 28, 2012]).

Wherever there is a spot on the earth where enormous amounts of vegetation have been buried to petrify into coal and oil, there is the potential for volcanic eruptions and devastating earthquakes. The evidences still existing today show that Sodom and Gomorrah and their associated villages and towns were located over just such a spot.

They were in danger constantly, for they were living over a powder keg, a disaster that was only waiting to happen. But the Lord desired their salvation. He was as loathe to see them perish as He is to see anyone destroyed. So He filled His usual role of Protector of those wicked cities, while His Spirit pleaded with them to repent and escape the wrath to come. But they would not, and the time came when finally the protecting Presence had to be withdrawn, leaving no power to control the seething elements beneath the ground. Long held back, when released they exploded in one spectacular and all-consuming fireball of destruction that filled the heavens above where they stood and the earth where they rested.

It was not something that God sent in the sense that He decreed what should happen to them and then personally used His power to see that it happened. Rather it came, not because the Lord brought it, but because He could not hold it back any longer. There was no one the Sodomites could blame for their destruction but themselves.

The burning of the cities of the plain is not an event singular to them. There is a modern counterpart to this in the destruction of St. Pierre on May 8, 1902. The story is told in a book by Hal Butler titled *Nature at War.*

> It was on May 8, 1902, that the town of St. Pierre, on the lush West Indies island of Martinique, abruptly died. At exactly 7:50 A.M. on that disastrous morning, 4,583-foot Mont Pelee—a long-dormant volcano—blew its top in one of the world's most cataclysmic explosions.
>
> The French-held island of Martinique shuddered like a stricken giant at the violent eruption. From the yawning mouth of the volcano, a huge black cloud of superheated air and gas emerged that rolled down the sloping side of the mountain like a monstrous tumbleweed. In its path, at the foot of the mountain, lay the harbor town of St. Pierre. Within seconds the cloud swept over the city. Street by street, buildings leaped into instant flame and people were turned into human torches. The hideous black ball—its core later estimated to have been at least 1,500 degrees Fahrenheit— quickly reduced St. Pierre to smoldering ashes. Only two people survived the fiery devastation, and the rest of the populace— more than 30,000—died.
>
> Elapsed time from the moment of eruption to extinction of the city was less than two minutes! (pp. 131, 132).

We have no eyewitness accounts of the destruction of the ancient cities as we have here of the modern decimation of St. Pierre, only the terse Bible statement of what God did there.

Yet the similarities between the two situations are very obvious. Both were located in an area of intense volcanic and earthquake activity and both were suddenly overcome by the descent of fire upon them of such ferocity and intensity that the cities were obliterated, never to be rebuilt, and the population was exterminated but for very few survivors. In the case of Sodom, there were only three, Lot and his two daughters. In St. Pierre, only two in the city and the family who fled just in time escaped death.

Like Sodom, St. Pierre was a place of abandoned wickedness. Here is the description of it as given in our source by Hal Butler:

> In 1902, St. Pierre, on the western coast of the island and only four miles from Mont Pelee, was Martinique's major city. Twelve miles to the south was Fort-de-France, the capital of the island, but this was a small village that bore no resemblance to glittering St. Pierre. France was proud of St. Pierre; indeed, the French often referred to the city as the 'little Paris' or 'the Paris of the West' because of its sparkling social life.
>
> ...In addition to being the social capital of the island, St. Pierre was also

the commercial center. One of its major industries was the rum distillery, and its principal business street, Rue Victor Hugo, was lined with banks, stores and other commercial establishments. The 'Paris of the West' was also equipped to cater both to the welfare of the soul and the gratification of the flesh, for it boasted a stately Catholic cathedral and several parish churches, along with a theater where actors from France entertained, cafes, nightclubs and assorted emporiums designed specifically for uninhibited revelry.

The French colonists, whose ancestors had settled on Martinique generations before, represented the elite of the island. They owned and supervised plantations producing tobacco, coffee, cacao and sugarcane. Most of them had built ostentatious villas in the mountains and spent much of their time either relaxing at these summer homes or sipping cognac in St. Pierre's hotels and inns. This wealthy group of Pierrotins—as residents of St. Pierre were called—numbered about 7,000.

Most of the city's 23,000 other inhabitants were blacks. The men—usually bare-chested and dressed in canvas trousers and hats made of bamboo grass—were typically handsome; the women couched their natural beauty in colorful robes and turbans and strode the streets with trays and baskets of salable goods balanced on their heads. The waterfront was a scene of continuous activity as stevedores loaded and unloaded ships calling at what was one of the most profitable ports in the Caribbean.

This was St. Pierre in 1902—a city that had every reason to believe in its future but a city that had no future at all (*Ibid.*, pp. 132, 133).

Life in St. Pierre and Sodom followed a similar pattern. Sodom and Gomorrah were places where study was given to the development of every means whereby the desires of the flesh could be gratified and, from the description given here, so was St. Pierre. Thus the very things that caused the departure of the restraining and protecting Spirit of God in the ancient situation were also present in this fair city. In both cases the balmy climate and abundant wealth tended to stimulate this pursuit for the licentious, until a fever pitch was reached.

It is not to be supposed that Sodom was irreligious, for in those days worship of the sun god was the devoted spiritual exercise of those peoples. Wherever this religious influence has been present, it has encouraged licentiousness and immorality of all kinds. The Roman Catholic religion that dominated the spiritual life of St. Pierre is the modern counterpart of ancient sun-worship and has demonstrated that it, likewise, is the spawning ground for various types of sin and wickedness. The same religious influences, **therefore,** that brought Sodom and Gomorrah to the pitch of wickedness and total and unrestrained rejection of God also brought the inhabitants of St. Pierre to that point.

St. Pierre, then, provides us with a splendid illustration of the death of Sodom and Gomorrah. God did the same thing in both the ancient and the modern situation for the same reason. He left the rejecters of His mercy to themselves to reap that which they had sown and He did that because that was what the people in each case demanded of Him. Because the cities concerned were sitting over a time bomb just waiting to go off in the form of a volcanic eruption, that was the fate which overtook them. In other words, they died, not because God decreed that this was the way it should be but because that was the potential destructive threat under which they lived.

A wide variety of destructions befall the wicked. There are those who, as in the cases of Sodom, Gomorrah, and St. Pierre, are wiped out by volcanic eruptions, while others are taken by flood, earthquake, hurricane, hailstorm; accidents by air, sea, and land; giant conflagrations in forests and buildings; famine; or the savage outbursts of human wrath. The only consistent pattern through it all is that the disaster is according to the potential of destruction common to the area. This denies the charge that God personally takes hold of the powers of nature and manipulates them according to His design to punish sinners. God has the power to create any kind of destruction at will. He is not bound to the particular peril present in a given area. Being a God of utter justice and consistency would require Him to punish the same offenses with the same punishments. But this is not what happened. The same offenses are dealt with by widely varying punishments always according to the destructive potential of the place where the offenders reside.

The nature and location of these catastrophes are clear proof that they are not the work of God. They occur because of the presence, in scattered areas of the earth, of pockets of potential destruction seeded at the time of the flood. Those who live in such areas need the protecting care of God more than do others who live where there is a lesser threat. But by their impenitent living, they grieve away the shield of omnipotence, thereby exposing themselves to the terrible storms or earthquakes, fires, floods, volcanic eruptions, or whatever else is poised to obliterate them. Therefore, they suffer the awful consequences of the withdrawal of God's presence as others in more favorable places do not.

This does not infer that there are entirely safe places on earth, for this is not true. As the withdrawal of God's presence becomes more extensive, the powers of nature are reaching out to waste areas previously untouched. As we draw nearer to the end, this will become universal.

There is no problem in understanding what God did at Sodom, Gomorrah, and St. Pierre if care is taken to consider all the implications and if the principles that govern God's behavior are carefully kept in mind.

Chapter Thirty

An Execution

Study/Discussion Questions:

- What shall we say about all of the slaughters that took place not at the hand of God but at His command, such as at the rebellion of the golden calf?

- Did God fulfill the role of a destroyer at last?

- Did God put the sword in the hands of His people? How so? If not, then what was God's intent regarding how the inheritance of Israel, the Promised Land, was to be taken?

- Did the Israelites have any good reason to take up the sword? Did they know any better?

- What are the implications of Jesus' statement to Peter that he who lives by the sword dies by the sword? Was this a new principle? Why or why not?

The flood was the first occasion when nature out of God's control broke with cataclysmic fury on the unsheltered heads of humanity. Then there was the destruction of the tower of Babel by lightning. The next incident of great note was the incineration of Sodom and Gomorrah.

After this the list lengthens. There were the plagues upon Egypt; the returning waters of the Red Sea; various pestilences that smote the Israelites; the invasion of the fiery serpents; the swallowing of Korah, Dathan, and Abiram in the earthquake; the overthrow of the walls of Jericho; the great hailstorm in Joshua's day; the expiration of Sennacherib's army; the death of the children at the claws and jaws of the bears; the fire which consumed the men who came to take Elijah captive; and many more.

In our day one disaster follows another in steady succession until each new one brings no surprise.

To examine each case would be repeating the same arguments already advanced in respect to the flood, the fall of Sodom and Gomorrah, and the plagues of Egypt. Once the principle has been established, it can then be applied to all other situations.

Sometimes it is possible to see a scientific explanation of the disaster, but not always. Just what took the lives of Sennacherib's men is not revealed. The withholding of this information simply provides an exercise in faith, testing the grip held upon the principles of righteousness revealed in the Scriptures. Because no revelation is given of how they died, the temptation is to revert to the idea that God personally executed them.

Such a temptation must be positively rejected. Cling to the simple belief that God does not execute sinners but leaves them to themselves to reap that which they has chosen. This is so emphatically revealed in the inspired Word of God that there is no excuse for losing sight of it.

The consumption of Korah, Dathan, and Abiram presents no problem. The earth opened up and swallowed them. What neither they, nor the rest of Israel knew, was that they were encamped over a fault that so far only the sustaining presence of God had held in check. In like manner, human beings today are unable to predict just where and when these disasters will strike.

When those rebels sustained their defiance of God, they compelled Him to withdraw from where they were, leaving only one possible consequence. The earthquake so long restrained was unleashed.

But there are other occasions, in some respects different from those cited above, in which God's actions are most difficult to understand. They have so perplexed earnest Christians for centuries that some have been led to doubt the character of God and even to forsake His service. What God *appears* to have done denies every principle discussed so far in this study. These incidents are those in which God commanded the Israelites to take their weapons and slay men, women, children, infants, and all livestock of other neighboring people groups. The execution of the defiant people who worshiped the golden calf, the genocide of the Amalekites, and the extermination of the Canaanites were all accomplished in obedience to God's directions. While God Himself did not carry out the slaughtering, the Israelites followed His command. Considering that, in the natural order of things, he who orders the execution is the real executioner, it *appears* that God filled the role of a destroyer in these instances.

More than any other, the biblical recital of these events provides those who cling to the view that God inflicts judgments on those who offend Him with the justification for their stand. To them, these stories provide incontrovertible proof to their stance.

Indeed, these stories are difficult to understand, but not even in these situations has God acted as an executioner or destroyer. It cannot be overstressed that success in uncovering the real truth of God's part at the golden calf execution, the genocide of the Amalekites, the annihilation of the Canaanites, and so forth, depends upon there being complete confidence in God's consistency. There must be the unassailable conviction that there are no contradictions in the Word of God and that He does not make a declaration about His character and behavior in one place and then proceed to do the opposite in another.

To clarify the nature of the problem, three statements outlining God's commitment never to use force will be quoted. These will be immediately followed by the record of the golden calf incident so it can be plainly seen that one set of statements appears to be directly contradicted by the other.

> Rebellion was not to be overcome by force. Compelling power is found only under Satan's government. The Lord's principles are not of this order. His authority

rests upon goodness, mercy, and love; and the presentation of these principles is the means to be used. God's government is moral, and truth and love are to be the prevailing power I*The Desire of Ages*, p. 759).

Earthly kingdoms rule by the ascendancy of physical power; but from Christ's kingdom every carnal weapon, every instrument of coercion, is banished (*The Acts of the Apostles*, p. 12).

God does not stand toward the sinner as an executioner of the sentence against transgression; but He leaves the rejecters of His mercy to themselves, to reap that which they have sown (*The Great Controversy*, p. 36).

There is no ambiguity in these statements, but they do become a problem when brought into direct contact with a story such as the slaughter of the rebels at the golden calf. When these two are brought together, it appears that God states one thing in one place and then proceeds to do the opposite in another. Compare the record that follows with the statements quoted above.

And he [Moses] said to them, "Thus says the Lord God of Israel: 'Let every man put his sword on his side, and go in and out from entrance to entrance throughout the camp, and let every man kill his brother, every man his companion, and every man his neighbor.'" So the sons of Levi did according to the word of Moses. And about three thousand men of the people fell that day. Then Moses said, "Consecrate yourselves today to the Lord, that He may bestow on you a blessing this day, for every man has opposed his son and his brother" (Exod. 32:27-29).

Those who performed this terrible work of judgment were acting by divine authority, executing the sentence of the King of heaven. Men are to beware how they, in their human blindness, judge and condemn their fellow men; but when God commands them to execute His sentence upon iniquity, He is to be obeyed. Those who performed this painful act, thus manifested their abhorrence of rebellion and idolatry, and consecrated themselves more fully to the service of the true God. The Lord honored their faithfulness by bestowing special distinction upon the tribe of Levi.

The Israelites had been guilty of treason, and that against a King who had loaded them with benefits and whose authority they had voluntarily pledged themselves to obey. That the divine government might be maintained justice must be visited upon the traitors. Yet even here God's mercy was displayed. While He maintained His law, He granted freedom of choice and opportunity for repentance to all. Only those were cut off who persisted in rebellion.

It was necessary that this sin should be punished, as a testimony to surrounding nations of God's displeasure against idolatry. By executing justice upon the guilty, Moses, as God's instrument, must leave on record a solemn and public protest against their crime. As the Israelites should hereafter condemn the idolatry of the neighboring tribes, their enemies would throw back upon them the charge that the people who claimed Jehovah as their God had made a calf and worshiped it in Horeb. Then though compelled to acknowledge the disgraceful truth, Israel could point to the terrible fate of the transgressors, as evidence that their sin had not been sanctioned or excused.

Love no less than justice demanded that for this sin judgment should be inflicted. God is the guardian as well as the sovereign of His people. He cuts off those who are determined upon rebellion, that they may not lead others to ruin. In sparing the life of Cain, God had demonstrated to the universe what would be the result of permitting sin to go unpunished. The influence exerted upon his descendants by his life and teaching led to the state of corruption that demanded the destruction of the whole world by a flood. The history of the antediluvians testifies that long life is not a blessing to the sinner; God's great forbearance did not repress their wickedness. The longer men lived, the more corrupt they became.

So with the apostasy at Sinai. Unless punishment had been speedily visited upon transgression, the same results would again have been seen. The earth would have become as corrupt as in the days of Noah. Had these transgressors been spared, evils would have followed, greater than resulted from sparing the life of Cain. It was the mercy of God that thousands should suffer, to prevent the necessity of visiting judgments upon millions. In order to save the many, He must punish the few. Furthermore, as the people had cast off their allegiance to God, they had forfeited the divine protection, and, deprived of their defense, the whole nation was exposed to the power of their enemies. Had not the evil been promptly put away, they would soon have fallen a prey to their numerous and powerful foes. It was necessary for the good of Israel, and also as a lesson to all succeeding generations, that crime should be promptly punished. And it was no less a mercy to the sinners themselves that they should be cut short in their evil course. Had their life been spared, the same spirit that led them to rebel against God would have been manifested in hatred and strife among themselves, and they would eventually have destroyed one another. It was in love to the world, in love to Israel, and even to the transgressors, that crime was punished with swift and terrible severity (*Patriarchs and Prophets*, pp. 324-326).

The people's behavior can only be classified as rebellion. In the case of those who refused to repent of it, it was persistent and incurable. It is clearly seen that the insurrection was overcome by force. The Levites took their swords and slaughtered the rebels. Thus, by force alone the rebellion was overcome.

What makes this critically different from the numerous other occasions when rebellion has been overcome by force is that God ordered this solution to be applied. The sinners were not left to themselves to reap that which they had sown. Rather, a direct sentence was formulated against them and summarily carried into effect.

Thus, at first observation, every step God is reported to have taken denies what He laid out as His principles in the first three references quoted. God declared that it is not His way to overcome rebellion by force, yet He directed that it be done in just that way. He claims that He leaves the sinners to themselves to reap what they have sown, but He certainly did not do that here.

It is simple to see how quite a case can be built up against God by using this evidence. It is argued by those who believe that God executes those who disobey Him that the only way to deny this is to make the Bible read as we wish it to be read. Before this study is over, it will become evident that those who make this charge are, in fact, the ones who are guilty of doing this.

When rightly understood, scriptural records will show that at the golden calf God did nothing in violation of His stated principles.

How is it, though, that the vast majority have failed to rightly perceive the work of God at the base of the mountain? Why has He been viewed as the maker and executioner of the sentence? Why has no real difference been made between the behavior of God and earthly monarchs?

It is because one vital factor, being completely overlooked, is never taken into consideration. When it is, it makes all the difference to understanding the case. Then the charges leveled against God will be redirected where they rightly belong.

The factor that we will be discussing is the Israelites introduction of the sword into their lives. Adopting the sword was an extremely serious and tragic step that placed them on a different relationship with their divine Leader. It amounted to the institution of humanity's procedures in the place of God's. Israel exercised their freedom of choice, and Jehovah could not and, therefore, did not compel them to discard it. All He could do was to labor to save them from the worst effects of what they had elected to do.

Their decision to take up weapons of coercion and destruction was not made in complete ignorance of God's will. Their heavenly Father had faithfully communicated to them that the sword was to find no place among them whatsoever.

They were named after their revered father Israel, whose history of victory over his foes was well known to them. God designed that this should be a witness to them of His ways. The lesson was especially pertinent, for there was a distinct parallel existing between Israel's situation and theirs. As he was a prisoner of his scheming uncle, Laban, and desired to depart for the promised land, so they were held in Egyptian bondage and longed to leave for Canaan's land.

When the patriarch set forth on his journey, he was pursued by Laban who was determined to bring his son-in-law back with him. It cost Laban seven days to overtake Jacob, seven days in which his temper had time to reach fever heat. When he found Jacob,

> He was hot with anger, and bent on forcing them to return, which he doubted not he could do, since his band was much the stronger. The fugitives were indeed in great peril (*Patriarchs and Prophets*, p. 193).

Jacob, knowing full well that he would be pursued, made every provision possible to prevent his being forced to return. But in all his careful planning for the security of the ones he loved so dearly, he made no move to arm his servants with swords and spears. He put his entire trust in God as his Protector, and the Lord filled that commission so effectively that not only did Jacob not go back to Laban's home but not one of his household was even so much as scratched.

This peril gone, with the pacified Laban returning to his place, Jacob pressed on to meet the greater peril of Esau who reportedly was coming to meet him with six hundred armed men. Esau had only one objective in mind—to ensure that Jacob could never dispossess him of their father's wealth. The only way to assure this was to slaughter Jacob and his band. That would settle the question for all time.

As this deadly peril threatened Jacob, there were at least two different courses he could have adopted. The common human reaction is to turn to the power of weapons. Accordingly, Jacob could have chosen to divert from his course to spend time in arming and training his servants. He did not do this, for he rightly understood that this was not God's way. Instead, he continued without deviation, his entire confidence resting in the assurance that God would faithfully fulfill His responsibility of protecting him and his entourage. On the night before the encounter, he turned aside to pray, his deep concern arising from the fear that unconfessed sin would obstruct God's work and leave him exposed to his enemy. There was no lack of faith in God's power to deliver him. His only fear was that his own spiritual condition would make that power unavailable. The long hours of agonized wrestling brought the victory.

God did not force Esau to leave his brother unmolested. Instead, He sent an angel to reveal to him the true character of Jacob, his sufferings, his spirit, and his intentions. Thus Esau was led to view Jacob in a new light. He realized that Jacob was not a threat to him and, therefore, did not need to be eliminated. His rage was replaced by sympathy, and the outcome again was that not a single one from Jacob's household received so much as a scratch.

Here is a point worthy of emphasis. Whenever the children of Israel gave God the task of protecting them, not one of them lost their lives or suffered injury, but when they took the sword, there was nearly always loss of life, which in some cases was very heavy.

From Jacob's experience, we gain a vision of how we should rely on God for deliverance. It is the same message reiterated by the psalmist.

> God is our refuge and strength, a very present help in trouble. Therefore we will not fear, even though the earth be removed, and though the mountains be carried into the midst of the sea; though its waters roar and be troubled, though the mountains shake with its swelling (Ps. 46:1-3).

> The angel of the Lord encamps all around those who fear Him, and delivers them (Ps. 34:7).

The great controversy is not between us and Satan but between Christ and Satan. We do not have the power to overcome the enemy. God alone can do that and has undertaken to do so. Our task is to leave Him to do what He has promised. The victory is ours as a gift, which is demonstrated in the wonderful experience of Jacob.

Through this experience, God provided the Israelites with a perpetual testimony of the security available to them if they trustingly committed the keeping of their lives to Him. As a preparation for their departure from Egypt, it was sufficient to assure them that they were to make no provision for acquiring and using swords. They were to entrust that task to God as fully as Jacob did, knowing they could expect the same results.

God, knowing that the success of the great venture depended on their strict adherence to these principles, reiterated the lesson repeatedly during the exodus and the period leading up to it.

Moses had been thoroughly trained in the art of war and had proved himself on the battlefield to be a brilliant tactician.

> His ability as a military leader made him a favorite with the armies of Egypt, and he was generally regarded as a remarkable character (*Patriarchs and Prophets*, p. 245).

Moses, therefore, naturally expected that the Lord would deliver them by force of arms. He saw in his Egyptian education a divinely provided training for such a campaign. Had God purposed to do things this way, no better man than Moses could have been found anywhere in history. It is significant that God made no use of this ability in Moses at any time in his life, for not once did Moses lead the armies of Israel into battle.

> The elders of Israel were taught by angels that the time for their deliverance was near, and that Moses was the man whom God would employ to accomplish this work. Angels instructed Moses also that Jehovah had chosen him to break the bondage of His people. He, supposing that they were to obtain their freedom by force of arms, expected to lead the Hebrew host against the armies of Egypt, and having this in view, he guarded his affections, lest in his attachment to his foster mother or to Pharaoh he would not be free to do the will of God (*Ibid.*).

Thus Moses was dedicated to the divine purpose for himself and Israel and longed for the fulfillment of the plan. When he saw the Israelite being oppressed by the Egyptian, he slew the persecutor, **supposing that thereby he had** initiated the armed struggle which would liberate the slave nation. But even though the Israelites were aware of God's appointment of Moses, there was not a man inspired to rise with him. Instead, he was forced into precipitous flight to Midian. This unexpected development caused Moses a great deal of deep heart-searching, providing God with the needed opportunity to teach him that it was not by warfare that Israel was to be delivered.

Forty years later he returned, clad, not in the shining armor of a military leader, but in the simple garb of an eastern shepherd with a staff in his hands. Before all Israel, God was proclaiming the way by which they would be taken out of bondage and preserved forever from their enemies. It was a reminder to them of the same truth as revealed in God's dealings with Jacob.

In all of this we are to clearly see that God did not intend to free them by His providence only to change His method and have them fight their own way to the Promised Land under His guidance. God started the exodus upon principles that were to be forever preserved and maintained. At no time did He deviate from His established course of action. During the reign of sorrow, as plague followed plague, the Israelites had no part to play other than merely standing by and letting the Lord handle everything.

When, just before their final departure, God impressed the Egyptians to liberally provide the travelers with everything they would ever need on their journey, He did not put it in the hearts of their former masters to give them weapons of war. It was a people for whom God had made *every* provision, who went out of Egypt, "unarmed and unaccustomed to war" (*Ibid.*, p. 282). If the Lord had intended a change from His fighting their battles to their doing this work for themselves, then He certainly would have made sure they were equipped for this role. The fact that He did not impress the Egyptians to arm them is clear proof that He never intended they should be. As the exodus began, so it was to continue.

How much happier their subsequent history would have been had they learned from Jacob and their recent experience of God's deliverance. There would have been no substitution of human, faithless methods in place of the infallible, divine procedures. God would never have commanded them to take their swords and slaughter men, women, and children. In every situation He would have been their Defender and Deliverer.

When they came to the Red Sea, the Lord once more demonstrated the way in which the power of their enemies would be broken if they relied on God. There it was shown in the most vivid way that the rejecters of God's mercy were simply left to themselves to perish.

When Pharaoh led his army into the corridor between those standing walls of water, it was an act of terrible presumption on his part. The only way in which the Israelites could pass safely over was by remaining within the circle of God's protection. But the Egyptians had deliberately and defiantly cast off that protection, and therefore, the Spirit of the Lord could not maintain the waters in their position. As the army advanced, the Spirit of God had no choice but to retire before it. As that power was withdrawn, the waters simply rushed back to their original position, overwhelming the enemies of God and delivering His people.

God's commitment to offering His creatures freedom of choice would be no more than empty words if there was no opportunity to choose another course. Accordingly, in order to give full support to His declared principles, the Lord is careful not to deprive the people of the means whereby they could go in another direction if they wished.

So while the Lord had made it absolutely clear that they were not to carry the sword in their journey from Egypt, they had the same freedom to obey or disobey as did their first parents in Eden. The opportunity for them to take the sword was afforded when the armor-clad bodies of the Egyptian soldiers were washed up at their feet.

> As morning broke it revealed to the multitudes of Israel all that remained of
> their mighty foes—the mail-clad bodies cast upon the shore (*Ibid.*, pp. 287, 288).

Here was the great test for the men of Israel. They were tempted with a veritable arsenal of weapons—swords, spears, helmets, shields, and breastplates. They could either rush down and take the spoils, thus equipping themselves to fight as other nations fought, or they could turn their backs upon it and leave their protection in the Lord's hands.

There are no direct records confirming that they rushed down and took the armor from the Egyptians, but all the evidence points strongly in that direction. Here are the facts. They approached, crossed, and emerged from the Red Sea without implements of war. Shortly after leaving the Red Sea, they engaged in warfare against the Amalekites in which they did not use sticks and stones. As there were no swordsmiths between the Red Sea and the location of their first battle, the only way they could have become equipped was by salvaging the weaponry washed ashore.

It was a critical point in their history, for the sad decision made there influenced the full span of their future. The real issue involved whether the people were going to trust God as their sole Protector or whether they were going to take His work into their own hands. It was the question of implicit trust in God versus greater confidence in the power of their own fighting abilities. They introduced a new order into the camp, replacing the divine arrangement. Thus they prevented the nation from giving a true representation of God's character, and this eventually led to their final dismissal as the channel of God's communication to the world.

What makes their decision so significant are the circumstances under which it was made. God had just demonstrated to them the most thrilling and convincing display of His ability and willingness to deal with their enemies according to the principles of eternal righteousness. With a God like that, what need did they have of weapons? In taking up the sword at that point, Israel failed tragically.

That it was not His intent for them to make war is proved by direct statements as well as by all the principles which undergird God's character.

> The Lord had never commanded them to "go up and fight." *It was not His purpose that they should gain the land by warfare*, but by strict obedience to His commands (*Ibid.*, p. 392, emphasis added).

The use of force is exclusive to Satan's kingdom. It has no part in God's order. They were to possess the Promised Land by strict obedience to His commands, one of which prohibits killing.

So while it is true that they gained the land by force, contrary to God's way, let it not be forgotten that they also lost it in the same manner. Their sad history confirms the truth of Christ's words to the valiant and belligerent Peter: "Put your sword in its place, for all who take the sword will perish by the sword" (Matt. 26:52).

Jesus did not give these words a limited application in time. He was not saying, "From this time forward, all who take the sword will thereby perish." What He stated is an *eternal* truth. It is a statement of the fact that the use of force engenders counterforce.

God, understanding perfectly that those who live by the sword will perish by it, knew that for Israel to use weaponry was to ensure their destruction. God did not desire such an outcome. Therefore, from this motivation alone, it is certain that He never gave them the sword. More than this, if He had done so, then He would be responsible for their destruction, for he who gives to another that which will assuredly effect his death must carry the blame for that demise.

It follows then that it was never in God's purpose that Israel or anyone else should ever carry the sword. It has no place in His character and corresponding methods, and therefore, it is to find no acceptance in the character and behavior of His people.

The recognition of this truth is essential to understanding the directives from God which sent the Israelites forth with the sword to utterly destroy the peoples who opposed them. The institution of this form of government was entirely the people's work, the expression of their having more faith in themselves than in God. It was the establishment of human principles and procedures in place of the divine.

Therefore, in every instance where the Israelites went to war or executed the wrongdoers among themselves, their actions were not a revelation of the character of God. There has been a universal readiness to conclude that they were acting in complete righteousness by simply doing as the Lord told them. If they had been a *truly obedient* people, they would *not have had the swords at all* and, therefore, would never have gone forth to slay their enemies.

Yet God did give directions to them. There is no denying this, nor is there any desire to do so, for *the nature* of those commands reveals a very wonderful and beautiful Father in heaven who is ever reaching out to save and never to destroy. The tragic error is that He has been terribly misunderstood to the point where the actions designed to minimize the evil effects of the slaughtering to which they were committed have been judged in an altogether different and wrong light.

The purpose here is to establish that it was in spite of God's best efforts to the contrary that the sword became an establishment in the encampment of Israel. The recognition of this truth is essential to understanding the directives given to Israel, which have long been viewed as an indication that He was personally using them as executioners.

Again, if God's will had been respected, they would never have used the sword, and God would have been free to do His work for them according to the eternal principles of righteousness. The command given by God at various times in connection with the various slayings during the sojourn of Israel makes it difficult for the average person to see anything but that God was personally and directly involved and that He decided the particular sentence and then ordered its execution.

But God does not give orders contrary to the principles of righteousness. Therefore, more study is required to remove the seeming inconsistencies. This may be done with the sweet consciousness that there are no contradictions in the Word of God and that God's character is perfectly consistent in all its behavior.

Chapter Thirty-One

The Ever-loving, Saving Father

Study/Discussion Questions:

- If you had a son or daughter of accountable age who made a choice in life contrary to principles of righteousness as taught in your home, would you have any other options than to:

    a. abandon them to their choice;

    b. employ force to correct them; or

    c. love them and try to lessen or delay the pain of the consequences of their error?

- What do the stories of the ministry of Jeremiah to God's people, the prodigal son, and the rebellion of Lucifer all have in common?

- What kind of war was waged in heaven, resulting in the "casting out" of Lucifer and his angels?

- Does arbitrary (discretionary; externally decreed and enforced) punishment for breaking the law have any place in God's government?

When the Israelites took the sword, thus rejecting God's way in favor of their own, the Lord was faced with several possible courses.

First, He could have simply abandoned them to their own devices. This would have been perfectly just and righteous on His part, though it would have been justice without mercy. The result would have been the speedy disappearance of the household of Israel from the face of the earth. Second, God had the physical power to force the Israelites to continue in His way, but He could not do this from the moral point of view. Third, God could have simply ignored the sin, pretended that it did not exist. To do this would be to condone it, and this God cannot do, for life cannot exist apart from God. He will not sustain sinful life for the purpose of continuance in sin.

These are three obvious alternatives, but none of them are possible with God. In the first, God has to be something He is not, unmerciful. God cannot be anything He is not, for He is unchangeable. In the second, God cannot do anything immoral. In the third, God is not the author of sin. But there is another "possibility" that is normally overlooked. Herein, the Lord recognizes that He has failed to save them from taking the wrong turn;

therefore, the work calculated to save them from that is now valueless. Because they have not yet tasted the bitter experience of the consequences of their apostasy, they are not disposed to come back. But they have not gone beyond the possibility of restoration. So God, in His infinite love, will not abandon them and thus cut off their opportunity to rectify their misdemeanors.

If no saving help is provided to draw them back from experiencing the worst effects of their choice, then they would not survive long enough to ever return to God. Therefore, the Lord works to save them from those evil results both to make their sufferings as mild as possible and to extend the time in which they may learn and repent. It is because this aspect of God's working has not been understood that He has been so seriously misjudged in the Old Testament.

By illustration, picture a small town located in an area where wild animals such as bear, deer, mountain sheep, and various big cats abound. As is to be expected, the majority of men in the town are keen hunters who never miss the opportunity to take their guns out and track down the game.

But one man is different. He has the love of God in his heart, and to kill the beautiful dwellers in the forests and mountains is contrary to his nature. So he is never seen in company with the men trailing off on another hunting adventure. For the other men in town, they were troubled by this odd man, and they never lost an occasion to persuade him, if possible, to join them.

This man had a fine son whom he was most anxious to protect from the influence of the hunters around. He worked untiringly to instill in him the same love of the wildlife that he possessed and was gratified to see that he was having good success in this direction.

But the father did not take away the boy's freedom of choice. When he eventually reached later youth, he became answerable for himself and was no longer under the direct control and discipline of his father. He received an invitation to spend some weeks away from home with his friends on a camping and hunting adventure, and eager to see new country, he accepted the kind offer. They urged him to try hunting with them just once to see how he liked it.

His first reaction was unfavorable, but something about the challenge, thrill, and excitement drew him in, and soon he was an enthusiastic devotee. He went to the sports store, selected a beautifully engineered weapon, and in due time returned with it to the dismay of his father. He had exercised his choice, and now the father was confronted with a situation that required a response. How would he now relate himself to this turn of events? Clearly the young man had instituted in his life a course contrary to the ways of his father and of God.

For the father, as for God, the choice lay between several alternatives. The first option was to disown the son, forbidding his entrance into the home and requiring that he go his own separate way. Another course would have called for the use of force to coerce the lad's surrender to his father's wishes and ways. This was not the answer, for the youth had achieved the age of independence, and it was not in this father's nature, anymore than it is in the character of God, to use force. To them, the only acceptable service is that which springs from an educated heart of love. A third alternative was to quietly ignore the change, pretend that the rifle had never been brought into the home, and act as if all were well. Again, this was no way out, for sin cannot be ignored. Neither love nor justice will permit it. Iniquity demands attention. A response to it will always be forthcoming whether it be the saving outreach of love or the vindictive reaction of destructive hate.

Having considered and rejected each of these possibilities, what would have been left for this godly man to do? What would God do in the same situation?

First, the older man recognized that his son had placed himself, other people, domestic livestock, and wild animals in a position of great danger. Being an inexperienced and untrained rifleman, he did not understand the necessity of looking beyond the target to ensure that there were no buildings, people, or farm animals in the line of fire. He needed to understand how to carry the weapon so that in climbing through fences, for instance, he did not, as so many have done, shoot himself or his friends. He must be made aware of the awful potential of the ricochet when a bullet, glancing from rock or tree, will embed itself in a target far to the right or left of the original sighting. He must come close enough to the game to eliminate the possibility of only wounding the animal, which would then drag itself away to suffer a lingering death. These and other things he could be taught in order to save himself and others from the worst effects of what he had chosen.

While the father could no longer save the youth from taking the gun, he could, if permitted, provide the instruction needed to save him from these serious consequences. Even the wild animals would benefit from this saving ministry, for, while they could not be saved from death, they could be delivered from a painful and lingering one.

The response of God and those who walk with Him will always be saving love; therefore, there is only one course among those suggested above that the Lord, or this father, would follow. God is by nature a Savior. So too was the father pictured in this illustration. When God is blocked from saving people in one area, He will still exercise His saving power in whatever possibilities remain. Thus, when the boy's father found that his long pursued objectives of saving the youth from taking up weapons had failed, he still recognized that there was much he could do to save the boy from the worst effects of what he had chosen.

So, sadly, but with tender dignity, the father drew his son aside and spoke with him. He expressed disappointment that the younger man had chosen to go the way he had, but he assured him that he would respect his decision fully. He gently suggested that there were dangers associated with the use of such a weapon, from which perils he could only be safeguarded by receiving and obeying a number of specific precautions. The father intimated that he was more than willing to carefully instruct the son in these things so that he would be saved from the worst results of what he had chosen.

The father introduced the training session by emphasizing that nothing he was about to do or say indicated that he had changed in any way, even though it could be interpreted that way.

God, who has been placed in the same position by the determination of His children to take up weapons of destruction, has likewise solemnly warned that His effort to save them from the worst effects of what they have chosen does not indicate any change in Him, even though His actions could and have been interpreted otherwise.

"For I am the Lord, I do not change" (Mal. 3:6). "Jesus Christ is the same yesterday, today, and forever" (Heb. 13:8) "with whom there is no variation or shadow of turning" (James 1:17).

Despite the fact that people know that before sin entered God never destroyed, and despite these solemn declarations from God that no change has ever occurred in Him, human beings still look on His everlasting efforts to save and interpret them as being the actions of one who has become like them.

The father in our story did not have to change his ways in order to instruct the son how to be a kind hunter, neither did God have to change His ways to save Israel from being cruel users of the sword. Neither of them took life. They were only bent on saving it, or, if that were no longer possible, to save it from as much suffering as possible.

Now suppose that one of the villagers had happened to come down the lane as the father was instructing his son in the use of firearms. The villager would have interpreted what he saw as sure proof that the father had changed. This man would have lost no time in returning to his hunting companions to announce the father's conversion. He would have told them that he was now one of them—a gunman. He would have offered as proof to his incredulous listeners what he had seen of the father actually instructing the boy in gun handling. The evidence he offered was factually true, for this is exactly what he had seen the father doing, but the conclusions drawn from those evidences were the opposite from the truth.

Even as that father was misjudged, so God has likewise been.

At the golden calf, God gave direct instructions through Moses for the Levites to take their swords and execute the unrepentant rebels. People have taken these facts and from them have drawn their own conclusions. While the facts are correct, the conclusions drawn from them are wholly wrong. They have declared with great satisfaction that God has become one of them—a destroyer.

They could not be more mistaken.

Thankfully, God has not changed. He has not become like humanity; He is not a destroyer. Sin has not changed Him, neither have sinful human beings. When His character and work are correctly understood, it will be seen that He did nothing differently at the golden calf than He did when Adam and Eve elected to go their own way.

In His great love and mercy, God does not leave people to themselves to reap the worst consequences of what he has sown. To whatever extent humanity will accept it, God provides them with counsel and blessing so that their lives are less severe and painful.

The golden calf episode is not the easiest place in the biblical record to see this principle. There are others where it is more clearly revealed. Therefore, it is better that they be studied first. Then a preparation will have been made for an enlightened reassessment of God's part at the golden calf.

The outstanding example is God's behavior before and after the Israelites went into Babylonian captivity.

Never did a nation pursue a more provocative course toward God than did Israel in those years of apostasy, rebellion, and idolatry between the reigns of David and Zedekiah. After an excellent beginning in Joshua's time, there had been the heartbreaking frustrations of Israel's vacillation between good and evil during the period of the judges, but in David's day, the kingdom had reached its pinnacle of glory. The people were basking in the manifold blessings of the Lord, and everything was set for the most glorious reign of righteousness yet to be witnessed in the world. Unfortunately, the people took the gifts of the Lord and transferred their trust from God to them, thus entering into the worst period of their history up to that point. It had cost heaven a great deal to bring Israel to this hour of promise and opportunity only to see it all thrown away so despitefully, selfishly, and irresponsibly.

From the human point of view, God would have been entirely justified if He had destroyed Israel when they pursued so daring and insulting a course as they did during that great apostasy.

But the Scriptures do not reveal any such disposition developing on God's part as the fateful years dragged on. Instead, they reveal Him in an entirely different attitude. He is shown as a compassionate Savior; seeing the dreadful, self-imposed plight of His people, He worked to deliver them from the power of the Babylonians and the sufferings that would follow their overthrow. Hear Him speaking through the prophet Jeremiah.

> "Hear the word of the Lord, all you of Judah who enter in at these gates to worship the Lord!" Thus says the Lord of hosts, the God of Israel: "Amend your ways and your doings, and I will cause you to dwell in this place. Do not trust in these lying words, saying, 'The temple of the Lord, the temple of the Lord, the temple of the Lord are these.' "For if you thoroughly amend your ways and your doings, if you thoroughly execute judgment between a man and his neighbor, if you do not oppress the stranger, the fatherless, and the widow, and do not shed innocent blood in this place, or walk after other gods to your hurt, then I will cause you to dwell in this place, in the land that I gave to your fathers forever and ever" (Jer. 7:2-7).

As these words were spoken, the mighty nation of Babylon was rising spectacularly in power, and nation after nation was succumbing to it. Israel, weakened by years of idol worship and sin, could not hope to resist the northern tide. If God had possessed even the slightest traces of the spirit people think He has, His attitude would have been very different at this time. He would have declared to Israel, "For centuries I have blessed, protected, and prospered you, and all I get in return is insult, disobedience, disrespect, and rejection. The might of Babylon is coming against you in the very near future. They will savage you, and you will deserve all you get and more. I wash My hands of you and leave you to your fate."

But we do not find such an attitude on God's part. If we did, then God's love must be less than infinite. There would be a limit to it. It would go so far and then stop, to be replaced by a spirit of revengeful reciprocation. Such is the changing nature of man's love, but it is never the way of God's infinite love. Nothing can change that.

In the face of all their rebellion, God could truthfully say, "For I am the Lord, I do not change; therefore you are not consumed, O sons of Jacob" (Mal. 3:6).

His relationship to them was the same at the end of this trying experience as it had been at the beginning. It is true that at the end they were not recipients of His blessings to the same extent as when their relationship with Him had been so good, but that was not because the Lord had retaliated by withdrawing those blessings. It was only because they had shut themselves away from them.

God did not call on them to endure appropriate punishments or a period of penance before they were reinstated in their land and in His favor. This is very difficult to accept, for humanity's philosophy demands that if a person sins, he or she pays for it.

There is a double motivation behind this human disposition. One is the spirit of rendering evil for evil, the other is the impulse for self-protection and security. Accordingly, courts of justice seek to measure an evil to the person equal to the evil he or she has committed. This satisfies the requirement for revenge. At the same time, the penalty is administered in such a way that the public is aware of it. The example of the wrongdoer serves as a warning deterrent to other would be offenders. By this means the hope is entertained that security will be guaranteed.

But this is not God's order. He does not mete out evil for evil. He returns good instead. Though this is the truth, it is exceedingly difficult for earthlings to grasp. So deeply ingrained is the concept of meeting evil with evil that it cannot be understood how God can operate on opposite principles.

Yet the case under study here verifies that this is His way. To prove otherwise will necessitate finding scriptures that record God's demands that they endure a series of punishments before they could regain His favor. But such references are not to be found. The only chastisements they suffered were those they had brought upon themselves but from which God had worked to save them.

If any doubt this beautiful attribute of God, let him study the story of the prodigal son, which is expressly designed to teach this truth. In this parable, both the sons exhibited the same belief that appropriate punishments must be endured before there could be a restoration. The erring son asked for it, and the other demanded it. The father, who directly represents God's behavior, would not hear of it. All he required was true repentance.

When the prodigal returned to his father, he asked only a place as the least of the servants. This, he felt, would be a humiliation so great as to be a punishment befitting his case. He was sure he was asking for his just reward.

The elder brother was incensed when he heard of the complete restoration of the sinner to the place from which he had gone. He thought of the prodigal's wasteful expenditure of health, money, time, and the father's reputation. He did not mind the repentance and the return, but he did object to the reinstatement. To be accorded the same place as he had left, *without being sentenced to an appropriate punishment*, was too much for his human morality to accept.

The father accepted the boy back into the household *as if he had never sinned*. Exactly so, God receives sinners back and accepts them as though they had never sinned.

> If you give yourself to Him, and accept Him as your Saviour, then, sinful as your life may have been, for His sake you are accounted righteous. Christ's character stands in place of your character, and you are accepted before God just as if you had not sinned (*Steps to Christ*, p. 62).

> There is therefore now no condemnation to those who are in Christ Jesus, who do not walk according to the flesh, but according to the Spirit (Rom. 8:1).

This is the truth expressed through Jeremiah to Israel when the Lord said that if they would repent they would stay in their own land forever. In other words, He would treat them as though they had never sinned. No clearer view could be given of the unchanging nature of God. His blessings never cease to flow toward humanity. His attitude is always the same. When people turn away from Him, they place themselves out of touch with those blessings, but the moment they return, they find themselves back in the same position they were in when they left.

In the great, original rebellion, this truth is revealed with clarity and force. Lucifer had served God with unfailing devotion for what must have been a long period of time. Throughout his service, he received the fullness of God's blessings and the joy of fellowship. Eventually, he lost confidence in God and consequently entered into rebellion against Him. If he had gone no further, it would have been bad enough, but he added greater offense by enlisting as many as possible in the same spirit of disaffection. A threat was thus directed against the entire kingdom. When this happens in an earthly dominion, the monarch speedily deals with the offender, making such an example of him or her in an attempt to effectively deter others from a similar course.

But the ways of human beings are not God's ways. Consequently, God did not relate Himself to Lucifer by making an example of him, by administering disciplinary actions, or by changing in His relationship toward him in any way. Instead, all the loving agencies of heaven were put in motion to plead with him not to persist in a course that could only propel him into deadly ruin. "But the warning, given in infinite love and mercy, only aroused a spirit of resistance" (*Patriarchs and Prophets*, p. 36).

God did not even demote the covering cherub. He did not take this type of action no matter how far the bright one departed from Him. The initial vacating of his position and later of heaven itself was Lucifer's own action. It was never the work of God.

In a loving effort to save both Lucifer and the angels who were coming under his influence, "the King of the universe summoned the heavenly hosts before Him, that in their presence He might set forth the true position of His Son and show the relation He sustained to all created beings" (*Ibid.*).

That was a marvelous sermon on the divine order and organization in which was revealed the love of God toward every one of His creatures. They were brought to see that the position occupied by Christ was one of great personal sacrifice, made for their good from a heart warmed by infinite love and wisdom.

Lucifer came close to sharing the adulation of the other angels, but the strange, fierce conflict raged within him until self and pride obtained the mastery. It was then that he left his place in the throne room of God. God did not dismiss him and require his departure. Lucifer took himself away as it is written:

> Leaving his place in the immediate presence of the Father, Lucifer went forth to diffuse the spirit of discontent among the angels (*Ibid.*, 37).

The time had surely come for positive preventive action such as the extermination or, at least, expulsion of the rebel. After all, it is sound policy to throw out the rotten apple to prevent corruption of the remainder. But God did not do this. It would have been a denial of the principle that He had given complete freedom to serve or not to serve Him. Therefore, He would not take any action requiring force. He would use only the outreach of saving love to draw His much-loved creature back from destruction.

> A compassionate Creator, in yearning pity for Lucifer and his followers, was seeking to draw them back from the abyss of ruin into which they were about to plunge (*Ibid.*, p. 39).

The result of this was that he came close to the point of yielding and coming back to God. Quite a time had elapsed, and he had done a tremendous amount of damage in God's kingdom. From the human point of view he deserved a great deal of punishment, but "though he had left his position as covering cherub, yet if he had been willing to return to God, acknowledging the Creator's wisdom, and satisfied to fill the place appointed him in God's great plan, he would have been reinstated in his office" (*Ibid.*).

In other words, he would have been accepted before God as though he had never sinned. He would have gone back to his place in God's presence and would have continued there as if he had never left it. Lucifer was not required to suffer any punishments, endure penance, or pass through a period of probation before being readmitted to his place. He was not even called upon to accept a lowly position from which he could work his way back to the top.

Therefore, when Christ revealed His Father in the parable of the returning prodigal, He was not simply telling what the Father would do to the repentant. He was confirming what He had always done. What Jesus told of the father's attitude toward the prodigal son is exactly how God related Himself to Lucifer. The only difference is that the prodigal son was repentant, Lucifer was not.

The Bible requires two or three witnesses to confirm any truth: "by the mouth of two or three witnesses every word may be established" (Matt. 18:16). Here are the three needed witnesses to confirm this truth about God's character. The case of Lucifer, the experience of the Israelites as they faced Babylonian oppression, and the parable of the prodigal son all confirm that God does not administer punishments to sinners but seeks to save them from the chastisements which they are about to inflict upon themselves. If they will only repent and return to the circle of His blessings, then they will be accepted back as if they had never sinned.

But those who do not really believe that God's love is infinite and that He never changes by so much as a hair's breadth will argue that there was a limit to His patience, and when that limit was exhausted with Lucifer, He turned to active warfare to run him out of heaven.

Their proof text is Revelation 12:7-9, which states, "And war broke out in heaven: Michael and his angels fought against the dragon; and the dragon and his angels fought, but they did not prevail, nor was a place found for them in heaven any longer. So the great dragon was cast out, that serpent of old, called the Devil, and Satan, who deceives the whole world; he was cast to the earth, and his angels were cast out with him."

To millions, these words have pictured an intense physical struggle between the forces loyal to heaven and the rebels. It has been seen as a conflict involving the use of physical power versus physical power. Great artists have portrayed Christ at the head of hordes of shining angels standing with an unsheathed sword before which Lucifer is plunging downward into the darkness of empty space.

But this is a superficial and inaccurate view of the nature of that struggle. It is a view consequent with the practice of seeing God's behavior as being identical to humanity's. There was war in heaven; it is true, but not war as human beings fight. Satan was cast out, but it was God's way of doing it, not humanity's.

> God could have destroyed Satan and his sympathizers as easily as one can cast a pebble to the earth; but He did not do this. Rebellion was not to be overcome by force. Compelling power is found only under Satan's government. The Lord's principles are not of this order. His authority rests upon goodness, mercy, and love; and the presentation of these principles is the means to be used. God's government is moral, and truth and love are to be the prevailing power (*The Desire of Ages*, p. 759).

In that struggle then, God did not use force. This weapon is never found in His kingdom but only in that of Satan's. Therefore, it was by another way that Satan was cast out of heaven, never to return. God fought with none other than the weapons consistent with His kingdom.

The struggle in heaven was a very real one nonetheless. It was war—a total effort on Satan's part to change the entire structure of heaven's order and organization. In order to succeed, he needed to convert the angels' allegiance away from God to himself. At that time the only sword Satan could use was that of deception, against which God used only the weapon of truth. The battle raged on over a considerable period of time until the point was reached where the devil had penetrated as far as he could. Each angel had made his choice with sufficient numbers standing for the truth to enable God to maintain His position as Protector of the heavenly hosts. With God's continued presence assured, there was no hope of the proposed new order being established. The old and proven order would remain. But Satan's deformation had brought him into such disharmony with those principles that he found it impossible to remain where they continued to operate. To him, heaven had become a place that was foreign, unacceptable, and unendurable, and he could not leave it quickly enough.

It was the truth of God that drove him out, not the use of any kind of physical force. The same reason for Satan's leaving heaven is the reason why the wicked would never be happy if they were to return there. They would not be able to tolerate the place and would want to leave it as soon as possible. They would be driven out by their sheer unfitness to remain.

> Could those whose lives have been spent in rebellion against God be suddenly transported to heaven and witness the high, the holy state of perfection that ever exists there,—every soul filled with love, every countenance beaming with joy, enrapturing music in melodious strains rising in honor of God and the Lamb, and ceaseless streams of light flowing upon the redeemed from the face of Him who sitteth upon the throne,—could those whose hearts are filled with hatred of God, of truth and holiness, mingle with the heavenly throng and join their songs of praise? Could they endure the glory of God and the Lamb? No, no; years of probation were granted them, that they might form characters for heaven; but they have never trained the mind to love purity; they have never learned the language of heaven, and now it is too late. A life of rebellion against God has unfitted them for heaven. Its purity, holiness, and peace would be torture to them; the glory of God would be a consuming fire. They would long to flee from that holy place. They would welcome destruction, that they might be hidden from the face of Him who died to redeem them. The destiny of the wicked is fixed by their own choice. Their exclusion from heaven is voluntary with themselves, and just and merciful on the part of God (*The Great Controversy*, pp. 542, 543).

Confirmation of this is already available. The worldly and ungodly today find that the society of true Christians engaged in devoted worship of God is intolerable to them, and they desire only to leave such society. They are happier elsewhere.

As Pharaoh's heart was hardened by his continual resistance to God's efforts to save him, so Lucifer's whole being was warped as he fought off God's loving efforts to draw him and his followers back from the abyss into which their steps were surely taking them. This is how Satan was driven from heaven, not by God directly driving him out but by His efforts to save him.

So then, in all of this we find that if Israel had repented and turned away from idol worship and all the licentiousness and evil that goes with it, they would have been delivered from the Assyrians and the Babylonians as if they had never sinned. The certainty of this is contained in the Word of God as quoted above in Jeremiah.

That these were not mere words with God is proven by the fact that when He was given the opportunity to carry them out, He surely did so. The mighty Sennacherib marched victoriously against the whole idol-worshiping world. The ten tribes of Israel fell before him, and he intended to add Judah as a further prize to his conquests. But there was a king on the throne who believed God. Hezekiah came to power after a succession of very wicked and idolatrous rulers. The land had been filled with images and the sanctuary was in a sorry state.

Over the whole land loomed the dark shadow of Assyrian global conquest, demanding that instant action be taken to meet the threat. Many a man would have concentrated on the formation of military preparedness by gathering, equipping, and training the largest army possible in the shortest time. The restoration of the sanctuary and the obliteration of the images could wait until a later date.

But not this king. First, he set to work to cleanse and restore the sanctuary and its services. With his whole heart he turned to the Lord and put his trust there. He claimed the promise that they would be protected and saved in their own land, and they were. God dismissed the Assyrian threat with such totality that it never assailed Judah again. Study the story with care, and see how the Lord did not demand that they pay their debt to Him. He did not require a long period of proving before He would act on their behalf. As soon as they repented, He stepped back into His rightful place as their Protector and Savior and delivered them as if they had never sinned.

Had Zedekiah been a king of Hezekiah's character then Nebuchadnezzar would never have had any hope of overcoming the Israelites. But despite the fact that the King of heaven sent His prophet Jeremiah to him with the assurance that if he would repent the Lord would work for him as if he had never sinned at all, and despite the fact that the history of Judah's deliverance from Sennacherib proved this, the king elected to reject God's counsels and go his own way, thus frustrating any hope of God doing what His loving heart longed to do, namely, to save them from the cruel oppressor.

What the Lord would have done for Lucifer and Zedekiah, He did for good king Hezekiah and for countless others who have believed the Lord. These experiences are the proof that the portrayal of God rendered in the parable of the prodigal son is the truth. Satan is desperate in his fear that people will become acquainted with such a God, for he knows they will then have confidence to come to Him for deliverance from his machinations. Therefore, he presents God as a being no different from sinful individuals—severe, exacting, and determined that the full measure of punishment for sin be borne before mercy can be extended. Then the devil leads the soul into sin so terrible that the victim knows he can never serve out the sentence and is thus discouraged from ever seeking God.

Let God's wonderful willingness to forgive and restore Israel in the face of their sad and desperate apostasy be to every man and woman an inspiring encouragement to come back to the God of mercy and light.

God says to the sinner:

I have blotted out, like a thick cloud, your transgressions, and like a cloud, your sins (Isa. 44:22).

I will forgive their iniquity, and their sin I will remember no more (Jer. 31:34).

Let the wicked forsake his way, and the unrighteous man his thoughts; let him return to the Lord, and He will have mercy on him; and to our God, for He will abundantly pardon (Isa. 55:7).

"In those days and in that time," says the Lord, "the iniquity of Israel shall be sought, but there shall be none; and the sins of Judah, but they shall not be found" (Jer. 50:20).

Do not listen to the enemy's suggestion to stay away from Christ until you have made yourself better; until you are good enough to come to God. If you wait until then, you will never come. When Satan points to your filthy garments, repeat the promise of Jesus, "Him that cometh to Me I will in no wise cast out." John 6:37. Tell the enemy that the blood of Jesus Christ cleanses from all sin. Make the prayer of David your own, "Purge me with hyssop, and I shall be clean; wash me, and I shall be whiter than snow" Psalm 51:7 (*Christ's Object Lessons*, pp. 205, 206).

Those who rejoice in deliverance from the old Satan-inspired concepts of God will know Him as He is presented in the parable of the prodigal son. They will have the faith and courage to bring their sins for pardon and cleansing and to thus stand before Him as if they had never sinned. These are they in whom true love for God will be found and from whom a stream of dedicated service will flow. Such will inhabit the universe throughout eternity to experience the fullness of eternal joys and pleasures. There is small wonder then that heaven will be a place of perfect bliss and security.

Chapter Thirty-Two

God Goes the Second Mile

Study/Discussion Questions:

- When the Jews disregarded God and were carried into Babylonian captivity, He did not forsake them but worked with them to mitigate the effects of their wrong choices. How?

- It is seen that when Israel decided to take up the sword they were acting contrary to God's intent and desire for them to rely upon Him in all things. He then gave them directives within that choice. Does this mean that God intended to destroy the enemies of Israel directly but had to revert to an alternative, or "plan b" approach, and use their sword when the Israelites got into the work of helping Him to fulfill His plan for them?

- If Israel had been abandoned by God to their own way with no directives or assistance, what would the outcome have been for them? For us?

- What other options could God have exercised beside total and immediate abandonment of His people?

We are still seeking Bible evidence to throw sufficient light on the incident at the golden calf to enable us to see clearly that God did not violate one principle of His character there. When the light of the Word of God shines with force and clarity on the situation, it will be seen that not only was God still acting as a Savior at the golden calf slaughter but that He has also been seriously misunderstood in that role.

The truth being developed here is that Israel elected to reject God's way when they took up the sword. Not only had the Lord not given this weapon to them, but He had done all in His power short of direct compulsion to prevent them from taking it. But once they made that choice, they instituted their way in place of God's way.

It is impossible for both the way of God and of human beings to operate within a society at the same time. It can be only one or the other, never both. So, when they elected to institute their way in place of God's, then God's methods could not be used in dealing with the rebellion at Sinai. Therefore, what happened at Mt. Sinai was not after the order of God. It was the application of the procedures that Israel had instituted by adding the sword to their way of life. The only part God filled was to apply some restraint and guidance to their use of it to minimize its evil effects.

What complicates the problem, making it difficult for many to understand God's behavior, is that Israel was still reckoned to be His people. Therefore, it is reasoned, if God was still their leader and, from that position, instructed them to execute the rebellious, then He was responsible for the slaughter. If this is correct reasoning, then it can only be concluded that this was the divinely instituted solution to the problem. Rebellion, therefore, was to be overcome by force.

The superficial thinker is satisfied with the serious, clashing contradictions in the Bible that result from such conclusions. The careful student cannot accept this. He or she will search with faith-filled, intensive dedication until the problem is resolved according to Bible principles.

The fact that the Israelites were God's people only to whatever extent they permitted Him to be their Sovereign is overlooked. This is the sad tragedy of their history. While in large areas they retained God as their leader, followed His ways, and served Him fully, there were others where they took His work to themselves. For instance, they still followed the pillar of cloud by day and fire by night, faithfully respected the Sabbath, were custodians of His law, and continued the services of the sanctuary according to the divine blueprint.

But, by taking up the sword, they deprived the Lord of His position as their Defender and Protector from enemies within and without. While it is true that they expected God to assist them in this work, it does not alter the fact that they were doing it in His stead and according to their own human principles. Therefore, their actions, as such, were not the revelation of God's character but of their own. It was the manifestation of the outworking of such wicked unbelief that led them to have more confidence in their own power to protect themselves than in God's.

Yet, God did something in this domain where they had taken the work to themselves. Inasmuch as His every act is a revelation of His character, God revealed Himself by what He did in directing the Levites to cut down the rebels. Unfortunately, the majority have seen His actions in a very different light from reality and consequently have retained an erroneous concept of His character.

It must be recognized that God is a Savior. He worked intensely to save them from taking the sword in the first place, but when they despitefully did so, then the best He could do was to give counsel designed to save them from the worst consequences of their choice. They were not compelled to obey His counsel, but they were well advised to do so if they wished to save themselves from terrible evils. It is interesting to note the perversity of humanity that will refuse to obey God in some things and yet implicitly follow His guidance in others. Thus, while Israel did not have the faith to leave their protection to God, they were prepared to follow to the letter His directions in dealing with crime in the camp.

It is doubtful if a better illustration of this exists than can be found in the relationship of God to the Israelites when they went into captivity. The evidence presented in the previous chapter shows that right up until Israel was carried into Babylon the Lord did His best to save them from it. He sent messages of warning and entreaty. He assured them that if they would only repent, then, even at the last moment, they would be delivered as if they had never sinned and would be kept safely and prosperously in their own land. He did not show the least trace of vindictiveness or desire to retaliate. He did not demand that they serve out a sentence of punishment for their evil deeds.

But they would neither heed nor repent. Because they would not, the Lord could not save them from that captivity. So they became captives. Their going into captivity effectively terminated God's efforts to save them from it. But this did not mean that the Lord ceased to act as a Savior to them. Certainly He could no longer act the role of a Savior to save them from going into captivity, for that possibility was past. They were now captives. But He could save them from the worst effects of that which they had chosen, and this is what He did.

The record of God's doing this is beautifully recorded in the Scriptures. Not only is He revealed there as an unchanging and ever-loving Savior, but, by contrast, the devil is shown in his work of destroying. The evil one had worked incessantly to deliver Israel into captivity and had succeeded. Then, when he got them there, he worked with equal frenzy to make that captivity as destructive to their physical and spiritual comfort and welfare as possible.

Thus we find God and Satan working in exactly opposite roles as we have been informed that they do. This truth is clearly portrayed in the inspired record of the way in which Satan and God related themselves to the people who had been carried captive into Babylon.

> Zedekiah at the beginning of his reign was trusted fully by the king of Babylon and had as a tried counselor the prophet Jeremiah. By pursuing an honorable course toward the Babylonians and by paying heed to the messages from the Lord through Jeremiah, he could have kept the respect of many in high authority and have had opportunity to communicate to them a knowledge of the true God. Thus the captive exiles already in Babylon would have been placed on vantage ground and granted many liberties; the name of God would have been honored far and wide; and those that remained in the land of Judah would have been spared the terrible calamities that finally came upon them.
>
> Through Jeremiah, Zedekiah and all Judah, including those taken to Babylon, were counseled to submit quietly to the temporary rule of their conquerors. It was especially important that those in captivity should seek the peace of the land into which they had been carried. This, however, was contrary to the inclination of the human heart; and Satan, taking advantage of the circumstances, caused false prophets to arise among the people, both in Jerusalem and in Babylon, who declared that the yoke of bondage would soon be broken and the former prestige of the nation restored.
>
> The heeding of such flattering prophecies would have led to fatal moves on the part of the king and the exiles, and would have frustrated the merciful designs of God in their behalf. Lest an insurrection be incited and great suffering ensue, the Lord commanded Jeremiah to meet the crisis without delay, by

warning the king of Judah of the sure consequence of rebellion. The captives also were admonished, by written communications, not to be deluded into believing their deliverance near. "Let not your prophets and your diviners, that be in the midst of you, deceive you," he urged. Jeremiah 29:8. In this connection mention was made of the Lord's purpose to restore Israel at the close of the seventy years of captivity foretold by His messengers.

With what tender compassion did God inform His captive people of His plans for Israel! He knew that should they be persuaded by false prophets to look for a speedy deliverance, their position in Babylon would be made very difficult. Any demonstration or insurrection on their part would awaken the vigilance and severity of the Chaldean authorities and would lead to a further restriction of their liberties. Suffering and disaster would result. He desired them to submit quietly to their fate and make their servitude as pleasant as possible; and His counsel to them was: "Build ye houses, and dwell in them; and plant gardens, and eat the fruit of them; ... and seek the peace of the city whither I have caused you to be carried away captives, and pray unto the Lord for it: for in the peace thereof shall ye have peace." Verses 5-7 (*Prophets and Kings*, pp. 440-442).

How clearly and wonderfully God's behavior is revealed in this story, in contrast to Satan's. While Satan was working to make their captivity as unpleasant and terrible as possible, the Lord sent Jeremiah with messages to the people that, if heeded, would have made their enforced stay in that foreign land "as pleasant as possible." He also specifically warned them against heeding the messages from the professed prophets of the Lord. Thus, while Satan was working to effect the destruction of the deserving, the Lord was striving to deliver them.

Once this view of God is grasped and understood, then the key has been obtained that will perfectly explain the true nature of the command to the Levites to go and destroy all those who worshiped at the golden calf.

However, before the application is fully made to that situation, let this story be developed a little further. Even though the Lord's behavior toward apostate Israel is sufficient evidence to make the point that God acts out only the role of a Savior, yet more evidence is provided. This time, though in the same story, it concerns other people outside the family of Israel. They were the people of Edom, Moab, Tyre, and other nations.

Of all the people in the ancient world, none had been more committed to an aggressive and hostile war against God and His cause than these people. The Edomites were descendants of Esau and the Moabites of Lot, but leading encyclopedias such as The Britannica are unable to give any origin to the people of Tyre. However, in Ezekiel 28 the wickedness of the king of Tyre was so great that he was spoken of as being the personification and direct instrument of the devil, so much so that no distinction is made between them.

While we may be able to accept the idea that God could retain some favor toward the Jews, we cannot think of any such thing being still available for the Moabites, Edomites, and the people of Tyre. We would not expect that God would act toward them as a Savior too. Yet the Lord made no distinction between them and the Israelites. When they too were in great danger because of their willingness to listen to the voice of Satan and their own wretched human desires, God sent them the same message He had given to His own people. Through Jeremiah, He warned them not to resist the king of Babylon, for their cause was hopeless, but to be discreet and cooperative so that they might be saved undue suffering and further loss.

God did not go so far as to send Jeremiah to those nations, for they had long since made it clear that neither God nor His servants were welcome among them. But when ambassadors from those lands visited the king of Judah to discuss the possibility of combined revolt against Nebuchadnezzar, they then placed themselves where the Lord could give them a message. God made use of the opportunity to stretch out a hand to save them.

> From the first, Jeremiah had followed a consistent course in counseling submission to the Babylonians. This counsel was given not only to Judah, but to many of the surrounding nations. In the earlier portion of Zedekiah's reign, ambassadors from the rulers of Edom, Moab, Tyre, and other nations visited the king of Judah to learn whether in his judgment the time was opportune for a united revolt and whether he would join them in battling against the king of Babylon. While these ambassadors were awaiting a response, the word of the Lord came to Jeremiah, saying, "Make thee bonds and yokes, and put them upon thy neck, and send them to the king of Edom, and to the king of Moab, and to the king of the Ammonites, and to the king of Tyrus, and to the king of Zidon, by the hand of the messengers which come to Jerusalem unto Zedekiah king of Judah." Jeremiah 27:2, 3.
>
> Jeremiah was commanded to instruct the ambassadors to inform their rulers that God had given them all into the hand of Nebuchadnezzar, the king of Babylon, and that they were to "serve him, and his son, and his son's son, until the very time of his land come." Verse 7.
>
> The ambassadors were further instructed to declare to their rulers that if they refused to serve the Babylonian king they should be punished "with the sword, and with the famine, and with the pestilence" till they were consumed. Especially were they to turn from the teaching of false prophets who might counsel otherwise. "Hearken not ye to your prophets," the Lord declared, "nor to your diviners, nor to your dreamers, nor to your enchanters, nor to your sorcerers, which speak unto you, saying, Ye shall not serve the king of Babylon: for they prophesy a lie unto you, to remove you far from your land; and that I should drive you out, and ye should perish. But the nations that bring their neck under the yoke of the king of Babylon, and serve him, those will I let remain still in their own land, saith the Lord; and they shall till it, and dwell therein." Verses 8-11. The lightest punishment that a merciful God could inflict upon so rebellious a people was submission to the rule of Babylon, but if they warred against this decree of servitude they were to feel the full vigor of His chastisement.

The amazement of the assembled council of nations knew no bounds when Jeremiah, carrying the yoke of subjection about his neck, made known to them the will of God.

Against determined opposition Jeremiah stood firmly for the policy of submission (*Ibid.*, pp. 442-444).

Here is the revelation of God the Savior at work. This story shows with great clarity the contrast between Satan's work as the destroyer and God's work as the restorer. It is a thing of beauty and wonder that the Lord would do this for Israel, but it is an even greater wonder that He would do it for the people of Tyre, Edom, and Moab.

Here it is shown that the behavior of God and Christ is indeed identical. Jesus both taught and lived the principle of loving your enemies, going the second mile, and of doing good forever to those who have done evil to you. God had gone the first mile by doing His very best to save them from captivity. Then, when they were captured, in spite of His efforts for them, He went the second mile by giving them guidance on how they could make their captivity as pleasant and short as possible.

But their rebellious hearts were no more prepared to accept God's saving efforts when He went the second mile with them than when He went the first. Thus they deprived God of any hope of saving them from their own foolish selves. The disasters that befell them were not from God, but from the natural reactions of those to whom they should have been subservient. They sowed the seed, and they reaped the harvest. All that happened to them was the inevitable outworking of their own course of action. They provided the cause, and the effect was determined.

The tragedy was that they did not understand God's character. Instead of seeing in those loving efforts a strong work of salvation springing from a heart of infinite, unfathomable love, they saw God and Jeremiah as being in league with the Babylonian king, and they openly accused them of this.

This is just the problem with God in the Old Testament. Humanity has consistently misunderstood what He really did and seen Him as doing something entirely different. This is why He has come to be looked upon as a God of terrible destruction.

But He is not. In the Old Testament, He behaved toward His people and others always and only as Christ did in the New Testament. He loved His enemies, blessed those who cursed and despitefully used Him, and went the second mile. He was ever and only the Savior to all. When destruction came upon them, it was only because they had rejected His efforts to save them, leaving no alternative. Thus God never determined their punishment, nor did He personally exercise His power to administer it.

Now that this principle of God's workings has been seen in the experience of Jeremiah with the last king of Judah and the ambassadors of the other nations, there should be no further problem in seeing what the Lord really did back in the days of the golden calf.

In that situation God went the second mile as surely as He did in Israel's captivity to Babylon. But whereas the children of Israel and the surrounding nations would not accept God's counsel during the second mile, the Israelites at Mount Sinai did. While neither heeded the efforts God expended during the first mile, the Levites did obey the second mile counsel, while Zedekiah and his contemporaries would not.

In at least four ways, God's efforts during the first mile back in Moses' day were directed at saving them from taking the sword. By upholding the illustrious witness of Jacob's double deliverance (his emancipation from the ill intent of his Uncle Laban and subsequent safe encounter with the hostility of his brother, Esau), God's rebuke to Moses when he set out to deliver the Israelites by the sword, the instruction to the Egyptians *not* to provide them with weapons, and then the marvelous deliverance at the Red Sea, the Lord told them as plainly as it could ever be told that they should not take the sword because they would never need it while they walked in His ways.

While He could teach the truth of His way both by declaration and demonstration, He would not make the choice for them, neither would He deprive them of the opportunity to make it. Thus it was that on the shore of the Red Sea, when they saw displayed the armor-clad bodies of the Egyptians, they were forced to make a decision. School had ended for the moment, and the examination had begun. How would they choose? Would the Lord's saving efforts indeed prove the effective means of keeping them from taking up the sword?

We could well wish that this had been so, but the sad record of history is that they took up the sword. There is no direct statement to say that they armed themselves on the shores of the Red Sea, but there are statements which prove that just before then they were still an unarmed people, while shortly after that we find them locked in physical combat with the Amalekites, with sword clashing against sword and spear against spear.

The exact point of time is not the most important item in this discussion. The vital factor is that after all God's efforts to save them from taking the weapons of destruction they chose to take them. When they did that, they chose to institute their way in place of God's. This fact is critical in understanding God's character in this situation.

God did not institute an alternative to His first and best procedure. He does not operate after this fashion, for His way is so perfect that it requires no provisions for failure. In fact, to supply any secondary system would be to admit that the first was faulty and, **therefore**, needing adjustment. Neither God nor His principles have ever failed or appeared in any way defective. The problem lies only in the refusal of some of His creatures to abide by them. Whenever this happens, they replace His perfect codes with their destructive ones. Therefore, on every occasion when the sword was used in Israel, it was humanity acting in humanity's way, not the carrying out of an alternative that God was obliged to accept because His way of perfection had failed. Human beings were the destroyers. God had not compromised in the least. With undeviating consistency, He had continued His eternal role of being the Savior.

But what makes God appear to have changed is the misunderstanding of His action in going the second mile, the further work of salvation. That which in actuality was God's continued effort to save is viewed all too often as His turning into a destroyer. No greater misconstruction of God's acts could be imagined.

When Israel took the sword, the Lord was left with four alternative courses of action.

He could simply have said that He would walk with them no more, that they were now on their own and what happened to them was entirely their own fault. This was the same course open to Him in the Garden of Eden. There He could have argued that He had given them everything, including adequate warnings of the cost of disobedience. Having shown their ingratitude, they were undeserving of any further help from Him, so He would have been entirely justified if He had left them to their fate. This is how He could have chosen to act.

If God had abandoned humanity, it would have passed speedily out of existence.

Likewise, if the Lord had turned away when Israel took the sword, the nation would have been quickly destroyed. First, they would have fought with their weapons among themselves. Second, they were no match for the highly trained and experienced Canaanites who, as Satan's allies, longed for nothing more than to remove Israel from the face of the earth. For God to have walked out on the Israelites would have committed them to certain death.

If the Israelites had elected to completely go their own way, then God would have had no choice but to leave them to themselves with all the consequences. But in many things they were still prepared to go God's way. They accepted the Sabbath institution, the sanctuary service, the general leadership of God, the provision of their daily bread, and even His counsel on how to best use their swords.

Therefore, in the very nature of His character, God could not leave them because they had departed from His ways in one thing or even in a number of things. He would stay with them, as with any person, while there was still some place where He could bless and heal them. He will never leave us nor forsake us. It is the person who leaves and forsakes God. When God separates from humanity, it is only because humanity has gone away from Him, never He from them.

The second option was for God to use force or arbitrarily manipulate events so that they would not have any opportunity to acquire the sword nor the skill to use it, thus insisting upon delivering them by His own method. But this was not an option, for by His withholding the sword from them, He would have consigned them to a quick extinction. Additionally, to suggest that God could have insisted upon using His own method of deliverance breaks with logic, for God's method is to never use force. Either way, Satan would have had grounds to claim a victory in his accusation.

The third option was for God to simply ignore the people's sin—to pretend that it had not happened. But He certainly could not do this. Sin demands attention. It imposes a situation that cannot be left unattended. The reality of sin is that to ignore it, for God, would be to let it do its work of separating the soul from God, which results in cessation of that soul's existence. In order to prevent this from happening, God would have to exercise mercy and interpose Himself between the consequence and the sinner. How He did this, while being true to justice and not interfering with the free choice of human beings, is the study of the gospel plan of salvation.

This leaves the fourth and only viable possibility. The others end in either a quick death or in God abandoning His principles and acting out of character, which is impossible. God would remain with His people to whatever extent they would have Him in their midst. He would lead, protect, forgive, bless, and teach them. In those areas where they chose their own way, He would offer them counsel that, if received and obeyed, would save them from the worst effects of what they had chosen. In the meantime, they might be led to see the error of choosing their own course of action and return entirely to the Lord's way.

This is how God handles the situation in the incident of the golden calf and in all the conquests and their attendant slaughters in the land of Canaan. What they did in all this was their doing, not His. They had established their own codes, and God had no choice but to let them have it their way. But He could and did counsel them on how they could operate in their own way without it being the worst of that way. This was love. This was returning good for evil. This is going the second mile.

Chapter Thirty-Three

The Consistency of God

Study/Discussion Questions:

The Israelites, by taking up the sword, declared that they themselves would handle matters involving any threat to their government. They now had a choice to wield the sword entirely according to their own wisdom or to hear God's instructions given to them within their own paradigm of self-defense. However, we find that on certain occasions justice according to God's way—departing where He is not wanted—is administered, even while Israel was still holding the sword. How can we maintain that God was being consistent in all of this?

Having searched out the general principles that underlie God's behavior at the golden calf incident, the time has come to look at this and other specific incidents in detail.

One of the great characteristics that sets God apart from all others is His utter consistency and total reliability. He is "the Father of lights, with whom there is no variation or shadow of turning" (James 1:17). With such a God there can be no capriciousness, no acting from the motivation of self-interest, no disregard of the principles involved in the law, no seeking to justify certain means because of a desired end result.

In the history of Israel and of humankind in general, there are two different kinds of situations in which sin develops. One is where God alone is in the position of leadership so that the sole responsibility of dealing with the problem rests with Him. Should the sinners be unrepentant then the Lord simply leaves them to themselves to reap that which they have sown. They then perish at the hands of whatever calamity is brooding over the situation, be it fire, earthquake, pestilence, invaders, or plagues. Examples of these types of calamities are the flood; the destruction of Sodom and Gomorrah; the plagues of Egypt; the overwhelming of the Egyptians in the Red Sea; the death of Korah, Dathan, and Abiram; the attack by the serpents in the wilderness; the death of Sennacherib's army; the destruction of Jerusalem in AD 70; the coming plagues; and the final destruction of this solar system. None of these calamities befall humanity until every possible avenue of divine mercy has been exhausted and there is nothing more that people will let God do for them.

Another situation exists when individuals replace God with themselves as the determiner of their fate and the administrator of their own affairs, thus establishing themselves as the investigator, judge, and executioner of those who sin against him. Because God has given the right of choice to His creatures and because He will never use compulsion, He has no choice other than to let them have their own way and manage their own institutions. However, He knows that human beings, left to themselves, are very foolish and cruel administrators who will unwisely adopt a course that brings fearful consequences. The Lord was in a position to see this and to offer counsel, which the Bible calls, "commands," which, if heeded, would enable people to take actions that would save them from the worst effects of their chosen course.

Examples of these are the golden calf, the conquest of Canaan, the wars of David and subsequent kings, the captivity in Babylon, and others.

In the golden calf incident, Israel had broken the law in the worst way. They had made another god in place of the true God, thus separating themselves from Him entirely. They had entered into the licentious practices of the heathen until they had become utterly debauched and depraved.

They could not so wantonly and defiantly break God's law without sowing seeds that, in this case, would bring a very speedy harvest. The harvest would not be something the Lord imposed upon them. It would be the simple and natural outworking of the breaking of the law.

Those who, at the base of Sinai, worshiped the golden calf laid themselves open to terrible consequences. At first they joined in a unified revelry, which they thoroughly enjoyed. It gave them the wild stimulation, feverish excitement, and heady intoxication so loved by humans. After the intensity of saturating the senses with sinful pleasures, there comes a depressing letdown, an emotional and physical low that can give rise to destructive behaviors. Destitute of the restraining Spirit of God yet desperately in need of Him to quiet and control jaded nerves and ugly feelings, there was nothing to stop the outbreak of bitter strife in the camp. It is a characteristic of the heathen that their revelries are usually succeeded by intense conflicts among themselves.

As strife broke out, the swords were unsheathed. One or more would be killed. Then the relatives of the dead would engage in a vendetta of revenge. More would be slain, calling for still further retaliation until it would escalate into a destructive outburst so great as to threaten to wipe out the entire encampment. Their ever-vigilant enemies would recognize the opportunity to launch a surprise attack on the confused mass, and the nation would be decimated. In the meantime, as revenge was sought by this or that person, family, or faction, they would study the most cruel and prolonged ways of executing those unfortunate enough to fall under their power. The witness of history convincingly declares that the further a people move away from God, the more cruel they are in the treatment of their captives. On the other side, the closer they follow the Lord, the more humane they are.

It is written regarding the apostasy at Sinai:

> Unless punishment had been speedily visited upon transgression, the same results would again have been seen. The earth would have become as corrupt as in the days of Noah. Had these transgressors been spared, evils would have followed, greater than resulted from sparing the life of Cain. It was the mercy of God that thousands should suffer, to prevent the necessity of visiting judgments

upon millions. In order to save the many, He must punish the few. Furthermore, as the people had cast off their allegiance to God, they had forfeited the divine protection, and, deprived of their defense, the whole nation was exposed to the power of their enemies. Had not the evil been promptly put away, they would soon have fallen a prey to their numerous and powerful foes. It was necessary for the good of Israel, and also as a lesson to all succeeding generations, that crime should be promptly punished. And it was no less a mercy to the sinners themselves that they should be cut short in their evil course. Had their life been spared, the same spirit that led them to rebel against God would have been manifested in hatred and strife among themselves, and they would eventually have destroyed one another. It was in love to the world, in love to Israel, and even to the transgressors, that crime was punished with swift and terrible severity (*Patriarchs and Prophets*, pp. 325, 326).

These then are the terrible things that would have come upon the transgressors themselves, the Israelites as a nation, and the world in general if God had done nothing for them. The worst possible results would have eventuated.

The love of God, that marvelous, infinite, and unchangeable love, drove Him to tell them how they could save themselves from so terrible a fate. He could no longer do it for them for they had taken over the work themselves, but they could save themselves from the worst effects of their own choice provided they would listen to and follow His counsels.

Whether they followed those counsels or not was as much a matter of their own choice as when they were faced with the alternative of leaving the swords with the dead Egyptians or of appropriating them. At the Red Sea they elected to take the wrong course by which they supplanted God as their Protector. But while not prepared to obey Him in this area, they were not rendered incapable of accepting His guidance in other matters. They could, if they would, adhere to His directions outlining how they could minimize the evil they had chosen.

In effect, as they faced the crisis occasioned by the worshiping of the golden calf, they were confronted with two possibilities. If they did not take some action, millions would perish. If they followed the Lord's suggestions, then only a few would die by comparison, and a great deal of tragedy would be averted. But, if anything was done at all, it had to be by them because they had deprived God of any opportunity to take appropriate action Himself.

Great care must be taken not to slide into the trap of supposing that because force was necessary to put down the rebellion, God compromised His principles on this occasion and resorted to force by using the righteous Levites as His direct instruments. God does not change His principles for anything or anybody. With Him there is no variableness or shadow of turning.

The exercise of force is contrary to the principles of God's government (*The Desire of Ages*, p. 22).

Compelling power is found only under Satan's government. The Lord's principles are not of this order (*The Desire of Ages*, p. 759).

Earthly kingdoms rule by the ascendancy of physical power; but from Christ's kingdom every carnal weapon, every instrument of coercion, is banished (*The Acts of the Apostles*, p. 12).

Had the Israelites been careful never to take up the sword, while fully trusting the Lord to take care of their needs, the problem would have been speedily resolved in accordance with divine methods of working. By their utter refusal to repent, the rebels would have certified that they wanted no more of God. He would have respected this decision and left them to themselves to reap what they had sown. Then, whatever impending disaster was present, would have taken them as the earthquake took Korah, Dathan, and Abiram, the fire destroyed Sodom and Gomorrah, or the Red Sea drowned the Egyptians.

But the situation was not such. Israel had taken the sword, and thereby, they made it their responsibility to take care of their own problems of defense against enemies within and without the camp. It was not possible for them to do this and for God, simultaneously, to still hold His position as their Protector. This could not be, for either they did that work or they trusted Him to do it. But because they had not entirely cast off their allegiance and respect for Him, He was afforded the opportunity of retaining the position of adviser to them. They did not have the wisdom to understand the results of one usage of the sword as distinct from another. He did. If they would listen and obey, He would teach them the differences so that they could save themselves, and the world, from much unnecessary sorrow and loss. It was for this reason that He counseled them that it was better to destroy the incurably affected than to leave the cancer to contaminate millions more.

Exactly as the father in the hunting story knew that killings were inevitable once his son had taken the gun, so God knew that there was going to be unpreventable slaughtering. It was no longer a matter of attempting to prevent the killings. All that could now be done was to work to make them as merciful and minimal as possible. God worked here just as at the later time of the Babylonian conquest when He sought to direct Israel into a course that would enable them to "make their servitude as pleasant as possible" (*Prophets and Kings*, p. 441). The unvarying consistency of God is truly remarkable.

It must be stressed that while the Lord commanded the Levites to kill the rebels, and much later told Zedekiah, the Ammonites, the Edomites, the people of Tyre, and the other nations concerned to submit quietly and cooperatively to the king of Babylon, He did not compel them to do it. The Levites chose to obey, but the others did not. By so doing, the Levites saved themselves, the whole of Israel, and the world from the most terrible consequences. By refusing to obey, Zedekiah and his contemporaries brought upon themselves dreadful reprisals.

Before the Levites was a third course. They could, then and there, have repented of ever taking up the weapons of destruction. Had they truly done this, they would have cast away those swords, bowed before the Lord, and confessed that they had erred. They would have given back to Him the sole responsibility of caring for them against enemies without and within the camp.

The Levites did not have sufficient understanding to do this, but they did know enough to obey the instructions God gave them and thus to avert the terrible consequences of not doing it. Unfortunately, by the time we come to the captivity in Babylon, the people were too blind to even follow the Lord's counsels, so they suffered the terrible wrath of Babylon for their continued spirit of rebellion and insurrection. There were some who obeyed, however. Daniel and his companions gave a living demonstration of the honor and freedom to be enjoyed by those who were obedient to God's command.

A question must arise here. Why were the people themselves left by God to destroy the rebels in the camp at the golden calf but not so with Korah, Dathan, and Abiram? In the instance of Korah, Dathan, and Abiram, the people were simply called upon to separate themselves from the rebels and watch them die at the hands of a terrible natural calamity. Why is there this difference? Israel still carried the sword, so it would be expected that God would have to call upon them to slay the rebels.

Once the principle governing God's actions in dealing with situations such as the rebellion at Sinai is learned, it would be expected that every disorder in the camp was resolved in the same way. It would be anticipated that, until Israel handed back to Him the position of full administrator of all their affairs, God would direct them to slay the rebels.

This is precisely what happened on numerous occasions. Notable examples were the stoning of the man who gathered sticks on the Sabbath, the adulterer, Achan who stole the Babylonian garment from Jericho, and the extermination of the Canaanites.

But it was not always done after this fashion. When Korah and his companions arose in defiance of God, when Miriam and Aaron rebelled, when the people murmured against Moses and God, the people were not commissioned to go out and strike down the offenders. They were taken by an earthquake, the infliction of leprosy, plagues, and the invasion of fiery serpents. In none of these punishments did the people have a part. Yet there had been no change in the situation of government. The people still carried the sword. So why was it done one way on certain occasions and differently on others? Is there an underlying principle that decides what it will be each time?

God is neither capricious nor inconsistent. Indeed, there was an underlying principle that determined how each problem should be dealt with. Within the structure of the camp, two different situations existed. One concerned the people in general, and the other, the position of Moses, God's personal appointee.

The people had placed themselves under the protection of the sword. By doing this they had reconstituted their government accordingly; therefore, when any offenses threatening that government were committed, they had to be dealt with by weapons of force wielded by the people. Those threats could be internal or external. In the case of worshiping the golden calf, it was internal, but when the Amalekites came against them, it was external. Because they did not have faith to accept God as their protector, they were left with self-protection as their only recourse. They became still further entrenched in this when they chose to have a king like the nations around them.

But there was another area in the encampment not under the jurisdiction of the people. This was the office of Moses. No one stood between him and God. God had appointed him his work so that he was answerable to the Lord and no one else. Furthermore, Moses had never joined with the people in taking up the sword. Even though he was the best-trained military man of all, he had so learned the lessons of trust in God while in the wilderness of Midian that when the opportunity came to take up weapons, he chose not to. Not once do we read of him leading Israel into battle with a sword in his hand.

Therefore, when Moses himself sinned by striking the rock, the people could not touch him. He was not under their government, in any sense. Only God could deal with him, and He would do it according to His righteous procedures and principles.

In like manner, when the people sinned against Moses and against God, they transgressed in a realm that had not come under their jurisdiction, for the sovereignty of the sword did not reach that far. So whenever the people sinned in this area, the punishment came by God's departing from them and leaving them exposed to the surrounding perils.

Consider the rebellion of Korah, Dathan, and Abiram. It was specifically a challenge to God's appointment of Moses, as was the protest of Miriam and Aaron and Israel's miserable complaints of which the following is typical:

> And the people spoke against God and against Moses: "Why have you brought us up out of Egypt to die in the wilderness? For there is no food and no water, and our soul loathes this worthless bread" (Num. 21:5).

All of these were in the same category. They were outside the jurisdiction taken over by the people when they took up the sword. Therefore, God was free and unhampered in dealing with these problems. In every such case He worked in the same way. Korah and his supporters were swallowed up by an earthquake; Miriam was afflicted with leprosy; and Israel suffered from plagues and the invasion of fiery serpents.

The same principle applies in the case of David. When he committed adultery and murdered Bathsheba's husband to cover up their sin, he would have been stoned to death had he been an ordinary citizen. But the people had made him a king like the kings around him. This placed him above the law of the land, for the kings of those days were exempt from obedience to that law. Therefore, he was outside the domain in which the people had taken authority to themselves, so they were not able to punish him for his crimes. He was thus placed in a position where his sin had separated him from God's protection. The troubles that overtook him were the direct outworking of his departure from the paths of righteousness.

Thus each situation in the camp was met in the way appropriate to it. When the people sinned within the area taken over by them when they acquired swords, they had to administer the punishment to assure their continued protection. God's work was limited under these circumstances to offering them the counsel He was so capable of giving, whereby they would be delivered from the worst effects of their chosen order.

When they sinned outside this area of jurisdiction, the matter could not be settled by them, for they had neither right nor power to deal with it. All God could do was to accept their insistence that He separate from them, and they were thus left exposed to the perils continually threatening them. God did not depart from them prompted by a hurt or revengeful spirit. It was with infinite sorrow and only with the greatest reluctance when every saving effort had been rejected that God accepted the necessity to withdraw. A careful study of the various incidents confirms that, with the utmost consistency, God dealt with each situation according to its nature. How the Israelites perished depended on whether they fell into the hands of their own established governmental system or whether they sinned outside of that and fell under the powers of nature released from God's control and direction.

The question of God's methods of dealing with such problems as the worshiping of the golden calf has now been thoroughly explored. It is thus made evident that, when rightly understood, the Old Testament records do not reveal a different God from the One portrayed by Christ during His earthly sojourn. "Hear, O Israel: The Lord our God, the Lord is one" (Deut. 6:4).

Chapter Thirty-Four

The Wars of Israel

Study/Discussion Questions:

- How did God intend that Israel should be victorious over their enemies?
- Whose idea was it that spies be sent in to inspect the land before sending in the entire people?
- Forty years later, they went into the land under Joshua. What was God trying to tell the people in the way they were instructed to take Jericho?
- Permissive will is not merely functioning in a paradigm that is less than God's ideal; it is deadly. It is putting our ways in place of God's ways, and it is a downward path. Israel took the path. After taking the sword, they moved into another realm of self-governance. What was that?
- The ultimate outcome of the path of permissive will is embodied in what declaration made by the Jews?

The fact that Israel went to war and slaughtered their enemies, ofttimes to the last man, woman, child, and animal, is not the real problem. That arises when God "commanded" they do it. When they did, they received His approval, but when they did not, He reproved them strongly. For instance, when Saul did not utterly destroy the Amalekites, he received a very severe rebuke from God through the prophet Samuel.

Despite the Lord's clear instructions, supported and illustrated by frequent demonstrations of His way of doing things, the Israelites showed a persisting disposition to take matters more and more into their own hands, thereby denying the manifestations of God's character and ways.

It all began when they took the sword after crossing the Red Sea. Between that time and their arrival at Kadesh Barnea in readiness for the border crossing, there had not been a great deal of bloodshed. The two most notable incidents were the battle with the Amalekites and the slaughter of the worshipers of the golden calf.

Yet God had never intended that they should gain the land of promise through the use of the sword. He told them how it would be done and assured them that He would do it, not they. Long before they reached the Promised Land, it was all spelled out.

I will send My fear before you, I will cause confusion among all the people to whom you come, and will make all your enemies turn their backs to you. And I will send hornets before you, which shall drive out the Hivite, the Canaanite, and the Hittite from before you. I will not drive them out from before you in one year, lest the land become desolate and the beast of the field become too numerous for you. Little by little I will drive them out from before you, until you have increased, and you inherit the land. And I will set your bounds from the Red Sea to the sea, Philistia, and from the desert to the River. For I will deliver the inhabitants of the land into your hand, and you shall drive them out before you (Exod. 23:27-31).

Thus the Lord emphasized that *He* would drive out the inhabitants of the land. Earlier, we have found that such expressions must be understood differently when describing God's actions from when they describe people's actions. Therefore, God driving them out would not have been by His using compelling power. Rather, as He came to them with His offerings of love, their resistance to and rejection of these would have placed them outside God's protective circle leaving nothing to save them from the destructive forces in the hands of the destroyer.

But they decided that displacing the inhabitants of the land was something they could not leave to God. They must do it themselves. This spirit really came to the forefront when they reached Kadesh Barnea. God's plan was to fulfill His promise to lead them directly into the land. Accordingly, as recalled by Moses, God told them to go in under His leadership and possess it. Here are Moses' words as he reminded the children of Israel of the event.

"So we departed from Horeb, and went through all that great and terrible wilderness which you saw on the way to the mountains of the Amorites, as the Lord our God had commanded us. Then we came to Kadesh Barnea. And I said to you, 'You have come to the mountains of the Amorites, which the Lord our God is giving us. Look, the Lord your God has set the land before you; go up and possess it, as the Lord God of your fathers has spoken to you; do not fear or be discouraged'" (Deut. 1:19-21).

Had they had the spirit of trust in and submission to the Lord of heaven, they would have responded by following without doubt or question where the Lord led. The inhabitants of the land would have fearfully retreated or would have attacked them with a rashness born of desperation. Such an action would have been one of complete and final defiance against heaven, whereby their separation from God would have been so total as to remove all divine protection from them. Speedily they would have perished as did the Egyptians, Korah and his company, or the Israelites themselves when a plague broke out among them.

But the Jews did not trust God, as is evident from their response to His directions. Here is their answer:

"And every one of you came near to me and said, 'Let *us* send men before *us*, and let *them* search out the land for *us*, and bring back word to *us* of the way by which *we* should go up, and of the cities into which *we* shall come'" (verse 22).

Here indeed was the substitution of man in place of God. Divine leadership was discarded in favor of the human.

How did God react to such a development? Was He offended? Did He demand His rights, insisting they do it His way? Not for one moment. If that was the way they chose to go, then all He could do was respect their choice and bless them as far as remained possible in their execution of their plan.

> Eleven days after leaving Mount Horeb the Hebrew host encamped at Kadesh, in the wilderness of Paran, which was not far from the borders of the Promised Land. Here it was proposed *by the people* that spies be sent up to survey the country. The matter was presented before the Lord by Moses, and permission was granted, with the direction that one of the rulers of each tribe should be selected for this purpose. The men were chosen as had been directed, and Moses bade them go and see the country, what it was, its situation and natural advantages; and the people that dwelt therein, whether they were strong or weak, few or many; also to observe the nature of the soil and its productiveness and to bring of the fruit of the land (*Patriarchs and Prophets*, p. 387, emphasis added).

Thus it was that "the Lord spoke to Moses, saying, 'Send men to spy out the land of Canaan, which I am giving to the children of Israel; from each tribe of their fathers you shall send a man, every one a leader among them.' So Moses sent them from the Wilderness of Paran according to the command of the Lord, all of them men who were heads of the children of Israel" (Num. 13:1-3).

If the reference in Numbers was read without considering the other statements, it would appear that the whole idea was from God. But it was *from the people*, which was contrary to God's plans. Yet it declares that Moses, by the *commandment* of the Lord, sent the twelve men. When the word "commandment" is used in connection with human behavior, it indicates an authoritative statement that is to be obeyed, irrespective of whether the recipient likes it or not. It becomes clear, however, that when used by the Lord it is more in the form of instruction or counsel with the choice of whether to obey or disobey being left with the people.

Thus the people took over their own leadership from God's hands. This was a further step in the wrong direction. Taking the sword had given them their own government in place of God's, but they had still followed the pillar of cloud by day and the pillar of fire by night. The time had now come when their self-confidence and their corresponding lack of faith in God led them to reject even that leadership. God was not offended. He behaved with perfect consistency. He gave them the liberty to choose whether they would follow His plans or their own.

If they wanted to send men in before them, they were free to do so. Of course, the situation could be worsened if poorly suited men were to go. Once again, in His love for them, God gave them directions to bring about the best outcome—thus He instructed that responsible men should be elected for the task.

But what a disaster it proved to be. It was a mistake that prevented that entire generation from entering the Promised Land. During the following forty years, everyone who had been twenty years old and above at the time was to die in the wilderness, except, of course, Caleb, Joshua, and members of the unnumbered tribe of Levi.

When they did finally follow the Lord into the land of Canaan, they did not send twelve spies first. It is true that Joshua sent out two spies, but the basis of their being sent was completely different from that of the previous experience. It had to be different for, whereas the people forty years before had placed their faith in themselves, Joshua had no confidence in himself. He placed his entire trust in God.

> Joshua was a wise general because God was his guide.... This was the secret of Joshua's victory. He made God his Guide (*The SDA Bible Commentary*, vol. 2, p. 993).

Whereas the people called for the spies to go forth at Kadesh Barnea, no such call came from them at Gilgal. This was from Joshua, and it was not motivated from any distrust in the Lord's leading. It is much more likely that the Spirit of God directed him to do it for the salvation of Rahab and her family. It gave her the opportunity to recognize God's power as being supreme and to demonstrate her faith in that power by hiding the two men. As a wonderful reward for that faith, she was accorded the high honor of being a mother in the direct line of the promised Messiah.

In sending those spies into the city, God demonstrated His character of wonderful, saving love. Inasmuch as Joshua had made the Lord his guide, it was God who chose to send the men in. He knew the heart of Rahab and her household. He knew she would respond to His call of salvation, but she was imprisoned within the walls of Jericho, and by no means could she go out to the Israelites. Therefore, the Lord sent those two men to her. She responded to the divinely provided opportunity and showed where her faith was. Thus she became known to the Israelites so that, when the city was destroyed, she survived and was rescued.

Thus far we have traced Israel's persistent tendency to replace the Lord's leadership and management with their own. It is now to be shown that God, with loving regard for His erring people, was trying to bring them back to the only safe path, which involved laying down their swords, thus giving God His rightful place as Guide, Protector, and Provider for His people. As a result, they did not need to fight, break the law, or stand sadly by the graves of those slain in battle.

As they crossed the Jordan and marched on to Jericho, the Lord spoke to them once more in a mighty demonstration designed to reveal His full capacity to fulfill His promises to give them the land. It was a hopeful attempt to establish their faith in Him that they would abandon all confidence in self, lay down the sword, and permit God to do His work in His own way. It was a reiteration of the same lessons that God had sought to teach their fathers as they left the land of Egypt.

As the waters of the Red Sea were opened to them by the miraculous power of God, so were the flooded waves of the Jordan rolled back to make a safe path for the people. As the Egyptians had been prevented from coming near, so, in that crossing, the Canaanites made no approach to them. Yet, from the military point of view, it would have been an excellent time to attack. With half of Israel on one side and half on the other, their forces were divided. The enemy could have speedily reduced their army portion by portion. But they did not come near them.

Then the Lord commissioned the Israelites to march around the city once per day until the seventh day when they were to march around it seven times. Then the massive walls came crashing down.

It should have been enough. They had the mighty promises of God; they had the multiplied lessons of the past, which are at all times easier to read and understand than those of the present; they had God's clear instructions that the land was not to be taken by warfare; and now, once more, they had a personal demonstration of God's tremendous power doing His promised work.

God gave them specific instructions for taking the city. In this He had a purpose. Desiring to deliver them from their own self-destructive ways, He organized an exercise in faith designed to develop in them the sense of utter distrust in human power and planning on one hand and of total committal to God's leadership and instruction on the other.

> "By faith the walls of Jericho fell down." Hebrews 11:30. The Captain of the Lord's host communicated only with Joshua; He did not reveal Himself to all the congregation, and it rested with them to believe or doubt the words of Joshua, to obey the commands given by him in the name of the Lord, or to deny his authority. *They* could not see the host of angels who attended them under the leadership of the Son of God. They might have reasoned: "What unmeaning movements are these, and how ridiculous the performance of marching daily around the walls of the city, blowing trumpets of rams' horns. This can have no effect upon those towering fortifications." But the very plan of continuing this ceremony through so long a time prior to the final overthrow of the walls afforded opportunity for the development of faith among the Israelites (*Patriarchs and Prophets*, p. 493).

God's whole design in this adventure was to call them back to a nonbelligerent status. Through this means "it was to be impressed upon their minds that their strength was not in the wisdom of man, nor in his might, but only in the God of their salvation. They were thus to become accustomed to relying wholly upon their divine Leader" (*Ibid*).

Indeed, it should have been enough.

Right then and there they ought to have stripped off their armor, laid it in a great heap, confessed the sovereignty of God, and expressed their complete trust in Him to give them the land He had promised in the way He had said He would.

But they did not do it. They rushed into the city, and soon their swords were dripping with the shed blood of men, women, and children. What a terrible, scarring effect that must have had upon their souls! Such a work could not lift people nearer to God. It would tend to brutalize them, to make them callous of life, and benumbed to the finest, most uplifting attributes of the divine character. With increasing clarity it must be seen that such actions on the people's part were never intended by God. (There are some statements in regard to the overthrow of the walls of Jericho that make it appear that God was a direct destroyer in this case. We will examine these later when other difficult statements are discussed.)

But against every effort and good intention by God, the people did not see the implications of clinging to the sword, which their fathers had taken up. They could not feel secure without it. They depended upon it to protect them from their enemies. They wanted to care for their own protection with the *help* of the Lord.

As surely as they clung to the sword, they came under the inexorable law that declares that all who take the sword will as surely perish by the sword. Their history after Jericho gives the clearest vindication to this principle.

It may be argued that it was not taking the sword but their loss of faith in God which occasioned their destruction as a nation, for whenever they, with the sword in their hands, put their trust in the Lord, they were victorious. This is true, but what has to be seen is that the act of taking the sword was the fruit of their loss of faith in God. Only a people who did not wholly and totally trust God to be their protector would take the sword. That first downward step into unbelief must inevitably be followed by others, especially as the practice of warfare would brutalize the warrior and make him still less receptive to the call and ways of God.

So, the Israelites at Jericho came to a point of decision, a crossroads. They could have let God finish the work of conquest for them, or they could use the brutal sword. Tragically, they made the wrong choice—the one that was the fruit of unbelief. Palestine was not conquered in harmony with God's principles but according to the Israelites'. Because they still retained His presence and leadership in some parts of their lives, a measure of His power remained among them so that they were often victorious. Apart from that, all He could do was to give them instructions for conducting the war mercifully. There was to be no torturing of their victims, and they were to obliterate specific nations that were given completely over to their own gods, being completely closed to God and the principles of His kingdom. Here are some examples of the explicit instructions He gave Israel regarding military rules of engagement, *their* chosen method of operation:

> "When you go near a city to fight against it, then proclaim an offer of peace to it. And it shall be that if they accept your offer of peace, and open to you, then all the people who are found in it shall be placed under tribute to you, and serve you. Now if the city will not make peace with you, but makes war against you, then you shall besiege it. And when the Lord your God delivers it into your hands, you shall strike every male in it with the edge of the sword. But the

women, the little ones, the livestock, and all that is in the city, all its spoil, you shall plunder for yourself; and you shall eat the enemies' plunder which the Lord your God gives you. Thus shall you do to all the cities which are very far from you, which are not of the cities of these nations.

"But of the cities of these peoples which the Lord your God gives you as an inheritance, you shall let nothing that breathes remain alive, but you shall utterly destroy them: the Hittite and the Amorite and the Canaanite and the Perizzite and the Hivite and the Jebusite, just as the Lord your God has commanded you, lest *they teach you to do according to all their abominations* which they have done for their gods, *and you sin against the Lord* your God" (Deut. 20:10-18).

The utter destruction of the people of Jericho was but a fulfillment of the commands previously given through Moses concerning the inhabitants of Canaan: "Thou shalt smite them, and utterly destroy them." Deuteronomy 7:2. "Of the cities of these people, ... thou shalt save alive nothing that breatheth." Deuteronomy 20:16. To many these commands seem to be contrary to the spirit of love and mercy enjoined in other portions of the Bible, but they were in truth the dictates of infinite wisdom and goodness. God was about to establish Israel in Canaan, to develop among them a nation and government that should be a manifestation of His kingdom upon the earth. They were not only to be inheritors of the true religion, but to disseminate its principles throughout the world. *The Canaanites had abandoned themselves to the foulest and most debasing heathenism, and it was necessary that the land should be cleared of what would so surely prevent the fulfillment of God's gracious purposes* (Patriarchs and Prophets, p. 492, emphasis added).

We can see from these instructions that even within the paradigm of their choice to take up weapons and engage in violent combat, God wanted to direct them to seek peace instead of war. He would have delivered the land up to them by different methods had they left the sword alone (Deut. 7:20). Yet, He also instructed them in how to conduct warfare in the best way possible, as a concession to their choice to choose to take up weapons and go into warfare. The instructions given on how they were to conduct different military campaigns were never arbitrary but were directly related to the spiritual realities of the people who they were coming against. God alone knew whose "cup of iniquity" was full and who would not be receptive to Him, His people, or His ways. God alone could know their condition.

Ever since God's instructions for civil rule had been delivered to Israel from Mt. Sinai, they had mistakenly regarded them as being exactly what God, in His heart, had planned for them. Like so many millions since, they showed a sad ignorance of what God's righteousness really is. They did not understand that these instructions were not the expression of His principles but merely an improved version of their own chosen course. The same applies for the instructions given for conducting the wars of Israel.

God delivered such counsel only to those whose unbelief had caused them to depart from the pathway of faith to self-protection dependent upon their utilizing the instruments of coercion. It was out of loving consideration for the victims of those in power that He admonished them to limit the exaction of their ideas of revenge and dominance. Their human tendencies would place them at the opposite end of the scale from God but in between these two choices there was a situation which, though it still could not be God's perfect plan, was considerably better than the one where they were left to their own devices.

The three positions were as follows:

First, there is God's perfect way, which Jesus lived and taught. It calls upon the manifestation of that love which never retaliates, always turns the other cheek, goes the second mile, loves all enemies, and does good to those who do evil. Weapons of force have no use under these principles. This requires a real and abiding faith in God to successfully operate. The children of Israel lacked that faith and discarded these ideas as impractical and dangerous. They were, in short, foolishness to them. They could not see how survival was possible under these conditions.

At the other end of the scale is the behavior of those who have no regard for God and consequently pay no heed to His counsels. They are ruthless, cruel, and revengeful. They torture their enemies, extracting the utmost suffering to satisfy their revengeful passions. The death camps of Germany during World War II—Auschwitz, Dachau, and Belsen—were demonstrations of this kind of spirit. Tremendous privation and suffering was experienced by those who fell into the terrible hands of the Third Reich. It was impossible for God to save them from this because the powers that were in charge had no disposition to obey God in anything.

The intermediate situation operates because of two things. First, there is God's compassion for the oppressed, leading Him to seek to minimize as far as possible their suffering and loss. Second, those who are doing the destroying are willing to obey Him in some things at least. So, throughout the world those nations and individuals who do respect God and profess to be His people accept and follow these counsels even though they do not have the faith to trust Him implicitly as their Judge and Protector.

While Israel maintained some connection with God and was prepared to obey Him at least in some things, they also insisted on carrying out their own ways, resulting in bloodshed and brutality, which cannot be considered as the perfect display of the righteousness of God.

Human brutality is exactly what the Lord was seeking to save them and their enemies from when they took up the weapons of destruction. This is why He gave them specific instructions regarding warfare. This is because they had chosen their own ways over God's ways and decided not to heed His voice in all things. If they *had* heeded His perfect will for them, they would have chosen to be obedient to the principle of love for one's enemies and returned good for evil, which Christ explained in the Sermon on the Mount.

God's way does not use force to put down rebellion, and it has no retaliation, no exacting of retributions, no violence, no use of the sword, and, therefore, no killing. Jesus identified this alone as being God's pattern of behavior by advising that those who did likewise would be like His Father who is in heaven (Matt. 5:48).

Humanity's way, if left entirely to themselves, is such that they will love their friends but will hit their enemies as hard as they can. The objective is actually to hit them much harder than they hit you so as to convince them permanently that it would be suicidal to launch any further assaults against you. This system of violence for violence continues in fearsome escalation as each seeks to guarantee their own security by the rule of fear.

When God was not able to hold them safely in His way, then He worked to save them from their way. This is why the compromise situation exists. What God is really saying by this is, "Very well, you have made your decision to take the sword and thereby depart from My ways. I cannot change your decision. You made it and in freedom it stands. But I can save you from the worst effects of that choice if you will accept and respect the advice I now give you. Do not be wanton and revengeful killers. Exact only an equal payment for what has been taken from you. Let there be no more than one eye for one eye, and one tooth for one tooth. Meanwhile, I will ever seek to win you back to the way of faith and obedience, back to the pathway where there is no killing or revenge but only the manifestation of My character of love."

Note that continuing in the middle of permissive will is not the way of salvation. It is only a temporary measure to prevent escalation of violence unto extinction, until such a body of faithful believers may develop in the earth as will understand His perfect way and return to it. These permissive laws are not good. They are not the way of life. They are only a measure of control on wickedness.

If the relationship between these three ways can be clearly discerned, and if it can be recognized that only the first of them is God's way, then it will be seen that there is not a single story in the Old Testament to prove that God destroys. Satan destroys and people destroy, but never God. He is the Savior who is only working to restore and to heal. He knows no other work than that. The whole history of His dealings with ancient Israel, rightly understood, testifies to this.

Thus far in Israel's history, we have seen a number of incidents in every one of which, to a larger or lesser extent, the Israelites chose to go the way of unbelief. There was that persistent tendency to cast off God's leadership and ways and to substitute their own.

Bad as those choices in the past had been, a worse step was yet to be taken. It was when the people came to Samuel and asked him to ask God to give them a king. This king was to judge them like all the nations. The people insisted on this, saying: "No, but we will have a king over us, that we also may be like all the nations, and that our king may judge us and go out before us and fight our battles" (1 Sam. 8:19, 20).

Again the people were making decisions, and again God had to relate Himself to them in their decisions. With unvarying consistency He did here what He had done in every other such situation. He gave them full liberty to make that choice. He made no moves to forcibly stop them. All He did was to outline in vivid terms what they were bringing upon themselves, but when, after that revelation of horror, they still stood by their decision, He gave them what they wanted.

God did not threaten them with personal punishments if they rejected Him. A careful reading of 1 Samuel 8:6-18 will show that the Lord outlined only the results of their taking that course. He told them that the king would do terrible things until they would wish that they had never taken the king to rule them.

> And he said, "This will be the behavior of the king who will reign over you: He will take your sons and appoint them for his own chariots and to be his horsemen, and some will run before his chariots. He will appoint captains over his thousands and captains over his fifties, will set some to plow his ground and reap his harvest, and some to make his weapons of war and equipment for his chariots. He will take your daughters to be perfumers, cooks, and bakers. And he will take the best of your fields, your vineyards, and your olive groves, and give them to his servants. He will take a tenth of your grain and your vintage, and give it to his officers and servants" (1 Sam. 8:11-15).

This is the description of heavy oppression indeed. The king would build up a court of great luxury and ease for himself, but it was the people who would be paying the accounts. Taxation would become increasingly severe until the people were poverty-stricken. All this did come to pass, but not by the imposition of God. They had brought it on themselves by their own waywardness.

The decision made in Samuel's day was a duplication of the step taken at Kadesh Barnea. It was a direct and specific replacement of the Lord as their leader. In the first case, it was a committee of twelve men while, in the second, it was with the king. Both led to disastrous consequences. In the first, it led to their being unable to enter the Promised Land and thus being forced to wander for forty years in the wilderness.

In the second case, it was followed by still further departures from God. Soon they were not only looking to man as their leader but, worse still, to gods of wood, stone, brass, gold, and silver. The futility of such gods was demonstrated as they became the slaves of their enemies, captives in the land of Babylon.

But they would never learn. They persisted in their determination to rule themselves and go their own way until, in the end, they cried out their total rejection of God and His ways in these words, "We have no king but Caesar!" (John 19:15). This was the final step in that long, long road of persistent and determined substitution of God's ways with their own ways. They had finally stepped outside the circle of God's presence and protection. The fearful consequences were delayed only for the sake of those who, like Rahab in Jericho, were still open to hear the voice of entreaty and love. That accomplished, the destruction of the city, the temple, and the nation was no longer preventable.

The history of that unfortunate nation, rightly understood, places God in His true light. Whereas there has been the tendency in the past to see Him as being in total control of that nation so that what they did was the expression of His character and will, it becomes very evident that this was not so. Rather, they had stubbornly refused to allow Him His full and rightful place in their community. They had substituted *their way* in place of *His way* so that what they did in the slaughter of the wicked was anything but the expression of His character and methods.

Chapter Thirty-Five

Difficult Statements

Study/Discussion Questions:

- What is the destroying angel and how do holy angels destroy?

- The Creator has power to speak worlds into existence. If God destroys by the same fiat word, if He punishes by arbitrary action, why would He use the relatively puny powers of demons, nature, and people?

- There are things God cannot do, such as lie. It is also said that He will do as He pleases. But He takes no pleasure in the death of the wicked. Does He kill the wicked?

- The walls of Jericho are represented as having fallen by the action of holy angels. Did these angels exert their physical might on the walls? We are told that Jerusalem also fell down by the action of holy angels. The Roman armies did the physical work. What is the difference between these two events?

The great truths of the Bible are not established by collecting a series of statements. They are built on solid foundational principles. Once these are ascertained, the super-structure can be accurately and safely constructed. When searching out the truth of God's character, the guiding principles are found in the nature of His government, the purpose of the law, Christ's revelation of His Father, and the role of the cross as the expression of God's methods of dealing with the unrepentant sinner. The mighty witnesses of God contained in these statements are more than sufficient to certify the loving, merciful, righteous, and just character of God. They effectively prove that He does not stand as an executioner toward the rejecters of His mercy.

But, as with every other Bible topic, certain statements seem to utterly contradict the witnesses mentioned above. These constitute a serious problem to many who cannot feel at rest with the message until every statement has been explained. This attitude is a detriment to spiritual advancement because living faith does not wait until every problem has been solved before grasping precious truths.

The life and teachings of Christ are the final, comprehensive declaration of what God is and does. It is the standard by which every argument about the Father's character is tested. If the argument presented cannot find support in Jesus Christ then, no matter how logical it may seem to be or how convincing it may appear, the faithful student of God's character will reject it even though there may be no apparent explanation for it as yet. Faith grasps the reality of Christ's mission as the outshining of the Father's countenance. It believes that God sent His Son into the world for the express purpose of penetrating the mists of error and delusion that Satan cast around His character of righteousness. The confirmation of that faith is expressed in the resolution to accept nothing about God except that which is in total agreement with the witness of the Father attested to by His Son.

Therefore, if anyone wishes to successfully prove that God destroyed the sinner, offering as evidence the overthrow of Sodom and Gomorrah or any other punishments of the Old Testament era, he or she must be able to bring proof that Christ, during His earthly mission, did the same thing. Indeed, ultimately he or she must be able to prove that God destroyed Christ on the cross. This will also demonstrate that it is God who will personally act to execute the impenitent. It is so impossible to do this that those who cling to the erroneous view that God executes the sinner claim that the revelation of God, as given by Christ, is only a partial manifestation of the Father, which omits the sterner roles of judge and executioner.

There are not two different revelations of God, the one given in Old Testament times versus that given by Christ. There are no contradictions in the Word of God. True Bible students are not afraid of difficult statements. They may have to admit, for the moment, that the true meaning eludes them, but they know that it will not be for long since the Holy Spirit leads each trusting student along the glorious corridors of unfolding light.

Not every statement that can be presented has as yet been resolved. The fact that they cannot be explained just yet is no cause for fear or doubt. There is more than sufficient evidence in the great foundation principles to establish, beyond doubt, the truth of God's character.

But most have been unraveled and, for the help of those still struggling with some of them, an examination of the most commonly quoted will be undertaken. These types of statements must be examined to see exactly what they say and, just as importantly, what they do not say. All too often the problem of interpretation lies in a tendency to assume that a statement infers something it does not. If this inference can be cleared away, the words will then be left free to say what they were intended to say.

The Same Powers

What I would rate as one of the most difficult statements to interpret is the following:

> A single angel destroyed all the first-born of the Egyptians and filled the land with mourning. When David offended against God by numbering the people, one angel caused that terrible destruction by which his sin was punished. The same destructive power exercised by holy angels when God commands, will be exercised by evil angels when He permits. There are forces now ready, and only waiting the divine permission, to spread desolation everywhere (*The Great Controversy*, p. 614).

The portion of this statement causing the most difficulty is this, "The *same* destructive power exercised by *holy* angels when God *commands*, will be exercised by *evil* angels when *He permits.*"

When a person does not have a clear grasp of the principles underlying God's character, it is easy to see how this statement could leave him or her with the conviction that holy angels destroy exactly as do evil angels. It would appear that the only difference is that holy angels destroy by God's command while the evil do it with His permission.

What happens is that almost everyone tends to read into this statement more than it actually says. Here is what the statement does not say: "The same destructive power exercised by holy angels when God commands, will be exercised in *the same way* by evil angels when He permits."

These four words, "in the same way," are not in the statement, neither are they inferred there. Furthermore, every principle of God's character forbids them being there. Yet, despite multiplied evidences to this effect, this is exactly what most people read into the reference. They make no distinction between the work of God and of Satan, and therefore, they make no distinction between the character of each. This is serious.

As we have examined this text in *The Great Controversy*, page 614, we have isolated the portion that causes confusion. However, if we were to back up even one sentence and obtain a wider context, we would find the introductory concept spelled out clearly:

> As the *angels of God* cease to hold in check the fierce winds of human passion, all the elements of strife will be let loose. The whole world will be involved in ruin more terrible than that which came upon Jerusalem of old (*Ibid.*, emphasis added).

By this and similar statements we find that destructive power is indeed unleashed by God's command to holy angels. Angels are appointed as ministers to those who shall be heirs of salvation as we read in Hebrews 1:14. When they can no longer function in a given situation because there are no heirs of salvation found in sufficient number, angels must abandon their heaven appointed post of holding back the winds of strife and leave the forces of evil and natural chaos to bear sway, such as we find in the major catastrophes of the flood and the conflagration upon Sodom and Gomorrah.

The angels only release the destructive forces when God judges that any further remaining on station will impose their presence where it is not desired and make Him into something which He is not—a God of force. There are many inspired passages that teach this.

> After these things I saw four angels standing at the four corners of the earth, holding the four winds of the earth, that the wind should not blow on the earth, on the sea, or on any tree (Rev. 7:1).

> We are today under divine forbearance; but how long will the angels of God continue to hold the winds, that they shall not blow? (*Testimonies for the Church*, vol. 6, p. 426).

Angels are now restraining the winds of strife, that they may not blow until the world shall be warned of its coming doom; but a storm is gathering, ready to burst upon the earth; and when God shall bid His angels loose the winds, there will be such a scene of strife as no pen can picture (*Education*, pp. 179, 180).

I saw four angels who had a work to do on the earth, and were on their way to accomplish it. Jesus was clothed with priestly garments. He gazed in pity on the remnant, then raised His hands, and with a voice of deep pity cried, "*My blood, Father, My blood, My blood, My blood!*" Then I saw an exceeding bright light come from God, who sat upon the great white throne, and was shed all about Jesus. Then I saw an angel with a commission from Jesus, swiftly flying to the four angels who had a work to do on the earth, and waving something up and down in his hand, and crying with a loud voice, "*Hold! Hold! Hold! Hold!* until the servants of God are sealed in their foreheads."

I asked my accompanying angel the meaning of what I heard, and what the four angels were about to do. He said to me that it was God that restrained the powers, and that He gave His angels charge over things on the earth; that the four angels had power from God to hold the four winds, and that they were about to let them go; but while their hands were loosening, and the four winds were about to blow, the merciful eye of Jesus gazed on the remnant that were not sealed, and He raised His hands to the Father and pleaded with Him that He had spilled His blood for them. Then another angel was commissioned to fly swiftly to the four angels, and bid them hold, until the servants of God were sealed with the seal of the living God in their foreheads (*Early Writings*, p. 38).

> Satan is the destroyer. God cannot bless those who refuse to be faithful stewards. All He can do is to permit Satan to accomplish his destroying work. We see calamities of every kind and in every degree coming upon the earth, and why? *The Lord's restraining power is not exercised.* The world has disregarded the word of God. They live as though there were no God. Like the inhabitants of the Noachic world, they refuse to have any thought of God. Wickedness prevails to an alarming extent, and the earth is ripe for the harvest (*Testimonies for the Church,* vol. 6, pp. 388, 389, emphasis added).

Every one of these and many other similar statements confirm that the angels' role is to hold back those terrible powers that are only awaiting release to destroy the earth and the heavens. Angels are righteous. They have not instituted their ways in place of God's. Accordingly, they do only what the Lord would have them do. As surely as the God of heaven never destroys by direct action, neither do the angels. Therefore, the way in which they exercise those powers is by the withdrawal of their restraint upon them. The released energies pass from an inactive state into one of intense activity and, consequently, of exercise.

This is the way in which the powers are brought into active exercise by holy angels when God *commands*, but it is not *the way* evil angels exercise them when God *permits*. Satan and his followers have studied the secrets of the laboratories of nature and the turbulent forces within human beings until they know just how to activate them into destructive intensities. Thus, while God's angels are working to hold back these fearful elements, Satan and his company are working in the opposite direction. It is the evil powers that are standing by with bloodlust, "now ready, and only waiting the divine permission," to exercise their destructive power everywhere (*The Great Controversy*, p. 614).

But whether they are released into active exercise by the holy angels or manipulated by evil angels, *they are the same powers*. This is the principal thought that the statement conveys when interpreted according to the principles of God's government and character. It does not discuss *the way* in which those powers are exercised. When it is recognized that this is the subject matter of the statement, there will be no problem in understanding it.

Far from proving that good angels, at God's command, sally forth and execute the unrighteous, this statement, by emphasizing that it is the *same power* in any case, verifies that they do not. If God undertook the work of executioner, He would not bother to use anything less than the greatest powers at His command. These certainly are not those in nature and in humanity. They are the almighty forces within Himself, forces so great that He merely has to speak and whole worlds appear and, in turn, disappear. Therefore, if God was the destroyer, it would *not* be the *same powers* as those used by the evil angels who have nothing of themselves but are dependent on what God has invested in them, in nature, and in human beings to do their work of destruction. God has almighty omnipotence and is not in any sense dependent on the relatively puny potentials He has given to this earth and its inhabitants. If these facts are kept in mind, then the statement presents no problem.

Doing as He Pleases

Here is another statement that has been a problem to some.

> Moses commanded the men of war to destroy the women and male children. Balaam had sold the children of Israel for a reward, and he perished with the people whose favor he had obtained at the sacrifice of twenty-four thousand of the Israelites. The Lord is regarded as cruel by many in requiring His people to make war with other nations. They say that it is contrary to his benevolent character. But he who made the world, and formed man to dwell upon the earth, has unlimited control over all the works of his hands, and it is his right to do as he pleases, and what he pleases with the work of his hands. Man has no right to say to his Maker, Why doest thou thus? There is no injustice in his character. He is the Ruler of the world, and a large portion of his subjects have rebelled against his authority, and have trampled upon his law.... He has used his people as instruments of his wrath, to punish wicked nations, who have vexed them, and seduced them into idolatry (*Spiritual Gifts*, vol. 4a, pp. 50, 51).

The main message of this statement is a warning that humankind is in no position to question the actions of God. If God does it, it is right and just. This rightness is not just because God is the Creator but because His character is righteous and there is no injustice with Him. We are not to question His *motives*, saying, "Why doest Thou thus?" but we are to understand His *methods*. He invites us to ask "*How* doest Thou thus?"

The greatest revelation of God's character and motives is portrayed in Christ Jesus, and there is no question that everything He does is motivated by *agape* love and based upon the principle that He does not kill the sinner but hands the sinner over to the results of free choice. We are given all that we need to understand that His government is rooted in the twin principles of freedom of choice and noncoercion. God has not withheld from us the "why" of what He does. Jesus came to suffer the full penalty of transgression that He might in justice reinstate us to eternal life; in fact, to an even higher station than if we had not sinned. He has shown us that His mercy and generosity are more than exceedingly abounding.

He, therefore, tells us not to question whether He is just or whether He has the full prerogative to exercise His justice. However, we do have much to learn and even more to unlearn in regard to "how" He exercises justice, not only in saving sinners but in destroying them, for it is the same justice that works for all, righteous and wicked. He wants us to know it. That is why we are given so many principle statements and why the curtain is drawn back on so many of the "God-did-it" depictions, revealing the mechanics of destruction, as in the classic case of "God slew Saul."

He desires that we would apply the principles across the whole of inspiration. Reading that God "uses His people as instruments of His wrath, to punish the wicked" is startling if we do not understand the mechanics of it in the context of the proper view of His character. This is what has happened in religion, and we have ended up with a view of God that presents Him as a frightening and capricious Deity.

When it comes to our handling of inspired text, there are two pitfalls to avoid: 1) vacillating between plenary (thought) and verbal (literal, verbatim) modes of viewing inspiration, and 2) holding prophets up on such a high pedestal as to make them infallible communicators of the mind of God. We are told that God is not represented in inspiration, as a writer, and that the prophets are His penmen, not His pen. We are to understand that God's thoughts are given through a medium that "diffuses" them. That medium is the minds of humans (see *Selected Messages,* book 1, p. 21).

If you have ever looked through a frosted window on a cold day, you will understand that you do not have twenty/twenty vision of what is really out there. What appears as an "elephant" in the yard could just be that old stump covered up by a tarp that the wind blew over it.

We have to give the prophets some space and keep them in place as men and women who lived in certain contexts of culture, education, prevailing tradition, and understandings, and they were given as much light as God could reveal through them in those contexts. God does not overwhelm, for that would be more than men and women could bear, causing them to reject His guidance and teaching. We must even be careful with an "I saw" or "I beheld" type of statement. Sometimes the prophets did not themselves fully understand what they were seeing or what they wrote.

These thoughts are developed and demonstrated in many worthy studies available to us, and you should avail yourself of this knowledge as it is highly relevant to the subject of understanding God's character through the language of inspired writing.

> Even the prophets who were favored with the special illumination of the Spirit did not fully comprehend the import of the revelations committed to them. The meaning was to be unfolded from age to age, as the people of God should need the instruction therein contained (*The Great Controversy,* p. 344).

We have to give prophets room to grow in understanding, even shifting beliefs and practices throughout the course of their walk with God. This may be a strange thought to some, but just because a man or woman receives a call from God to a special office in the exercise of a high calling or gift does not mean they have a perfect understanding or theology, and it does not mean they would not ever express something differently in the latter end of their experience than they would have in the former days.

These thoughts from the Bible come down to us from an inspired writer. Let's decide if it accurately represents the heart and mind of God:

> Break their teeth in their mouth, O God!… The righteous shall rejoice when he sees the vengeance: he shall wash his feet in the blood of the wicked (Ps. 58:6, 10).

Even though the psalmist had Deuteronomy 31:17, 18 and other defining passages available to him, it is not likely that he understood the wrath of God according to the biblical key depicting it as the "hiding of His face," nor is it probable that he would have intelligently used what we call today the "language of wrath," which portrays God as doing that unpleasant and punitive thing to which He hands over the sinner. This writer probably had every intention of rejoicing in bloody vengeance, according to the unrighteous wrath of man, as we read in James 1:20.

Although David was inspired and "a man after God's own heart," he was not to build the temple of the Lord. God told him why:

> And David said to Solomon: "My son, as for me, it was in my mind to build a house to the name of the Lord my God; but the word of the Lord came to me, saying, 'You have shed much blood and have made great wars; you shall not build a house for My name, because you have shed much blood on the earth in My sight'" (1 Chron. 22:7, 8).

The full light of the character of God has been largely misunderstood by God's people even after the cross. It is yet to unfold further through His church. Because Jesus gave us Himself in the Holy Spirit, we can do an even greater work than He—He was one, but we are many.

> "And greater works than these shall he do; because I go unto My Father." By this Christ did not mean that the disciples' work would be of a more exalted character than His, but that it would have greater extent. He did not refer merely to

miracle working, but to all that would take place under the working of the Holy Spirit (*The Desire of Ages*, p. 664).

Keeping all of these thoughts about prophets and inspiration in mind, we return to the lines about God doing as He pleases, and we work with the text in the context of the advancing light that is being given to us in the present. It is understandable that many are troubled by the part which reads: "But He who made the world, and formed man to dwell upon the earth, has unlimited control over all the works of His hands, and it is His right to do *as He pleases*, and *what He pleases* with the work of His hands" (*Spiritual Gifts*, vol. 4a, p. 50, emphasis added).

No problem would exist here if it were not for the persistent tendency of people to think of God as if He, too, was a man. When people have the power to do as they please and what they please, then their behavior becomes dependent on how they feel on a given day and what they want on that day. They do all things in reference to their own likes and dislikes and not according to unvarying principles. This is the behavior pattern with which we are most familiar, and we tend to think of the unknown and unfamiliar in God as if it were the same.

So we see individuals sinning against God and His people. Whereupon, we visualize God as being highly incensed and angered by this so that it becomes His pleasure to exact a revenge against those who have treated Him so shabbily.

But, unlike human beings, God is never motivated by feelings. He finds no pleasure in unrighteousness in any form. Therefore, *it does not please Him* to kill, to lie, to steal, to bear false witness, or to break any other of the commandments, which are the transcript of His wondrous character. We need never fear then that the Lord will destroy us because He has the right to do "as He pleases, and what He pleases." On the other hand, if we become subject to human beings with limitless power to do "what they please, and as they please," we can know that, unless we are able to serve them to their entire satisfaction all the time, sooner or later we are doomed.

In other words, this and any other statement must be understood in the light of what it pleases God to do, not in the light of what it would please human beings to do if they were in the same position.

Those Walls of Jericho

There are a number of statements in respect to the overthrow of the walls of Jericho, which, if understood in the way human beings naturally understand such words, would mean that God and His angels personally exercised the power of force to bring down those mighty battlements.

> How easily the armies of heaven brought down the walls that had seemed so formidable to the spies who brought the false report! The word of God was the only weapon used. The Mighty One of Israel had said: "I have given into thine hand Jericho." If a single warrior had brought his strength to bear against the walls,

the glory of God would have been lessened and His will frustrated. But the work was left to the Almighty; and had the foundation of the battlements been laid in the center of the earth, and their summits reached the arch of heaven, the result would have been the same when the Captain of the Lord's host led His legions of angels to the attack (*Testimonies for the Church,* vol. 4, pp. 161, 162).

The city of Jericho was devoted to the most extravagant idolatry. The inhabitants were very wealthy, but all the riches that God had given them they counted as the gift of their gods. They had gold and silver in abundance; but, like the people before the Flood, they were corrupt and blasphemous, and insulted and provoked the God of heaven by their wicked works. God's judgments were awakened against Jericho. It was a stronghold. But the Captain of the Lord's host Himself came from heaven to lead the armies of heaven in an attack upon the city. Angels of God laid hold of the massive walls and brought them to the ground (*Testimonies for the Church,* vol. 3, p. 264).

The Lord marshaled his armies about the doomed city; no human hand was raised against it; the hosts of heaven overthrew its walls, that God's name alone might have the glory (*The Review and Herald*, March 15, 1887).

The most significant sentence in these statements is the one that says: "Angels *of God* laid hold of the massive walls and brought them to the ground."

It would seem that these words allow only one interpretation, which is that the angels of God, with Christ at their head, took hold of those walls with their hands and literally threw them to the ground. In doing so they did more than tear down buttresses of stone. There were people on those high walls (see *Patriarchs and Prophets*, p. 491). Furthermore, there were people who actually lived in the wall as did Rahab who delivered the spies from her countrymen (see Josh. 2:15).

It follows that if the angels did in fact throw down those walls as we tend to understand those words as saying then they took the lives of a great number of people.

If this is so, then we have finally found the long looked for evidence to prove that God changed because of sin and became a destroyer of life.

God has gone on record to say that He does not deal with the sin problem by the use of physical force. We have shown the various principle statements repeatedly:

He does not stand toward the sinner as the executioner of the sentence against transgression.

He leaves the rejecters of His mercy to themselves to reap that which they have sown.

Compelling power is found only under Satan's government.

God does not destroy. He destroys no one.

From His kingdom, every weapon of coercion is banished.

If the Lord were to violate those principles in just one situation, it would be all that was necessary to give Satan the victory in the great controversy. Therefore, our understanding of the principles that govern God's character compels us to look more deeply into the problem in an endeavor to see in what sense the angels laid hold of the walls and brought them to the ground.

However, if such a search, for the moment at least, fails to bring to light exactly what the angels did then we cannot lose faith in the great principles. We simply understand that this is but one of the hooks left to hang our doubts on if we want to do so. God always leaves some points unexplained to see if we will trust Him in the unknown from what we know of Him already.

The explanation for any difficult scripture must be found in some other part of the Word of God. In a problem like this, the most likely place to find such an explanation is in a similar incident. Such is to be found in the fall of Jerusalem, which, like Jericho, had filled up the cup of iniquity. From it, the Spirit of God had also departed. Its walls were likewise torn to the ground with not one stone being left upon another. It is to be expected that the Lord would describe its destruction in the same language as in Jericho's fall. Research quickly shows that He does.

> Men will continue to erect expensive buildings, costing millions of money; special attention will be called to their architectural beauty, and the firmness and solidity with which they are constructed; but the Lord has instructed me that despite the unusual firmness and expensive display, these buildings will share the fate of the temple in Jerusalem. That magnificent structure fell. *Angels of God were sent to do the work of destruction, so that one stone was not left one upon another that was not thrown down* (*The SDA Bible Commentary,* vol. 5, pp. 1098, 1099, emphasis added).

Consider how explicitly it declares that "angels of God were sent to do the work of destruction, so that one stone was not left upon another that was not thrown down." Before He was crucified, Jesus solemnly declared that not one stone would be left upon another in the temple. Now it is declared that the angels were sent to do this work of destruction so that the fulfillment of Christ's words was assured. Just as the language used in the fall of Jericho tends to give the picture of angels personally laying hold of the stones and throwing them down, so this statement tends to give the same impression as far as the fall of Jerusalem is concerned.

But a study of history shows that those stones were cast down by human hands. The Romans, once they had captured the temple, razed it and much of the city to the ground, making certain that not one stone was left upon another (see *The Great Controversy,* p. 35). Perhaps the greatest authority on Jewish history is Josephus who was actually present at the fall of Jerusalem. His record of the event testifies to the work of the Roman soldiers in the destruction of Jerusalem and is found in *Wars of the Jews,* book VII, chapter one, as translated by William Whiston.

This notable historian's report is confirmed in *The Great Controversy*: "Both the city and the temple were razed to their foundations, and the ground upon which the holy house had stood was 'plowed like a field'" (p. 35).

Here we have two records of what took place back there. One declares that the angels did the work of destruction, while the other clearly shows that it was at Caesar's orders and by the strength and activity of his soldiers that the city was razed.

This would be a hopeless contradiction if we had not studied the way in which the Bible is its own dictionary and the way in which God is said to destroy. First, it is clear that the angels did not do the work of destruction as people do it. That is, they did not themselves take those stones and throw them to the ground. Yet, at the same time, it must be recognized that they did a work which resulted in those walls being thrown to the ground until not one single stone was left upon another. But they certainly did not use the soldiers as direct servants at their personal direction and command to tear down those mighty bastions.

So what did the angels do? How did they go about a mission of destruction?

As already shown by a number of earlier quotations, the angels' role is to hold back the four winds of strife so that they might not blow on the earth. Let those winds be released, and there is a terrible outbreak of human anger and natural power. In this way, the angels come from heaven on a mission of destruction. Let it be emphasized once more that while this involves a judgment on God's part, it is not His arbitrary act. He assesses the situation to be such that to remain any longer would be to force His presence where it is totally unwanted, and this He cannot do. The restraining angels feel this pressure on them to leave, but they await God's command before they do so. These instructions are conveyed to them by messenger angels who, because of this responsibility, are called messengers of destruction, which in fact they are.

The picture of this holding and releasing by one body of angels upon receipt of a clearance to do so by other angels is clearly shown in *Early Writings*, pages 36-38.

The chronicle of Jerusalem's destruction bears out the facts recited above. The tearing down of that city into individual stones was the end result of a series of causes. The Romans did it as the expression of their white-hot anger and hatred for the Jews. That, in turn, was the result of the behavior of the Jews who had given the Romans so much trouble, had shown such a spirit of rebellion, and had been so ungrateful for the favors the Romans desired to show them.

That spirit, consequently, was the result of the Jews' persistent determination to institute their ways in the place of God's and of their continual rejection of the appeals of mercy to them.

For the apostasy of the Jew and the fury of the Romans to race away uncontrolled, the angels of God had to fully and totally withdraw their restraining power over the evil passions of humanity. This they did. That accomplished, the infuriated Roman soldiery was so totally uncontrolled that not even their officers, generals, or Titus himself could control or restrain them. Titus had determined to preserve the temple and had given specific orders that it should not be burned, but his orders were flouted. Even though he rushed in among them and demanded obedience, it was as if he was not even there. Here is part of Josephus' account of the burning of the temple.

And now a certain person came running to Titus, and told him of this fire, as he was resting himself in his tent after the last battle; whereupon he rose up in great haste, and as he was, ran to the holy house, in order to have a stop put to the fire; after him followed all his commanders, and after them followed the several legions, in great astonishment; so there was a great clamour and tumult raised, as was natural upon the disorderly motion of so great an army. Then did Caesar, both by calling to the soldiers that were fighting, with a loud voice, and by giving a signal to them with his right hand, order them to quench the fire; but they did not hear what he said, though he spake so loud, having their ears already dinned by a greater noise another way; nor did they attend to the signal he made with his right hand neither, as still some of them were distracted with fighting, and others with passion; but as for the legions that came running thither, neither any persuasions nor any threatenings could restrain their violence, but each one's own passion was his commander at this time; and as they were crowding into the temple together, many of them were trampled on by one another, while a great number fell among the ruins of the cloisters, which were still hot and smoking, and were destroyed in the same miserable way with those whom they had conquered: and when they were come near the holy house, they made as if they did not so much as hear Caesar's orders to the contrary; but they encouraged those that were before them to set it on fire. As for the seditious they were in too great distress already to afford their assistance [toward quenching the fire]; they were everywhere slain, and everywhere beaten; and as for a great part of the people, they were weak and without arms, and had their throats cut wherever they were caught. Now, round about the altar lay dead bodies heaped one upon another; as at the steps going up to it ran a great quantity of their blood, whither also the dead bodies that were slain above [on the altar] fell down (*Wars on the Jews*, book VI, chapter four, paragraph six).

The blind obstinacy of the Jewish leaders, and the detestable crimes perpetrated within the besieged city, excited the horror and indignation of the Romans, and Titus at last decided to take the temple by storm. He determined, however, that if possible it should be saved from destruction. But his commands were disregarded. After he had retired to his tent at night, the Jews, sallying from the temple, attacked the soldiers without. In the struggle, a firebrand was flung by a soldier through an opening in the porch, and immediately the cedar-lined chambers about the holy house were in a blaze. Titus rushed to the place, followed by his generals and legionaries, and commanded the soldiers to quench the flames. His words were unheeded. In their fury the soldiers hurled blazing brands into the chambers adjoining the temple, and then with their swords they slaughtered in great numbers those who had found shelter there. Blood flowed down the temple steps like water. Thousands upon thousands of Jews perished. Above the sound of battle, voices were heard shouting, "Ichabod!"—the glory is departed.

"Titus found it impossible to check the rage of the soldiery; he entered with his officers, and surveyed the interior of the sacred edifice. The splendor filled them with wonder; and as the flames had not yet penetrated to the holy place, he made a last effort to save it, and springing forth, again exhorted the soldiers to stay the progress of the conflagration. The centurion Liberalis endeavored to force obedience with his staff of office; but even respect for the emperor gave way to the furious animosity against the Jews, to the fierce excitement of battle, and to the insatiable hope of plunder" (*The Great Controversy*, pp. 33, 34).

When soldiers who have had instilled into them the strongest discipline of respect and obedience to the emperor are so totally maddened with rage that they completely ignore orders he has personally given, it is manifested that human passion is rioting in its most unrestrained form. Such outrage was possible only if the angels had vacated their positions as withholders of the winds of strife. They had no further influence over those men.

They never step down of their own volition, but only on the receipt of orders from on high. These are brought to them by messenger angels commissioned to fly swiftly with the advice that the time has come when the people have chosen to reject God so utterly that He can no longer provide them with protection. The advent of these messengers at the outposts heralds the unleashing of destructive forces, thus making them, in a certain sense, angels on a mission of destruction. The result was the full release of the Romans' infuriated hostility toward the Jews, which would not be appeased even when, with their own hands, they had torn the city apart.

This casts great light on the fall of Jericho, teaching how the same descriptions are to be understood in the destruction of the Canaanite city. The only difference between the overthrow of Jericho as compared to Jerusalem is that, while in the latter it was the unleashing of the furies in men that did the work, at Jericho it was the release of the pent-up forces of nature. The role of the angels in both instances was the same. They acted only and entirely in harmony with the principles of God's kingdom. Christ, Himself, led the messengers to the walls of Jericho to give the sad message that that people had forfeited all divine protection, leaving God with no option but to call away the restraining angels. Then the furies of nature, hitherto held under control, burst forth to flatten the proud metropolis. The walls were hurled to the ground. Yet, the Word of God says that the angels did it. Surely, from the way in which inspired text interprets itself, the time has come when it is clearly understood in what sense the angels did this.

If careful comparison is made between the language used to describe the destructions of both Jericho and Jerusalem, all difficulties will disappear. Just what the angels did will be quite clear. Once more, it will be confirmed that they did not act any differently from the revelation of God's character as given by Christ when He came to the earth.

The Wrath of God

The wrath of God is referred to frequently in the Scriptures. It is an expression describing the savage fury of demons, humanity, or nature, or any of these working in concert, in a rampage of destruction. The seven last plagues are referred to specifically as the wrath of God, which is to be poured upon those who worship the beast and his image.

There is very real danger that God's wrath will be understood to be exactly what humanity's wrath is. People's wrath is the development within them of fury, anger, and a desire to retaliate against those who have hurt or offended them. God's wrath is not the expression of His personal feelings, for, while His wrath is busily destroying people and the world, God is feeling anything but wrathful. He is pained with sorrow and distress to see His handiwork and children being committed to so terrible a fate. The wrath of God is an expression of the very opposite from what He is feeling.

Yet without question it is wrath. See the blasting might of the roaring hurricane, the thunder of a thousand falling buildings and opening crevasses as the earthquake strikes, the crackling roar of the blazing inferno, the shriek of the storm, and even the fiendish fury of individuals at war. This is wrath. It is the complete picture of anger and fury, and these are the events that the Bible terms "the wrath of God."

From the message God gave through Moses' rod, He plainly showed that when nature is in this state it has passed out of His control. Therefore, it is not the expression of God's feelings. Why then is it called "the wrath *of God*"? It is God's wrath simply because every power that has is released in wrath is through God's power being withdrawn, which is of God. They are the powers of God in a wrathful state; therefore, it could be called the wrath of the powers of God. Instead, it is simply and more briefly called "the wrath of God."

Other Difficult Statements

There will come many times, as the Bible record is studied, when situations will confront us for which the Lord has not yet revealed any specific explanation or at least it has not been revealed to our individual mind. Someone else may have studied it out. This is why those who are advancing in this light must communicate, study, and fellowship together in this special time and final generation (Mal. 3:16-18). True faith knows that the absence of the correct explanation does not compel us to accept the one which readily presents itself to human logic, or as would be interpreted by thinking in a mode of verbal inspiration, or by using human language dictionary definitions of terms and concepts, even though these are the first tools for which we would reach based on years of conditioning in the world and in the traditional understandings of religion. True faith rests in the knowledge that God does nothing out of character, nothing arbitrary, and nothing outside of the principles of His law. We can rest and trust Him in the unknown because of what we have learned and know of Him.

Chapter Thirty-Six

The Seven Last Plagues

Study/Discussion Questions:

- In what way are the destructions of the plagues upon Egypt and upon Jerusalem in AD 70 the same in character as the seven last plagues?

- The wrath of God is released when Jesus steps out of his mediatory role at the closure of probation. Does this mean that the Father and the Son take different roles; that Jesus is keeping the Father back from heaping wrath upon the sinner?

- God's wrath is expressed by a removal of restraint upon destructive forces. Therefore, is Satan's fury the wrath of God?

Thus far, study has been given only to events that are in the past. The attention is now directed to events that are in the future. Their coming is known through the prophetic revelations, while the nature of them is shown through the types of the past, of which they are the antitypes.

The greatest destruction yet to eventuate before the second coming of Christ will result from the outpouring of the seven last plagues. The impenitent will finally "drink of the wine of the wrath of God, which is poured out *full strength* into the cup of His indignation" (Rev. 14:10).

Up until the end time the judgments of God have always been mixed with mercy so that the wicked were shielded from the full penalty of their guilt.

> All the judgments upon men, prior to the close of probation, have been mingled with mercy. The pleading blood of Christ has shielded the sinner from receiving the full measure of his guilt; but in the final judgment, wrath is poured out unmixed with mercy (*The Great Controversy*, p. 629).

The same language used in Scripture to describe the destructions on men in the past, is employed to portray this terrible future desolation. It is depicted as being "the wrath of God," administered by destroying angels. The incineration of Sodom and Gomorrah; **the flooding of Noah's world**; the plaguing of the Egyptians; the invasion of the serpents into Israel's encampment; the overthrow of Jericho, Nineveh, and Jerusalem; and many more such catastrophes are consistently detailed in the same terms employed to prophesy the coming seven last plagues.

Harmony of interpretation insists that the scriptural portrayal of events yet future must be understood in the same way as the Word of God reveals that the description of events in the past be understood. The Bible abounds in explanations of how we are to interpret the declarations describing the punishment to befall the wicked. By this means we have no excuse for failing to understand that when God is said to destroy the result of His efforts to save have resulted in *the withdrawal of the impenitent* from Him to the place where no protection from destruction remains to them. This is the way it has always been in the past. So it must be in the seven last plagues.

We are greatly assisted in the study of the seven last plagues by two events in the past. The first is the plagues of Egypt and the second, the fall of Jerusalem. Scripture declares that each of these events was a preview of what is to happen in the final scourges.

> The plagues upon Egypt when God was about to deliver Israel were similar in character to those more terrible and extensive judgments which are to fall upon the world just before the final deliverance of God's people (*The Great Controversy*, pp. 627, 628).

While the seven last plagues will not be an exact repetition of the Egyptian scourges, they will be similar in character. The Egyptian devastations possessed the character they had because of the situation out of which they were born and by which they were shaped. The people's continued determination to shut God out of their lives had brought them to the place where God was compelled to accept their desires and leave them to reap their harvest of pain and loss. God released His hold on the rod so that it passed out of His direction and control. Thus the character of the plagues was that they were natural forces possessed of the fury of destruction.

The same character will be manifested in the seven last plagues because they will be the offspring of exactly the same conditions. As the nation of Egypt threw off all connection with God, so the people of the whole world will separate from God, rejecting every principle of righteousness and association with Him. The last appeals of mercy scorned, God will be left with no option but to leave humanity alone. Once again, nature will be out of control and will smite them until none remain.

The second preview of the seven last plagues is given in the destruction of Jerusalem.

> The Saviour's prophecy concerning the visitation of judgments upon Jerusalem is to have another fulfillment, of which that terrible desolation was but a faint shadow. In the *fate of the chosen city* we may behold the *doom of a world* that has rejected God's mercy and trampled upon His law (*The Great Controversy*, p. 36, emphasis added).

The Spirit of God, persistently rejected and abused, had at last no choice but to leave the people to themselves. With nothing to restrain the fierce passions of the Jews, they rebelled so treacherously and seditiously against the Romans that they stirred up the worst spirit of retaliation in their enemies. This brought the mighty power of Rome to bear upon the city of Jerusalem. With the continued resistance of the Jews and the prolonged attack by the Romans, the spirits of all became so intensified that in the final scenes the powers in those people simply ran riot. The resulting slaughter and atrocities were worse than human language can picture. When the city had been conquered and there were no more to be slain, the Romans then systematically tore the city stone from stone until the destruction was virtually absolute.

In that fate the doom of the world is to be read. Exactly what befell Jerusalem will befall the whole earth. The time is coming when the sins of humanity will compel the Spirit of God to totally depart. With nothing to hold in check the deadly powers in nature and human beings, the earth will be plunged into a time of trouble such as never was. The seven last plagues will in no sense of the word be the manipulation of those powers by the hands of God. Instead, just as in Egypt and in Jerusalem, God will not even be there. Everything that happens will be because of His absence, not because of His presence. Once again the rod will have passed out of Moses' hand.

These direct statements will verify the truth of the above principles and the conclusions drawn from them.

> When He leaves the sanctuary, darkness covers the inhabitants of the earth. In that fearful time the righteous must live in the sight of a holy God without an intercessor. The *restraint* which has been upon the wicked is *removed*, and Satan has *entire control* of the finally impenitent. God's long-suffering has ended. The world has rejected His mercy, despised His love, and trampled upon His law. The wicked have passed the boundary of their probation; the Spirit of God, persistently resisted, has been at last withdrawn. Unsheltered by divine grace, they have no protection from the wicked one. Satan will then plunge the inhabitants of the earth into one great, final trouble. As the angels of God cease to hold in check the fierce winds of human passion, all the elements of strife will be let loose. The whole world will be involved in ruin more terrible than that which came upon Jerusalem of old (*The Great Controversy*, p. 614, emphasis added).

While Jesus had been standing between God and guilty man, a *restraint* was upon the people; but when He stepped out from between man and the Father, *the restraint was removed* and Satan had entire control of the finally impenitent. It was impossible for the plagues to be poured out while Jesus officiated in the sanctuary; but as His work there is finished, and His intercession closes, *there is nothing to stay the wrath of God*, and it breaks with fury upon the shelterless head of the guilty sinner, who has slighted salvation and hated reproof (*Early Writings*, p. 280, emphasis added).

This statement verifies the truth that it is the removal of God's restraining power that releases the powers of individuals and nature into Satan's hands. They then burst with destructive fury upon the shelterless heads of the wicked.

Let the expression, "there is nothing to stay the wrath of God," be guarded from misunderstanding. Before the principles in regard to God's character are understood, this would be taken to mean that God was personally angered and, therefore, anxious to smite the offenders but is restrained by the intercession of His Son until Jesus finishes His work in the sanctuary.

If this interpretation is correct, then Christ and His Father are working against each other. God is longing to destroy humanity while Christ is restraining Him. However, it is impossible to believe this and at the same time hold to the great and precious truth that Christ and the Father are one and that, far from working against each other, they are fully united in the task of saving their creation—"God was in Christ reconciling the world to Himself" (2 Cor. 5:19).

There could be nothing closer than the unity of the Father and the Son in the work of salvation. God is not seeking to destroy sinners while the Son works to delay the unleashing of the Father's fury. They are working together to the limit of their resources to bring people back to eternal life, and only when people utterly reject those saving measures, do the Father and Son jointly leave the rebellious to their chosen fate.

Also, as we see that the wrath of God functions through the work of Satan, we are given a clear understanding of what His wrath is and what it is not, for God does not work *with* Satan to achieve a destructive purpose. Rather, as people reach a point of total rejection of God, in the granting of freedom to choose their path, He has no choice but to give them over to Satan, who is then released to do his own work, to God's sorrow.

> Men have reached a point in insolence and disobedience which shows that their cup of iniquity is almost full. Many have well-nigh passed the boundary of mercy. Soon God will show that He is indeed the living God. He will say to the angels, "No longer combat Satan in his efforts to destroy. Let him work out his malignity upon the children of disobedience; for the cup of their iniquity is full. They have advanced from one degree of wickedness to another, adding daily to their lawlessness. I will no longer interfere to prevent the destroyer from doing his work" (*The Review and Herald*, September 17, 1901).

> It is God that shields His creatures and hedges them in from the power of the destroyer. But the Christian world have shown contempt for the law of Jehovah; and the Lord will do just what He has declared that He would—He will withdraw His blessings from the earth and remove His protecting care from those who are rebelling against His law and teaching and forcing others to do the same. Satan has control of all whom God does not especially guard. He will favor and prosper some in order to further his own designs, and he will bring trouble upon others and lead men to believe that it is God who is afflicting them (*The Great Controversy*, p. 589).

> God does not stand toward the sinner as an executioner of the sentence against transgression; but He leaves the rejectors of His mercy to themselves, to reap

that which they have sown. Every ray of light rejected, every warning despised or unheeded, every passion indulged, every transgression of the law of God, is a seed sown which yields its unfailing harvest. The Spirit of God, persistently resisted, is at last withdrawn from the sinner, and then there is left no power to control the evil passions of the soul, and no protection from the malice and enmity of Satan (*The Great Controversy*, p. 36).

The wicked have sown the seed. The harvest is inevitable. But it is not the work of God. It is the work of people against themselves. They sowed the seed. They reap the harvest.

Chapter Thirty-Seven

The Brightness of His Coming

Study/Discussion Questions:

- **The brightness of His coming is a consuming fire to the wicked. Does this apply only to those alive at the second coming?**

- **What is the nature of this brightness?**

- **Certainly there is physical glory surrounding His being, but is this the aspect that destroys?**

"And then the lawless one will be revealed, whom the Lord will consume with the breath of His mouth and destroy with the brightness of His coming" (2 Thess. 2:8).

This scripture has been usually understood to portray the picture of Christ descending in the advent skies while before Him precedes great flowing sheets of devouring fire that reaches out to consume whoever of the impenitent have somehow managed to survive the plagues.

Such an interpretation of this Scripture, obvious as it may appear, is out of harmony with the character of God and Christ. If fire emanating from Him kills the wicked, then there is a direct, destructive work associated with His presence. Therefore, He would be an executioner after all. But He is not, nor will He ever be.

When He came to this earth the first time, Jesus testified that He had not come to destroy people's lives but to save them, and that purpose does not change with His second coming. Once again, His intention is to deliver His people from an earth that has been reduced to almost nothing by the final disasters. Certainly, He would save every individual who has ever been born if this were possible, but tragically, so few are prepared to accept His saving grace. He does nothing to them. He has not come for them. They have taken themselves out of the circle of His responsibility, and their fate is entirely a matter of their own appointment.

There are statements that explain this text and which harmonize with this principle.

> Then shall they that obey not the gospel be consumed with the spirit of His mouth and be destroyed with the brightness of His coming. 2 Thessalonians 2:8. Like Israel of old the wicked destroy themselves; they fall by their iniquity. By a life of sin, they have placed themselves so out of harmony with God, their natures have become so debased with evil, that the manifestation of His glory is to them a consuming fire (*The Great Controversy*, p. 37).

It is most important to note the parallel drawn between the way in which Israel perished and the destruction in the last days. As the one perished, so will the other. This is to indicate that the Israelites were likewise destroyed with the brightness of His coming. This is true, for that is exactly how they did come to their end. It may be immediately objected that Jesus did not come with outshining glory at His first advent. Furthermore, He was far away in the distant heavens when the Jews met their fate, so there is no visible evidence of their having been consumed with the brightness of His glory. Such an interpretation depends on the understanding of what the brightness of His glory is and how humans are consumed by it. Defining that expression is the key to solving the problem.

The factor that above all others brought the Jews to their untimely end was the manifestation of the brightness of God's character or glory in Christ. Before Christ came the Jews were in a serious state of apostasy, but even so, they were not totally separated from God, for they had not taken the final steps in rebellion. But as the light of Christ's glorious character shone on them, they were driven to desperate lengths of resistance until they were pushed to the extremes of apostasy. God did not intend that such be the result of this revelation, but once they determined to reject Him, it became the only possible outworking of that decision. They were destroyed, and it was by the brightness of His coming.

The sequence was as follows:

- The Jews were in a state of apostasy.
- Christ shone on them the brightness of His coming, the glory of His character.
- They rejected this influence and thus separated themselves from His protection.
- The actual destruction was accomplished by the unleashed natural forces.
- In exactly the same way, there is recorded the identical procedure that leads to the destruction of the wicked in the final overthrow of humankind.
- They will be in a state of deep apostasy.
- The brightness of His coming will be revealed to them in the loud cry.
- Their rejection of this influence will drive them to separate themselves from God's protection.

The actual destruction to befall them will be accomplished by the unleashing of the wild passions within them and by the unrestrained forces of nature.

Basically then, it is the brightness of His coming that destroys them, but not in the sense that they are struck down by it. That is left to the unrestrained forces in humanity and nature, the destruction from which the brightness of His coming would have saved them if they had related to it correctly.

The sacred writings reveal the entire sequence.

> In the mad strife of their own fierce passions, and by the awful outpouring of God's unmingled wrath, fall the wicked inhabitants of the earth—priests, rulers, and people, rich and poor, high and low. "And the slain of the Lord shall be at that day from one end of the earth even unto the other end of the earth: they shall not be lamented, neither gathered, nor buried." Jeremiah 25:33.

At the coming of Christ the wicked are blotted from the face of the whole earth—consumed with the spirit of His mouth and destroyed by the brightness of His glory. Christ takes His people to the City of God, and the earth is emptied of its inhabitants (*The Great Controversy*, p. 657).

Placing these two statements in this order side by side perfectly expresses the destiny of the unrepentant. The immediate and seemingly obvious means of their destruction will be the terrible onslaught of maddened human beings and nature. But the deeper, underlying cause is not to be overlooked. *Prior to the coming of the physical calamities, divine love will have sent the revelation of Christ's character in the brightness of His soon coming. Their rejection of those saving provisions will place them where destruction is free to descend upon them.*

Those who do not understand this and believe that the death of the wicked will be directly and physically accomplished by flaming fire emanating from the person of Christ would need to have the statement written differently to justify their stance. For them it should appear as follows:

> In the mad strife of their own fierce passions, and by the awful outpouring of God's unmingled wrath, fall [*the larger proportion of*] the wicked inhabitants of the earth—priests, rulers, and people, rich and poor, high and low. "And the slain of the Lord shall be at that day from one end of the earth even unto the other end of the earth: they shall not be lamented, neither gathered, nor buried." Jeremiah 25:33.
>
> At the coming of Christ [*the remainder of*] the wicked are blotted from the face of the whole earth—consumed with the spirit of His mouth and destroyed by the brightness of His glory. Christ takes His people to the City of God, and the earth is emptied of its inhabitants (*Ibid.*).

The second version provides for the theory that when Christ appears there will be such an outshining of flaming power that the wicked who manage to survive the seven last plagues and the bloody internecine warfare will be consumed by it. If the statement was written in this way, those who believe that would have an incontrovertible proof for their belief.

But it is not written that way. Instead, we have the truth stated and then repeated in different words of just how the wicked will perish. They are parallel declarations, each saying the same thing in different words. *To be slain by the brightness of His coming is to perish under the seven last plagues and the fierce battles they will fight.*

In all of the discussion of the brightness of His coming at the second advent we have only been touching upon the penultimate destruction of the wicked who are alive to witness the second coming. The ultimate destruction of the wicked comes at the second death, which is after the third coming at the end of the millennium. This destruction is also effected by the brightness of His coming, which, by definition, is the final outworking of their rejection of the light of His character as seen at the time of His first and second advents. In fact, for every one that is finally lost, including those who lived before the first advent, it will be this same brightness of His coming that destroys them, according to the same principles as discussed here. For the gospel of Christ has been in the world since sin entered through Adam.

It is shown in inspiration how at the final coronation of Christ and the Great White Throne judgment the full implications of their rejection of the Savior are brought to their realization. They see the full righteousness of His character in contrast to their own cherished attributes. By their lives they have declared, "We will not have this Man [Jesus] to reign over us" (*The Great Controversy*, p. 668). It is at this time that the emotional agonies of their chosen fate calls for the full separation from the life of God, and they receive the second death, which culminates in the lake of fire in which all of the elements melt with fervent heat, going into dissolution. There comes at this time the full wrath of God, an actual cessation of entire existence, mind, soul, and body, but this is not due to fire emanating from the person of God or Christ.

It is revealed in inspiration how, at the end of the millennium, in the final confrontation around the city of God, it is not the pulsing forth of some kind of blinding physical energy from Christ that destroys the wicked. The wicked will come quite close to the presence of Christ, who is just as powerful then as when He returns the second time. But they are able to march against the city in which resides the presence of God and of Christ. They are able to stand there right through the revelation of the mystery of Christ, and they are able to see all that God wants them to see without being consumed with physical fire from the presence of God and His Son. (Read the last chapter of *The Great Controversy*.)

Therefore, if the fire surrounding Christ does not consume them at the end of the thousand years, why should it do so at the beginning unless Christ personally decided that it should? If He did, then of course He would be acting arbitrarily, which God never does, and He would become a direct destroyer which, for Him, is impossible.

It is argued that fire comes from God to kill the impenitent in certain instances, such as when the drunken sons of Aaron—Nadab and Abihu—went into the sanctuary without the protection of the incense. In this case it is found that they entered into God's presence with their own fire, their own righteousness, which cannot endure before Him.

The same principle applies to the two hundred and fifty princes in the story of the rebellion of Korah, Dathan, and Abiram. These men had also come before the Lord with their own fire. Such is done by the rebel, as if to state, no, as truly stating, "We will not have this Jesus reign over us." They are making a fundamental statement of intent to stand on their own and in defiance of God's righteousness as their only covering they boldly try to come before Him on their own merits. God honors their final choice in the matter, and we have then a dramatic example of the withdrawal of His word, the fire of the Holy Spirit, from them, and they are "consumed," not in a physical rapid oxidation from great heat, but they die immediately by the cessation of God's sustaining power within their being.

Chapter Thirty-Eight

The Final Showdown

Study/Discussion Questions:

- Most have gone to their graves with the wrong view of God. At the end of the millennium all of the wicked are resurrected because the controversy cannot be ended until every mind is satisfied. Why is that?

- In the final showdown, God will be making the ultimate demonstration of the principles of His government, which are freedom of choice and noncoercion. How does the destruction of the wicked do this?

- Satan and his host lay plans for the biggest war ever seen in history. They build weapons. They march against the city. Are the weapons fired?

The earth is the proving ground for the validity, power, indestructibility, justice, and perfect righteousness of the principles upon which God's kingdom is built. During the span of history from the beginning of the world until now, Satan and his hosts have mounted every possible assault in their desperate search for that one weakness or flaw needed to supply the evidence to prove that God's ways are not perfect and need to be reformed. They have worked to provoke God to the point where He would arise and sweep humankind off the face of the earth. They have subjected Him to the greatest test that could ever come upon Him at their hands and devices.

This has been no light test for God. He is a being of infinite power and love. The witness of human history shows that the more power a person possesses, the greater the danger of his corruption. A great many have successfully endured privation and poverty only to be destroyed by coming into possession of riches and power. Furthermore, the intense sensitivity of God's nature and perceptions causes Him to view sin with a hatred and detestation that no human being could either know or understand. Throughout the entire period of the great controversy, God has been suffering intense anguish.

> All heaven suffered in Christ's agony; but that suffering did not begin or end with His manifestation in humanity. The cross is a revelation to our dull senses of the pain that, from its very inception, sin has brought to the heart of God. Every departure from the right, every deed of cruelty, every failure of humanity to reach His ideal, brings grief to Him. When there came upon Israel the calamities that were the sure result of separation from God,—subjugation by their en-

emies, cruelty, and death,—it is said that "His soul was grieved for the misery of Israel." "In all their affliction He was afflicted: … and He bare them, and carried them all the days of old." Judges 10:16; Isaiah 63:9.…

Our world is a vast lazar house, a scene of misery that we dare not allow even our thoughts to dwell upon. Did we realize it as it is, the burden would be too terrible. Yet God feels it all (*Education*, pp. 263, 264).

Christ feels the woes of every sufferer. When evil spirits rend a human frame, Christ feels the curse. When fever is burning up the life current, He feels the agony (*The Desire of Ages*, p. 823).

The depth of God's continual suffering needs to be better realized and appreciated. There has been the inclination to think that Jesus came to this earth, suffered with increasing intensity for thirty-three years, and then returned to the perfect bliss and painlessness of heaven. This is anything but the truth. The Father and Son have suffered to a depth of which we have neither knowledge nor experience.

This personal pain is distasteful to God who desires the end of all suffering more than we ever could. He has the power to end it in an instant by simply obliterating it. Yet He does not yield to the pressure of His own feelings and desires. He is prepared to suffer in order to maintain the principles of His government, whereby we will be assured eternally the happiness and security of all the universe. If we could enter into the full extent of God's sufferings and, at the same time, possess the power He has then we would know something of the pressure exerted on Him throughout the great controversy.

But during all those ages of darkness and death, of temptation and suffering, God has never deviated from the stated and perfect principles of His government and kingdom. He has never violated the freedom given to any individual, has never taken a person's life, has never destroyed, and has never in the smallest particular broken the law. He has been strictly impartial and just. He has been the Savior, ever and only working to bless, heal, and restore. Satan has never gained a point over the Lord in the battle. From it all, God emerges as untouched by sin as if it had never entered the universe. He is immaculate.

But while God has been immaculately perfect in all His activities, He has not been seen as such. In the eyes of humanity, Satan has dressed the pure and holy God in his own evil garments. Millions upon millions have gone to their graves with a decidedly reversed view of the true nature of righteousness and the God of righteousness. The great controversy cannot be settled until every one of those minds sees the true nature of our heavenly Father and confesses His perfect justice and righteousness.

God is not concerned about clearing His name for His own personal interest. He is not proud. He does not take personal offense. But He does understand that His character and the principles of righteousness are one and the same. Therefore, the justification of one assures the establishment of the other. He further knows that *the eternal happiness and security of the universe depend on the vindication of those principles*. Inasmuch as His everlasting and infinite love for all His children will not permit Him to provide anything less than perfection for them, He is determined not to permit the ultimate desecration of righteousness. He will establish it eternally.

Because of this, every person who has ever lived must be assembled for the final showdown in the great controversy. Every principle upon which the kingdom of God is built and operates must be revealed in sharply defined contrast to the principles of Satan's government.

It follows then that if it was important for God never to violate the laws of His government during the active controversy, then it is of multiplied importance that He strictly adhere to them in the final confrontation around the city after the thousand years have expired.

In this last showdown He is afforded His final opportunity to confirm that He is not an executioner. Instead, He has given to all the freedom to choose what they want, and He will not interfere with that choice. To make the least concession then, after so perfectly demonstrating the contrary over the previous millenniums, would nullify all that has been achieved. It would be as if a man spent a lifetime building a splendid edifice and then burned it to the ground. It is certain that this is not what God will do. There is no possibility of His having faithfully resisted every pressure to provocation for so long only to give way to it at the last. The final eradication of the wicked will happen exactly as lesser decimations occurred in human history. As Jerusalem was overthrown by the Jews themselves, as Sodom and Gomorrah perished as a harvest of their own seed-sowing, as the flood came, not because God sent it but because He could not prevent it without violating His righteous principles, so the final end will come. It will not be because God sent it, but because He cannot prevent it without taking away people's freedom to choose what they want.

These principles are poorly understood by earth-dwellers, most of whom have gone to their dusty beds with distorted understandings of God's character. This is not God's fault, for He has provided in nature, in His Word, and in the revelation given by Christ all that is necessary for understanding His righteous principles. Therefore, in His great love and mercy, He will especially raise up every human being so that once more they can be shown God's workings and their own rejection of them. This time they will have no arguments with which to counter the witness of God. Every person, from Satan down, will acknowledge that God has been just and that the loss of their own souls is their own doing.

After one thousand years, during which there will not be a living soul upon this earth apart from the devil and his evil angels, the wicked of every generation will be raised up for this final showdown. They come up resuming "the current of their thoughts just where it ceased. They are actuated by the same desire to conquer that ruled them when they fell" (*The Great Controversy*, p. 664).

Satan is astir at once and marshals the mighty hosts into the most prodigious, prestigious army ever to tramp the earth. It will be a most impressive sight as they drill and train day after day. How long a time will be involved in this mammoth preparation, we are not told. According to the principle of freedom that the Lord extends to all, they will be given as much time as they wish to take. Satan knows this, and while he is anxious to see the struggle over, at the same time he knows that it will be a titanic struggle. Therefore, he will direct that the preparations be as thorough as possible.

They do not intend to advance to the hoped-for conquest of the city with bare hands. "Skillful artisans construct implements of war" (*The Great Controversy*, p. 664). Just how sophisticated the weapons will be, we are not told. It is possible that they will be as highly technical as the scientific men can assemble. The atomic scientists will be there, remembering all they learned while still living on this earth. They will think in terms of conducting nuclear warfare against the city so that, if it is at all possible to prepare such tools of destruction, they certainly will do so. With Satan having full control of all of the people on the earth except those in the safety of the ark of the New Jerusalem, there will be no restrictions upon the development of his war machine. There will undoubtedly be weaponry such as we have never before seen deployed upon the earth, far in advance even of nuclear technology. The advancing hordes will carry such weaponry with them as they move up to the jasper walls.

But no battle ensues. It has been suggested that the battle of Armageddon begins before Christ's coming and is completed around the New Jerusalem. A little careful thought will show that there is no battle in the end. The struggle between God and His people on one side and Satan and his on the other will all end before Christ comes the second time. At the end of the thousand years, God will have at His command the revelations of the principles of righteousness as embodied in His character, which have been provided by His dealings with the rebellion in heaven; the temptation and fall of humanity; the course of His leading and dealings with human beings through all of the pre-first advent history; the life and teachings of Christ upon this earth; and at last, the witness of the translated saints as given during the time of Jacob's trouble.

These witnesses will be fully unfolded before the entire multitude. Their advance against the Holy City is arrested. The coronation of Christ takes place. A panoramic view above the throne plays out for every individual to review the history of the great rebellion and their place in it. As scene after scene passes before them, they will see the great controversy in its true light. They will realize just what God stands for. They will see the true nature of Satan's rebellion against Him. They will recognize that His law was provided for them as a life preserver; that disregard of the divine precepts did not bring them release from an arduous bondage, but opened the floodgates of woe upon them. They will understand, at last, that every woe and trouble they have experienced has been the result of their own course of action. They will know that they have abused the gift of freedom to their own miserable hurt (see The Great Controversy, pp. 666-668).

They will see things as they have never seen them before, things the devil was determined they should never see. As soon as they do, *all intent* to continue the rebellion against God is *ended*. The principle here is that when a misrepresentation of God's character begins rebellion against God likewise begins. So when the character of God is fully revealed for what it is, rebellion against God then comes to its end.

This is precisely why there is no war between the wicked and God over the New Jerusalem. In the beginning of the great controversy, God had not yet been afforded the opportunity to set forth so clear a manifestation of His character as would settle the problem right then and there. But at the end of the thousand years, He *will* have such revelations, which He will use, not only to ensure that there is no war but to bring, from the least person to Satan himself, the frank and open confession that *they* have held wrong concepts of God, that *they* have been responsible for rejecting His salvation, and that *their* doom is deserved.

The picture is so clear. The wicked see things exactly as they are, and instead of rushing in to attack the city, they fall "prostrate" and "worship the Prince of life" (*The Great Controversy*, p. 669).

Satan also sees it all. His mind travels back over the full span of his life. He sees again those days when he was the covering cherub. He remembers the first thoughts of doubt and then the open rebellion. He surveys the long centuries in between, comparing the loving patience and forgiving power of the Eternal in contrast to his own mean, destructive spirit.

> Satan sees that his voluntary rebellion has unfitted him for heaven. He has trained his powers to war against God; the purity, peace, and harmony of heaven would be to him supreme torture. His accusations against the mercy and justice of God are now silenced. The reproach which he has endeavored to cast upon Jehovah rests wholly upon himself. And now Satan bows down and confesses the justice of his sentence (*The Great Controversy*, p. 670).

The great moment has come. There is not a single intelligent being in the universe whose mind has the slightest question remaining as to the perfect righteousness of God's character. Even the arch-rebel himself will bow down to acknowledge the truth of God's ways and the falsity of every other system.

> "Who shall not fear Thee, O Lord, and glorify Thy name? for Thou only art holy: for all nations shall come and worship before Thee; for Thy judgments are made manifest." [Revelation 15:4]. Every question of truth and error in the long-standing controversy has now been made plain. The results of rebellion, the fruits of setting aside the divine statutes, have been laid open to the view of all created intelligences. The working out of Satan's rule in contrast with the government of God has been presented to the whole universe. Satan's own works have condemned him. God's wisdom, His justice, and His goodness stand fully vindicated. It is seen that all His dealings in the great controversy have been conducted with respect to the eternal good of His people and the good of all the worlds that He has created. "All Thy works shall praise Thee, O Lord; and Thy saints shall bless Thee." Psalm 145:10. *The history of sin will stand to all eternity as a witness that with the existence of God's law is bound up the happiness of all*

the beings He has created. With all the facts of the great controversy in view, the whole universe, both loyal and rebellious, with one accord declare: "Just and true are Thy ways, Thou King of saints" (*The Great Controversy*, pp. 670, 671, emphasis added).

In the day of final judgment, every lost soul will understand the nature of his own rejection of truth. The cross will be presented, and its real bearing will be seen by every mind that has been blinded by transgression. Before the vision of Calvary with its mysterious Victim, sinners will stand condemned. Every lying excuse will be swept away. Human apostasy will appear in its heinous character. *Men will see what their choice has been.* Every question of truth and error in the long-standing controversy will then have been made plain. *In the judgment of the universe, God will stand clear of blame for the existence or continuance of evil. It will be demonstrated that the divine decrees are not accessory to sin. There was no defect in God's government, no cause for disaffection.* When the thoughts of all hearts shall be revealed, both the loyal and the rebellious will unite in declaring, "Just and true are Thy ways, Thou King of saints. Who shall not fear Thee, O Lord, and glorify Thy name?... for Thy judgments are made manifest." Revelation 15:3, 4 (*The Desire of Ages*, p. 58, emphasis added).

We tend to think of the post-millennial judgment primarily as a judgment of the wicked, but what is really going on here in this "day of final judgment"? Who and what is actually being judged? Notice that the *universe* is doing the judging! *God* is the One who is cleared of blame and His government stands unblemished!

The wicked are part of the universe; they too are standing in judgment of God and declaring His name as "just and true." But their confession is bitter, unlike that borne of the work of the Holy Spirit, which brings the sinner to repentance. The hardened impenitent masses still hate God, every one of them. Now they hate Satan also, and they abandon their loyalty to him and his government. Their end has come. There is nowhere to turn. There is no hope.

Though God stands vindicated by this confession, there is one more grand demonstration of the truth about God and the nature of His government. The wicked will die, and there will be a cleansing fire. It will be seen that sin destroys the wicked, not God. God will emerge from this scenario with His character and the nature of His justice standing unimpeachable for eternity.

Chapter Thirty-Nine

The Fires

Study/Discussion Questions:

- Fire destroys the wicked. Fire comes from nature gone to wrath. Fire utterly dissolves all things. Are these all the same fires?

- At the final revelation to the wicked, they will be convinced about the righteousness of God, but they will not be converted by it. Why is this witness important to the saved and the unfallen universe? Why is it important that the lost also realize this?

- The Scriptures depict the wicked coming against Satan in the end. How do they turn on him?

- The unquenchable fire is what destroys the sinner at last. What is it?

- Some are going to suffer longer than others. How is this accomplished by natural outcome rather than by arbitrary judgment and execution by Deity?

- Judas is a type of the death of the wicked. How?

- Jesus' descent into the second death experience on the cross is a type of the death of the wicked. Do we attribute the second death to mental stress producing physical trauma (i.e., the "broken heart syndrome"), or is there something more?

- During the millennium the redeemed judge the wicked and determine the sentence. Explain how this is so.

- Peter speaks about a reservoir of fire in the earth. What is this fire, and what place does it have in the final dissolution of all that is associated with sin?

- What is "fervent heat" that "melts" all matter, in other words, how do all of the elements burn to a total consumption?

- What smoke and ash are made by stones? By helium? By diamonds?

Once Satan and his followers have been brought to acknowledge the justice and righteousness of God, the stage is set for the final act—the expiration of the wicked on the earth and the purification of the earth and heavens from the presence and stain of sin.

This will be accomplished by fire. The Scriptures say, "And fire came down from God out of heaven and devoured them. The devil, who deceived them, was cast into the lake of fire and brimstone where the beast and the false prophet are. And they will be tormented day and night forever and ever.... Then Death and Hades were cast into the lake of fire. This is the second death. And anyone not found written in the Book of Life was cast into the lake of fire" (Rev. 20:9-15).

> "Every battle of the warrior is with confused noise, and garments rolled in blood; but this shall be with burning and fuel of fire." "The indignation of the Lord is upon all nations, and His fury upon all their armies: He hath utterly destroyed them, He hath delivered them to the slaughter." "Upon the wicked He shall rain quick burning coals, fire and brimstone and an horrible tempest: this shall be the portion of their cup." Isaiah 9:5; 34:2; Psalm 11:6, margin. Fire comes down from God out of heaven. The earth is broken up. The weapons concealed in its depths are drawn forth. Devouring flames burst from every yawning chasm. The very rocks are on fire. The day has come that shall burn as an oven. The elements melt with fervent heat, the earth also, and the works that are therein are burned up. Malachi 4:1; 2 Peter 3:10. The earth's surface seems one molten mass—a vast, seething lake of fire. It is the time of the judgment and perdition of ungodly men—"the day of the Lord's vengeance, and the year of recompenses for the controversy of Zion." Isaiah 34:8.
>
> The wicked receive their recompense in the earth. Proverbs 11:31. They "shall be stubble: and the day that cometh shall burn them up, saith the Lord of hosts." Malachi 4:1. Some are destroyed as in a moment, while others suffer many days. All are punished "according to their deeds." The sins of the righteous having been transferred to Satan, he is made to suffer not only for his own rebellion, but for all the sins which he has caused God's people to commit. His punishment is to be far greater than that of those whom he has deceived. After all have perished who fell by his deceptions, he is still to live and suffer on. In the cleansing flames the wicked are at last destroyed, root and branch—Satan the root, his followers the branches. The full penalty of the law has been visited; the demands of justice have been met; and heaven and earth, beholding, declare the righteousness of Jehovah (*The Great Controversy*, pp. 672, 673).

These texts and statements are familiar to Bible students. Invariably they have given a picture of God personally pouring down fire upon the wicked and thus bringing about their final end. This is no problem to average people, for they consider that God has a perfect right to destroy those who have rebelled against Him. Furthermore, they know of no other way whereby the problem can be solved. The criminals must be executed or they will go on making trouble forever. Of course, this is humanity's thinking, but it is neither the thinking nor the way of God.

There is no difference in the language used in Revelation or *The Great Controversy* from that used in other parts of the inspiration describing the outpouring of terrible judgments.

> Then the Lord rained brimstone and fire on Sodom and upon Gomorrah, from the Lord out of the heavens (Gen. 19:24).

> And I will harden Pharaoh's heart, and multiply My signs and My wonders in the land of Egypt (Exod. 7:3).

> So the Lord sent fiery serpents among the people, and they bit the people; and many of the people of Israel died (Num. 21:6).

> But the Spirit of the Lord departed from Saul, and a distressing spirit from the Lord troubled him (1 Sam. 16:14).

> But when the king heard about it, he was furious. And he sent out his armies, destroyed those murderers, and burned up their city (Matt. 22:7).

We have already considered each of these statements from the Lord. It has been demonstrated that there must be a different definition of the terms and expressions used to describe the behavior of human beings. Trouble is experienced in understanding these expressions in regard to God's character when no distinction is made between humanity's ways and God's ways.

Those previous studies into these verses confirmed the truth that when God pours out fire, sends serpents, or such things, it is not something dispensed from His hands as a response to His personal decree. Rather, it happens only when He is obliged to depart from the scene, thus leaving matters in the hands of individuals and devils and to nature given over to chaos. Then, being out of His control, the rod of power descends in merciless might upon the defenseless heads of the self-willed.

There is no reason to suppose that these verses in Revelation are to be understood any differently. What those expressions mean throughout the remainder of the Scriptures, they must still mean at the end of them. Therefore, in the end, God does not decree that the wicked shall die by fire and then set about executing this decree by personally exercising His power. God does not decree what punishment shall befall the evildoer. He foresees what will happen and *foretells* it, but He neither chooses nor organizes it to be just that way.

In the light of all the truths learned so far in this study, consider the sequence of events in the drama of destruction outside the city. When the wicked are raised at the close of the millennium, it is only possible for them to live safely upon the earth by God holding firm to the rod of power. All the mighty forces of nature are thus held in restraint in order to afford to the lost the opportunity of seeing the true nature of the great controversy. Thus, there is no outburst of fire and brimstone during the time that they make their preparations and advance upon the city.

But when the revelations of the mystery of God have been completed while simultaneously they have been convincingly shown where they have rejected the loving appeals of God, the time has come for the final settlement. Every one of these individuals has, during this life, made an irrevocable decision rejecting salvation in preference for Satan's kingdom. God knows that once this point has been reached, the wicked will never change no matter what opportunity may be given to them. It is for this reason that Jesus solemnly intones as He leaves the sanctuary, "He who is unjust, let him be unjust still; he who is filthy, let him be filthy still; he who is righteous, let him be righteous still; he who is holy, let him be holy still" (Rev. 22:11).

This is the declaration of Jesus Christ in evaluating the condition of the wicked. It is not to be supposed that Christ says this because He and the Father have decided that probation can no longer be continued, and for this reason those who have not availed themselves of salvation during the designated time limit are lost forever. It is because, no matter what revelations might be made to them or opportunities given, their decision is final.

But it is one thing for this to be so and for Christ to say it is so. It is something else for God's true children to see it. How often in this life have we looked upon a person who appears to be so sincere and honest and yet who makes no evident move toward the messages of truth. We feel that if only this person had been given more opportunity to see it, he or she would have come to Christ. We find it difficult to accept the idea that when this person goes to the grave he or she should remain unjust forever.

The declaration made by Christ will be vindicated by the demonstration of its truthfulness at the close of the millennium. Those whom we thought had gone down to their graves without the necessary chance to see the light will then be afforded the most comprehensive, clear, and wonderful revelation of the truth. They behold, with transfixed eye, the entire story of rebellion and redemption and see their own place in relation to it and how their attitude toward God's way played out in their relations to their fellow humankind. It will convince but not convert them. Their rejection of such light as came to them in this life will have hardened them beyond any possibility of change.

Their conviction that God is right after all will be expressed by their bowing before Him and saying so, but they do not plead His forgiveness nor ask to be accepted into His kingdom. All of that is foreign and distasteful to them. They still want to live but on their own terms. Knowing that this cannot be and that, accordingly, they are eternally to be deprived of any life, they rise from their knees in a frenzy of disappointment and rage and turn upon him who has robbed them of everything.

This rage is a part of a process that will begin at the time of the panoramic view of salvation history above the throne, and it is the fire unquenchable. To the righteous, this revelation of God's character is called the everlasting burnings. This is their eternal dwelling place, in joy and peace.

> The sinners in Zion are afraid; fearfulness has seized the hypocrites: "Who among us shall dwell with the devouring fire? Who among us shall dwell with

everlasting burnings? He who walks righteously and speaks uprightly, He who despises the gain of oppressions, Who gestures with his hands, refusing bribes, who stops his ears from hearing of bloodshed, and shuts his eyes from seeing evil: He will dwell on high; his place of defense will be the fortress of rocks; bread will be given him; his water will be sure. Your eyes will see the King in His beauty; they will see the land that is very far off (Isa. 33:14-17).

Inspiration explicitly declares what is the torment of the wicked and how they are destroyed.

But those who refuse the gift of Christ will one day *feel the sting of remorse.* Entire obedience to the law of God is the condition of salvation. Those who refuse this, who refuse to accept Christ, will *become embittered against God.* When punished for transgression, they will *feel despair and hatred.* This will be the experience of all who do not enter into Christ's suffering; for it is the sure consequence of sin.

We read of chains of darkness for the transgressor of God's law. We read of the worm that dieth not, and of *the fire that is not quenched.* Thus is represented the experience of every one who has permitted himself to be grafted into the stock of Satan, who has cherished sinful attributes. When it is too late, *he will see* that sin is the transgression of God's law. *He will realize* that because of transgression, his soul is cut off from God, and that God's wrath abides on him. *This is a fire unquenchable, and by it every unrepentant sinner will be destroyed.* (*Signs of the Times*, April 14, 1898, emphasis added).

These "chains of darkness" are the realization of the hopeless condition of their souls. They see clearly that their wills are fixed in a bent toward self-governance and selfishness and that there is no way out of their terrible dilemma. This is what it is to be "grafted into the stock of Satan." As a branch grafted into its host, they are now part of Satan's fixed and determined rebellion against the law of God, the character of God. They understand this.

In effect, at the climax of the revelation of the gospel, God will ask them to confirm their intentions. Hitherto they have reiterated their wish to live without God. The time will have come when they must either confirm or deny the plan to continue that way. *If it were possible* for them to relinquish every desire to be separate from God, then God would save them, even then, for "His mercy endures forever" (Ps. 106:1).

But no person will be saved at this time, for they will not show any disposition to change. Their consciences have been seared. Their rebellion is incurable. Christ's declaration will be proven correct. As God waits for their answer, they will confirm in the most emphatic terms that they want nothing to do with Him; they will choose to be left entirely to their own way. They want the world and life under their own terms.

"Then death shall be chosen rather than life by all the residue of those who remain of this evil family, who remain in all the places where I have driven them," says the Lord of hosts (Jer. 8:3).

What can God do under these circumstances?

He has made it very plain that everyone has full liberty to choose what they want. If they prefer to go it alone without Him, then this is what they shall have. When Israel wanted their king, He gave them one; when they wanted flesh, He let them have it; and whenever individuals have wanted this or that, the Lord has never stood in their way, no matter what dire results might follow their foolish choosing.

At the end of the millennium, He cannot change. So when they choose to go alone, He will simply say to them, "Then I respect your choice, and I will set you completely free from My presence and control. All the earth and the mighty powers surrounding it are going to be relinquished. The rod of power is to pass out of My hands and control and all of that which has been marred by sin will evaporate back into the void from whence it came by my original word."

They will be given into the hands of their god—self. The qualifications for godhood are to be eternally existent and self-sustaining. The wicked will understand this truth. They will know with certainty that they are not gods, and they will know without any doubt that Satan is no god, only a thief, a liar, and a murderer. The time for the full reckoning of these verities, as well as the reality that they are fixed in their own determination not to live under the rule of Christ, is all rolled together with the weight of the guilt of every sin ever committed.

Satan will try to stir the wicked to continue the battle plan to take the city, but the wicked will be finished with him. The lies will be all fully revealed. Satan had convinced them that God was a tyrant Who would rule over them with an iron fist, requiring them to live a life of joyless servitude and preventing them from any real progress out of a motivation of jealousy for His own power and control. Satan had promised them a New World Order wherein they would enjoy power and prosperity, living as they pleased. They will see that they gave in to their desire for self and sin and chose Satan as their ruler. By their lives they declared, "We will not have this Jesus to reign over us."

They have no help for Satan. Their refusal to go into battle with him is the result of their full realization that he has used them miserably in his own personal vendetta against God. They had once thought him so wise, as they banded together in secret societies, partook of hidden (occult) wisdom, and communicated with the "ascended masters." They had believed, as did Eve when she partook of the occult philosophy at the forbidden tree, that he was taking them to new and exalted heights of existence and would even evolve upward into a super species of humanity.

An end! The end is come upon the four corners of the land (Eze. 7:2).

"They have blown the trumpet and made everyone ready, but no one goes to battle: for My wrath is on all their multitude" (verse 14).

At last, the wicked will cut Satan and his philosophies to pieces, not literally, for he is a spirit being, and no human can lay hands on angels, but they will bring him down in their bitter expressions borne of revelation.

"Those who see you will gaze at you, and consider you, saying: 'Is this the man who made the earth tremble, Who shook kingdoms, Who made the world as a wilderness, and destroyed its cities, Who did not open the house of his prisoners?" (Isa. 14:16, 17).

Saith the Lord: "Because thou hast set thine heart as the heart of God; behold, therefore I will bring strangers upon thee, the terrible of the nations: and they shall draw their swords against the beauty of thy wisdom, and they shall defile thy brightness. They shall bring thee down to the pit." "I will destroy thee, O covering cherub, from the midst of the stones of fire…. I will cast thee to the ground, I will lay thee before kings, that they may behold thee…. I will bring thee to ashes upon the earth in the sight of all them that behold thee…. Thou shalt be a terror, and never shalt thou be any more." Ezekiel 28:6-8, 16-19 (*The Great Controversy*, p. 672).

As they work through this terrible time of reckoning with their own death, Satan's brightness is defiled by their withdrawal from him. It is the ultimate "drying up of the Euphrates." They do not turn on him with weapons of warfare. Even if they could, they know it would be pointless and futile. There is no bloody battle of the warrior, as humans wage war. They know Satan has nothing to offer. Satan is laid bare in the global reckoning of the bankruptcy of his ideology. The *burning* is the agony of loss, hatred, rage, and the realization of the burden, or the wages, of sin in their soul. It is a burning that only death can relieve. When this burning is done, the fuel of fire will dissolve the elements with fervent heat in the lake of fire.

This final dissolution of the elements is referred to as the "fire in the midst," which comes out of Satan. More on this is mentioned further on.

Every battle of the warrior is with confused noise, and garments rolled in blood; *but this* shall be with *burning* and *fuel of fire* (Isa. 9:5, KJV).

The wicked will die in the same way as did Christ. His sufferings are a type of the death of the wicked in the second death.

But bodily pain was but a small part of the agony of God's dear Son. The *sins* of the world were *upon Him*, also the *sense of* His Father's *wrath* as He suffered the penalty of the law transgressed. It was *these* that crushed His divine soul. It was the *hiding of His Father's face*—a *sense* that His own dear Father had *forsaken* Him—which *brought despair*. The *separation* that sin makes between God and man was *fully realized* and keenly felt by the innocent, suffering Man of Calvary. He was *oppressed* by the powers of *darkness*. He had *not one ray of light* to brighten the future (*Testimonies for the Church*, vol. 2, p. 214, emphasis added).

Like this, the wicked also are consumed with their anguish, suffering the absolute coming to terms with the fact that only in God is there life and that they will not have it or abide in Him ever; therefore, they must acknowledge their hopeless condition and go away. This is how they expire.

"Praise the Lord! Blessed is the man who fears the Lord, Who delights greatly in His commandments. His descendants shall be mighty upon earth; the generation of the upright will be blessed. Wealth and riches will be in his house, and his righteousness endures forever.... *The wicked will see it, and be grieved; he will gnash with his teeth and melt away; the desire of the wicked shall perish* (Ps. 112:1-3, 10).

"Those who reject the mercy so freely proffered, will yet be made to know the worth of that which they have despised. They will feel the agony which Christ endured upon the cross to purchase redemption for all who would receive it. And they will then realize what they have lost—eternal life and the immortal inheritance.... When sinners are compelled to look upon Him who clothed His divinity with humanity, and who still wears this garb, their confusion is indescribable. The scales fall from their eyes, and they see that which before they would not see. They realize what they might have been had they received Christ, and improved the opportunities granted them. They see the law which they have spurned, exalted even as God's throne is exalted. They see God Himself giving reverence to His law. What a scene that will be! No pen can describe it! The accumulated guilt of the world will be laid bare, and the voice of the Judge will be heard saying to the wicked, "Depart from me, ye that work iniquity" (*The SDA Bible Commentary*, vol. 6, pp. 1069, 1070).

Notice the language of awakened understanding, of revelation and realization, of *seeing*. These are all the ones of whom it was once spoken that "seeing they would not see and hearing they would not hear." They had the chance to see and hear with spiritual senses that they might be drawn to repentance and be saved, but now they see and hear in the visible presence of the target of their murderous designs: the New Jerusalem, Christ, the angels, and the redeemed.

In this final sinking to the eternal night of death, the wicked do not all take the same time to perish. There is a direct relationship between the extent to which they have sinned and the length of time they suffer.

"I saw that some were quickly destroyed, while others suffered longer. They were punished according to the deeds done in the body. Some were many days consuming, and just as long as there was a portion of them unconsumed, all the sense of suffering remained. Said the angel, "The worm of life shall not die; their fire shall not be quenched as long as there is the least particle for it to prey upon."

Satan and his angels suffered long. Satan bore not only the weight and punishment of his own sins, but also of the sins of the redeemed host, which had been placed upon him; and he must also suffer for the ruin of souls which he had caused. Then I saw that Satan and all the wicked host were consumed, and the justice of God was satisfied; and all the angelic host, and all the redeemed saints, with a loud voice said, "Amen!" (*Early Writings*, pp. 294, 295).

Again, the language of the unquenchable fire is used, and the worm, which we saw explained in the *Signs of the Times* quote above. Here is a repetition of the key ideas in that same quote:

We read of the worm that dieth not, and of the fire that is not quenched. Thus is represented the experience of every one who … has cherished sinful attributes (*Signs of the Times*, April 14, 1898).

He will realize that … his soul is cut off from God, and that God's wrath abides on him. *This is a fire unquenchable, and by it every unrepentant sinner will be destroyed.* (*Signs of the Times*, April 14, 1898, emphasis added).

Note the language of experiential realization. *This* is the final outworking of eating the fruit of the tree of knowledge of good and evil. This is intimate knowledge, experiential knowledge, which God never intended any of His creatures to have. This is the day that they are eating it and swallowing it down, the day that God had declared would be the day of their death (Gen. 2:17) *This* is what destroys the wicked.

"The worm of life shall not die; their fire shall not be quenched as long as there is the least particle for it to prey upon" is what the angel said, in direct quote. Here, the metaphor of Isaiah 66:24 is expanded to include the "particles" that are preyed upon by the fire. The worm refers to the life of the being itself. This is interesting as the worm is usually thought of as preying upon something already dead, but in this statement the angel is emphasizing that the being suffers consciously until the last particle of sin—don't miss this point—is consumed by the fire (see Job 18; Ps. 22:6; Isa. 41:14). Remember, this is a fire of realization of the end of the soul, of being cut off from the life of God, as He must be released, in righteousness, from maintaining the sinner. The sinner will then die, in effect, by suicide, saying, "God, you are right, but I don't want you. Let me go." Then it is fulfilled as it is written,

But he who sins against me wrongs his own soul; all those who hate me love death (Prov. 8:36).

His own iniquities entrap the wicked man, and he is caught in the cords of his sin (Prov. 5:22).

Judas is a primary illustration of this anguish leading to a wish for death. Although he was sorry for the results of his way, he was not about to change his way. He threw the blood money back to the priests, as surely as the wicked will cast their gold and silver to the moles and the bats (Isa. 2:20). Riches hold no allure in the face of the loss of the soul. They are useless to a dead person, and Judas knew that he was just that. Judas wanted a different God. He wanted one who would let him live for self, power, glory, honor, and wealth. The principles of God's kingdom were made clear to him, but he would rather die than have that. So he hung himself. He realized who Jesus was and understood his own role. He was convinced of God's goodness and righteousness, but he remained unrepentant. All that was left for him was to go away.

It must be seen by all that the actual cause of death of the wicked is sin. There must be no question that it is their choice to reject God, to be separate from Him, to live by Satan's law, to "do as thou wilt." As the reality of the nature of sin is processed, along with the burden of its guilt and the coming to an acceptance of the impossibility of continued existence in sin and the realization that there is life only in God, they suffer extreme anguish. They will at last give over to the inevitable; they will at last want death, and this will be their acknowledged position, while at the same time proclaiming God just and true. This is how the great controversy can close and all potential seeds of rebellion be sterilized, forever.

While great mental anguish can cause great physical stress, even death, and while God's release on the forces of nature will cause fires in the earth to erupt, the cause of death will not, and cannot, be seen as any of these things. We confirm the truth that the cause of death is the burden of sin and the giving over of the soul unto it by going to the ultimate revelation of it at the cross of Christ.

> The mystery of the cross explains all other mysteries. In the light that streams from Calvary the attributes of God which had filled us with fear and awe appear beautiful and attractive (*The Great Controversy*, p. 652).

It is true that Christ suffered greatly in Gethsemane as the weight of the world's guilt was rolled onto Him. It caused Him to sweat blood, a condition known in the medical field as hematidrosis, where the capillaries in the sweat glands rupture and blood mixes with perspiration. The agony of great emotional stress will cause trauma on the heart, known as acute stress cardiomyopathy or "broken heart syndrome." Many in the past have seen that it was not the physical rigors of the cross that killed Him in such a short time, but they have fallen short in claiming that it was the broken heart syndrome that killed Him. We cannot focus on this as the cause of death. Sin destroys; in the ultimate sense, let us not get sidetracked in looking for physical manifestations.

> He guards all his bones; not one of them is broken. Evil shall slay the wicked, And those who hate the righteous shall be condemned [desolate, KJV] (Ps. 34:20, 21).

As the Type of the finally impenitent going to second death, we see Him giving up His life. John 10:15, 17, 18 reveals that Jesus laid down His life of His own volition. In three gospels it is recorded that He "gave up the ghost." He was not yet physically shutting down, as with strong voice he shouted from His cross, "My God, My God, why have You forsaken Me?" (Matt. 27:46). Then, at the stroke of the hour for the Passover sacrifice, He prayed, "Father, into Your hands I commit My spirit" (Luke 23:46).

It was not the dread of death that weighed upon Him. It was not the pain and ignominy of the cross that caused His inexpressible agony. Christ was the prince of sufferers; but *His suffering was from a sense of the malignity of sin….*

Upon Christ as our substitute and surety was laid the iniquity of us all. He was counted a transgressor … *The guilt of every descendant of Adam was pressing upon His heart.* The wrath of God against sin, the terrible manifestation of *His displeasure because of iniquity, filled the soul of His Son with consternation.* All His life Christ had been publishing to a fallen world the good news of the Father's mercy and pardoning love. Salvation for the chief of sinners was His theme. But now with the terrible weight of guilt He bears, He cannot see the Father's reconciling face. The withdrawal of the divine countenance from the Saviour in this hour of supreme anguish pierced His heart with a sorrow that can never be fully understood by man. So great was this agony that His physical pain was hardly felt….

Christ felt the anguish which the sinner will feel when mercy shall no longer plead for the guilty race. It was the sense of sin, bringing the Father's wrath upon Him as man's substitute, that made the cup He drank so bitter, and *broke the heart of the Son of God* (*The Desire of Ages,* pp. 752, 753, emphasis added).

But your iniquities have separated you from your God, and your sins have hid His face from you, so that he will not hear (Isa. 59:2).

Are you able to drink the cup that I am about to drink? (Matt. 20:22).

For as you drank on My holy mountain, so shall all the nations drink continually; Yes, they shall drink, and swallow, and they shall be as though they had never been (Obad. 1:16).

During His thirty years of life on earth His heart was wrung with inconceivable anguish. The path from the manger to Calvary was shadowed by grief and sorrow. He was a man of sorrows, and acquainted with grief, enduring such heartache as no human language can portray. He could have said in truth, "Behold, and see if there be any sorrow like unto my sorrow" (Lamentations 1:12) (*Selected Messages,* book 1, p. 322).

Is it nothing to you, all you who pass by? Behold and see if there is any sorrow like my sorrow, which has been brought on me, which the Lord has inflicted in the day of His fierce anger. From above *He has sent fire into my bones*, and it overpowered them; He has spread a net for my feet, and turned me back; He has made me desolate and faint all the day (Lam. 1:12, 13).

Notice here that this suffering is depicted as a fire. This desolating effect of the processing of sin is a very real horror, and the trauma of it has physical effect leading to death, but this death will not break upon the sinner until there is a surrender to the blackness of sin's consequences. A strict adherence to the witness of Christ's descent to second death on the cross is the proof of how the finally impenitent will expire.

The question must arise as to how the wicked will suffer according to what they deserve unless some intelligence calculates the measure of their individual punishments and so controls events that they will be kept alive until the full punishment has been exacted. On the surface, this would seem to be impossible. Therefore, it is considered that God, being the only one with the power to either estimate the deserved chastisement or to control its administration, must surely be the one who executes the sinners in the end. In fact, in the language of inspiration, it is represented as exactly that way:

> In union with Christ they judge the wicked, comparing their acts with the statute book, the Bible, and deciding every case according to the deeds done in the body. Then the portion which the wicked must suffer is meted out, according to their works; and it is recorded against their names in the book of death (*The Great Controversy*, p. 661).

This would appear in an obvious sense to be an arbitrary assignment of suffering. But we know that whatever they suffer will be directly related to their own choices in rebellion. Some will be much more hardened in their course than others. Not that any have any potential to repent. They don't. All are hardened irrevocably. Yet evil brings its own reward, and it follows a law: "the Lord shall repay the evildoer according to his wickedness" (2 Sam. 3:39). The key to understanding how this may come upon them is that the consciousness of sin, its burden and its guilt, was taken up by Christ for every person when He became sin for us, but this is now rolled back onto the hardened sinner. They must bear the burden of sin for themselves.

> As soon as the books of record are opened, and the eye of Jesus looks upon the wicked, they are conscious of *every sin* which they have ever committed. *They see* just where their feet diverged from the path of purity and holiness, just how far pride and rebellion have carried them in the violation of the law of God. The seductive temptations which they encouraged by indulgence in sin, the blessings perverted, the messengers of God despised, the warnings rejected, the waves of mercy beaten back by the stubborn, unrepentant heart—all appear as if written in letters of fire (*The Great Controversy*, p. 666, emphasis added).

Then you will remember your evil ways and your deeds that were not good; and you will loathe yourselves in your own sight, for your iniquities and your abominations (Eze. 36:31).

The heaviest burden that we bear is the burden of sin. If we were left to bear this burden, it would crush us. But the Sinless One has taken our place. "The Lord hath laid on Him the iniquity of us all." Isaiah 53:6 (*The Ministry of Healing*, p. 71).

"The spotless Son of God took upon Himself the burden of sin. He who had been one with God, felt in His soul the awful separation that sin makes between God and man. This wrung from His lips the anguished cry, "My God, my God, why hast thou forsaken me?" Matthew 27:46. It was the burden of sin, the sense of its terrible enormity, of its separation of the soul from God— *it was this that broke the heart of the Son of God* (*The Faith I Live By*, p. 101, emphasis added).

So, we see that the burden of sin is a cumulative burden. The wicked are "conscious of *every* sin." The conscious awareness of all of its guilt must be owned entirely by the bearer. Jesus took our guilt and shame so that we never have to bear it. We cannot bear it because it kills. It killed Him. As we apply the cumulative principle to the wicked, we find that the more intensively wicked the being, the more guilt they bear with all of the suffering that is implied.

Yet, in all of this bearing of guilt, the flesh is very much alive and screaming to live. Humanity's biggest drive is to hold on to life and their biggest fear is death. So, there is a tenacious clinging to the life of the flesh, which is somehow relative to the degree of wickedness, a perverse clinging to the desire to yet go on in it while fully realizing that this is an impossibility. It is insanity and an extreme mental crisis that we hope to never know.

Yet this has all been but a feeble attempt to describe with words something that is yet a mystery. To understand all of this, how sin can selectively punish one more than another, requires knowledge of laws that as yet are beyond our ken. One thing we do know, however, is that the more sinful people are the more desperately they struggle to live in the face of death. The true children of God do not fight the Grim Reaper. They know that their time has come and that their life is safe in the hands of God. But not so with the rebels against God's laws and government. They resist with all the power of their soul and are able to prolong their life beyond its natural span.

That the righteous, in the millennial judgment, "mete out" any durations or intensities of suffering is the language of predestination. As God foreknows all things, He is said to predestine them. But He does not interfere with free choice. He merely knows what choices are to be made in the context of the freedom by which He runs His universe. Therefore, the righteous, as they review the courses of the lost souls, will come to vindicate God's righteous judgment and will see how much suffering is going to be endured by the finally impenitent, and in their agreement with it, they are said to record the same "against their names in the book of death" (*The Faith I Live By*, p. 216). In this they are saying, "just and true are Your ways" (Rev. 15:3), which is merely an echo in advance, a prefiguring of the utterance made by the wicked themselves in the final scenes:

> The whole wicked world stand arraigned at the bar of God on the charge of high treason against the government of heaven. They have none to plead their cause; they are without excuse; and the sentence of eternal death is pronounced against them.
>
> It is now evident to all that the wages of sin is not noble independence and eternal life, but slavery, ruin, and death. The wicked see what they have forfeited by their life of rebellion. The far more exceeding and eternal weight of glory was despised when offered them; but how desirable it now appears. "All this," cries the lost soul, "I might have had; but I chose to put these things far from me. Oh, strange infatuation! I have exchanged peace, happiness, and honor, for wretchedness, infamy, and despair." *All see that their exclusion from heaven is just. By their lives they have declared, "We will not have this Man [Jesus] to reign over us."*
>
> As if entranced, the wicked have looked upon the coronation of the Son of God. They see in His hands the tables of the divine law, the statutes which they have despised and transgressed. They witness the outburst of wonder, rapture, and adoration from the saved; and as the wave of melody sweeps over the multitudes without the city, all with one voice exclaim, "Great and marvelous are Thy works, Lord God Almighty; just and true are Thy ways, Thou King of saints" (Revelation 15:3); and, falling prostrate, they worship the Prince of life (*The Great Controversy*, p. 668, emphasis added).

This worship is not one of love and adoration. They have only bitterness and hatred in their hearts. It is wrung from a heart of anguish, through guilty lips; it is the same "worship" as the false teachers will display as they fall at the feet of the saints at the time of the midnight deliverance when the captivity of God's people is turned, and it is realized that God has loved those whom they hate and that they have been fighting God (see *Early Writings*, p. 124; *The Great Controversy*, pp. 653-655).

One thing must be very clear. It is that God does not execute the sinner, now or in the past or ever. Nor do God or His saints arbitrarily predetermine the punishment that is to fall on the wicked. *It is sin that does that.* By their own works will they receive the measure of their reward.

> Evil shall slay the wicked: and they that hate the righteous shall be desolate (Ps. 34:21, KJV).

> The wages of sin is death (Rom. 6:23).

"But as for those whose hearts follow after the desire for their detestable things and their abominations, I will recompense their deeds on their own heads," says the Lord God (Eze. 11:21).

The wicked fall in death as they come to their surrender. Some give over immediately, some with greater struggle, some a very long time. The bodies accumulate over the earth.

And they shall go forth and look upon the corpses of the men who have transgressed against Me. For their worm does not die, and their fire is not quenched. They shall be an abhorrence to all flesh (Isa. 66:24).

Then I saw an angel standing in the sun; and he cried with a loud voice, saying to all the birds that fly in the midst of heaven, "Come and gather together for the supper of the great God, that you may eat the flesh of kings, the flesh of captains, the flesh of mighty men, the flesh of horses and of those who sit on them, and the flesh of all people, free and slave, both small and great" (Rev. 19:17, 18). [Note that the birds are not actual birds but a metaphor for the cleansing action of the final fires upon the remains of the wicked. See Jeremiah 4:25, 27 and Zephaniah 1:2, 3.]

And at that day the slain of the Lord shall be from one end of the earth even to the other end of the earth. They shall not be lamented, or gathered, or buried; they shall become refuse on the ground (Jer. 25:33).

No one has been so great a sinner as Satan, and no one will fight the inevitability of death with greater determination than he. His has been a most determined struggle—in his character manifesting the ultimate in stubbornness, pride, and rebellion, for he is truly the dark father of all wickedness. Thus he will prolong his life far beyond that point where he would have died if he had resigned himself to his fate. In so doing he will extend his suffering until he has suffered for all the sins he has committed and caused others to commit.

As the process of unquenchable fire progresses, the forces of nature are let loose so that they go into chaos. Peter spoke of this as a "fire reservoir" when he wrote:

By the word of God the heavens were of old, and the earth standing out the water and in the water, by which the world that then existed perished, being flooded with water. But the heavens and the earth which are now preserved by the same word, are reserved for fire until the day of judgment and perdition of ungodly men (2 Pet. 3:5-7).

Earlier we talked about how the reservoir of water above and under the earth broke loose and destroyed the world and how that this event set up the conditions in the earth such as we have today. Storms, extreme temperatures, earthquakes, volcanoes, and so on are all the offspring of the flood. The reservoir of fire is held in check, ready to spring forth with spectacular force the next time God's wrath is manifest on a global scale. It will manifest both at the second coming and at the end of the millennium, after the Great White Throne judgment.

As in the flood of water when the fountains of the earth were broken up so that water rushed out from beneath the surface, so the stores of oil and coal still hidden from human beings in the bowels of the earth will burst forth in flaming torrents upon the surface.

> Those majestic trees which God had caused to grow upon the earth, for the benefit of the inhabitants of the old world, and which they had used to form into idols, and to corrupt themselves with, God has reserved in the earth, in the shape of coal and oil to use as agencies in their final destruction. As he called forth the waters in the earth at the time of the flood, as weapons from his arsenal to accomplish the destruction of the antediluvian race, so at the end of the one thousand years he will call forth the fires in the earth as his weapons which he has reserved for the final destruction, not only of successive generations since the flood, but the antediluvian race who perished by the flood (*Spiritual Gifts*, vol. 3, p. 87).

In the original flood, water also poured down from above. Likewise, it is to be expected that fire will rain down from the heavens. The great source of this would be from nature spiraling into chaos since we know that it does not come from God personally. When God's presence was withdrawn from the earth in Noah's day, both the sun and the moon were affected. Therefore, when God's presence is again withdrawn in the same way at the close of the millennium, the sun could very well again be affected. In its final stages of decay, resulting from the effects of sin in this earth, it could erupt in great explosions, projecting streams of fire far out into the solar system and onto this earth. If this is to be so, then fire from above would mingle with the fire from beneath exactly as the waters did when this earth was flooded. The great emissions from the broken crust of the earth would spew high into the air, raining back down upon the earth, enveloping the whole earth in a sea of flame on which the Holy City will ride as did the ark. Within it, the ransomed will be safe and secure until the destruction is completed.

But these geophysical and perhaps solar fires are not of sufficient heat to dissolve the elements of creation. Also, what kind of heat is it that takes spirit beings out of existence? We do not know what kind of material a spiritual being is made from, but the substance of wicked angels will also be dissolved along with the substance of the human bodies.

Just as at the showdown between God and Baal on Mount Carmel, where the fire of God burned up the sacrifice, the wood, the rocks, and the water, so also will the final fire utterly consume all matter itself. This would be a nuclear fire. It is the energy that sustains all of matter, all of the universe. It is the word of God, by whom all things consist (see Col. 1:16, 17; John 1:1-3; Acts 17:28).

This nuclear binder is represented in Scriptures as "fire from the midst," and when it is brought forth, it is as the Word of God being withdrawn, His sustaining power being removed from matter itself. All that would have been damaged by being in contact with sin will be left to dissolution and will "consume away" "into smoke," as depicted in the biblical language of the process of oxidation or burning of fire.

> You defiled your sanctuaries by the multitude of your iniquities, by the iniquity of your trading; *therefore I brought fire from your midst; it devoured you, and I turned you to ashes upon the earth in the sight of all who saw you.* All who knew you among the peoples are astonished at you; you have become a horror, and shall be no more forever (Eze. 28:18,19).

Satan, having the greatest measure of iniquity upon himself, will be the last wicked being alive. Dying alone, with no place left for him anywhere in God's universe and with none to stand with him in his attempted kingdom, (for a kingdom requires subjects), he utters his final desperate gasp, requesting release from life. He now expires of the unquenchable fire and simultaneously goes to the physical annihilation of the "lake of fire," the "fire from the midst," the total meltdown of all things that sin has marred, where it is also said that the beast and the false prophet, the wicked host, already are (Rev. 20:10).

(There are two senses in which these are depicted as already in the lake of fire. In the first sense, the earth is by now already well on its way to being converted to a seething molten mass by the fire reservoir. In the second sense, where the lake would be defined as the fire of nuclear dissolution, they are said to be in the lake already in that they have been utterly consigned to the ultimate cessation of being, i.e., although their consciousness and breath are gone, the substance of their bodies, even though perhaps vaporized into steam and smoke, must now go out of actual existence.)

In Jeremiah 48 we have a prophecy against the latter day judgment of Moab, and here also is represented a destruction by this same fire: "But a fire shall come out ... a flame from the midst ... and shall devour the brow [region] of Moab, the crown of the head of sons of tumult" (verse 45).

This will be the last fire, the cleanup fire, the very ultimate manifestation of wrath, after all of the wicked have perished in the unquenchable fire of emotional agony and as the physical fires of nature gone to wrath have also broken forth and escalated unto this fervent heat of "atomic meltdown." Peter speaks also of this fire, which ends with a new heaven and a new earth being created:

> The heavens will pass away with a great noise, and the elements will melt with fervent heat; both the earth and the works that are in it will be burned up. Therefore, since all these things will be dissolved, what manner of persons ought you to be in holy conduct and godliness, looking for and hastening the coming of the day of God, because of which the heavens will be dissolved, being on fire, and the elements will melt with fervent heat? Nevertheless we,

according to His promise, look for new heavens and a new earth, in which righteousness dwells (2 Pet. 3:10-13).

The deadly experiment will be ended, and it will be demonstrated eternally that through it all God did not change. When sin entered it changed angels, human beings, the animals, and the operations of nature, *but it did not change God.* Nothing was introduced into His ways after the coming of sin that was not there before. He never destroyed before sin entered, never executed, never punished, and never forced. The entry of sin did not cause Him to begin doing any of these things in order to solve the problems sin imposed upon Him.

Satan and evil angels did their utmost to provoke Him to anger and arise to sweep away the rebellious inhabitants of the earth, but He would not be provoked, angered, insulted, or hurt. He emerges from the whole miserable test as immaculate as He entered it. Satan has not been able to sustain a single point against Him, and it is shown that the way of the cross—the power of self-sacrificing love, which serves, no matter what the cost to the server—is stronger than all the ways of force combined.

Chapter Forty

In Conclusion

Study/Discussion Questions:

- **What will be the theme of eternity?**
- **Is there any study greater than that of knowing and understanding the Creator and Life-giver of the universe?**
- **The final generation must have a message and an experience that will move the world. How does this message regarding the true light on God's character fit the requirement?**

The redeemed will spend the coming eternity studying the wonderful depths, breadths, and heights of the character of the Infinite. The mental, physical, and spiritual energies and attendant capacities of these people will far surpass the capabilities of earthbound students by at least twenty to one. In the original creation, Adam and his wife possessed twenty times the electrical energy possessed by us today.

> God endowed man with so great vital force that he has withstood the accumulation of disease brought upon the race in consequence of perverted habits, and has continued for six thousand years. This fact of itself is enough to evidence to us the strength and electrical energy that God gave to man at his creation. It took more than two thousand years of crime and indulgence of base passions to bring bodily disease upon the race to any great extent. If Adam, at his creation, had not been endowed with twenty times as much vital force as men now have, the race, with their present habits of living in violation of natural law, would have become extinct (*Testimonies for the Church,* vol. 3, pp. 138, 139).

In eternity eager students will possess at least twenty times the vital energy possessed today and will be under the direct tutelage of Christ. It would be impossible to conceive of the enormous amount of light gathered by such in the first million years, for instance, of their celestial sojourn. That, in turn, will be but the beginning of what will be learned as successive millions of years roll by devoted to the continued contemplation of God's character of love. In comparison with that, a microscopic fragment of the knowledge of God's character is contained in this book. It is but cradle roll level at best. It is nothing more than a start, albeit, a very necessary and vital one.

It is important that this be realized by the hungry seekers after God, for thereby they will be encouraged to press on, ever reaching for the richer and more beautiful revelations of God yet to come. They will be impressed to immerse themselves in the contemplation of the life of Jesus Christ, the complete and perfect revelation of the Infinite One. Every contact with the spiritual vitality of His life, with its marvelous consistency, tenderness, saving power, and a thousand other blessed qualities, will create an even more intense thirsting to know and experience its elevating power. The things of this world will wane in interest and value until they have no drawing influence left.

The benefit to be gained is not limited to acquiring information. Vital and basic as this is, it is but the doorway to a character development such as no other factor can produce. There is no possibility of coming in contact with God without being dramatically changed in nature. Consciously and unconsciously, the patterns of behavior, the attitudes, the spirit, the motivation, the work, and every aspect of the life will be purified, ennobled, sanctified, vitalized, prolonged, and enriched.

> Thus says the Lord: "Let not the wise man glory in his wisdom, let not the mighty man glory in his might, nor let the rich man glory in his riches; But let him who glories glory in this, that he understands and knows Me, that I am the Lord, exercising lovingkindness, judgment, and righteousness in the earth. For in these I delight," says the Lord (Jer. 9:23, 24).

Nebuchadnezzar ruled the world and gloried in the power by which he did it. Other men and women have been unbelievably rich, possessing treasures, lands, and money beyond computation. This is their glory and honor, but all the power and wealth that this world could ever give can never compare to the riches contained in knowing God. Search for this treasure. Dig deeply, earnestly, relentlessly, until the golden veins are opened wide and the greatest riches in the universe become your possession. Here is true value, which, if possessed, will bring all other treasures in its train. Those who have it are rich; the remainder are impoverished. This is a treasure available to all.

This book purposes to set the learner on the right track; to clear away the tragic misconceptions of God, which Satan has foisted on the human family to its hurt; to open to view God as He really is; and thus to introduce the blessings that are awaiting those who dig deeply into the mines of truth.

No attempt has been made to examine every incident in the Bible where God has been involved in one way or another. There is no necessity to do so. Once the application of divine principles has been applied to typical cases, anyone who has thoroughly grasped them will have no difficulty in solving most problems. There will always be one or two that defy solution, the simple reason being that God will never remove the opportunity for doubt, for to do so would take away the right of choice. He desires our spiritual education to come to the place where we will learn to trust Him in the unknown on the basis of what we have learned in the known.

Learn to expect that seeming contradictions will manifest themselves as study progresses. The solution of one problem only exposes another. This is a normal development. Some claim that they have never found anything in the Bible that sounded contradictory, but this only admits that they have never really studied it. People who dig deeply will be confronted with what *appears* to be insoluble problems. But, if aware that this is normal rather than abnormal, and if faith has attended the research, these seekers will rest in the comfort of knowing that there are no real contradictions in God's Word, only beautiful harmonies, even if they are not seen as such at the moment.

Train the mind not to think of God as if He were a man. Glaringly evident in every false concept of God's character is the disposition to see God operating on the same procedures as human beings. There is no greater stumbling block than this in the way of a correct comprehension of God. It must first be recognized as such, after which it will take protracted effort in retraining the thinking to automatically recognize that God works along lines that are opposite from humanity's way of working.

As a gift to every creature, there is nothing that God desires more than for them to have the knowledge of His character of righteousness.

When consideration is given to the magnitude of the task of understanding the Infinite, discouragement might well possess the soul. But be assured that there is nothing God is more anxious to supply than this knowledge, not only as a store of precious information but, more importantly, as a personal experience. He longs that the same character which is in Him be also in every one of His creatures, for only then is it possible for all to enter into the blessed fellowship that makes heaven be heaven.

Therefore, the blessed assurance is to accompany the spiritual wayfarer every moment that the full resources of heaven are devoted to unfolding these things to the eager mind. With pitying tenderness, God stoops low to unveil these mysteries to our dull human senses, and He is grieved when we learn so little so slowly. Before those who will press forward with unabated determination are possibilities beyond the outreach of our imaginations and aspirations. Higher and still higher, the Lord will personally elevate the mind until it is overwhelmed with the revelation of divine things. Sweeter and sweeter will be the love implanted within the heart, more and more intense the spirit of self-sacrificing service, and more exalted and profound the response of praise and joy. Earthly things will appear in their true light, with luster dimmed and attractiveness gone. Sin will no longer masquerade in garments of light but will be exposed for what it is—a hideous, deceptive, and unwanted perversion of all things good and true. There will be no more glorying in power and riches but in the possession of the knowledge of God, the greatest power and riches of all.

When God has a people upon this earth equipped with this then He will have the instrumentalities whereby He will move the world. It is for this reason that the loud cry under the power of the latter rain cannot come until such qualifications are possessed by a living church. God desires to dispense to that church the very best gifts heaven can bestow, that its members, in turn, may render the finest saving service possible to the desperately needy and perishing millions of earth's population.

God's people have long professed to desire nothing more than the outpouring of the latter rain whereby the work can be finished and the way prepared for Christ's return. To such, then, comes the challenge of the truth that this can never be accomplished until the knowledge of God's character fills them and subsequently lightens the whole earth with its glory. It is the failure of God's church to know by text and by experience the truth of His character that is retarding the finishing of God's work in the earth today. While His children enjoy the comforts of this life, making little effort to penetrate the mysteries of infinite love, which have been revealed and are for them to understand, sin continues to trample the oppressed on its missions of death and destruction.

Men and women of God, it is time to arise to the full stature of God's plan, to measure up to the exacting demands of this climactic hour. For six thousand years now our loving heavenly Father has been earnestly entreating His people to learn of Him that they might embark on their appointed mission and the earth be delivered from its oppression.

Let each person come to a full realization of these issues and arouse every faculty and power to a profound and total consecration in the devoted study and experience of the character of God.

We invite you to view the complete
selection of titles we publish at:

www.TEACHServices.com

Scan with your mobile
device to go directly
to our website.

Please write or email us your praises, reactions,
or thoughts about this or any other book we publish at:

TEACH Services, Inc.
P U B L I S H I N G

www.TEACHServices.com

P.O. Box 954
Ringgold, GA 30736

info@TEACHServices.com

TEACH Services, Inc., titles may be purchased in bulk for
educational, business, fund-raising, or sales promotional use.
For information, please e-mail:

BulkSales@TEACHServices.com

Finally, if you are interested in seeing
your own book in print, please contact us at:

publishing@TEACHServices.com

We would be happy to review your manuscript for free.

CPSIA information can be obtained
at www.ICGtesting.com
Printed in the USA
FFOW04n0611010817
38171FF